LEADERS OF THE WORLD
General Editor: **ROBERT MAXWELL, M.C.**

M. S. GORBACHOV

Speeches and Writings

LEADERS OF THE WORLD

General Editor: ROBERT MAXWELL, M.C.

MIKHAIL SERGEYEVICH GORBACHOV.

M. S. GORBACHOV

*General Secretary of the CPSU and
Member of the Presidium of the Supreme
Soviet of the USSR*

Speeches and Writings

PERGAMON PRESS

OXFORD · NEW YORK · BEIJING · FRANKFURT
SÃO PAULO · SYDNEY · TOKYO · TORONTO

U.K.	Pergamon Press, Headington Hill Hall, Oxford OX3 0BW, England
U.S.A.	Pergamon Press, Maxwell House, Fairview Park, Elmsford, New York 10523, U.S.A.
PEOPLE'S REPUBLIC OF CHINA	Pergamon Press, Qianmen Hotel, Beijing, People's Republic of China
FEDERAL REPUBLIC OF GERMANY	Pergamon Press, Hammerweg 6, D-6242 Kronberg, Federal Republic of Germany
BRAZIL	Pergamon Editora, Rua Eça de Queiros, 346, CEP 04011, São Paulo, Brazil
AUSTRALIA	Pergamon Press Australia, P.O. Box 544, Potts Point, N.S.W. 2011, Australia
JAPAN	Pergamon Press, 8th Floor, Matsuoka Central Building, 1-7-1 Nishishinjuku, Shinjuku-ku, Tokyo 160, Japan
CANADA	Pergamon Press Canada, Suite 104, 150 Consumers Road, Willowdale, Ontario M2J 1P9, Canada

Copyright © 1986 Pergamon Books Ltd.

First edition 1986

Library of Congress Cataloging-in-Publication Data

Gorbachov, Mikhail Sergeyevich, 1931–
Speeches and writings.

(Leaders of the world)
Translated selections from various sources.
1. Soviet Union—Politics and government—
1982–   .   2. Soviet Union—Foreign relations—
1975–   .   I. Title.   II. Series.
DK290.3.G67A25   1986   327.47   86–12270

British Library Cataloguing in Publication Data
Gorbachov, M.S.
Speeches and writings.
1. Soviet Union—Politics and
government—1953-
I. Title
947.085′4′0924   DK290.3.G6

ISBN 0–08–034266–3

Printed in Great Britain by A. Wheaton & Co. Ltd., Exeter

Preface

As I agreed to write a preface to my selected works to be published in Great Britain, I recollected the impressions of my visit to your country in 1984. My discussions with British statesmen and businessmen and members of the public reaffirmed my conviction that great unused opportunities exist in Soviet-British relations. This is true of all areas, ranging from politics to sport and tourism.

Needless to say, the social systems in our two countries are different and they are divided in their approach to vital international problems. The Soviet Union and Great Britain belong to opposing military-political alliances. These are the hard facts. However, they should not make us blind to what is immeasurably more important; namely, the possibility and necessity of fruitful and full-blooded co-operation between the Soviet Union and Great Britain to promote peace in Europe and throughout the world. This co-operation could include broad mutual ties in the economic, scientific, technological and cultural fields and, of course, in politics. The benefits would be mutual.

At our 27th Congress, the documents of which are partly included in this collection, we made decisions of principle on the need to organize constructive and fruitful co-operation of states and peoples on a worldwide scale.

Our own plans are truly great. We expect to double the country's productive potential towards the end of the century and to advance the Soviet people's standards of life to a new level of quality. Our strategic line of boosting the country's socio-economic development integrates emphasis on scientific and technological progress with radical economic reform and a widening of democracy; that is, the broadest possible involvement of the working people in the management of affairs of state and society. Now that the Congress is over, I believe we are entitled to say that by ridding ourselves of whatever hindered our development and by reviewing realistically our achievements, as well as our errors and setbacks, we have laid the groundwork for using the enormous constructive potential of the socialist system much more efficiently than before.

Naturally, we have no intention to restrict ourselves to self-isolation. The Soviet Union is a member of the world community of nations fully aware of the responsibility this fact involves. We proceed from the principle that an interdependent world, torn by contradictions yet integral in many ways, is taking shape through a dielectical conflict of opposites, feeling its way as it were. The formation of this interdependent and integral world is the essence of present-day social development and requires a new approach to international relations, a new philosophy of world politics. In other words, it is a question of working out a concept of international security to be adopted by all to enable us to retreat from the brink of nuclear war.

The realities of the nuclear age prove conclusively that military technology alone, even the most sophisticated kind, cannot guarantee national security. The advancement of weaponry is reducing to nil the significance of the vast oceans and enormous land distances, let alone mere straits. Modern weapons have turned military power into a veritable boomerang, a nuclear one moreover, that is as sure to hit the thrower as his adversary. Therefore, concern for national security now demands the most scrupulous consideration of the security interests of other states. Mutual and equal security of all is imperative. This is our final conclusion.

The world is in a state of rapid change. Any social status quo is simply impossible. The existence of antagonisms in our complex and many-faceted world makes it incumbent on states to realize their common interest and, most important of all, to learn the science and art of peaceful coexistence, to exercise restraint and circumspection on the international scene, to behave in a civilized manner — that is, to observe the rules of correct international intercourse and co-operation.

In short, it is imperative to renounce resolutely and for good the ways of thinking and acting that have taken shape over the centuries on the principle that war, armed conflicts and a contest in armaments are permissible in the conduct of national policy. It is impossible to win such a contest, let alone a nuclear war. Contradictions should be settled on the lines of peaceful competition alone.

Such is our concept of national security in broad outline. It is the basis for the programme of establishing a comprehensive system of international security advanced by the 27th Congress of the CPSU.

I realize that the ideas we put forward at our Party Congress may give rise to counter-proposals. We would welcome peace initiations by other states.

I want to note at the same time that our proposals mean more than the offer of a dialogue. There is a dialogue in progress, although it is rather half-hearted at times. We invite other countries, including Great Britain of course, to take part in a collective effort to avert the danger of nuclear or any other war. It is the common duty of all states regardless of their social systems to deal effectively with the global problems facing mankind.

Great Britain has long been a great power. Mankind owes to British genius many of its cultural achievements, great scientific discoveries and brilliant inventions. I am not just paying compliments. The history of Great Britain, like that of many other countries, does not consist merely of bright pages. However, our common concern for the future of mankind has come to the forefront.

I am confident that fruitful Soviet–British co-operation could greatly contribute to normalizing international relations and changing over from confrontation and suspicion to goodneighbour-liness and mutual trust. The Soviet Union is prepared for such a new deal.

I avail myself of this opportunity to reaffirm the Soviet people's willingness to develop friendly ties with the people of Great Britain and I wish them peace and prosperity.

March 1986   M. S. Gorbachov

Contents

Introduction by Robert Maxwell

On 11 March 1985, a few days after his fifty-fourth birthday, Mikhail Sergeyevich Gorbachov was elected General Secretary of the CPSU. He succeeded to this unique position of power, the youngest person ever to do so, at a time of increasing world tension and will undoubtedly have a major influence on superpower relations over the next twenty years. The third leader of the Soviet Union in as many years, he succeeded at a time of doubt and uncertainty of direction for one of the world's mightiest nations. His opportunity to promote change both at home and abroad, to modernise the Soviet Union and to develop lasting world peace is unprecedented in history.

Mikhail Gorbachov is an unusual and remarkable man. As a young man of peasant stock, he left his collective farm to read law at the Lomonosov State University in Moscow in September 1950. In those days few students specialised in law and his pursuit of it allowed him to explore different theories on the origin of the state which others could not. As a young Party official back in his native Stavropol in the northern Caucasus, he specialised in agriculture — a key sector in the Soviet economy. This was to stand him in good stead for, years later, when his Party career took him to Moscow, he was to become Central Committee Secretary for Agriculture. This was an unusual springboard for higher office given the background of disappointing harvests, but with his first-hand experience and knowledge (enhanced by a second degree in Agricultural Economics), he was able to turn it to his advantage.

Although he is the eighth leader of the Soviet Union, he is the first not to have fought in the Great Patriotic War (1941–1945), and so his formative years were spent in postwar Soviet society. His personal experience equips him to look forward to the future, instead of backward to the devastating losses suffered by the Soviet Union at the hands of Nazi Germany.

On reaching Moscow in 1978 he gained rapid promotion to become both Central Committee Secretary and Politbureau member in less than two years, a position of power equalled only by four other members of the Politbureau at that time: Suslov and Kirilenko, neither of whom were candidates for the succession by reason of age, Chernenko, who was to become briefly Soviet leader after Andropov, and Brezhnev himself. At a time when the average age of the Politbureau was over seventy, Gorbachov was not yet fifty, and he had already harnessed to himself considerable power.

In the year before his election he visited both Canada and Britain. It was the first such visit by a high-ranking Soviet politician since Kosygin came to London in 1967. The Western media was initially quite taken aback, but they soon warmed to the man whose poise, calm self-assurance and mastery of media skills had so disarmed them. Since then he has continued to develop those attributes with some striking results, most notably in the lead-up to last November's Summit in Geneva.

In power, he has already set about major changes with conspicuous campaigns against corruption and alcoholism, driven both by the need for greater efficiency in the economy and to confront inertia in the bureaucracy. As a statesman, he seeks peace not only for reasons of mutual survival, but also because only in that way can resources be redirected to bring about the consumer-led expansion and revitalisation he is impatient to achieve.

In his own preface to this work, Mikhail Gorbachov notes that the world is in a state of rapid change. Looking to the future, it is imperative, he says, to renounce once and for all the sort of thinking that allows war and armed conflict to be used in the resolution of problems between states. Even limited contests of this kind cannot be won, "let alone a nuclear war". These are the words of a man who wants to bring about a new world order, "a new philosophy of world politics" and a world of lasting peace.

Two biographies of Gorbachov have recently been published in Britain. Compelling and useful they may be, complete with their commentary and analysis. But for the serious student, politician, diplomat, journalist or other interested reader there is no substitute for an examination of original sources and materials. This work brings together a selection of documents and speeches chosen by

Mikhail Gorbachov personally. It is essential reading for all those who need to know more about the man who will lead the Soviet Union into the twenty-first century.

Oxford, May 1986   ROBERT MAXWELL

1.

Report to the 27th Congress of the Communist Party of the Soviet Union
25 February 1986

Comrade Delegates,
Esteemed guests,

The 27th Congress of the CPSU has gathered at a crucial turning point in the life of the country and the contemporary world as a whole. We are beginning our work with a deep understanding of our responsibility to the Party and the Soviet people. It is our task to elaborate a broad conception, in the Leninist way, of the times we are living in, and to work out a realistic, well-thought-out programme of action that would organically blend the grandeur of our aims with our real capabilities, and the Party's plans with the hopes and aspirations of every person. The resolutions of the 27th Congress will determine both the character and the rate of our movement towards a qualitatively new state of the Soviet socialist society for years and decades ahead.

The Congress is to discuss and adopt a new edition of the Programme of the CPSU, amendments to the Party Rules, and Guidelines for Economic Development for the next five years and a longer term. I need hardly mention what enormous importance these documents have for our Party, our state, and our people. Not only do they contain an assessment of the past and a formulation of the urgent tasks, but also a glimpse into the future. They speak of what the Soviet Union will be like as it enters the 21st century, of the image of socialism and its positions in the international arena, of the future of humanity.

SW-A

Soviet society has gone a long way in its development since the currently operative Party Programme was adopted. In fact, we have built the whole country anew, have made tremendous headway in the economic, cultural, and social fields, and have raised generations of builders of the new society. We have blazed the trail into outer space for humanity. We have secured military strategic parity and have thereby substantially restricted imperialism's aggressive plans and capabilities to start a nuclear war. The position of our Motherland and of world socialism in the international arena have grown considerably stronger.

The path travelled by the country, its economic, social and cultural achievements convincingly confirm the vitality of the Marxist–Leninist doctrine, and socialism's tremendous potential as embodied in the progress of Soviet society. We can be justly proud of everything that has been achieved in these years of intensive work and struggle.

While duly appraising our achievements, the leadership of the CPSU considers it its duty to tell the Party and the people honestly and frankly about the shortcomings in our political and practical activities, the unfavourable tendencies in the economy and the social and moral sphere, and about the reasons for them. For a number of years the deeds and actions of Party and Government bodies lagged behind the needs of the times and of life — not only because of objective factors, but also for reasons above all of a subjective nature. The problems in the country's development grew more rapidly than they were being solved. The inertness and rigidity of the forms and methods of management, the decline of dynamism in our work, and increased bureaucracy — all this was doing no small damage. Signs of stagnation had begun to surface in the life of society.

The situation called for change, but a peculiar psychology — how to improve things without changing anything — took the upper hand in the central bodies and, for that matter, a local level as well. But that cannot be done, comrades. Stop for an instant, as they say, and you fall behind a mile. We must not evade the problems that have arisen. That sort of attitude is much too costly for the country, the state and the Party. So let us say it loud and clear!

The top-priority task is to overcome the negative factors in society's socio-economic development as rapidly as possible, to accelerate it and impart to it an essential dynamism, to learn from the lessons of the past to a maximum extent, so that the decisions we adopt for the future should be absolutely clear and responsible, and the concrete actions purposeful and effective.

The situation has reached a turning point not only in internal but also in **external** affairs. The changes in current world developments are so deep-going and significant that they require a reassessment and a comprehensive analysis of all factors. The situation created by the nuclear confrontation calls for new approaches, methods, and forms of relations between the different social systems, states and regions.

Owing to the arms race started by imperialism, the 20th century, in the field of world politics, is coming to an end burdened with the question: will humanity be able to avert the nuclear danger, or will the policy of confrontation take the upper hand, thus increasing the probability of nuclear conflict. The capitalist world has not abandoned the ideology and policy of hegemonism, its rulers have not yet lost the hope of taking social revenge, and continue to indulge themselves with illusions of superior strength. A sober view of what is going on is hewing its way forward with great difficulty through a dense thicket of prejudices and preconceptions in the thinking of the ruling class. But the complexity and acuteness of this moment in history makes it increasingly vital to outlaw nuclear weapons, destroy them and other weapons of mass annihilation completely, and improve international relations.

The fact that the Party has deeply understood the fundamentally new situation inside the country and in the world arena, and that it appreciates its responsibility for the country's future, and has the will and resolve to carry out the requisite change, is borne out by the adoption at the April 1985 Plenary Meeting of the **decision to accelerate the socio-economic development of our society**.

Formulating the long-term and fundamental tasks, the Central Committee has been consistently guided by Marxism–Leninism, the truly scientific theory of social development. It expresses the vital interests of the working people, and the ideals of social justice. It derives its vitality from its everlasting youthfulness, its constant capacity for development and creative generalization of the new facts and phenomena, and from its experience of revolutionary struggle and social reconstruction.

Any attempt to turn the theory by which we are guided into an assortment of rigid schemes and formulas which would be valid everywhere and in all contingencies is most definitely contrary to the essence and spirit of Marxism–Leninism. Lenin wrote back in 1917 that Marx and Engels rightly ridiculed the "mere memorising and repetition of 'formulas', that at best are capable only of marking out **general** tasks, which are necessarily modifiable by the **concrete** economic and political conditions of each particular **period** of the historical process". Those are the words, comrades, that everyone of us must ponder and act upon.

The **concrete** economic and political situation we are in, and the particular **period** of the historical process that Soviet society and the whole world are going through, require that the Party and its every member display their creativity, their capacity for innovation and ability to transcend the limits of accustomed but already outdated notions.

A large-scale, frank and constructive examination of all the crucial problems of our life and of Party policy has taken place during the discussion of the pre-Congress documents. We have come to the Congress enriched by the wisdom and experience of the whole Party, the whole people. We can now see more clearly what has to be done and in what order, and what levers we must set in motion so that our progress will be accelerated at a desired pace.

These days, many things, in fact everything, will depend on how effectively we will succeed in using the advantages and possibilities of the socialist system, its economic power and social potential, in updating the obsolescent social patterns and style and methods of work, in bringing them abreast of the changed conditions. That is the only way for us to increase the might of our country, to raise the material and spiritual life of the Soviet people to a qualitatively new level, and to enhance the positive influence of the example of socialism as a social system on world development.

We look to the future confidently, because we are clearly aware of our tasks and of the ways in which they should be carried out. We look to the future confidently, because we rely on the powerful support of the people. We look to the future confidently, because we are acting in the interests of the socialist Homeland, in the name of the great ideals to which the Communist Party has dedicated itself wholeheartedly.

I. THE CONTEMPORARY WORLD:
ITS MAIN TENDENCIES AND CONTRADICTIONS

Comrades, the draft new edition of the Programme of the Party contains a thorough analysis of the main trends and features of the development of the world today. It is not the purpose of the Programme to anticipate the future with all its multiformity and concrete developments. That would be a futile exercise. But here is another, no less important point: if we want to follow a correct, science-based policy, we must clearly understand the key tendencies of the current reality. To penetrate deep into the dialectic of the events, into their objective logic, to draw the right conclusions that reflect the motion of the times, is no simple matter, but is is imperatively necessary.

In the days before the October Revolution, referring to the capitalist economy alone, Lenin noted that the sum-total of the changes in all their ramifications could not have been grasped even by seventy Marxes. But, Lenin continued, Marxism has discovered "the **laws** . . . and the **objective** logic of these changes and of their historical development . . . in its chief and basic features".

The modern world is complicated, diverse and dynamic, and shot through with contending tendencies and contradictions. It is a world of the most difficult alternatives, anxieties and hopes. Never before has our home on earth been exposed to such great political and physical stresses. Never before has man exacted so much tribute from nature, and never has he been so vulnerable to the forces he himself has created.

World developments confirm the fundamental Marxist–Leninist conclusion that the history of society is not a sum of fortuitous elements, that it is not a disorderly "Brownian motion", but a law-governed onward process. Not only are its contradictions a verdict on the old world, on everything that impedes the advance; they are also a source and motive force for social progress. This is progress which takes place in conditions of a struggle that is inevitable so long as exploitation and exploiting classes exist.

The liberation revolutions triggered by the Great October Revolution are determining the image of the 20th Century. However considerable the achievements of science and technology, and however great the influence which rapid scientific and technological progress has on the life of society, nothing but the social and spiritual emancipation of man can make him truly free. And no matter what difficulties, objective and artificial, the old world may create, the course of history is irreversible.

The social changes of the century are altering the conditions for the further development of society. New economic, political, scientific, technical, internal and international factors are beginning to operate. The interconnection between states and between peoples is increasing. And all this is setting knew, especially exacting demands upon every state, whether it is a matter of foreign policy, economic and social activity, or the spiritual image of society.

The progress of our time is rightly identified with socialism. **World socialism** is a powerful international entity with a highly developed economy, substantial scientific resources, and a reliable military and political potential. It accounts for more than one-third of the world's population; it includes dozens of countries and peoples advancing along a path that reveals in every way the intellectual and moral wealth of man and society. A new way of life has taken shape, based on the principles of socialist justice, in which there are neither oppressors nor the oppressed, neither exploiters nor the exploited, in which power belongs to the people. Its distinctive features are collectivism and comradely mutual assistance, triumph of the ideas of freedom, unbreakable unity between the rights and duties of every member of society, the dignity of the individual, and true humanism. Socialism is a realistic option open to all humanity, an example projected into the future.

Socialism sprang up and was built in countries which were far from being economically and socially advanced at that time and which differed greatly from one another in mode of life and their historical and national traditions. Each one of them advanced to the new social system along its own way, confirming Marx's prediction about the "infinite variations and gradations" of the same economic basis in its concrete manifestations.

The way was neither smooth nor simple. It was exceedingly difficult to rehabilitate a backward or ruined economy, to teach millions of people to read and write, to provide them with a roof over their heads, with food and free medical aid. The very novelty of the social tasks, the ceaseless military, economic, political, and psychological pressure of imperialism, the need for tremendous efforts to ensure defence — all this could not but influence the course of events, their character, and the rate at which the socio-economic programmes and transformations were carried into effect. Nor were mistakes in politics and various subjectivist deviations avoided.

But such is life; it always manifests itself in diverse contradictions, sometimes quite unexpected ones. The other point is much more important: socialism has demonstrated its ability to resolve social problems on a fundamentally different basis than previously, namely a collectivist one; it has brought the countries to higher levels of development, and has given the working people a dignified and secure life.

Socialism is continuously improving social relations, multiplying its achievements purposefully, setting an example which is becoming more and more influential and attractive, and demonstrating the real humanism of the socialist way of life. By so doing, it is erecting an increasingly reliable barrier to the ideology and policy of war and militarism, reaction and force, to all forms of inhumanity, and is actively furthering social progress. It has grown into a powerful moral and material force, and has shown what opportunities are opening for modern civilization.

The course of social progress is closely linked with **anti-colonial** revolutions, national liberation movements, the renascence of many countries, and the emergence of dozens of new ones. Having won political independence, they are working hard to overcome backwardness, poverty, and sometimes extreme privation — the entire painful legacy of their past enslavement. Formerly the victims of imperialist policy, deprived of all rights, they are now making history themselves.

Social progress is expressed in the development of the **international communist and working-class movement** and in the growth of the new massive democratic movement of our time, including the anti-war and anti-nuclear movement. It is apparent, too, in the polarization of the political forces of the capitalist world, notably in the USA, the centre of imperialism. Here, progressive tendencies are forcing their way forward through a system of monopolistic totalitarianism, and are exposed to the continuous pressure of organized reactionary forces, including their enormous propaganda machine which floods the world with stupefying misinformation.

Marx compared progress in exploitative society to "that hideous pagan idol, who would not drink the nectar but from the skulls of the slain". He went on: "In our days everything seems pregnant with its contrary. Machinery, gifted with the wonderful power of shortening and fructifying human labour, we behold starving and overworking it. The new-fangled sources of wealth, by some strange weird spell, are turned into sources of want. The victories of art seem bought by the loss of character. At the same pace that mankind masters nature, man seems to become enslaved to other men or to his own infamy. Even the pure light of science seems unable to shine but on the dark background of ignorance. All our invention and progress seem to result in endowing material forces with intellectual life, and in stultifying human life into a material force."

Marx's analysis is striking in its historical sweep, accuracy, and depth. It has, indeed, become still more relevant with regard to bourgeois reality of the 20th century than it was in the 19th century. On the one hand, the swift advance of science and technology has opened up unprecedented possibilities for mastering the forces of nature and improving the conditions of the life of man. On the other, the "enlightened" 20th century is going down in history as a time marked by such outgrowths of imperialism as the most devastating wars, an orgy of militarism and fascism, genocide, and the destitution of millions of people. Ignorance and obscurantism go hand in hand in the capitalist world with outstanding achievements of science and culture. That is the society we are compelled to be neighbours of, and we must look for ways of co-operation and mutual understanding. Such is the command of history.

The progress of humanity is also directed connected with the **scientific and technological revolution**. It matured slowly and gradually, and then, in the final quarter of the century, gave the start to a gigantic increase of man's material and spiritual possibilities. These are of a twofold nature. There is a qualitative leap in humanity's productive forces. But there is also a qualitative leap in means of destruction, in the military sphere, "endowing" man for the first time in history with the physical capacity for destroying all life on earth.

The facets and consequences of the scientific and technological revolution differ in different socio-political systems. Capitalism of the 1980s, the capitalism of the age of electronics and information science, computers and robots, is throwing more millions of people, including young and educated people, out of jobs. Wealth and power are being increasingly concentrated in the hands of a few. Militarism is thriving on the arms race greatly, and also strives gradually to gain control over the political levers of power. It is becoming the ugliest and the most dangerous monster of the 20th century. Because of its efforts, the most advanced scientific and technical ideas are being converted into weapons of mass destruction.

Before the developing countries the scientific and technological revolution is setting this most acute question: are they to enjoy the achievements of science and technology in full measure in order to gain strength for combatting neocolonialism and imperialist exploitation, or will they remain on the periphery of world development? The scientific and technological revolution shows in bold relief that many socio-economic problems impeding progress in that part of the world are unresolved.

Socialism has everything it needs to place modern science and technology at the service of the people. But it would be wrong to think that the scientific and technological revolution is creating no problems for socialist society. Experience shows that its advance involves improvement of social relations, a change of mentality, the forging of a new psychology, and the acceptance of dynamism as a way and a rule of life. It calls insistently for a continuous reassessment and streamlining of the prevailing patterns of management. In other words, the scientific and technological revolution not only opens up prospects, but also sets higher demands on the entire organization of the internal life of countries and international relations. Certainly, scientific and technological progress cannot abolish the laws of social development or the social purpose and content of such development. But it exercises a tremendous influence on all the processes that are going on in the world, on its contradictions.

It is quite obvious that the two socio-economic systems differ substantially in their readiness and in their capacity to comprehend and resolve the problems that arise.

Such is the world we are living in on the threshold of the third millennium. It is a world full of hope, because people have never before been so amply equipped for the further development of civilization. But it is also a world over-burdened with dangers and contradictions, which prompts the thought that this is perhaps the most alarming period in history.

The first and most important group of contradictions in terms of humanity's future is connected with the **relations between countries of the two systems, the two formations**. These contradictions have a long history. Since the Great October Revolution in Russia and the split of the world on the social-class principle, fundamental differences have emerged both in the assessment of current affairs and in the views concerning the world's social perspective.

Capitalism regarded the birth of socialism as an "error" of history which must be "rectified". It was to be rectified at any cost, by any means, irrespective of law and morality: by armed intervention, economic blockade, subversive activity, sanctions and "punishments", or rejection of all co-operation. But nothing could interfere with the consolidation of the new system and its historical right to live.

The difficulty that the ruling classes of the capitalist world have in understanding the realities, the recurrence of attempts at resolving by force the whole group of contradictions dividing the two worlds are, of course, anything but accidental. The intrinsic mainsprings and socio-economic essence of imperialism prompt it to translate the competition of the two systems into the language of military confrontation. Owing to its social nature, imperialism ceaselessly gives rise to aggressive, adventurist policy.

Here we can speak of a whole complex of motives involved: the predatory appetites of the arms manufacturers and the influential military-bureaucratic groups, the selfish interest of the monopolies in sources of raw materials and markets for their goods, the bourgeoisie's fear of the ongoing changes, and, lastly, the attempts to resolve its own increasingly acute problems at socialism's expense.

Such attempts are especially typical of US imperialism. It was nothing but imperial ideology and policy, the wish to create the most unfavourable external conditions for socialism and for the USSR that prompted the launching of the race of nuclear and other arms after 1945, just when the crushing defeat of fascism and militarism was, it would seem, offering a realistic opportunity for building a world without wars, and a mechanism of international co-operation — the United Nations — had been created for this purpose. But imperialism's nature asserted itself that time again.

Today, too, the right wing of the US monopoly bourgeoisie regards the stoking up of international tensions as something that justifies military spending, claims to global supremacy, interference in the affairs of other states, and an offensive against the interests and the rights of the American working people. No small role seems to be played by the idea of using tensions to put pressure on the allies, to make them absolutely obedient, to subordinate them to Washington's dictation.

The policy of total contention, of military confrontation has no future. Flight into the past is no answer to the challenges of the future. It is rather an act of despair which, however, does not make this posture any less dangerous. By its deeds Washington will show when and to what extent it will understand this. We, for our part, are ready to do everything we can in order radically to improve the international situation. To achieve this, socialism need not renounce any of its principles or ideals. It has always stood for and continues to stand for the peaceful coexistence of states with different social systems.

As distinct from imperialism, which is trying to halt the course of history by force, to regain what it had in the past, socialism has never, of its own free will, related its future to any military solution of international problems. This was borne out at the very first big discussion that took place in our Party after the victory of the Great October Revolution. During that discussion, as we may recall, the views of the "Left Communists" and the Trotskyites, who championed the theory of "revolutionary war" which, they claimed, would carry socialism to other countries, were firmly rejected. This position, as Lenin emphasized in 1918, "would be completely at variance with Marxism, for Marxism has always been opposed to 'pushing' revolutions, which develop with the growing acuteness of the class antagonisms that engender revolutions". Today, too, we are firmly convinced that promoting revolutions from outside, and even more so by military means, is futile and inadmissible.

The problems and crises experienced by the capitalist world arise within its own system and are a natural result of the internal antagonistic contradictions of the old society. In this sense, capitalism negates itself as it develops. Unable to cope with the acute problems of the declining phase of capitalism's development, the ruling circles of the imperialist countries resort to means and methods that are obviously incapable of saving the society which history has doomed.

The myth of a Soviet or communist "threat" that is being circulated today, is meant to justify the arms race and the imperialist countries' own aggressiveness. But it is becoming increasingly clear that the path of war can yield no sensible solutions, either international or domestic. The clash and struggle of the opposite approaches to the perspectives of world development have become especially complex in nature. Now that the world has huge nuclear stockpiles and the only thing experts argue about is how many times or dozens of times humanity can be destroyed, it is high time to begin an effective withdrawal from the brink of war, from the equilibrium of fear, to normal, civilized forms of relations between the states of the two systems.

In the years to come, the struggle will evidently centre on the actual content of the policy that can safeguard peace. It will be a hard and many-sided struggle, because we are dealing with a society whose ruling circles refuse to assess the realities of the world and its perspectives in sober terms, or to draw serious conclusions from their own experience and that of others. All this is an indication of the wear and tear suffered by its internal "systems of immunity", of its social senility, which reduces the probability of far-reaching changes in the policy of the dominant forces and augments its degree of recklessness.

That is why it is not easy at all, in the current circumstances, to predict the future of the relations between the socialist and the capitalist countries, the USSR and the USA. The decisive factors here will be the correlation of forces on the world scene, the growth and activity of the peace potential, and its capability of effectively repulsing the threat of nuclear war. Much will depend, too, on the degree of realism that Western ruling circles will show in assessing the situation. But it is unfortunate when not only the eyesight but also the soul of politicians is blind. With nuclear war being totally unacceptable, peaceful coexistence rather than confrontation of the systems should be the rule in inter-state relations.

The second group of contradictions consists of the **intrinsic contradictions of the capitalist world itself**. The past period has amply confirmed that the **general crisis of capitalism** is growing keener. The capitalism of today, whose exploitative nature has not changed, is in many ways different from what it was in the early and even the middle 20th century. Under the influence and against the background of the scientific and technological revolution, the conflict between the productive forces, which have grown to gigantic proportions, and the private-owner social relations, has become still more acute. Here there is growth of unemployment and deterioration of the entire set of social problems. Militarism, which has spread to all areas, is applied as the most promising means of enlivening the economy. The crisis of political institutions, of the entire spiritual sphere, is growing. Reaction is exerting fierce pressure all along the line — in domestic and foreign policy, economy and culture, and the use of the achievements of human genius. The traditional forms of conservatism are giving place to authoritarian tendencies.

Special mention should be made of such dangerous manifestation of the crisis of capitalism as anti-communism and anti-Sovietism. This concerns not only foreign policy. In the present-day system of imperialism it is also a very important aspect of domestic policy, a means of exerting pressure on all the advanced and progressive elements that live and fight in the capitalist countries, in the non-socialist part of the world.

True, the present stage of the general crisis does not lead to any absolute stagnation of capitalism and does not rule out the possibilities for economic growth, and the mastering of new scientific and technical fields. This stage "allows for" sustaining concrete economic, military, political and other positions, and in some areas even the possibility for social revenge, for regaining what has been lost before. Because capitalism lacks positive aims and orientations, capable of expressing the interests of the working masses, it now has to cope with the unprecedented interlacement and mutual exacerbation of all of its contradictions. It faces more social and other impasses than it has ever known before in all the centuries of its development.

The contradictions **between labour and capital** are among the first to grow more acute. In the 1960s and 1970s, with the onset of a favourable economic situation, the working class and working people managed to secure a certain improvement of their condition. But from the mid-1970s on, the proliferation economic crises and another technological modernization of production changed the situation, and enabled capital to go on the counter-offensive, depriving the working people of a considerable part of their social gains. For a number of standard of living indicators, the working people were flung many years back. Unemployment has reached a postwar high. The condition of peasants and farmers is deteriorating visibly: some farms are going backrupt, with their former owners joining the ranks of hired workers, while others become abjectly dependent on large agricultural monopolies and banks. The social stratification is growing deeper and increasingly striking. In the United States, for example, 1 per cent of the wealthiest families own riches that exceed by nearly 50 per cent the aggregate wealth of 80 per cent of all American families, which make up the lower part of the property pyramid.

Imperialism's ruling circles are doubtlessly aware that such a situation is fraught with social explosions and political destabilization. But this is not making their policies more considered. On the contrary, the most irreconcilable reactionary groups of the ruling class have, by and large, taken the upper hand in recent years. This period is marked by an especially massive and brutal offensive by the monopolies on the rights of the working people.

The whole arsenal of means at capitalism's disposal is being put to use. The trade unions are persecuted and economically blackmailed.

Anti-labour laws are being enacted. The left and all other progressives are being persecuted. Continuous control or, to be more precise, surveillance of people's state of mind and behaviour has become standard. The deliberate cultivation of individualism, of the principle that might makes right in the fight for survival, of immorality and hatred of all that is democratic — this is practised on an unprecedented scale.

The future, the working people's fight for their rights, for social progress, will show how that basic contradiction between labour and capital will develop and what conclusions will be drawn from the prevailing situation. But mention must be made of the serious danger to international relations of any further substantial shift of policy, of the entire internal situation in some capitalist countries, to the right. The consequences of such a development are hard to predict, and we must not underrate their danger.

The last decades of the century are marked by new outbreaks of **inter-imperialist contradictions** and the appearance of their new forms and tendencies. This group of capitalist contradictions has not been eliminated either by class affinity, the interest in uniting forces, by military, economic and political integration, or by the scientific and technological revolution. The latter has incontestably accelerated the internationalization of capitalist production, has given added impetus to the evening up of levels as well as to the leap-like development of capitalist countries. The competition that has grown more acute under the impact of scientific and technological progress, is affecting those who have dropped behind ever more mercilessly. The considerable complication of the conditions of capitalist reproduction, the diversity of crisis processes, and the intensification of international competition have made imperialist rivalry especially acute and bitter. The commercial and economic struggle on the world market is witnessing ever greater reliance on the power of national state-monopoly capitalisms, with the role of the bourgeois state becoming increasingly aggressive and egoistic.

The **transnational monopoly capital** has gained strength rapidly. It is seizing control of, and monopolizing, whole branches or spheres of production both on the scale of individual countries and in the world economy as a whole. By the early 1980s, the transnational corporations accounted for more than one-third of industrial production, more than one half of foreign trade, and nearly 80 per cent of the patents for new machinery and technology in the capitalist world.

The core of the transnational corporations consists of American firms. Their enterprises abroad use an additional army of wage and salary workers, whose number is half of those employed in manufacturing in the USA. At present, they produce something like 1.5 trillion dollars worth of goods and services a year, or nearly 40 per cent of gross US output.

The size of the "second economy" of the United States is double or triple that of the economies of such leading West European powers as the FRG, France, and Britain, and second only to that of Japan. Today, the biggest US transnational monopolies are empires whose scale of economic activity is comparable to the gross national product of an entire country.

A new knot of contradictions has appeared and is being swiftly tightened **between the transnational corporations and the nation-state form of society's political organization**. The transnational corporations are undermining the sovereignty both of developing and of developed capitalist countries. They make active use of state-monopoly regulation when it suits their interests, and come into sharp conflict with it when they see the slightest threat to their profits from the actions of bourgeois governments. But for all that, the US transnational supermonopolies are, as a rule, active conductors of state hegemonism and the imperial ambitions of the country's ruling circles.

The relations between the three main centres of present-day imperialism — the USA, Western Europe and Japan — abound in visible and concealed contradictions. The economic, financial, and technological superiority which the USA enjoyed over its closest competitors until the end of the 1960s has been put to a serious trial. Western Europe and Japan managed to outdo their American patron in some things, and are also challenging the United States in such a traditional sphere of US hegemony as that of the latest technology.

Washington is continuously calling on its allies not to waste their gunpowder on internecine strife. But how are the three centres of present-day imperialism to share one roof if the Americans themselves, manipulating the dollar and the interest rates, are not loath to fatten their economy at the expense of Western Europe and Japan? Wherever the three imperialist centres manage to co-ordinate their positions, this is more often than not the effect of American pressure or outright dictation, and works in the interests and aims above all of the United States. This, in turn, sharpens, rather than blunts, the contradictions.

It appears that people are beginning to wonder about this cause-and-effect relationship. For the first time, governments of some West European countries, the social democratic and liberal parties, and the public at large have begun to discuss openly whether present US policy coincides with Western Europe's notions about its own security and whether the United States is going too far in its claims to "leadership"? The partners of the United States have had more than one occasion to see that someone else's spectacles cannot substitute for one's own eyes.

The clash of centrifugal and centripetal tendencies will, no doubt, continue as a result of changes in the correlation of forces within the imperialist system. Still, the existing complex of economic, politico-military and other common interests of the three "centres of power" can hardly be expected to break up in the prevailing conditions of the present-day world. But within the framework of this complex, Washington should not expect unquestioning obedience to US dictation on the part of its allies and competitors, and especially when this is to the detriment of their own interests.

The specificity of the inter-imperialist contradictions in the current period also includes the possibility for changes in their configuration in the coming decades, with new capitalist "centres of power" coming on the scene. This will doubtless lead to a further growth of the bulk of contradictions, to their closer interlacement and aggravation.

A new, complex and changing set of contradictions has taken shape between imperialism, on the one hand, and the developing countries and peoples, on the other. The liberation of former colonies and semi-colonies was a strong political and ideological blow to the capitalist system. It has ceased to exist in the shape that it assumed in the 19th century and which extended into the first half of the 20th. A slow, arduous, but irreversible process of socio-economic transformations is under way in the life of nations comprising the majority of mankind. This process, which has brought about not a few fundamental changes, has also encountered considerable difficulties.

By political manoeuvring, blandishments and blackmail, military threats and intimidation, and all too often by direct interference in the internal affairs of the newly free countries, capitalism has in many ways managed to sustain the earlier relationships of economic dependence. On this basis, imperialism managed to create and run the most refined system of neocolonialist exploitation, and to tighten its hold on a considerable number of newly free states.

The consequences of this are tragic. The developing countries with a population of more than two billion, have, in effect, become a region of wholesale poverty. In the early 1980s, the per capita income in the newly free countries was, on the whole, less than 10 per cent that of the developed capitalist states. And in the past thirty years, far from shrinking, the gap has grown wider. Nor is it a question of just comparative poverty. There is illiteracy and ignorance, chronic undernourishment and hunger, appalling child mortality, and epidemics that afflict hundreds of millions of people.

This is a disgrace for civilized humanity! And its culprit is imperialism. Not only from the point of view of history, that is, of colonial plunder on entire continents which left behind a heritage of unbelievable backwardness, but equally in terms of present-day practices. In just the past ten years, the profits squeezed out of the developing countries by US corporations exceeded their inputs fourfold. And in Latin America and the Caribbean, in the same period, the profits of US monopolies were over eight times greater than their inputs.

It is no exaggeration to say that, to a large extent, the imperialist system still lives by plundering the developing countries, by mercilessly exploiting them. The forms and methods are changing, but the essence remains the same. In the United States, for example, a tangible portion of the national income comes from these very sources. The developing countries are being exploited by all the imperialist states, but, unquestionably, US imperialism is doing it with the greatest impudence. Non-equivalent exchange, unequal trade, manipulations and arbitrary actions regarding interest rates and the pump of the transnational corporations are being used to one and the same end. They are adding still more to the poverty and misery of some, and to the wealth of others, and increasing the polarization in the capitalist world economy.

The distressing condition of the developing countries is a major worldwide problem. This and nothing else is the true source of many of the conflicts in Asia, Africa, and Latin America. Such is the truth, however hard the ruling circles of the imperialist powers may invoke the "hand of Moscow" in order to vindicate their neocolonialist policy and global ambitions.

Take the problem of debts. Together with the profits shipped out yearly from the developing countries, the accumulated debt means just one thing: the prospects for their development have shrunk, and a further aggravation of the already grave social, economic, and other problems is inevitable.

In the existing circumstances, these countries will not, of course, be able to repay their debts. And if no fair solution is devised, the situation will be fraught with grave socio-economic and political consequences on the international scene. It would be wrong to say that the imperialist ruling circles are blind to the underlying danger here. But all their concerns boil down to one thing – how to save the present system of enriching themselves through the exploitation and super-exploitation of the peoples of the developing countries.

This other thing is certain as well: there is an irrefutable causal connection between the trillion-sized debt of these countries and the more than trillion-sized growth of US military expenditures in the past ten years. The 200-odd billion dollars that are being annually pumped out of the developing countries and the practically equal size of the US military budget in recent years, are no coincidence. That is why militarism has a direct stake in maintaining and tightening the system of neocolonial super-exploitation.

It is also obvious that with capitalism's contradictions growing sharper and its sphere of predominance shrinking, neocolonialism is becoming an increasingly important source of means that provide monopoly capital with the possibility for social manoeuvring, reducing social tensions in the leading bourgeois states, and for bribing some sections of the working people. It is a truly extraordinary source, for a worker's hourly rate in the advanced capitalist states is higher, some times several times higher, than a day's earnings in the countries of Asia, Africa and Latin America.

All this cannot go on forever. But, of course, no miracle can be expected: the situation is not going to straighten itself out on its own. The military force that the USA is counting on to maintain the status quo, to safeguard the interests of the monopolies and the military-industrial complex, and to prevent any further progressive change in the newly free countries, can only complicate the situation and precipitate new conflicts. The bags of money are liable to become kegs of gunpowder. Sooner or later, in this area too, capitalism will have to choose between the policy of force and shameless plunder, on the one hand, and the opportunity for co-operation on an equitable basis, on the other. The solutions must be radical — in the interests of the peoples of the developing states.

Analysis of yet another group of contradictions — those on a global scale, affecting the very foundations of the existence of

civilisation — leads to serious conclusions. This refers first of all to pollution of the environment, the air and oceans, and to the depletion of natural resources. The problems are aggravated not just by the excessive loads on the natural systems as a consequence of the scientific and technological revolution and the increasing extent of man's activity. Engels, in his time, foresaw the ill effects of subordinating the use of natural resources to the blind play of market forces. The need for effective international procedures and mechanisms, which would make for the rational use of the world's resources as an asset belonging to all humanity, is becoming increasingly apparent.

The global problems, affecting all humanity, cannot be resolved by one state or a group of states. This calls for co-operation on a worldwide scale, for close and constructive joint action by the majority of countries. This co-operation must be based on completely equal rights and a respect for the sovereignty of each state. It must be based on conscientious compliance with accepted commitments and with the standards of international law. Such is the main demand of the times in which we live.

Capitalism also causes an impoverishment of **culture**, an erosion of the spiritual values created over the centuries. Nothing elevates man more than knowledge. But in probably no other period of history has mankind experienced any stronger pressure of falsehood and deceit than it does now. Bourgeois propaganda foists cleverly doctored information on people all over the world, imposing thoughts and feelings, and inculcating a civic and social attitude advantageous to the ruling forces. What knowledge, what values and moral standards are implicit in the information dispensed to the people and in the system of education is, first and foremost, a political problem.

Life itself brings up the question of safeguarding culture, of protecting it from bourgeois corruption and vandalization. That is one of the most important worldwide tasks. We cannot afford to neglect the long-term psychological and moral consequences of imperialism's current practices in the sphere of culture. Its impoverishment under the onslaught of unbridled commercialism and the cult of force, the propaganda of racism, of lowly instincts, the ways of the criminal world and the "lower depths" of society, must be, and certainly will be, rejected by mankind.

The problems, as you see, comrades, are many, and they are large-scale and intricate. But it is clear that their comprehension is, on the whole, lagging behind the scope and depth of the current tasks. The imperative condition for success in resolving the pressing issues of international life is to reduce the time of search for political accords and to secure the swiftest possible constructive action.

We are perfectly well aware that not everything by far is within our power and that much will depend on the West, on its leaders' ability to see things in sober perspective at important cross-roads of history. The US President said once that if our planet were threatened by a landing from another planet, the USSR and the USA would quickly find a common language. But isn't a nuclear disaster a more tangible danger than a landing by extra-terrestrials? Isn't the ecological threat big enough? Don't all countries have a common stake in finding a sensible and fair approach to the problems of the developing states and peoples?

Lastly, isn't all the experience accumulated by mankind enough to draw well-substantiated practical conclusions today rather than wait until some other crisis breaks out? What does the United States hope to win in the long term by producing doctrines that can no longer ensure US security within the modest dimensions of our planet?

To keep in the saddle of history, imperialism is resorting to all possible means. But such a policy is costing the world dearly. The nations are compelled to pay an ever higher price for it. To pay both directly and indirectly. To pay with millions of human lives, with a depletion of national resources, with the waste of gigantic sums on the arms race. With the failure to solve numerous, increasingly difficult problems. And in the long run, perhaps, with the highest possible price that can be imagined.

The US ruling circles are clearly losing their realistic bearings in this far from simple period of history. Aggressive international behaviour, increasing militarization of politics and thinking, contempt for the interests of others — all this is leading to the inevitable moral and political isolation of US imperialism, widening the abyss between it and the rest of humanity. It is as though the opponents of peace in that country are unaware that when nuclear weapons are at the ready, for civilization time and space lose their habitual contours, and mankind becomes the captive of an accident.

Will the ruling centres of the capitalist world manage to embark on the path of sober, constructive assessments of what is going on? The easiest thing is to say: maybe yes and maybe no. But history denies us the right to make such predictions. We cannot take "no" for an answer to the question: will mankind survive or not? We say: the progress of society, the life of civilization, must and will continue.

We say this not only by dint of the optimism that is usual for Communists, by dint of our faith in people's intelligence and common sense. We are realists and are perfectly well aware that the two worlds are divided by very many things, and deeply divided too. But we also see clearly that the need to resolve the most vital problems affecting all humanity must prompt them towards interaction, awaken humanity's heretofore unseen power of self-preservation. And here is the stimulus for solutions commensurate with the realities of our time.

The course of history, of social progress, requires ever more insistently that there should be **constructive and creative interaction between states and peoples on the scale of the entire world**. Not only does it so require, but it also creates the requisite political, social and material premises for it.

Such interaction is essential in order to prevent nuclear catastrophe, in order that civilization could survive. It is essential in order that other worldwide problems that are growing more acute should also be resolved jointly in the interests of all concerned. The prevailing dialectics of present-day development consists in a combination of competition and confrontation between the two systems and in a growing tendency towards interdependence of the countries of the world community. This is precisely the way, through the struggle of opposites, through arduous effect, groping in the dark to some extent, as it were, that the controversial but **interdependent and in many ways integral world** is taking shape.

The Communists have always been aware of the intrinsic complexity and contradictoriness of the paths of social progress. But at the centre of these processes — and this is the chief distinction of the communist world outlook — there unfailingly stands man, his interests and cares. Human life, the possibilities for its comprehensive development, as Lenin stressed, is of the greatest value; the interests of social development rank above all else. This is what guides the CPSU in its practical activity.

As we see it, the main trend of struggle in contemporary conditions consists in creating worthy, truly human material and spiritual conditions of life for all nations, ensuring that our planet should be habitable, and in cultivating a caring attitude towards its riches, especially to man himself — the greatest treasure, and all his potentials. And here we invite the capitalist system to compete with us under the conditions of a durable peace.

II. THE STRATEGIC COURSE: ACCELERATION
OF THE COUNTRY'S SOCIO-ECONOMIC
DEVELOPMENT

Comrades, by advancing the strategy of accelerating the country's socio-economic development at the April Plenary Meeting, the Central Committee of the CPSU adopted a decision of historic significance. It won the wholehearted support of the Party, of the entire people, and is being submitted for discussion at the Congress.

What do we mean by acceleration? First of all, raising the rate of economic growth. But that is not all. In substance it means a new quality of growth: an all-out intensification of production on the basis of scientific and technological progress, a structural reconstruction of the economy, effective forms of management and of organizing and stimulating labour.

The policy of acceleration is not confined to changes in the economic field. It envisages an active social policy, a consistent emphasis on the principle of socialist justice. The strategy of acceleration presupposes an improvement of social relations, a renovation of the forms and methods of work of political and ideological institutions, a deepening of socialist democracy, and resolute overcoming of inertness, stagnation and conservatism — of everything that is holding back social progress.

The main thing that will ensure us success is the living creativity of the masses, the maximum use of the tremendous potentials and advantages of the socialist system.

In short, comrades, acceleration of the country's socio-economic development is the key to all our problems: immediate and long-term, economic and social, political and ideological, domestic and foreign. That is the only way a new qualitative condition of Soviet society can and must be achieved.

A. The Results of Socio-economic Development and the Need for Its Acceleration

Comrades, the programme tasks of the Party raised and discussed at our Congress necessitate a broad approach to the assessment of the results of the country's development. In the quarter of a century since the adoption of the third CPSU Programme, the Soviet Union has achieved impressive successes. The fixed production assets of our economy have increased seven times. Thousands of enterprises have been built, and new industries created. The national income has gone up by nearly 300 per cent, industrial production 400 per cent and agricultural production 70 per cent.

Before the war and in the early postwar years the level of the US economy appeared to us hard to attain, whereas already in the 1970s we had come substantially closer to it in terms of our scientific, technical and economic potential, and had even surpassed it in the output of certain key items.

These achievements are the result of tremendous effort by the people. They have enabled us to considerably enhance the wellbeing of Soviet citizens. In a quarter of a century real per capita incomes have gone up 160 per cent, and the social consumption funds more than 400 per cent. Fifty-four million flats have been built, which enabled us to improve the living conditions of the majority of families. The transition to universal secondary education has been completed. The number of people who finished higher educational establishments has increased fourfold. The successes of science, medicine, and culture are universally recognized. The panorama of achievements will not be complete if I say nothing about the deep-going changes in social relations, the relations between nations and the further development of democracy.

At the same time, difficulties began to build up in the economy in the 1970s, with the rates of economic growth declining visibly. As a result, the targets for economic development set in the CPSU Programme, and even the lower targets of the 9th and 10th five-year plans, were not attained. Neither did we manage to carry out fully the social programme charted for this period. A lag ensued in the material base of science and education, health protection, culture, and everyday services.

Certainly, the state of affairs was affected, among other things, by certain factors beyond our control. But they were not decisive. The main thing was that we had failed to produce a timely political assessment of the changed economic situation, that we failed to apprehend the acute and urgent need for converting the economy to intensive methods of development, and for the active use of the achievements of scientific and technological progress in the national economy. There were many appeals and a lot of talk on this score, but practically no headway was made.

By inertia, the economy continued to develop largely on an extensive basis, being oriented towards drawing additional labour and material resources into production. As a result, the rate of growth of labour productivity and certain other efficiency indicators dropped substantially. The attempts to rectify matters by undertaking new projects affected the problem of balance. The economy, despite the enormous resources at its disposal, ran into shortage of them. A gap appeared between the needs of society and the attained level of production, between the effective demand and the supply of goods.

And though efforts have been made of late, we have not succeeded in wholly remedying the situation. The output of most types of industrial and agricultural goods fell short of the targets set by the 26th Congress of the CPSU for the 11th five-year-plan period. There are serious lags in engineering, the oil and coal industries, electrical engineering, in ferrous metals and chemical industries, and in capital construction. Neither have the targets been met for the main indicators of efficiency and the improvement of the people's standard of living.

And we, comrades, must draw the most serious lessons from all this.

The **first** of them may be described as the lesson of truth. A responsible analysis of the past clears the way to the future, whereas a half-truth which shamefully evades the sharp corners holds down the elaboration of realistic policy, and impedes our advance. "Our strength", Lenin said, "lies in stating the truth." That is precisely why the Central Committee deemed it essential to refer once more in the new edition of the Party Programme to the negative processes that had surfaced in the 1970s and the early 1980s. That is why, too, we speak of them at the Congress today.

The **other lesson** concerns the sense of purpose and resolve in practical actions. The switchover to an intensive development of such an enormous economy as ours is no simple matter and calls for considerable effort, time, and the loftiest sense of responsibility. But once transformations are launched, we must not confine ourselves to half-hearted measures. We must act consistently and energetically, and must not hesitate to take the boldest of steps.

And **one more lesson** — the main one, I might say. The success of any undertaking depends to a decisive degree on how actively and consciously the masses take part in it. To convince broad sections of the working people that the chosen path is correct, to interest them **morally** and materially, and to restructure the psychology of the cadres — these are the crucial conditions for the acceleration of our growth. The advance will be all the more rapid, the tighter our discipline and organization will be, and the higher the responsibility of each for his job and its results.

Today, the prime task of the Party and the entire people is to reverse resolutely the unfavourable tendencies in the development of the economy, to impart to it the due dynamism and to give scope to the initiative and creativity of the masses, to truly revolutionary change.

There is no other way. In the absence of accelerated economic growth our social programmes will remain wishful thinking, even though, comrades, they cannot be put off. Soviet people must within a short time feel the results of the common effort to resolve cardinally the food problem, to meet the need for high-quality goods and services, to improve the medical services, housing, the conditions of life, and environmental protection.

The acceleration of socio-economic development will enable us to contribute considerably to the consolidation of world socialism, and will raise to a higher level our co-operation with franternal countries. It will considerably expand our capacity for economic ties with the peoples of developing countries, and with countries of the capitalist world. In other words, implementation of the policy of acceleration will have far-reaching consequences for the destiny of our Motherland.

B. Economic Policy Guidelines

Comrades, the draft Programme of the CPSU and the draft Guidelines define the main targets of our economic and social development. By the end of this century we intend to increase the national income nearly twofold while doubling the production potential and qualitatively transforming it. Labour productivity will go up by 2.3-2.5 times, energy consumption per rouble of national income will drop by 28.6 per cent and metal consumption by nearly 50 per cent. This will signify a sharp turn towards intensifying production, towards improving quality and effectiveness.

Subsequently, by intensifying these processes we intend to switch over to an economy having a higher level of organization and effectiveness, with comprehensively developed productive forces, mature socialist relations of production, and a smoothly-functioning economic mechanism. That is our strategic line.

As was emphasized at the conference in the Central Committee of the CPSU in June 1985, the main factors behind this line are scientific and technological progress and a fundamental transformation of society's productive forces. It is impossible to effect cardinal changes with the previous material and technical foundation. The way out, as we see it, lies in thorough modernization of the national economy on the basis of the latest scientific and technological advances, breakthroughs on the leading avenues of scientific and technological progress, and restructuring of the economic mechanism and management system.

1. Modernization of the National Economy on the Basis of Scientific and Technological Progress

The CPSU has tremendous experience in carrying out major scientific-technological and socio-economic transformations. However significant they are, the scale and complexity of the work we carried out in the past cannot be compared with what has to be done in the period ahead to modernise the national economy.

What do we need for this?

First of all, changing the structural and investment policy. The substance of the changes lies in shifting the centre of attention from quantitative indices to quality and efficiency, from intermediate results to end results, from building up production assets to renewing them, from expanding fuel and raw material resources to making better use of them, and also to speeding up the development of research-intensive industries and of the production and social infrastructures.

A big step forward is to be made in this direction in the current five-year period. It is intended to allocate upwards of 200 billion roubles of capital investments — more than during the past ten years — for modernizing and technically reequipping production. Sizeable though these amounts are, the planning and economic bodies will have to continue the search for additional resources for these purposes.

Large-scale integrated programmes in the strategic areas have been drawn up, and their implementation has begun. The industries that play the key role in scientific and technological progress, that assure a quick economic return and the solution of urgent social problems, will move ahead more dynamically. Substantial funds and material, scientific, and manpower resources are being concentrated to speed up their development.

It is clear that the effectiveness of modernization and also the economic growth rates depend to a crucial degree on **machine-building**. This is where the fundamental scientific and technological ideas are materialized, where new implements of labour and machine systems that determine progress in the other branches of the national economy are developed. Here the foundations are laid down for a broad advance to basically new, resource-saving technologies, higher productivity of labour and better quality of output.

The Congress delegates know that the CPSU Central Committee and the USSR Council of Ministers recently adopted a decision on the further development of machine-building. In substance, it is a national programme for modernising this essential sector of industry. A single management body has been set up in it. The machine-building complex has been set the goal of sharply raising the technical-economic level and quality of machines, equipment and instruments already by the end of the 12th five-year plan period. The capital investments allocated for modernising this industry will be 80 per cent greater than in the previous five years.

What, specifically, do we expect from the implementation of this programme? The output of machinery and equipment is to increase by more than 40 per cent, and their quality standards will be improved. The growing stream of machines of new generations will pave the way for a fundamental retooling of the national economy and a growth in its effectiveness. The resultant annual savings will amount to the labour of about 12 million people, more than 100 million tons of fuel, and many billions of roubles. Calculations show that the use of the Don-1500 harvester alone, for example, will lead to a considerable reduction in the number of grain harvesting machines, will release about 400,000 machine-operators, and will reduce grain losses by millions of tons.

Large-scale introduction of computers and comprehensive automation of production will tremendously influence the rate of technical modernization. Concrete targets in the development and large-scale application of modern computers and expansion of the manufacture of their components have been defined. The development of computer software and of management information systems is being put on an industrial footing. The Academy of Sciences of the USSR has set up an information science and computer technologies division to co-ordinate research and development.

Radical modernization of the fuel and energy complex is the keynote of the Energy Programme. The Programme puts the emphasis on energy-saving technologies, on the replacement of liquid fuel by natural gas and coal, and on more sophisticated methods of oil refining. Advanced technologies are also to be employed in the extraction industry: open-cast coal mining, the use of hydromonitors in coal extraction, the development of improved and more reliable oil extraction equipment and the universal introduction of automated systems. In the course of the current five-year period two and a half times more nuclear power plant generating capacities will be started up than in the previous five years, and outmoded units at thermal power stations will be replaced on a large scale.

A great deal will have to be done in the metal-making and chemical industries, in introducing more highly productive equipment there. The production of fundamentally new and improved structural and other advanced materials will accelerate the development of electronics, machine-building, construction, and other branches of the economy.

The Party attaches enormous importance to technical reequipment of the production infrastructure, in the first place, in transport and communications. Top priority will be given to the development of light industry and other industries that directly meet consumer demand. Advanced equipment for them is to be manufactured not only by specialized industries but also by other industries.

We will not be able to carry out technical modernization unless we radically improve capital construction. This calls for raising the entire building industry complex to a new industrial and organizational level, shortening the investment cycle by a minimum of 50 per cent both in modernizing enterprises and in the construction of new facilities. We cannot reconcile ourselves any longer to slow construction rates that freeze enormous sums and retard scientific and technological progress in the national economy.

All these tasks, comrades, are gigantic in scale and significance. How they are carried out will, in the final analysis, determine the fulfilment of our plans and the rates of our growth. Each sector and each enterprise must have a clear-cut programme for the continuous modernization of production. The responsibility of the planning and economic bodies for the achievement of planned targets will increase accordingly. Party organizations should also direct their activities towards this.

It is especially important to prevent window dressing and the use of palliative instead of substantive measures. There are disquieting instances, and by no means solitary ones, of ministries and departments erecting new facilities under the guise of modernization, of stuffing them with outdated equipment, and of drawing up costly projects that do not assure the rise of production to higher technical-economic levels.

Here is an illustration of that approach. The Bryansk Engineering Works, which puts out motors for diesel locomotives, is now in the middle of a 140-million rouble retooling programme. What results will this modernization of capacities yield? It turns out that the programme does not provide for the introduction of advanced technologies, the number of workers has already been increased by nearly 1,000, and the return on the assets has dropped. The worst part of it is that they intend to use the new capacities to manufacture an outdated motor, although a more efficient model has been designed and tested.

What does the stance of the executives of the Ministry of the Heavy Machine-Building Industry and of the Ministry of Railways mean? Evidently some comrades have failed to grasp the profound importance of the tasks confronting them. Such facts deserve stern condemnation as undermining the Party's policy of modernization and of accelerated scientific and technological progress. Such cases should be examined with all severity.

The need for modernization poses new tasks for **scientific research**. The CPSU will consistently pursue a policy of strengthening the material and technical base of scientific research to the maximum, of providing scientists with the conditions for fruitful work. However, our country is entitled to expect, from its scientists, discoveries and inventions that will bring about genuinely revolutionary changes in the development of machinery and production methods.

Important measures to make the work of research establishments more effective have been outlined lately. They deal with incentives for scientists and new forms of interaction between science and production. A decision was recently adopted to set up inter-sectoral research-and-technological complexes, including the large institutes that are leaders in their respective fields, among them institutes under Academies of Sciences, design organizations and pilot plants.

Steps are also being taken to intensify the work of sectoral research institutes and to increase their contribution to speeding up scientific and technological progress. However, this process is going ahead at an impermissibly slow pace. Many institutes are still an appendage of ministry staffs; not infrequently they support departmental interests and are bogged down in red tape and paper-work. The question of bringing science closer to production, of including sectoral research institutes into production and research-and-production associations, was forcefully raised at the June conference. We must ascertain who is opposing this, what stand the ministries and their Party committees take on this issue, and how they are reacting to life's demands.

The research potential of higher educational establishments must also be used more effectively. Upwards of 35 per cent of our country's research and educational personnel, including about half of the holders of doctoral degrees, are concentrated there but they carry out no more than 10 per cent of the research projects. The respective departments should draft and submit proposals for strengthening the links between university research and production. The proposals should also take into account the training of the next generation of researchers. Just as a forest cannot live on without undergrowth, a true scientist is inconceivable without students. This is a question of the future of science, and, therefore, of our country, too. Beginning with their freshman year, college and university students should be drawn into research work and into participation in applying research findings in production. This is the only way that real scientists and creatively-thinking specialists can be trained.

In sum, comrades, the orientation of science towards the needs of the national economy should be carried out more energetically. However, it is equally important to orient production towards science, to make it maximally receptive to scientific and technological advances. Regrettably, no few scientific discoveries and major inventions fail to find practical application for years, and sometimes for decades. I shall cite a few examples.

The non-wear and tear effect, which Soviet scientists discovered three decades ago, led to the development of fundamentally new lubricants that greatly increase the service life of machine parts subjected to friction and sharply reduce labour outlays. This discovery, which may yield a saving of many millions of roubles, has not yet been applied on a broad scale because of the inertness of some high-ranking executives of the USSR Ministry of Petrochemical Industry and of a number of other ministries and departments.

The Ministry of the Motor Vehicle Industry and planning bodies are to blame for the fact that for about ten years now a newly-invented anti-friction bearing, which makes machines more reliable and failure-safe under the most rigorous operating conditions, has not been applied on a large scale. The Ministry of the Machine-Tool Industry has impermissibly held up the manufacture of unique hydraulic motors enabling extensive use of hydraulic techniques in mining and elsewhere, to increase labour productivity several-fold and to improve working conditions.

Unfortunately, this list could be continued. This kind of attitude to new inventions is not infrequently based on the ambitions of some groups of scientists, on departmental hostility towards inventions made "by others", and a lack of interest on the part of production managers in introducing them. It is no secret that even the examination of invention applications is sometimes an ordeal that drags on for years.

We cannot reach our targets in accelerating scientific and technological progress unless we find levers that will guarantee priority only to those research establishments and industrial enterprises whose work collectives actively introduce whatever is new and progressive and seek ways and means of manufacturing articles of high quality and effective yield.

We have already accumulated a definite amount of experience in improving the economic mechanism in the sphere of science and its interaction with production. It must be thoroughly analysed and then applied without delay, closely linking up material incentives for research collectives and individual researchers with their actual contribution to the resolving of scientific and technological problems.

At all levels of economic management there should be a new attitude to the introduction of new methods and technology. This also refers to the State Planning Committee of the USSR, which should go over more boldly to all-inclusive planning of scientific and technological progress, as well as to the USSR State Committee for Science and Technology, which is reorganizing its work too slowly. The Academy of Sciences of the USSR, ministries and departments should pay more attention to basic research and to applying its findings in production. This is a sacred duty of every scientist, engineer, designer, and manager of an enterprise.

Our activity in the sphere of **foreign economic contacts** must be tied up more closely with the new tasks. There should be a large-scale, forward-looking approach to mutually advantageous economic relations. The member-countries of the Council for Mutual Economic Assistance have worked out a policy of this kind. It presupposes a switchover in economic relations among them from primarily trade relations to deeper specialisation and co-operation in production, above all, in machine-building, and to the establishment of joint associations and research-and-production complexes.

We have no few departments and organizations that are responsible for separate spheres of foreign economic relations but they do not always co-ordinate their work. In setting the aim of actively using foreign economic contacts to speed up our development we have in mind a step-by-step restructuring of foreign trade, of making our exports and imports more effective.

2. *Solving the Food Problem: A Top-Priority Task*

Comrades, a problem we will have to solve in the shortest time possible is that of fully supplying our country with food. This is the aim of the Party's present agrarian policy, formulated in the decisions taken by the CPSU. Central Committee at its May 1982 Plenary Meeting and in the Food Programme of the USSR. In the period since their adoption a good deal has been done to expand the material and technical base of agriculture and of the related industries. The economy of the collective farms, state farms, inter-farm enterprises and processing plants has become stronger; the productivity of crop-farming and livestock farming has risen.

There is progress, but the lag in agriculture is being overcome slowly. A decisive turn is needed in the agrarian sector to improve the food supply noticeably already during the 12th five-year plan period. It is planned to more than double the growth rate of farm production and to ensure a substantial increase in the per capita consumption of meat, milk, vegetables, and fruit.

Can we do this? We can and we must. The Party has therefore worked out additional measures to raise the efficiency of all sectors of the agro-industrial complex. Their substance consists in changing the socio-economic situation in the rural areas, in creating the conditions for greater intensification and guaranteed farm produce. The emphasis is put on economic methods of management, broader autonomy of collective farms and state farms and their higher responsibility for the results of their work.

In carrying out this policy we will have to make more effective use of the production potential in the agro-industrial complex and concentrate efforts and resources on the most important sectors providing the highest returns. It is a question, first and foremost, of increasing soil fertility and creating the conditions for stable farming. As the experience of recent years has shown, the key of success lies in large-scale application of intensive technologies. They have a tremendous effect. Their application made it possible to obtain, last year alone, an additional 16 million tons of grain and a substantial amount of other produce.

Reducing losses of farm produce during harvesting, transportation, storage, and processing is the most immediate source of augmenting food stocks. We have no small potentialities in this respect; an increase in consumption resources could amount to as much as 20 per cent, and in the case of some products to as much as 30 per cent. Besides, eliminating the losses would cost two to three times less than supplying the same amount of produce.

The Central Committee and the Government have now defined major steps to reduce losses. Rapid expansion of agricultural machine-building will make it possible to equip the collective farms and state farms with highly productive machines capable of performing all the field jobs faster and better. We have also made additional outlays to increase the manufacture of machinery for the food industry and facilities for the processing and storage of food.

The Party and the state will persistently continue to strengthen the material and technical base of the agro-industrial complex. It is equally clear, however, that people will, as before, be the mainspring and inspiration of progress. Today, more than ever before, agriculture needs people who want to work actively, who have a high level of professional skill and a feeling for the new. Constant attention to the working and living conditions of the people in rural areas is the best guarantee of all our successes. All our plans are geared to this, and it is important that they should be carried out unswervingly.

All these are urgent measures, but the programme of action is not confined to them. The switchover of the agrarian sector to new methods of administration and management has to be completed. The establishment, in the centre and in the localities, of unified management bodies of the agro-industrial complex, called upon to carry out genuine and effective integration of agriculture and of the related industries, is undoubtedly a step of fundamental significance.

The establishment of this organizational framework is backed up by an effective economic mechanism. Proposals on this score have already been drafted. The main idea is to give broad scope to economic methods of management, to substantially broaden the autonomy of collective farms and state farms, to increase their interest in and responsibility for the end results. In substance, it is a question of creatively applying, in the conditions of today, Lenin's idea of the food tax.

It is intended to establish fixed plans for the purchase of produce from the collective farms and state farms for each year of the five-year period; these plans will not be altered. Simultaneously, the farms will be given the opportunity to use all the produce harvested over and above the plan, and in the case of fruit and potatoes and other vegetables a considerable part of the planned produce, as they see fit. The farms can sell it, additionally the state, can sell it, either fresh or processed, on the collective-farm market or through co-operative trade outlets, or use it for other needs, including the needs of personal subsidiary holdings. Additional allocations of material resources for which there is a heightened demand, and also other incentives, will encourage farms to sell grain to the state over and above the plan.

In future, the republics, territories, and regions will be given fixed quotas for the delivery of produce to centralized stocks; everything produced over and above that will be kept for the local supply system.

There is to be a transition to improved planning methods based on advanced standards. The role of cost accounting will be substantially increased. Past experience shows that neglect of the principles of self-support, material interest and responsibility for performance led to a deterioration of the financial and economic position of collective farms and state farms and also to their considerable indebtedness. Genuine cost accounting, with the incomes of enterprises depending upon the end results, should become the rule for all links of the agro-industrial complex and, first and foremost, the collective farms and state farms. The contract and job-by-job systems of payment at the levels of terms, groups, and families to whom the means of production, including land, will be assigned for a period specified by contract, will become widespread.

There will be big opportunities for displaying initiative and resourcefulness. This also presupposes, however, a higher sense of responsibility for meeting the targets of the Food Programme, for the results of the financial and economic activity of collective farms, state farms, inter-farm enterprises and organisations. A reliable barrier must be erected in the way of mismanagement and parasitism, and an end must be put to excuses such as "objective circumstances", which some collective farms and state farms have been using to cover up their inaptitude and sometimes a lack of desire to work better. The farms will have to use chiefly their own funds to develop production, increase profits and incomes and provide incentives. The practice of providing bank loans will have to be substantially altered to stimulate a higher level of activity of collective farms and state farms.

As you see, comrades, conditions for rural economic management are undergoing a cardinal change. This calls for major changes in the style and methods of guidance of the agro-industrial complex. An end must be put to incompetent interference in production activity in rural areas. We expect the State Agro-Industrial Committee of the USSR and its local bodies to do everything so that our country receives weighty returns from the measures that are being taken.

3. Economic Management Must Measure Up to the New Demands

Comrades, the new economic tasks cannot be solved without an in-depth readjustment of the economic mechanism, without creating an integral, effective and flexible system of management that will make it possible to take fuller advantage of the possibilities of socialism.

It is obvious that economic management requires constant improvement. However, the situation today is such that we cannot limit ourselves to partial improvements. A radical reform is needed. Its meaning consists in truly subordinating the whole of our production to the requirements of society, to the satisfaction of people's needs, in orienting management towards raising efficiency and quality, accelerating scientific and technological progress, promoting a greater interest of people in the results of their work, initiative and socialist enterprise in every link of the national economy, and, above all, in the work collectives.

The Central Committee of the CPSU and its Political Bureau have defined guidelines for reorganizing the economic mechanism. We set ourselves the aims of:

—heightening the efficiency of centralized guidance of the economy, strengthening the role of the centre in implementing the main goals of the Party's economic strategy and in determining the rates and proportions of national economic growth, its balanced development.

Simultaneously, the practice of interference by the centre in the daily activities of the lower economic links must be overcome;

—resolutely enlarging the framework of the autonomy of associations and enterprises, increasing their responsibility for attaining the highest ultimate results. Towards this end, to transfer them to genuine cost accounting, self-support and self-financing, and to make the income level of collectives directly dependent on the efficiency of their work;

—going over to economic methods of guidance at all levels of the national economy, for which purpose to reorganize the system of material and technical supply, improve the system of price formation, financing and crediting, and work out effective incentives to eliminate overexpenditure;

—introducing modern organizational management structures, taking into account the trends towards concentration, specialization and co-operation of production. This is a question of setting up complexes of interconnected industries, research and technological inter-sectoral centres, various forms of economic associations and territorial-production associations;

—ensuring the best possible combination of sectoral and territorial economic management, integrated economic and social development of republics and regions, and the organization of rational inter-sectoral contacts;

—carrying out all-round democratization of management, heightening the part played in it by work collectives, strengthening control from below, and ensuring account-ability and publicity in the work of economic bodies.

Comrades, we now unquestionably stand before the most thorough reorganization of the socialist economic mechanism. The reorganization has begun. The direction along which work is going ahead in the agro-industrial complex has been already spoken about. Management of the machine-building complex is being upgraded. Industrial enterprises are being transferred, in the main, to a two-level system of management. Beginning with the current year, new economic management methods which have gone through experimental testing have been introduced in enterprises and associations that turn out half of the total industrial output. Their introduction in the service sphere, in construction and in transport has begun. Collective forms of organizing work and providing incentives, and economic contract systems are being applied on an ever wider scale.

We are only at the beginning of the road, however. Time and energetic efforts are needed to reorganize the economic mechanism in our country with its vast and complex economy. Difficulties may arise, and we are not guaranteed against miscalculations either, but still the main thing now is to move ahead purposefully, step by step, along the direction we have chosen, supplementing and perfecting the economic mechanism on the basis of the accumulated experience and eliminating everything that has outlived itself or has failed to justify itself.

Success will depend largely on the **reorganization of the work of the central economic bodies, first and foremost, the State Planning Committee of the USSR**. It must indeed become our country's genuine scientific and economic headquarters, freed from current economic matters. We have begun this work. New management bodies of the inter-sectoral complexes are being set up, and the major part of the day-to-day management functions is being delegated directly to the enterprises and associations. The State Planning Committee and other economic agencies must concentrate their efforts on long-term planning, on ensuring proportional and balanced economic development, on carrying out the structural policy, and on creating the economic conditions and incentives for attaining the best end results in each unit of the national economy. Considerable improvements are needed in the sphere of statistics.

Lately there has been a weakening of the **financial-credit influence on the economy**. The financial system does not sufficiently stimulate higher economic efficiency. The defective practice of income redistribution, with the losses of lagging enterprises, ministries and regions covered at the expense of those that operate profitably, has reached a large scale. This undermines cost accounting, promotes parasitism and prompts endless demands for assistance from the centre. Crediting no longer serves its purpose.

"Any radical reforms", said Lenin, "will be doomed to failure unless our financial policy is successful." Accordingly, we must radically change the substance, organization and methods of the work of the financial and credit bodies. Their chief aim is not to exercise petty control over the work of enterprises but to provide economic incentives and to consolidate money circulation and cost accounting, which is the best possible controller. Everything must be made dependent on the end result. The question of improving collection of the turnover tax, deductions from the profit and other budget revenues has obviously come on the agenda. Their size and the procedure for their payment should more effectively help reduce losses in production, raise quality of output and promote its sale.

Prices must become an active factor of economic and social policy. We shall have to carry out a planned readjustment of the price system as an integral whole in the interests of organizing effective cost accounting and in conformity with the aims of increasing the real incomes of the population. Prices must be made more flexible; price levels must be linked up not only with the outlays but also with the consumer properties of the goods, their effectiveness and the degree to which products meet the needs of society and consumer demand. Ceiling prices and contract prices are to be employed more widely.

The system of **material and technical supply** also needs thorough improvement. It must be turned into a flexible economic mechanism which helps the national economy to function rhythmically and steadily. It is the direct duty of the State Committee for Material and Technical Supply to contribute actively to the establishment of direct long-term relations between producers and consumers on a contractual basis, and to improve the observance of the terms of delivery. Wholesale trade in the means of production should be developed.

In the final analysis, everything we are doing to improve management and planning and to readjust organizational structures is aimed at creating conditions for the **effective functioning of the basic link of the economic system: the association or enterprise**.

As shown by analysis, the results of the experiments that have been carried out could have been much better, if, on the one hand, there had been a corresponding reorganization of the work of industrial ministries and central economic agencies, which continue their attempts to restrict the powers of enterprises, and, on the other hand, if the incentives for higher efficiency had been brought home to every section, work team and workplace. Special attention should be paid to this.

It is high time to put an end to the practice of ministries and departments exercising petty tutelage over enterprises. Ministries should concentrate their attention on technical policy, on intra-sectoral proportions, and on meeting the requirements of the national economy in high-quality products put out by their respective industries. Enterprises and organizations should be given the right independently to sell to one another what they produce over and above the plan, as well as raw and other materials, equipment, etc., which they do not use. They should also be given the legal right to make such sales to the population. What sense is there in destroying or dumping onto waste heaps articles that could come in useful in the household, in building homes, garages or cottages on garden and vegetable plots?

It would be difficult to overestimate the role of economic **standards**. When the work collectives of enterprises know, ahead of time, specifics of the planned period — delivery targets, prices, deductions from profits to the budget, standards for forming wage funds and cost-accounting incentives funds — they can draw up creatively plans which provide for higher production growth rates and much higher efficiency without being afraid to reveal their as yet untapped potentialities. Moreover, enterprises should be given the possibility — following the example of the Volga Auto Works and the Sumy Engineering Works — themselves to earn the funds needed to expand and retool production.

It is especially important to give enterprises and organizations greater autonomy in the sphere of consumer goods manufacture and services. Their task is to react quickly to consumer demand. It is along these lines that we are reshaping the economic mechanism of light industry. The range of targets approved from above is being sharply limited for enterprises in this sphere; their plans will be drawn up chiefly on the basis of contracts with trade organizations, which, in turn, must see to it that their orders conform to the actual consumer demand. In other words, the quantity, range, and quality of goods, that is, just what people need, will be the main thing, and not gross output. Besides, it is planned to establish inter-sectoral production and industrial-commercial associations for the manufacture and sale of light industry goods and to open more retail outlets operated by them.

The time has also come to solve another problem. An enterprise's wage fund should be directly tied in with the returns from the sale of its products. This will help to exclude the manufacture and supply of low-grade goods for which there is no demand, or, as they say, production for the warehouse. Incidentally, that approach should be applied not only in light industry. We can no longer reconcile ourselves to a situation in which the personnel of enterprises producing worthless goods lead an untroubled life, drawing their full pay and receiving bonuses and other benefits. Indeed, why should we pay for work which produces goods nobody wants to buy. One way or another all this goes against us, comrades! We must not forget about this.

A well-thought-out approach must also be taken to the question of a rational combination of **large, medium and small enterprises**. As experience shows, small, well-equipped plants have their own advantages in many cases. They can be quicker and more flexible in taking into account technological innovations and changes in demand, can meet the demand faster for small-batch and separate items, and can make better use of available manpower, especially in small towns.

Another substantial aspect of readjustment is consolidation of the territorial approach to planning and management. This is especially important for our vast and multi-national country with its diverse features. The actions of ministries and departments that neglect the conditions in and the requirements of regions, with resulting economic imbalances, were rightly criticised at Party conferences and at congresses of the communist parties of constituent republics.

Some suggestions are also being received on this score. It is evidently worthwhile giving thought to enlarging the powers of republican and local bodies — following the example of the agro-industrial complex — in the management of construction, inter-sectoral production units, the social and production infrastructures, and many consumer goods factories. The work of the State Planning Committee of the USSR and of the ministries should get a broader territorial orientation. The question of national-economic management on the basis of large economic areas deserves study.

Our short- and long-term plans are linked, to a considerable degree, with the tapping of the natural wealth of Siberia and the Soviet Far East. This is a very important matter that requires a statesmanlike approach ensuring integrated regional development. Special attention should be paid to providing people there with the conditions for fruitful work and a full-blooded life. That is the main question today, and fulfilment of the set targets depends on how it is solved.

Attention should be drawn at our Congress to the problems involved in the further socio-economic development of the Non-Black-Earth Zone of the Russian Federation. I will stress two points. The Central Committee of the CPSU and the Soviet Government have adopted special decisions for an upswing in the agriculture of the Non-Black-Earth Zone, and they must be carried out unswervingly and fully. That is in the first place. And in the second place, the local Party, government and economic bodies and work collectives must pay much more attention to making effective use of the potential accumulated there and of the allocated resources.

Consolidation of the territorial principle of management calls for a higher level of economic guidance in each republic, region, city, and district. Proposals that come from the localities are at times not thought out thoroughly, not dictated by the interests of the national economy but rather by a dependant's mentality and sometimes even by self-seeking interests, which draw the economy into capital-intensive and low-productive projects. Due attention is not paid everywhere to raising the efficiency of production. In Kazakhstan, for example, the share of national income per unit of fixed production assets is a third less than the average for the Soviet economy. In Turkmenia, the productivity of social labour has not grown at all in 15 years. Thought should be given to how to tie in the resources allocated for social needs more closely with the efficiency of the regional economy.

Comrades, every readjustment of the economic mechanism begins, as you know, with a readjustment of thinking, with a rejection of old stereotypes of thought and actions, with a clear understanding of the new tasks. This refers primarily to the activity of our economic personnel, to the functionaries of the central links of administration. Most of them have a clear idea of the Party's initiatives, actively support them, boldly tackle complicated assignments, and seek and find the best ways of carrying them out. This attitude deserves utmost support. It is hard, however, to understand those who adopt a wait-and-see policy or who, like the Gogol character that thought up all kinds of fanciful ideas, do not actually do anything or change anything. There will be no reconciliation with the stand taken by functionaries of that kind. We will simply have to part ways with them. All the more so do we have to part ways with those who hope that everything will settle down and return to the old lines. That will not happen, comrades!

In our work on restructuring the economy and the economic mechanism it is more important than ever to rely on science. Life prompts us to take a new look at some theoretical ideas and concepts. This applies to such major problems as the interaction of the productive forces and the production relations, socialist ownership and its economic forms, commodity-money relations, the co-ordination of centralism with the autonomy of economic organizations, and so on.

Practice has revealed the insolvency of the ideas that under the conditions of socialism **the conformity of production relations to the nature of the productive forces** is ensured automatically, as it were. In real life, everything is more complicated. Indeed, the socialist production relations open up broad vistas for development of the productive forces. However, they must be constantly improved. And that means outdated economic management methods must be noticed in good time and replaced by new ones.

The forms of production relations and the economic management and guidance system now in operation took shape, basically, in the conditions of extensive economic development. These gradually grew out of date, began to lose their stimulating effect and in some respects became a brake. We are now striving to change the thrust of the economic mechanism, to overcome its costliness and to orient it towards a higher level of quality and efficiency, acceleration of scientific and technological progress and enhancement of the human factor. This is the main thing that will, in practice, signify further improvement of the socialist production relations and will provide new scope for the growth of the productive forces.

In this work we must not be stopped by long-established ideas, let alone by prejudices. If, for example, it is necessary and justifiable to apply economic standards instead of targets that are sent down as directives, this does not mean a retreat from the principles of planned guidance but only a change in its methods. The same can be applied to the need to broaden the autonomy, initiative and responsibility of associations and enterprises, and to enhance their role as socialist commodity producers.

Unfortunately, there is a widespread view when any change in the economic mechanism is regarded as practically being a retreat from the principles of socialism. In this connection I should like to emphasize the following: socio-economic acceleration and the consolidation of socialism in practice should be the supreme criterion in the improvement of management and of the entire system of the socialist production relations.

The **aspects of socialist property** as the foundation of our social system acquire great relevance. Socialist property has a rich content; it includes a multi-faceted system of relations among people, collectives, industries and regions of the country in the use of the means of production and its results, and a whole range of economic interests. This complex of relations requires a definite combination and constant regulation, especially since it is in motion. Unless we gain a deep understanding of these changes in theoretical terms we cannot arrive at correct practical decisions and consequently take prompt steps to mould a genuine sense of responsibility to socialist property.

We must provide the working people with greater incentives for putting the national riches to the best possible use and multiplying them. How can this be done? It would be naive to imagine that the feeling of ownership can be inculcated by words. A person's attitude towards property is shaped, first and foremost, by the actual conditions in which he has been put, by his possibilities of influencing the organization of production, and the distribution and use of the results of work. The problem is thus one of further intensifying socialist self-government in the economic sphere.

The role of work collectives in the use of social property must be raised decisively. It is important to carry out unswervingly the principle according to which enterprises and associations are wholly responsible for operating without losses, while the state does not bear any responsibility for their obligations. This is where the substance of cost accounting lies. You cannot be a master of your country if you are not a real master in your factory or collective farm, in your shop or livestock farm. It is the duty of the work collective to answer for everything, to multiply the social wealth. Multiplication of the social wealth, as well as losses, should affect the income level of every member of the collective.

And, of course, a reliable barrier is needed against all attempts to extract unearned income from the social property. There are still "snatchers", persons who do not consider it a crime to steal from their plant everything that comes their way, and there are also sundry bribe-takers and grabbers who do not stop at using their position for selfish purposes. The full force of the law and of public condemnation should be applied to all of them.

Attention should also be paid to such a topical problem of regulating socialist property relations as ensuring unquestionable priority of the interests of the whole people over the interests of industries and regions. Ministries, departments and territorial bodies are not the owners of means of production but merely institutions of state administration responsible to society for efficient use of the people's wealth. We cannot allow departmental and parochial interests to hinder realization of the advantages of socialist property.

We also stand for full clarity on the question of co-operative property. It has far from exhausted its possibilities in socialist production, in providing better satisfaction of people's needs. Many collective farms and other co-operative organizations are managed effectively.

And wherever the need exists, utmost support should be given to the establishment and growth of co-operative enterprises and organisations. They should become widespread in the manufacture and processing of products, in housing construction and in construction on garden and vegetable allotments, and in the sphere of services and trade.

It is also time to overcome prejudices regarding **commodity-money** relations and underestimation of these relations in planned economic guidance. Refusal to recognize the importance of their active influence on people's interest in working better and on production efficiency leads to a weakening of the cost-accounting system and to other undesirable consequences. Conversely, sound commodity-money relations on a socialist basis can create a situation and economic conditions under which the results depend entirely on the standards of the work done by the collective and on the ability and initiative of the managers.

Thus, comrades, we are obliged to assess the situation again and again and to resolutely reorganize everything that has become out of date, that has outlived itself. A profound understanding of this task by Party activists and by all personnel, as well as its comprehension by the broad masses are indispensable for success, are the point of departure in the exceptionally important work of building up a new economic mechanism and management system.

4. *Putting Reserves of Economic Growth into Action*

Comrades, the Party has worked out a strategy of deep-going transformations in the national economy and has begun to effect them. They will undoubtedly enable us to speed up economic growth. As was noted, however, this will require a good deal of time, but we must increase the growth rates at once, today. The specific feature of the 12th five-year plan period consists in retooling the national economy on a new scientific and technological basis while simultaneously stepping up the rates of our advance.

Hence the need to utilise all of our reserves to the maximum. It is more sensible to start with those that do not require big outlays but yield quick and tangible returns. This is a matter of economic-organizational and socio-psychological factors, of making better use of the production capabilities that have been built up, of making the incentives more effective, of improving the level of organization and tightening discipline, and of eliminating mismanagement. Our reserves are at hand, and with a dedicated approach plus good management they promise high returns.

Just look at the capacities in operation. The value of our country's fixed production assets exceeds 1.5 trillion roubles, but they are not all being used properly. This applies to a number of industries — to machine-building, heavy industry, and power industry and agriculture. What is especially alarming is the fact that the most active assets — machinery, equipment, and machine-tools — often stand idle or else are operated at half capacity. In the engineering industry, for example, metalcutting machine-tools are in use only slightly more than one shift a day. On the whole, our country annually loses billions of roubles' worth of industrial output because capacities are underloaded. Planning and economic bodies and work collectives at enterprises must do everything possible to ensure the operation of existing capacities at the designed level. In heavy industry alone, this would nearly double the output growth rates.

Failure to meet component delivery obligations is another hindrance. A violation of this kind in one place has a ripple effect throughout the national economy and lowers its efficiency. Jerky production also does tangible damage. It is no secret that at the beginning of the month many plants stand idle longer than they function. But at the end of the month they begin a headlong rush, as a result of which output quality is low. This chronic disease must be eradicated. Strict observance of component delivery obligations is the duty of work collectives and also of management at all levels. We will not be able to achieve our aims unless we bring order into planning and supply, create the necessary stocks, and impose higher financial liability at all levels for failure to meet obligations and for spoilage.

There are also great reserves in the use of manpower. Some economic managers complain of a manpower shortage. I think the complaints are groundless in most cases. If you look into the matter more closely you will see that there is no shortage of labour. But there is a low level of labour productivity, inadequate work organization and ineffective incentive schemes. Add to this the creation of superfluous jobs by planning and economic bodies. It is a well-known fact that some of our enterprises, design offices and research institutes have considerably larger staffs than their counterparts abroad with the same work load.

Once people at enterprises get down in earnest to improving work organization and incentives, to tightening discipline and setting higher demands, reserves that had never been thought to exist previously are brought to light. Application of the Shchokino method and the certification of work places convincingly confirm this. When Byelorussian railwaymen went over to a new pay system, with one person doing two or more different jobs, about 12,000 workers were soon freed for jobs in other sectors.

Of course, more attention must also be paid to production mechanization and automation. In tackling this problem one does not have to wait for machines and devices to be designed and made somewhere else. A great deal can be accomplished by using one's own capabilities. For instance, efforts in this direction in Zaporozhye Region led, in three years, to a 9 per cent reduction in the number of workers employed in manual jobs in industry and a 15 per cent reduction in the number of those in similar jobs in the building trades. I think that other regions, territories, and republics have no fewer possibilities. The important thing is to put persistent and dedicated effort into this, showing consideration for the people who have to perform manual operations, and striving the reduce production outlays.

Generally speaking, comrades, there are enormous economic reserves. We have not yet really begun to use many of them. The mentality of a substantial section of the managerial personnel at various levels took shape against the background of an abundance of resources. Many were spoiled by these riches, and that led to wastefulness. However, the situation changed long ago. The former influx of manpower has dwindled, and we have begun to pay a heavy price for every ton of oil, ore, and coal we extract and deliver. We cannot close our eyes at these facts; we must reckon with them. We must economise everywhere and always: on the job and at home. We must not ignore mismanagement and wastefulness. Nearly the whole of this year's growth in the national income is to come from raising labour productivity and lowering materials and energy consumption.

That is not simple but wholly feasible. All the more so since our country has accumulated experience in making thrifty use of resources; but it is not being spread fast enough. Party, YCL, and trade union organizations should constantly promote thrift and encourage those who make economical and rational use of raw materials, electrical energy, and fuel. We must make it a firm rule that overexpenditure of resources is disadvantageous and savings are tangibly rewarded.

I would like to put special emphasis on the problem of **output quality standards**. This is more than our immediate and major reserve. Accelerated scientific and technological progress is imposs- ible today without high quality standards. We are sustaining great material and moral losses because of flaws in design, deviations from technology, the use of low-grade materials and poor finishing. This affects the precision and reliability of machines and instruments and hinders satisfaction of consumer demand for goods and services. Last year millions of metres of fabrics, millions of pairs of leather footwear and many other consumer items were returned to factories or marked down as inferior-grade goods. The losses are significant: wasted raw materials and the wasted labour of hundreds of thousands of workers. Radical measures must be taken to rule out the manufacture of defective or low-grade goods. The full force of pecuniary and admi- nistrative influence and legislation must be applied for this purpose. There is also evidently a need to adopt a special law on the quality of output.

Recently the Central Committee of the CPSU called upon Party committees, government and economic bodies, trade union and YCL organizations and all working people to make maximum efforts to radically improve the quality of goods. This must be a matter of concern for every Communist, for every Soviet citizen, for all who respect their own work, for all who cherish the honour of their enterprise, their industry, and the honour of our country.

A great deal of important and intensive work lies ahead of us. The first year of the five-year plan period is a year of persistent work, a year of tests for every manager and work collective. We must pass this test, draw all the reserves of the economy into production, and consolidate the foundation for further transformations.

The industry and talent of Soviet citizens are the key to attaining the goal that has been set. It is now up to efficient organization and precise direction of this great force. The part to be played by socialist emulation in this effort cannot be overestimated. It should be spear- headed at raising the standards of work, economising and thriftiness, and reaching the target set before each collective and at each work- place. Enthusiasm and the growing skills have been and, we are confident, will continue to be our reliable support.

C. The Basic Guidelines of Social Policy

Comrades, questions of social policy, concern for man's welfare, have always stood at the centre of our Party's attention.

The social sphere encompasses the interests of classes and social groups, nations and nationalities, the relationship between society and individual, the conditions of work and life, health and leisure. **It is the sphere in which the results of economic activity affecting the vital interests of the working people are realized, and the loftiest aims of socialism are carried into effect. It is the sphere in which the humanism of the socialist system, its qualitative difference from capitalism, is seen most distinctly and graphically**.

Socialism has eliminated the main source of social injustice — the exploitation of man by man, and inequality in relation to the means of production. Social justice reigns in all areas of socialist social relations. It is embodied in the real power of the people and the equality of all citizens before the law, the actual equality of nations, respect for the individual, and conditions for the all-round development of the personality. It is also embodied in broad social guarantees — employment, access to education, culture, medical care and housing, concern for people in old age, and mother and child welfare. Strict observance in life of the principle of social justice is an important condition for the unity of the people, society's political stability, and dynamic development.

But life, as they say, does not stand still. So we must look at the further development of the social sphere with new eyes, and appreciate the full measure of its increasing significance. We are obliged to do so in keeping with the general course worked out by the Party for the acceleration of socio-economic development, and with the programme aim of our Party, that of achieving the complete wellbeing and a free allround development of all members of society.

Lessons of the past, too, require that we pay greater attention to social issues. The Party's Central Committee holds that central and local bodies and underestimated relevant problems concerning the material base of the country's social and cultural sphere. As a result, residual principle had actually taken shape governing allocation of resources for its development. There was a certain overemphasis on technocratic approaches, blunting attention to the social aspect of production, to everyday life and leisure; this could not but reduce the interest of the working people in the results of their work, slacken discipline and lead to other negative developments.

We are not at all indifferent to what ways and means are used to improve the material and spiritual aspects of life and what social consequences this entails. If private-owner, parasitic sentiments, and levelling tendencies begin to surface, this means that something is wrong about the choice of ways and means in our work, and has got to be rectified. During the discussion of the pre-Congress documents, Party members and non-members spoke with concern of the slackening of control over the measure of labour and consumption, of infringements of socialist justice, and of the need for stepping up the fight against unearned incomes. The gravity and importance of these questions is more than obvious.

In short, the attained level of development and the magnitude of the new tasks call for a long-term, deeply considered, integral, and strong social policy that would extend to all aspects of the life of society. It is essential for the planning and management bodies, for central and local economic organizations to deal resolutely with the needs of the social sphere.

The objectives of social policy are thoroughly characterized in the drafts of the Party Programme and the Guidelines. Allow me to dwell on some issues related to its implementation.

1. Steady Improvement of the People's Standard of Living,
Consistent Application of Social Justice

The long-term plans for the country's social and economic development envisage **raising the people's wellbeing to a qualitatively new level**. In the coming fifteen years, the volume of resources allocated for the improvement of the conditions of life is to be doubled. Real per capita incomes are to go up 60 to 80 per cent. The rise in incomes in the 12th five-year period is to cover millions of people. Huge funds are being earmarked for increasing the construction of homes and social and cultural facilities. Those are the plans. But we must mention the main thing: these plans will become reality only if every Soviet person works hard and efficiently. This applies to every person wherever he may work and whatever post he may occupy. What we accomplish is what we are going to have, and how we are going to live.

Socialist transformations have radically changed both the purpose of work and the attitude to work of the mass of workers and peasants. This is vividly reflected in the massive growth of socialist emulation.

Relying on its wealth of experience, the Party intends to continue promoting these traditions, and to cultivate a conscious and creative attitude to work as the prime duty to society.

At election meetings and conferences, Communists have rightly raised the question of not only improving the forms of moral incentives, but also of greatly increasing material incentives and establishing due order in this important matter. It was rightly pointed out that the so-called "figure juggling", payment of unearned money and unmerited bonuses, and setting "guaranteed" pay rates unrelated to the worker's contributed work, are impermissible. It should be said quite emphatically on this score that when equal payments are fixed for the work of a good employee and that of a negligent one this is a gross violation of our principles. And first of all it is an intolerable distortion of socialism's basic principle: "From each according to his ability, to each according to his work", which expresses the substance of the social justice of the new social system.

It is essential that the government's wage policy should ensure that incomes strictly correspond to the quantity and quality of work done. Proceeding from this, the increase of wage rates and basic salaries of factory and office workers in productive fields envisaged in the 12th five-year period will be enacted for the first time essentially at the expense and within the limits of the sums earned by the enterprises themselves. This procedure will make a more active impact on the acceleration of technical progress and on heightening the efficiency of production.

Rates and salaries in the non-productive sphere will go up, drawing on centralized sources. A phased increase of the salaries of doctors and other medical workers was started last year. The increase of the rates and salaries of those employed in public education is to be completed in 1987, and a start is to be made that year in raising the salaries of cultural workers. Measures are being taken to extend the wage and salary advantages of factory and office workers in certain regions of Eastern Siberia and the Soviet Far East.

Many proposals made by working people refer to the role of social consumption funds in enforcing the principle of justice. These funds already account for nearly one-third of the consumed material goods and services. We hold that they are in no way charity. They play an important role in providing equal access for members of society to education and culture, equalising conditions for the raising of children, and easing the life of those who may, for one reason or another, need a grant or continuous assistance. At the same time, it is a means of encouraging and stimulating qualified, conscientious work. The Party intends to continue promoting the further growth and more effective use of these social funds. In the 12th five-year period they are to go up by 20 to 23 per cent.

Combatting unearned incomes is an important function of the socialist state. We must admit today that owing to a slackening of control and for a number of other reasons groups of people have appeared with a distinct proprietary mentality and a scornful attitude to the interests of society.

Working people have legitimately raised the question of rooting out such things. The Central Committee agrees completely with these demands. It is considered necessary, already in the immediate future, to carry out additional measures against parasites, plunderers of socialist property, bribe-takers, and all those who embarked on a path alien to the work-oriented nature of our system. We should also give thought to proposals about perfecting our tax policy, including the introduction of a progressive inheritance tax.

But while combatting unearned incomes, we must not permit any shadow to fall on those who do honest work to earn a supplementary income. What is more, the state will promote various forms of satis-fying popular demand and providing services. We must attentively examine proposals for regulating individual labour. It stands to reason that such labour must be in full conformity with socialist economic principles, and rest on either co-operative principles or on contracts with socialist enterprises. Society, the population only stand to gain from this.

All the efforts to perfect the distributive relations will have little effect and the objective of enhancing the people's wellbeing will not be attained if we fail to **saturate the market with diverse goods and services**. That, indeed, is the purpose of the Comprehensive Programme for the Development of the Production of Consumer Goods and the Services.

In the current five years it is planned to secure higher growth rates for output of consumer goods and retail trade, and to considerably improve the organization of trade and public catering. Heavy industry has been instructed to involve all enterprises in the production of manufactured goods and to ensure output of high-quality materials and equipment for light industry and the food industry.

We must build up an up-to-date services industry as quickly as possible. That is the job of central organizations, but also — no less, and perhaps even more — of the Councils of Ministers of Union Republics, and all bodies of local government. Resolute measures must be taken to eliminate the glaring disproportions between the supply and demand of services. This applies first of all to services that lighten domestic work and those connected with the improvement and renovation of flats, with tourism, and the servicing of cars the demand for which is increasing at an especially swift rate. Responding to the proposals of the working people, we are promoting broad expansion of collective gardening and vegetable growing. This has got off the ground. But the work must be continued, and all artificial obstacles must be removed.

The social importance and acuteness of the **housing problem** have predetermined our serious attitude to it. To provide every family with a separate flat or house by the year 2000 is, in itself, a tremendous but feasible undertaking. In the current five years, and especially in the five-year periods to follow, the scale of house-building and of modernizing available housing will increase. The building of co-operative and individual housing should be encouraged in every way. There are great reserves here for expanding the building of homes. Those who are backing the construction of youth complexes are doing the right thing. The motivation and energy of young people can do a lot in this respect.

Much is being said about the need for seriously improving the practice of distributing housing. These questions must be settled on a broad democratic basis and put under continuous public control. Proposals for fair changes in the system of house rents, by gearing them to the size and quality of all the occupied living space merit attention. There have been many complaints about the low quality of house-building. It is essential to work out measures that would stimulate a substantial improvement of quality, and also an improvement of the layout, the amenities, and architecture of our towns and villages.

Comrades, the qualitative changes in the social sphere are impossible without **deep-going changes in the content of labour**. The main role here is to be played by the technical reconstruction of the economy: mechanisation, automation, computerisation and robotization which, as I want to stress specially, must have an explicitly clear social orientation. Already in the current five years it is planned to sharply reduce the share of manual labour, and by the year 2000 to bring it down in the productive sphere to 15-20 per cent, relieving millions of people of manual operations. The further change of labour in the context of the scientific and technological revolution sets high demands on education and the professional training of people. In substance, the task of **establishing a single system of continuous education** is now on the agenda.

In recent years the Central Committee has taken important steps in that direction. A reform has been launched of the **general and vocational school**. It should be said that the rate and extent of the measures taken under the reform are not satisfactory as yet. A more profound approach is required to the study of the scientific basis of contemporary production and of the leading trends of its intensification. And what is especially urgent is that all pupils should learn the use of computers. In sum, it is essential that the Leninist principle of combining education with productive labour should be implemented more fully, that the effectiveness of education should be considerably raised, and that radical improvements should be carried out in the training of young people for independent life and labour and in bringing up politically conscious builders of the new society.

The Party is setting the task of **restructuring higher and specialized secondary education**. In recent years, the growing output of specialists was not accompanied by the requisite improvement in the quality of their training. The material base of the higher school is lagging behind gravely. The use of engineers and technicians must be considerably improved.

At present, proposals have been drawn up to alter the prevailing situation. It is in the interests of society to raise the prestige of the work of engineers. The structure of higher and specialised secondary education is to be revised, so that the training of specialists will be abreast of the times and they acquire substantial theoretical knowledge and practical skills. The relationship of higher educational institutions and specialized secondary schools with various branches of the economy should evidently follow new lines, and their mutual interest in raising the level of training and retraining of cadres, in cardinally improving their use in production, should be enhanced.

Nothing is more valuable to every person and, for that matter, to society than health. **The protection and improvement of the health of people** is a matter of cardinal importance. We must consider the problems of health from broad social positions. Health depends above all on the conditions of work and life, and on the standard of living. It stands to reason, of course, that the public health service is also of tremendous importance. We must meet the needs of the population in high-quality medical treatment, health protection and pharmaceuticals as quickly as possible, and, moreover, everywhere. All this puts the question of the material and technical base of the health service in a new way, calling for the solution of many urgent scientific, organizational, and personnel problems. Considerable funds will be needed, of course, and we must see to it that they are made available.

It has long since been noted, and most aptly, that health cannot be bought in a pharmacy. The main thing is a person's way of life and, among other things, how sensibly and wholesomely a person uses his or her spare time. The opportunities for this are at hand, but the organizational side of the matter is very poorly run. Much depends on the initiative of the public, on people's avocational activity. But in towns and villages, and within work collectives, they often wait for instructions and count on assistance from above. Why do we make poor use of what is already at our disposal — of palaces, clubs, stadiums, parks, and many other facilities? Why don't the Soviets, the trade unions, and the Komsomol tackle these questions properly? Why not start a movement for more active building of simple playgrounds and gymnasiums on the residential principle? And finally, why not organize sports, tourist and other clubs on a co-operative basis?

A fight has been mounted across the country against hard drinking and alcoholism. In the name of the health of society and of the individual we have taken resolute measures and started a battle against traditions that were shaped and cultivated over the centuries. While we should have no illusions about what has been accomplished, we can safely say that incidents of drunkenness on the job and in public places have become fewer. The situation within families is improving, the number of industrial injuries has gone down, and discipline has been tightened. But extensive, persevering and varied efforts are still needed to secure a final break with prevailing habits. There must be no indulgence here!

We face the acute task of ensuring the **protection of nature and rational use of its resources**. Socialism, with its plan-governed organization of production and humane world outlook, is quite capable of creating a harmonious balance between society and nature. A system of measures to that effect has already been implemented in our country, and quite considerable funds are being allocated for this purpose. There are also practical results.

Still, in a number of regions the state of the environment is alarming. And the public, notably our writers, are quite right in calling for a more careful treatment of land and its riches, of lakes, rivers, and the plant and animal world.

Scientific and technical achievements are being introduced much too slowly in nature protection. The projects of new and the reconstruction of operating enterprises are still being based on outdated notions, with wasteless and low-waste production techniques being introduced on too small a scale. During the processing of minerals, most of the extracted mass goes to waste, polluting the environment. More resolute economic, legal and educational measures are required here. All of us living today are accountable to our descendants and to history for the environment.

2. Improvement of Social-Class Relations and Relations Among the Peoples of the USSR

Comrades, analysing problems involved in **interrelationship of classes and social groups** is of vital importance for a Marxist-Leninist party. By carefully taking into account both the community and the specific nature of their interests in its policy, the Communist Party ensures society's strong unity and successful fulfilment of its most important and complex tasks.

The working class holds a vanguard place in Soviet society. Owing to its position in the socialist production system, its political experience, high political awareness, good organization, labour and political activity, the working class unites our society and plays the leading role in improving socialism, in communist construction. Constant concern for the consolidation of the alliance of the working class, the peasantry and the intelligentsia is the cornerstone of the policy pursued by the Communist Party of the Soviet Union. It is precisely this which enables us to muster forces for the speedy solution of the economic and social tasks we have set ourselves.

The unity of socialist society by no means implies a levelling of public life. Socialism encourages diversity of people's interests, requirements and abilities, and vigorously supports the initiative of social organizations that express this diversity. Moreover, socialism needs this diversity, which it regards as an essential condition for the further promotion of people's creative activity and initiative, and the competition of minds and talents, without which the socialist way of life and the movement forward would be inconceivable.

Generally speaking, the problem is as follows: unless we elevate emulation to a new, incomparably higher level in production, in the economy, as well as in the fields of science and the arts, we shall not be able to cope with the task of accelerating the country's socio-economic progress. To improve the socialist way of life is to ensure the maximum opportunities for fostering collectivism, the cohesion of society, and the individual's activity.

The **problems of consolidating the family** are attracting public attention. Our achievements in cultivating the new, socialist type of family are indisputable. Socialism has emancipated women from economic and social oppression, securing for them the opportunity to work, obtain an education and participate in public life on an equal footing with men. The socialist family is based on the full equality of men and women and their equal responsibility for the family.

Yet, the formation of the new type of family is no simple matter. It is a complicated process that involves many problems. In particular, although the divorce rate has dropped in the past few years, it is still high. There is still a large number of unhappy families. All this has a negative effect, above all, on the upbringing of children, as well as on the morale of men and women, on their labour and public activity. It stands to reason that society cannot be indifferent to such phenomena. The strong family is one of its principal pillars.

Young families need special care. Young people must be well prepared for family life. More thought should be given to the system of material assistance to newlyweds, above all in solving their housing and everyday problems. It would apparently be a good thing to consider the proposals for improving relevant legislation with a view to heightening the citizen's responsibility for consolidating the family. But that is not all. It is necessary to organise the practical work of state and public organizations so that it will promote in every way a strengthening of the family and its moral foundations. This means the creation of conditions for family participation in public festivities and in cultural and sports events, and for family recreation. Families in which successive generations work in a same profession should be widely honoured; good family traditions should be given every support and young people should be brought up on the basis of the experience of older generations. Here a big contribution can be made by the mass information media, television, literature, cinema and the theatre.

Securing living and working conditions for women that would enable them to successfully combine their maternal duties with active involvement in labour and public activity is a prerequisite for solving many family problems. In the 12th five-year period we are planning to extend the practice of letting women work a shorter day or week, or to work at home. Mothers will have paid leaves until their babies are 18 months old. The number of paid days-off granted to mothers to care for sick children will be increased. Lower-income families with children of up to 12 years of age will receive child allowances. We intend to fully satisfy the people's need for preschool children's institutions within the next few years.

Thought should also be given to appropriate orgnaizational forms. Why not reinstitute women's councils within work collectives or residentially, integrating them in a single system with the Soviet Women's Committee at its head? Women's councils could help to resolve a wide range of social problems arising in the life of our society.

Concern for the older generation, for war and labour veterans, should rank as one of the top priorities. The Party and the Soviet Government will do everything possible for the pensioners' wellbeing to rise with the growth of society's prosperity. In the 12th five-year period it is planned to increase the minimum old-age, disability, and loss-of-breadwinner pensions paid to factory and office workers, and to raise the previously fixed pensions of collective farmers. But man lives not by bread alone, as the saying goes. According to the information reaching the Central Committee, many retired veterans feel left out of things. Apparently, additional measures should be taken by government and public organizations, centrally and locally, to assist the veterans in becoming more actively involved in production and socio-political life. After all, more than 50 million Soviet people are veterans.

The setting up of a national mass organization of war and labour veterans could be a new step in this direction. It could be instrumental in involving highly experienced people in social and political affairs, and first of all in educating the rising generation. The pensioners' involvement, both on a co-operative and on an individual, family basis, in the services or trade, producing consumer goods or turning out farm produce could be highly useful. The new organization could be helpful in improving everyday and medical services for pensioners and expanding their leisure opportunities. As we see it, it will certainly have a lot of work to do.

Comrades, of tremendous importance for the multi-national Soviet state is **development of relations among the peoples of the USSR**. The foundation for solving the nationalities problem in our country was laid by the Great October Socialist Revolution. Relying on Lenin's doctrine and on the gains of socialism the Communist Party has done enormous transformative work in this area. Its results are an outstanding achievement of socialism which has enriched world civilization. National oppression and inequality of all types and forms have been done away with once and for all. The indissoluble friendship among nations and respect for national cultures and for the dignity of all peoples have been established and have taken firm root in the minds of tens of millions of people. The Soviet people is a qualitatively new social and international community, cemented by the same economic interests, ideology and political goals.

However, our achievements must not create the impression that there are no problems in the national processes. Contradictions are inherent in any kind of development, and are unavoidable in this sphere as well. The main thing is to see their emergent aspects and facets, to search for and give prompt and correct answers to questions posed by life. This is all the more important because the tendency towards national isolation, localism, and parasitism still persist and make themselves felt quite painfully at times.

In elaborating guidelines for a long-term nationalities policy, it is especially important to see to it that the republics' contribution to the development of an integrated national economic complex should match their grown economic and spiritual potential. It is in the supreme interests of our multinational state, and each of the republics, to promote co-operation in production, collaboration and mutual assistance among the republics. It is the task of Party organizations and the Soviets to make the fullest possible use of available potentialities in the common interests and to persistently overcome all signs of localism.

We are legitimately proud of the achievements of the multinational Soviet socialist culture. By drawing on the wealth of national forms and characteristics, it is developing into a unique phenomenon in world culture. However, the healthy interest in all that is valuable in each national culture must be on means degenerate into attempts to isolate oneself from the objective process by which national cultures interact and come closer together. This applies, among other things, to certain works of literature and art and scholarly writings in which, under the guise of national originality, attempts are made to depict in idyllic tones reactionary nationalist and religious survivals contrary to our ideology, the socialist way of life, and our scientific world outlook.

Our Party's tradition traceable to Lenin of being particularly circumspect and tactful in all that concerns the nationalities policy and the interests of every nation or nationality, national feelings, calls at the same time for resolute struggle against national narrow-mindedness and arrogance, nationalism and chauvinism, no matter what their guise may be. We Communists must unswervingly follow Lenin's wise teachings, must creatively apply them to the new conditions, and be extremely heedful and principled as regards relations among peoples in the name of the further consolidation of fraternal friendship among all the peoples of the USSR.

The social policy elaborated by the Party has many aspects to it and is quite feasible. However, its success will largely hinge on the social orientation of the cadres, on persistence and initiative in carrying out our plans. Concern for people's needs and interests must be an object of unflagging attention on the part of the Party, government and economic organizations, of trade unions and of each executive. If we succeed in securing a decisive switch to the social sphere, many of the problems that face us today and will face us tomorrow will be solved far more quickly and much more effectively than has so far been the case.

III. FURTHER DEMOCRATIZATION OF SOCIETY
AND PROMOTION OF THE PEOPLE'S
SOCIALIST SELF-GOVERNMENT

Comrades, Lenin regarded democracy, the creative initiative of working people, as the principal force behind the development of the new system. Unmatched in his faith in the people, he showed concern for raising the level of the political activity and culture of the masses, stressing that illiterate people were outside politics. Nearly seventy years have elapsed since then. The general educational and cultural level of Soviet people has risen immeasurably and their socio-political experience has grown richer. This means that the possibility and need of every citizen to participate in managing the affairs of the state and society have grown enormously.

Democracy is the wholesome and pure air without which a socialist public organism cannot live a full-blooded life. Hence, when we say that socialism's great potential is not being used to the full in our country, we also mean that the **acceleration of society's development is inconceivable and impossible without a further development of all the aspects and manifestations of socialist democracy**.

Bearing that in mind, the Party and its Central Committee are taking measures aimed at deepening the democratic character of the socialist system. Among them are steps to heighten the activities of the Soviets, the trade unions, the Komsomol, the work collectives and the people's control bodies, and to promote publicity. But all that has been and is being done should be assessed in terms of the scale and complexity of our new tasks, rather than by yesterday's standards. As stressed in the new edition of the Party Programme, these tasks call for consistent and unswerving development of the **people's socialist self-government**.

In socialist society, particularly under the present circumstances, government should not be the privilege of a narrow circle of professionals. We know from theory and from our extensive experience that the socialist system can develop successfully only when the people really run their own affairs, when millions of people are involved in political life. This is what the working people's self-government amounts to, as Lenin saw it. It is the essence of Soviet power. The elements of self-government develop within rather than outside our statehood, increasingly penetrating all aspects of state and public life, enriching the content of democratic centralism and strengthening its socialist character.

The Party is the guiding force and the principal guarantor of the development of socialist self-government. Playing the leading role in society, the Party is itself the highest form of a self-governing socio-political organization. By promoting inner-Party democracy and intensifying the activity of Communists at all levels of the political system, the CPSU sets the right direction for the process of furthering the people's socialist self-government and broadening the participation of the masses and of each person in the affairs of the country.

The result of the revolutionary creativity of the working people, the **Soviets of People's Deputies** have stood the test of time, displaying their viability and vast potentialities in securing full power for the people, in uniting and mobilizing the masses. The very logic of the development of socialist democracy shows the urgent need for making the maximum use of these potentialities of Soviet representative bodies.

The fact that the Supreme Soviet of the USSR and the Supreme Soviets of the Union and Autonomous Republics are becoming increasingly businesslike and effective in their activity with each passing year is most welcome. It is their duty to consistently improve legislation, supervise law enforcement and check on the actual outcome of the work done by each state body and each executive. At their sessions, the Supreme Soviets should place greater emphasis on discussing proposals submitted by trade unions, the Komsomol, and other public organizations, the reports of administrative bodies, the situation in different branches of the economy, and the development of the various regions.

I should like to draw special attention of Congress delegates to the activity of **local Soviets**. Today they can and must serve as one of the most effective means of mobilizing the masses for the effort to accelerate the country's socio-economic development. As they receive the electorate's mandate, local government bodies undertake responsibility for all aspects of life on their territory. If someone may be allowed to say, "This is none of my business", this approach is certainly unacceptable to the Soviets. Housing and education, public and health and consumer goods, trade and services, public transport and the protection of nature are principal concerns of the Soviets. Whenever we hear complaints from working people on these subjects, which is still fairly often, it means that the Soviets lack efficiency and initiative, and that their control is slack. But while making legitimate demands on the Soviets, we should not be blind to the fact that for the time being their ability to tackle many of the local problems is limited; there exists excessive centralization in matters which are not always clearly visible from the centre and can be much better solved locally.

That is why we resolutely follow a course of promoting the autonomy and activity of local government bodies. Proposals to this effect are currently being worked out by the CPSU Central Committee, the Presidium of the Supreme Soviet and the USSR Council of Ministers. Their goal is to make each Soviet a complete and responsible master in all things concerning the satisfaction of people's everyday needs and requirements; in using the allocated funds, the local potentialities and reserves; in co-ordinating and supervising the work of all organizations involved in servicing the population. In this connection, we must make a thorough examination of the relationship between Soviets and the centrally-managed enterprises in their territories, and increase the local governing bodies' interest in the results of their work.

The sessions of Soviets should be conducted far more effectively, the analytical and supervisory activity of standing committees should be more thorough, and the practice of deputies' enquiries should be improved. The committees' recommendations and the deputies' proposals and observations should be carefully considered and taken into account by the executive bodies.

While mapping out further improvements of the work of the Soviets, we should remember that none of them will yield the desired results unless backed by the deputies' initiative. The Party will continue to see to it that deputies are elected from among the worthiest people who are capable of effectively running state affairs, and that the composition of the Soviets is systematically renewed. In this connection, it is apparently time to make necessary corrections in our election procedures as well. There is quite a number of outstanding problems here awaiting solution.

The Party has always deemed it its duty to heighten the authority of the people's representatives, and, at the same time, to enhance their responsibility to the electorate in every way possible. The title of a deputy is not just something that goes with one's office; it is not an honorary privilege; it means a lot of hard work at the Soviet and among the population. And we must do all we can for the strict observance of the law on the status of deputies, and see to it that each deputy should be afforded every opportunity to exercise his or her authority.

The development of the people's self-government calls for **a further strengthening of democratic principles in administration**, in the activity of the Soviets' executive committees, of their apparatus, and of all other government bodies. Most of the people working in them are competent and take what they do close to heart. However, one should always remember that, even if its executives are masterminds, no apparatus will ever get what it wants unless it relies on the working people's motivated support and participation in government. The times are making increasingly exacting demands on the work of the apparatus. And there are quite a few shortcomings here; one often encounters departmental approach and localism, irresponsibility, red tape and formal indifference to people. One of the main reasons for this is the slackening of control over the activity of the apparatus by the working people, the Soviets themselves, and public organizations.

Bearing all this in mind, the Party has set itself the task of putting to use all the instruments that actually enable every citizen to actively influence administrative decision-making, verify the fulfilment of decisions, and receive necessary information about the activity of the apparatus. This should be the purpose of a system of regular reports to work collectives and general meetings by all administrative bodies. Much can be done in this area by people's control committees, groups and teams, by voluntary trade union inspectors, and the mass media.

The elective bodies themselves should be more exacting and strict towards their own apparatus. One cannot overlook the fact that executives who remain in office for long periods tend to lose their feel for the new, to shut themselves off from the people by instructions they have concocted themselves, and sometimes even hold back the work of elective bodies. Apparently it is time to work out a procedure which would enable Soviets, as well as all public bodies, to evaluate and certify the work of the responsible executives of their apparatus after each election, making desirable personnel changes.

Our time demands ever more active involvement on the part of **public organizations** in governing the country. When the work of our public organizations is considered from this angle, however, it becomes clear that many of them are lacking in initiative. Some of them try to operate above all through their regular staff, in a bureaucratic way, and lean only a little on the masses. In other words, the popular, creative, independent nature of public organizations is far from being fully realized.

In our country, the trade unions are the largest mass organization.

On the whole, they do a lot to satisfy the requirements of factory and office workers and collective farmers, to promote emulation, tighten discipline and heighten labour productivity. Still, trade union committees are in many cases lacking in militancy and resolve when it comes to defending the working people's legitimate interests, ensuring labour protection and safety, and constructing and running health-building, sports and cultural facilities. Understandably, such passivity suits those managers for whom production sometimes obscures the people. The trade unions, however, should always give priority to social policy objectives, to promoting the working people's interests. Properly speaking, this is the basic purpose of their activity. The All-Union Central Council of Trade Unions and other trade union bodies enjoy extensive rights and control considerable funds, both the state's and their own. It is up to them, therefore, to make extensive and confident use of them, instead of waiting for somebody else to fulfil the tasks they are charged with.

Comrades, our future largely depends on the kind of young people we are bringing up today. That is the task of the whole Party, of all the people. It is most important and fundamental task of the **Leninist Young Communist League**. Our young people are hard-working, ready for exploits and self-sacrifice, and devoted to socialism. Nonetheless, it is the duty of the older generations to do everything they can for those who will replace them to be still more intelligent, more capable and better educated, worthy of taking the baton and carrying into the future the ideals of justice and freedom bequeathed to us by the Great October Revolution.

As Lenin said, it is impossible to master communism through books alone, it is impossible to cultivate a sense of responsibility without charging people with responsible tasks. The young people of the 1980s are broad-minded, well-educated and vigorous. I should say, they are ready for action and look for a chance to show their worth in all areas of public life. So, the YCL must make every effort to support their drive in all areas — the national economy, science and engineering, in achieving high levels of knowledge and culture, in political life, and in defending the Motherland. This effort, more than any other, should be of a questing nature, interesting and appealing to young people, and closely linked to the needs of the young in production, study, home life, and leisure.

Together with the YCL, the Party, government and economic bodies should consistently seek to promote deserving young people to leadership positions in management, production, science and culture. We say: in our country, all roads are open to young people. That is true. But persistent efforts are needed for these words not to lose lustre and the road for young people to be really wide.

By and large, the CPSU Central Committee deems it advisable to take further steps to increase the role of the trade unions, the YCL, the unions of creative workers and voluntary societies in the system of the people's socialist self-government. In particular, it is planned to extend the range of questions which governmental bodies can settle only with the participation or prior agreement of trade union, YCL or women's organizations and to grant these organizations the right to suspend, in some cases, the implementation of administrative decisions.

Our Party Programme aims at the most effective exercise of all forms of **direct democracy**, of direct participation by the popular masses in the elaboration, adoption and execution of governmental and other decisions. An enormous role is played here by the **work collectives** operating in all spheres of the life of society, and chiefly in the national economy. The granting of broader powers to enterprises, the introduction of cost accounting, and promotion of the spirit of socialist enterprise will become truly effective only if the working man himself displays greater activity. We cannot put up with instances which still exist, where workers do not know the programmes of their own enterprises, where their suggestions do not receive due attention and are not taken into account. These instances show that in some places the force of inertia determines the state of affairs, hinders the involvement of factory and office workers in management and impedes the process of fostering among them the feeling that they are full-fledged masters of production.

The Law of Work Collectives adopted two years ago has indisputably stimulated initiatives by work collectives. But we cannot yet say this Law is producing the results we expected. This is evident from the CPSU Central Committee's examination of its application at the Minsk Motor Works and elsewhere. Our conclusion is unambiguous: it is necessary to radically improve the mechanism that enables us to make the democratic principles and norms of the Law operative in everyday practice. Step by step we must extend the range of issues on which the work collective's decisions are final, enhance the role of the general meetings of factory and office workers and raise responsibility for implementing their decisions. There has arisen an idea of having a council, say, of the work collective made up of representatives of the management, Party, trade union and YCL organizations, team councils, rank-and-file workers, and specialists, function, in the period between general meetings, both at the level of teams and the enterprise as a whole.

Today the advanced teams which apply the cost-accounting principle are already becoming primary self-government units with elected managers. Life shows the viability of this practice. It has confirmed that in developing democratic economic management principles it is advisable to extend the principle of electiveness to all team leaders and then gradually to some other categories of managerial personnel — foremen, shift, sector or shop superintendents, and state-farm department managers. Long years of experience testify that this is the direction in which we must look for modern forms of combining centralism and democracy, of combining one-man management and the principle of electiveness in running the national economy.

Undeviating observance of the democratic principles of guiding collective farms and other co-operative organizations, including observance of their rules, is a matter which receives our constant attention. In recent times our efforts in this sphere have somehow relaxed, and too many organizations have been interfering in the activities of co-operative societies. Party and government bodies must see to it that collective-farm or co-operative self-government is exercised unfailingly, that any attempts to resort to pressure or to practise armchair management are thwarted.

Our Constitution provides for nation-wide discussions and referendums on major issues of our country's life and for discussions on decisions to be passed by local Soviets. We must expedite the drafting of a law on this highly important question. We must make better use of such reliable channels for the development of direct democracy as citizens' meetings, constituents' mandates, letters from people, the press, radio, TV and all other means of eliciting public opinion and of quickly and sensitively responding to the people's needs and mood.

Broader publicity is a matter of principle to us. It is a political issue. Without publicity there is not, nor can there be, democracy, political creativity of the citizens and participation by the citizens in administration and management. This is an earnest, if you like, of a responsible statesmanlike attitude to the common cause on the part of millions upon millions of factory workers, collective farmers and members of the intelligentsia, and a point of departure in the psychological reorientation of our cadres.

When the subject of publicity comes up, calls are sometimes made for exercising greater caution when speaking about the shortcomings, omissions, and difficulties that are inevitable in any ongoing effort. There can only be one answer to this, a Leninist answer: Communists want the truth, always and under all circumstances. The experience of the past year has shown how forcefully Soviet people support an uncompromising appraisal of everything that impedes our advance. But those who have grown used to doing slipshod work, to practising deception, indeed feel really awkward in the glare of publicity, when everything done in the state and in society is under the people's control and is in full public view. Therefore, we must make publicity an unfailingly operative system. It is needed in the centre and no less, perhaps much more, in the localities, wherever people live and work. The citizen wants to know, and should know, not only decisions taken on a nation-wide scale but also decisions taken locally by Party and government bodies, factory managements and trade unions.

The whole range of the **Soviet citizen's socio-political and personal rights and freedoms** should promote the broadening and further development of socialist democracy. The Party and the state regard the deepening of these rights and freedoms and the strengthening of their guarantees as their primary duty. But the gist of socialism is that the rights of citizens do not, and cannot, exist outside their duties, just as there cannot be duties without corresponding rights.

It is essential to stimulate the activity of our citizens, of one and all, in constructive work, in eliminating shortcomings, abuses and all other unhealthy phenomena, all departures from our legal and moral standards. Democracy was and remains a major lever for **strengthening socialist legality**, and stable legality was and remains an inseparable part of our democracy.

A good deal of work has been done lately to strengthen law and order in all spheres of the life of society. But the efforts in this direction must not be slackened in any way. We must continue to improve Soviet legislation. Our legislation — the civil, labour, financial, administrative, economic and criminal laws — must help more vigorously in introducing economically viable management methods, in exercising effective control over the measure of labour and consumption and in translating the principles of social justice into reality.

We must persistently increase the responsibility of the law-enforcement and other bodies, and strengthen the legal service in the Soviets and in the national economy, and state arbitration, and also improve the legal education of the population. As before, full use must be made of Soviet legislation in combatting crime and other breaches of the law, so that the people in towns and villages know that the state is concerned about their peace and personal inviolability, and that not a single wrongdoer evades the punishment he deserves.

We must very strictly observe the democratic principles of justice, the equality of citizens before the law and other guarantees that protect the interests of the state and of every citizen. In this context it is necessary to take vigorous steps to enhance the role of the procurators' supervision, to improve the functioning of courts of law and the bar, and to complete, in the very near future, the drafting of a law, as provided for by the Constitution, on the procedure of filing appeals in court against unlawful actions by officials that infringe upon the rights of citizens. Naturally, the more vigorously Party and government bodies, trade unions, the YCL, work collectives, and volunteer public order squads, and the public at large, are involved in such effort, the more fully legality and law and order will be ensured.

In the context of the growing subversive activity by imperialist special services against the Soviet Union and other socialist countries, greater responsibility devolves upon the **state security bodies**. Under the Party's leadership and scrupulously observing Soviet laws, these bodies are conducting extensive work to expose enemy intrigues, to frustrate all kinds of subversion and to protect our country's sacred frontiers. We are convinced that Soviet security forces and border-guards will always meet the demands made of them, will always display vigilance, self-control and tenacity in the struggle against any encroachment on our political and social system.

Taking into account the complicated international situation and the growing aggressiveness of the reactionary imperialist quarters, the CPSU Central Committee and its Political Bureau pay unflagging attention **to our country's defence capability, to the combat might of the Armed Forces of the USSR**, to the tightening of military discipline. The Soviet Army and Navy had modern arms and equipment, well trained servicemen and skilled officers and political cadres who are completely dedicated to the people. They acquit themselves with honour in the most complicated, and at times rigorous situations. Today we can declare with all responsibility that the defence capability of the USSR is maintained on a level that makes it possible to protect reliably the peaceful life and labour of the Soviet people.

The Party and the Government have always been striving to ensure that the Soviet soldier and officer are constantly aware of our society's care and attention while performing their arduous duties, and that our Armed Forces are a school of civic responsibility, fortitude and patriotism.

It is clear, comrades, that here, at this Congress, we are merely charting the general framework and the main outlines for perfecting our democracy, statehood, and the entire Soviet political system. Implementation of the Congress decisions undoubtedly will bring about fresh manifestations of the people's initiative and new forms of mass social and political creative activity.

IV. BASIC AIMS AND DIRECTIONS OF THE
PARTY'S FOREIGN POLICY STRATEGY

Comrades,

The tasks underlying the country's economic and social development also determine the CPSU's strategy in the world arena. Its main aim is crystal clear — to provide the Soviet people with the possibility of working under conditions of lasting peace and freedom. Such, in essence, is the Party's primary programme requirement of our foreign policy. To fulfil it in the present situation means, above all, to terminate the material preparation for nuclear war.

After having weighted all the aspects of the situation that has taken shape, the CPSU has put forward a coherent programme for the total abolition of weapons of mass destruction before the end of this century, a programme that is historic in terms of its dimensions and significance. Its realization would open for mankind a fundamentally new period of development and provide an opportunity to concentrate entirely on constructive labour.

As you know, we have addressed our proposals not only through the traditional diplomatic channels but also directly to world public opinion, to the peoples. The time has come to realise thoroughly the harsh realities of our day: nuclear weapons harbour a hurricane which is capable of sweeping the human race from the face of the earth. Our address further underscores the open, honest, Leninist character of the CPSU's foreign policy strategy.

Socialism unconditionally rejects war as a means of settling political and economic contradictions and ideological disputes among states. Our ideal is a world without weapons and violence, a world in which each people freely chooses its path of development, its way of life. This is an expression of the humanism of communist ideology, of its moral values. That is why for the future as well the **struggle against the nuclear threat, against the arm race, for the preservation and strengthening of universal peace** remains the fundamental direction of the Party's activities in the international arena.

There is no alternative to this policy. This is all the more true in periods of tension in international affairs. It seems that never in the decades since the war has the situation on the world been so explosive, and consequently complex and uncongenial as in the first half of the 1980s. The right-wing group that came to power in the USA and its main NATO fellow-travellers made a steep turn from *détente* to a policy of military strength. They have adopted doctrines that reject good-neighbourly relations and co-operation as principles of world development, as a political philosophy of international relations. The Washington administration remained deaf to our calls for an end to the arms race and an improvement of the situation.

Perhaps it may not be worth churning up the past? Especially today when in Soviet–US relations there seem to be signs of a change for the better, and realistic trends can now be detected in the actions and attitudes of the leadership of some NATO nations. We feel that it is worthwhile, for the drastic frosting of the international climate in the first half of the 1980s was a further reminder that nothing comes of itself: peace has to be fought for, and this has to be a persevering and purposeful fight. We have to look for, find, and use even the smallest opportunity in order — while this is still possible — to reverse the trend towards an escalation of the threat of war. Realizing this, the Central Committee of the CPSU at its April Plenary Meeting once again analysed the character and dimensions of the nuclear threat and defined the practical steps that could lead to an improvement of the situation. We were guided by the following considerations of principle.

First. The character of present-day weapons leaves any country no hope of safeguarding itself solely with military and technical means, for example, by building up a defence system, even the most powerful one. The task of ensuring security is increasingly seen as a political problem, and it can only be resolved by political means. In order to progress along the road of disarmament what is needed is, above all, the will. Security cannot be built endlessly on fear of retaliation, in other words, on the doctrines of "containment" or "deterrence". Apart from the absurdity and amorality of a situation in which the whole world becomes a nuclear hostage, these doctrines encourage an arms race that may sooner or later go out of control.

Second. In the context of the relations between the USSR and the USA, security can only be mutual, and if we take international relations as a whole it can only be universal. The highest wisdom is not in caring exclusively for oneself, especially to the detriment of the other side. It is vital that all should feel equally secure, for the fears and anxieties of the nuclear age generate unpredictability in politics and concrete actions. It is becoming extremely important to take the critical significance of the time factor into account. The appearance of new systems of weapons of mass destruction steadily shortens time and narrows down the possibilities for adopting political decisions on questions of war and peace in crisis situations.

Third. The USA, its military-industrial machine remains the loco-motive of militarism, for so far it has no intention of slowing down. This has to be taken into consideration, of course. But we are well aware that the interests and aims of the military-industrial complex are not at all the same as the interests and aims of the American people, as the actual national interests of that great country.

Naturally, the world is much larger than the USA and its occupation bases on foreign soil. And in world politics one cannot confine oneself to relations with only one, even a very important, country. As we know from experience, this only promotes the arrogance of strength. Need-less to say, we attach considerable significance to the state and char-acter of the relations between the Soviet Union and the USA. Our countries coincide on quite a few points, and there is the objective need to live in peace with each other, to co-operate on a basis of equality and mutual benefit, and on this basis alone.

Fourth. The world is in a process of swift changes, and it is not within anybody's power to maintain a perpetual status quo in it. It consists of many dozens of countries, each having perfectly legitimate interests. All without exception face a task of fundamental signifi-cance: without neglecting social political, and ideological differences all have to master the science and art of restraint and circumspection on the international scene, to live in a civilized manner, in other words, under conditions of civil international intercourse and co-operation. But to give this co-operation with scope there has to be an all-embracing system of international economic security that would in equal measure protect every nation against discrimination, sancations, and other attributes of imperialist, neocolonialist policy. Alongside disarmament such a system can become a dependable pillar of inter-national security in general.

In short, the modern world has become much too small and fragile for wars and a policy of strength. It cannot be saved and preserved if the way of thinking and actions built up over the centuries on the acceptability and permissibility of wars and armed conflicts are not shed once and for all, resolutely and irrevocably.

This means the realization that it is no longer possible to win an arms race, or nuclear war for that matter. The continuation of this race on earth, let alone its spread to outer space, will accelerate the already critically high rate of stockpiling and perfecting nuclear weapons. The situation in the world may assume such a character that it will no longer depend upon the intelligence or will of political leaders. It may become captive to technology, to technocratic military logic. Consequently, not only nuclear war itself but also the preparations for it, in other words, the arms race, **the aspiration to win military superiority can, speaking in objective terms, bring no political gain to anybody**.

Further, this means understanding that the present level of the balance of the nuclear potentials of the opposite sides is much too high. For the time being it ensures **equal danger** to each of them. But only for the time being. Continuation of the nuclear arms race will inevitably heighten this equal threat and may bring it to a point where even parity will cease to be a factor of military-political deterrence. Consequently, it is vital, in the first place, greatly to reduce the level of military confrontation. In our age, genuine equal security is guaranteed not by the highest possible, but by the lowest possible level of strategic parity, from which nuclear and other types of weapons of mass destruction must be totally excluded.

Lastly, this means realising that in the present situation there is no alternative to co-operation and interaction between all countries. Thus, the objective — I emphasize, objective — conditions have taken shape in which confrontation between capitalism and socialism can proceed **only and exclusively in forms of peaceful competition and peaceful contest**.

For us peaceful coexistence is a political course which the USSR intends to go on following unswervingly, ensuring the continuity of its foreign policy strategy. The CPSU will pursue a vigorous international policy stemming from the realities of the world we live in. Of course, the problem of international security cannot be resolved by one or two, even very intensive, peace campaigns. Success can only be achieved by consistent, methodical, and persevering effort.

Continuity in foreign policy has nothing in common with a simple repetition of what has been done, especially in tackling the problems that have piled up. What is needed is a high degree of accuracy in assessing one's own possibilities, restraint, and an exceptionally high sense of responsibility when decisions are made. What is wanted is firmness in upholding principles and stands, tactical flexibility, a readiness for mutually acceptable compromises, and an orientation of dialogue and mutual understanding rather than on confrontation.

As you know, we have made a series of unilateral steps — we put a moratorium on the deployment of intermediate-range missiles in Europe, cut back the number of these missiles, and stopped all nuclear explosions. In Moscow and abroad there have been talks with leaders and members of the governments of many countries. The Soviet–Indian, Soviet–French, and Soviet–US summits were necessary and useful steps.

The Soviet Union has made energetic efforts to give a fresh impetus to the negotiations in Geneva, Stockholm, and Vienna, the purpose of which is to curb the arms race and strengthen confidence between states. Negotiations are always a delicate and complex matter. Of cardinal importance here is to make an effort to achieve a mutually acceptable balance of interests. To turn weapons of mass destruction into an object of political scheming is, to say the least, immoral, while in political terms this is irresponsible.

Lastly, concerning our Statement of January 15 this year. Taken as a whole, our programme is essentially an alloy of the philosophy of shaping a safe world in the nuclear-space age with a platform of concrete actions. The Soviet Union offers approaching the problems of disarmament in their totality, for in terms of security they are linked with one another. I am not speaking of rigid linkages or attempts at "giving way" in one direction in order to erect barricades in another. What I have in mind is a plan of concrete actions strictly measured out in terms of time. The USSR intends to work persever-ingly for its realization, regarding it as the **central direction of its foreign policy for the coming years.**

The Soviet military doctrine is also entirely in keeping with the letter and spirit of the initiatives we have put forward. Its orientation is unequivocally defensive. In the military sphere we intend to act in such a way as to give nobody grounds for fears, even imagined ones, about their security. But to an equal extent we and our allies want to be rid of the feeling that we are threatened. The USSR undertook the obligation not to be the first to use nuclear weapons and it will abide strictly by that obligation. But it is no secret that scenarios for a nuclear strike against us do exist. We have no right to overlook this. The Soviet Union is a staunch adversary of nuclear war in any variant. Our country stands for removing weapons of mass destruction from use, for limiting the military potential to reasonable adequacy. But the character and level of this ceiling continue to be restricted by the attitudes and actions of the USA and its partners in the blocs. Under these conditions we repeat again and again: **the Soviet Union lays no**

claim to more security, but it will not settle for less.

I should like to draw attention to the problem of verification, to which we attach special significance. We have declared on several occasions that the USSR is open to verification, that we are interested in it as much as anybody else. All-embracing, strictest verification is perhaps the key element of the disarmament process. The essence of the matter, in our opinion, is that **there can be no disarmament without verification and that verification without disarmament makes no sense.**

There is yet another matter of principle. We have stated our attitude to Star Wars quite substantively. The USA has already drawn many of its allies into this programme. There is the danger that this state of things may become irreversible. Before it is too late it is imperative to find a realistic solution **guaranteeing that the arms race does not spread to outer space**. The Star Wars programme cannot be permitted to be used as a stimulus for a further arms race or as a roadblock to radical disarmament. Tangible progress in what concerns a drastic reduction of nuclear potentials can be of much help in surmounting this obstacle. For that reason the Soviet Union is ready to make a substantial step in that direction, to resolve the question of intermediate-range missiles in the European zone separately — without linking it to problems of strategic armaments and outer space.

The Soviet programme has touched the hearts of millions of people, and among political leaders and public personalities interest in it continues to grow. The times today are such that it is hard to brush it off. The attempts to sow doubt in the Soviet Union's constructive commitment to accelerate the solution of the pressing problem of our day — the destruction of nuclear weapons — and to tackle it in practical terms are becoming less and less convincing. Nuclear disarmament should not be the exclusive domain of political leaders. The whole world is now pondering over this, for it is a question of life itself.

But, also, it is necessary to take into account the reaction of the centres of power that hold in their hands the keys to the success or failure of disarmament negotiations. Of course, the US ruling class, to be more exact its most egoistical groups linked to the military-industrial complex, have other aims that are clearly opposite to ours. For them disarmament spells out a loss of profits and a political risk, for us it is a blessing in all respects — economically, politically, and morally.

We know our principal opponents and have accumulated a complex and extensive experience in our relations and talks with them. The day before yesterday, we received President Reagan's reply our our Statement of January 15. The US side began to set forth its considerations in greater detail at the talks in Geneva. To be sure, we shall closely examine everything the US side has to say on these matters. However, since the reply was received literally on the eve of the Congress, the US administration apparently expects, as we understand it, that our attitude to the US stand will be made known to the world from this rostrum.

What I can say right away is that the President's letter does not give ground for amending in any way the assessment of the international situation as had been set forth in the report before the reply was received. The report says that the elimination of nuclear arms is the goal all the nuclear powers should strive for. In his letter the President agrees in general with some or other Soviet proposals and intentions as regards the issue of disarmament and security. In other words, the reply seems to contain some reassuring opinions and statements.

However, these positive pronouncements are drowning in various reservations, "linkages" and "conditions" which in fact block the solution of radical problems of disarmament. Reduction in the strategic nuclear arsenals is made conditional on our consent to the Star War programme and reductions, unilateral, by the way, in the Soviet conventional arms. Linked to this are also problems of regional conflicts and bilateral relations. The elimination of nuclear arms in Europe is blocked by the references to the stand taken by Great Britain and France and the demand to weaken our defences in the eastern part of the country, while the US military forces in that region remain as they are. The refusal to stop nuclear tests is justified by arguments to the effect that nuclear weapons serve as a factor of "containment". This is in direct contradiction with the purpose reaffirmed in the letter — the need to do away with nuclear weapons. The reluctance of the USA and its ruling cirlces to embark on the path of nuclear disarmament manifests itself most clearly in their attitude of nuclear explosions the termination of which is the demand of the whole world.

To put it in a nutshell, it is hard to detect in the letter we have just received any serious readiness by the US administration to get down to solving the cardinal problems involved in eliminating the nuclear threat. It looks as if some people in Washington and elsewhere, for that matter, have got used to living side by side with nuclear weapons linking with them their plans in the international arena. However, whether they want it or not, the Western politicians will have to answer the question: are they prepared to part with nuclear weapons at all?

In accordance with an understanding reached in Geneva there will be another meeting with the US President. The significance that we attach to it is that it ought to produce practical results in key areas of limiting and reducing armaments. There are at least two matters on which an understanding could be reached: the cessation of nuclear tests and the abolition of US and Soviet intermediate-range missiles in the European zone. And then, as a matter of fact, if there is readiness to seek agreement, the question of the date of the meeting would be resolved of itself: we will accept any suggestion on this count. But there is no sense in empty talks. And we shall not remain indifferent if the Soviet–US dialogue that has started and inspired some not unfounded hopes of a possibility for changes for the better is used to continue the arms race and the material preparations for war. It is the firm intention of the Soviet Union to justify the hopes of the peoples of our two countries and of the whole world who are expecting from the leaders of the USSR and the USA concrete steps, practical actions, and tangible agreements on how to curb the arms race. We are prepared for this.

Naturally, like any other country, we attach considerable importance to the security of our frontiers, on land and at sea. We have many neighbours, and they are different. We have no territorial claims on any of them. We threaten none of them. But as experience has shown time and again, there are quite a few persons who, in disregard of the national interests of either our country or those of countries neighbouring upon us, are endeavouring to aggravate the situation on the frontiers of the Soviet Union.

For instance, counter-revolution and imperialism have turned Afghanistan into a bleeding wound. The USSR supports that country's efforts to defend its sovereignty. We should like, in the nearest future, to withdraw the Soviet troops stationed in Afghanistan at the request of its government. Moreover, we have agreed with the Afghan side on the schedule for their phased withdrawal as soon as a political settlement is reached that will ensure an actual cessation and dependably guarantee the non-resumption of foreign armed interference in the internal affairs of the Democratic Republic of Afghanistan. It is in our vital, national interest that the USSR should always have good and peaceful relations with all its neighbours. This is a vitally important objective of our foreign policy.

The CPSU regards the **European direction** as one of the main directions of its international activity. Europe's historic opportunity and its future lie in peaceful co-operation among the nations of that continent. And it is important, while preserving the assets that have already been accumulated, to move further: from the initial to a more lasting phase of *détente*, to mature *détente*, and then to the building of dependable security on the basis of the Helsinki process and a radical reduction of nuclear and conventional weapons.

The significance of the **Asian and Pacific direction** is growing. In that vast region there are many tangled knots of contradictions and, besides, the political situation in some places is unstable. Here it is necessary, without postponement, to search for the relevant solutions and paths. Evidently, it is expedient to begin with the co-ordination and then the pooling of efforts in the interests of a political settlement of painful problems so as, in parallel, on that basis to at least take the edge off the military confrontation in various parts of Asia and stabilize the situation there.

This is made all the more urgent by the fact that in Asia and other continents the **flashpoints of military danger** are not being extinguished. We are in favour of vitalizing collective quests for ways of defusing conflict situations in the Middle East, Central America, Southern Africa, in all of the planet's turbulent points. This is imperatively demanded by the interests of general security.

Crises and conflicts are fertile soil also for international terrorism. Undeclared wars, the export of counter-revolution in all forms, political assassinations, the taking of hostages, the highjacking of aircraft, and bomb explosions in streets, airports, and railway stations — such is the hideous face of terrorism, which its instigators try to mask with all sorts of cynical inventions. The USSR rejects terrorism in principle and is prepared to co-operate actively with other states in order to uproot it. The Soviet Union will resolutely safeguard its citizens against acts of violence and do everything to defend their lives, honour, and dignity.

Looking back over the past year one will see that, by all the evidence, the prerequisites for improving the international situation are beginning to form. But prerequisites for a turn are not the turn itself. The arms race continues and the threat of nuclear war remains. However, international reactionary forces are by no means omnipotent. The development of the world revolutionary process and the growth of mass democratic and anti-war movements have significantly enlarged and strengthened the **huge potential of peace, reason, and good will**. This is a powerful counter-balance to imperialism's aggressive policy.

The destinies of peace and social progress are now linked more closely than ever before with the dynamic character of the **socialist world system's economic and political development**. The need for this dynamism is dictated by concern for the welfare of the peoples. But for the socialist world it is necessary also from the standpoint of counteraction to the military threat. Lastly, it helps demonstrate the potentialities of the socialist way of life. We are watched by both friends and foes. We are watched by the huge and heterogeneous world of developing nations. It is looking for its choice, for its road, and what this choice will be depends to a large extent on socialism's successes, on the credibility of its answers to the challenges of time.

We are convinced that socialism can resolve the most difficult problems confronting it. Of vital significance for this is the increasingly vigorous interaction whose effect is not merely the adding up but the multiplication of our potentials and which serves as a stimulus for common advancement. This is reflected also in joint documents of countries of the socialist community.

Interaction between governing communist parties remains the heart and soul of the **political co-operation** among these countries. During the past year there has been practically no fraternal country with whose leaders we have not had meetings and detailed talks. The forms of such co-operation are themselves being updated. A new and perhaps key element, the multilateral working meetings of leaders of fraternal countries, is being established. These meetings allow for prompt and friendly consultations on the entire spectrum of problems of socialist construction, on its internal and external aspects.

In the difficult international situation the prolongation of the **Warsaw Treaty** by a unanimous decision of its signatories was of great significance. This Treaty saw its second birth, so to speak, and today it is hard to picture world politics as a whole without it. Take the Sofia Conference of the Treaty's Political Consultative Committee. It was a kind of threshold of the Geneva dialogue.

In the **economic sphere** there is now the Comprehensive Programme of Scientific and Technological Progress. Its importance lies in the transition of the CMEA countries to a co-ordinated policy in science and technology. In our view, changes are also required in the work of the very headquarters of socialist integration — The Council of Mutual Economic Assistance. But the main thing is that in carrying out this programme there is less armchair administration and fewer committees and commissions of all sorts, that more attention is given to economic levers, initiative, and socialist enterprise, and that work collectives are drawn into this process. This would indeed be a Party approach to such an extraordinary undertaking.

Vitality, efficiency, and initiative — all these qualities meet the requirements of the times, and we shall strive to have them spread throughout the system of relations between fraternal parties. The CPSU attaches growing significance to live and broad communication between citizens of socialist countries, between people of different professions and different generations. This is a source of mututal intellectual enrichment, a channel for exchanges of views, ideas, and the **experience of socialist construction**. Today it is especially important to analyse the character of the socialist way of life and understand the processes of perfecting democracy, management methods and personnel policy on the basis of the development of several countries rather than of one country. A considerate and respectful attitude to each other's experience and the employment of this experience in practice are a huge potential of the socialist world.

Generally speaking, one of socialism's advantages is its ability to learn: to learn to resolve the problems posed by life; to learn to forestall the crisis situations that our class adversary tries to create and utilize; to learn to counter the attempts to divide the socialist world and play off some countries against others; to learn to prevent collisions of the interests of different socialist countries, harmonize them by mutual effort, and find mutually acceptable solutions even to the most intricate problems.

It seems to us that it is worth taking a close look also at the relations in the socialist world as a whole. We do not see the community as being separated by some barrier from other socialist countries. The CPSU stands for honest, aboveboard relations with all communist parties and all countries of the world socialist system, for comradely exchanges of opinion between them. Above all, we endeavour to see what unites the socialist world. For that reason the Soviet Communists are gladdened by every step towards closer relations among all socialist states, by every positive advance in these relations.

One can say with gratification that there has been a measure of improvement of the Soviet Union's relations with its great neighbour — **socialist China**. The distinctions in attitudes, in particular to a number of international problems, remain. But we also note something else — that in many cases we can work jointly, co-operate on an equal and principled basis, without prejudice to third countries.

There is no need to explain the significance of this. The Chinese Communists called the victory of the USSR and the forces of progress in the Second World War a prologue to the triumph of the people's revolution in China. In turn, the formation of People's China helped to reinforce socialism's positions in the world and disrupt many of imperialism's designs and actions in the difficult postwar years. In thinking of the future, it may be said that the potentialities for co-operation between the USSR and China are enormous. They are great because such co-operation is in accordance with the interests of both countries, because what is dearest to our peoples — socialism and peace — is indivisible.

The CPSU is an inalienable component of the international communist movement. We the Soviet Communists are well aware that every advance we make in building socialism is an advance of the entire movement. For that reason the CPSU sees its primary internationalist duty in ensuring our country's successful progress along the road opened and blazed by the October Revolution.

The communist movement in the non-socialist part of the world remains the principal target of political pressure and persecution by reactionary circles of the bourgeoisie. All the fraternal parties are constantly under fire from anti-communist propaganda, which does not scruple to use the most despicable means and methods. Many parties operate underground, and in situation of unmitigated persecution and repressions. Every step the Communists take calls for struggle and personal courage. Permit me, comrades, on behalf of the 27th Congress, on behalf of the Soviet Communists to express sincere admiration for the dedicated struggle of our comrades, and profound fraternal solidarity with them.

In recent years the communist movement has come face to face with many new realities, tasks, and problems. There are all indications that it has entered upon a qualitatively new phase of development. The international conditions of the work of communists are changing rapidly and profoundly. A substantial restructuring is taking place in the social pattern of bourgeois society, including the composition of the working class. The problem facing our friends in the newly independent states are not simple. The scientific and technological revolution is exercising a contradictory influence on the material condition and consciousness of working people in the non-socialist world. All this requires the ability to do a lot of reappraising and demands a bold and creative approach to the new realities on the basis of the immortal theory of Marx, Engels, and Lenin. The CPSU knows this well from its own experience.

The communist movement's immense diversity and the tasks that it encounters are likewise a reality. In some cases this leads to disagreements and divergences. The CPSU is not dramatising the fact that complete unanimity among communist parties exists not always and not in everything. Evidently, there generally cannot be an identity of views on all issues without exception. The communist movement came into being when the working class entered the international scene as an independent and powerful political force. The parties that comprise it have grown on national soil and pursue common end objectives — peace and socialism. This is the main, determining thing that unites them.

We do not see the diversity of our movement as a synonym for disunity, much as unity has nothing in common with uniformity, hierarchy, interference by some parties in the affairs of others, or the striving of any party to have a monopoly over what is right. The communist movement can and should be strong by virtue of its class solidarity, of equal co-operation among all the fraternal parties in the struggle for common aims. This is how the CPSU understands unity and it intends to do everything to foster it.

The trend towards strengthening the potential of peace, reason, and good will is enduring and in principle irreversible. At the back of it is the desire of people, of all nations to live in concord and to co-operate. However, one should look at things realistically: the balance of strength in the struggle against war is shaping in the course of an acute and dynamic confrontation between progress and reaction. An immutable factor is the CPSU's solidarity with the forces of national liberation and social emancipation, and our course towards close interaction with socialist-oriented countries, with revolutionary-democratic parties, and with the Non-Aligned Movement. The Soviet public is prepared to go on promoting links with non-communist movements and organizations, including religious organizations that are against war.

This is also the angle from which the CPSU regards its relations with the **social democratic movement**. It is a fact that the ideological differences between the Communists and the Social Democrats are deep, and that their achievements and experience are dissimilar and non-equivalent. However, an unbiased look at the standpoints and views of each other is unquestionably useful to both the Communists and the Social Democrats, useful in the first place for furthering the struggle for peace and international security.

We are living in a world of realities and are building our international policy in keeing with the specific features of the present phase of international development. A creative analysis of this phase and vision of prospects have led us to a conclusion that is highly significant. Now, as never before, it is important to find ways for closer and more productive co-operation with governments, parties, and mass organizations and movements that are genuinely concerned about the destinies of peace on earth, with all people in order to **build an all-embracing system of international security**.

We see the Fundamental Principles of this system in the following:

1. **In the military sphere**
— renunciation by the nuclear powers of war — both nuclear and conventional — against each other or against third countries;
— prevention of an arms race in outer space, cessation of all nuclear weapons tests and the total destruction of such weapons, a ban on and the destruction of chemical weapons, and renunciation of the development of other means of mass annihilation;
— a strictly controlled lowering of the levels of military capabilities of countries to limits of reasonable adequacy;
— disbandment of military alliances, and as a stage towards this — renunciation of their enlargement and of the formation of new ones;
— balanced and proportionate reduction of military budgets.

2. **In the political sphere**
— strict respect in international practice for the right of each people to choose the ways and forms of its development independently;
— a just political settlement of international crises and regional conflicts;
— elaboration of a set of measures aimed at building confidence between states and the creation of effective guarantees against attack from without and of the inviolability of their frontiers;
— elaboration of effective methods of preventing international terrorism, including those ensuring the safety of international land, air, and sea communications.

3. **In the economic sphere**

— exclusion of all forms of discrimination from international practice; renunciation of the policy of economic blockades and sanctions of this is not directly envisaged in the recommendations of the world community;
— joint quest for ways for a just settlement of the problem of debts;
— establishment of a new world economic order guaranteeing equal economic security to all countries;
— elaboration of principles for utilizing part of the funds released as a result of a reduction of military budgets for the good of the world community, of developing nations in the first place;
— the pooling of efforts in exploring and making peaceful use of outer space and in resolving global problems on which the destinies of civilization depend.

4. **In the humanitarian sphere**

— co-operation in the dissemination of the ideas of peace, disarmament, and international security; greater flow of general objective information and broader contact beween peoples for the purpose of learning about one another; reinforcement of the spirit of mutual understanding and concord in relations between them;
— extirpation of genocide, apartheid, advocacy of fascism and every other form of radical, national or religious exclusiveness, and also of discrimination against people on this basis;
— extension — while respecting the laws of each country — of international co-operation in the implementation of the political, social, and personal rights of people;
— decision in a humane and positive spirit of questions related to the reuniting of families, marriage, and the promotion of contacts between people and between organizations;
— strengthening of and quests for new forms of co-operation in culture, art, science, education, and medicine.

These Principles stem logically from the provisions of the Programme of the CPSU. They are entirely in keeping with our concrete foreign policy initiatives. Guided by them it would be possible to make peaceful coexistence the highest universal principle of relations between states. In our view, these principles could become the point of departure and a sort of guideline for a direct and systematic dialogue — both bilateral and multilateral — among leaders of countries of the world community.

And since this concerns the destinies of peace, such a dialogue is particularly important among the permanent members of the Security Council — the five nuclear powers. They bear the main burden of responsibility for the destinies of humankind. I emphasize — not a privilege, not a foundation for claims to "leadership" in world affairs, but responsibility, about which nobody has the right to forget. Why then should their leaders not gather at a **round table** and discuss what could and should be done to strengthen peace?

As we see it, the entire existing mechanism of arms limitation negotiations should also start to function most effectively. We must not "grow accustomed" to the fact that for years these talks have been proceeding on a parallel course, so to speak, with a simultaneous build-up of armaments.

The USSR is giving considerable attention to a joint examination, at international forums as well as within the framework of the Helsinki process, of the world economy's problems and prospects, the interdependence between disarmament and development, and the expansion of trade and scientific and technological co-operation. We feel that in the future it would be important to convene a **World Congress on Problems of Economic Security** at which it would be possible to discuss as a package everything that encumbers world economic relations.

We are prepared to consider seriously any other proposal aimed in the same direction.

Under all circumstances success must be achieved in the battle to prevent war. This would be an epoch-making victory of the whole of humanity, of every person on earth. The CPSU sees active participation in this battle as the essence of its foreign policy strategy.

V. THE PARTY

Comrades,

The magnitude and novelty of what we have to do make exceptionally high demands on the character of the political, ideological, and organizational work conducted by the CPSU, which today has more than 19 million members welded together by unity of purpose, will, and decipline.

The Party's strength is that it has a feel for the time, that it feels the pulse of life, and always· works among the people. Whenever the country faces new problems the Party finds ways of resolving them, restructures and remoulds leadership methods, demonstrating its ability to measure up to its historic responsibility for the country's destiny, for the cause of socialism and communism.

Life constantly verifies our potentialities. Last year was special in this respect. As never before there was a need for unity in the Party ranks and unity in the Central Committee. We saw clearly that it was no longer possible to evade pressing issues of society's development, to remain reconciled to irresponsibility, laxity, and inertness. Under these conditions the Political Bureau, the Central Committee Secretariat, and the Central Committee itself decided that the cardinal issues dictated by the times had to be resolved. An important landmark on this road was the April Plenary Meeting of the Central Committee. We told the people frankly about the difficulties and omissions in our work and about the plans for the immediate future and the long term. Today, at this Congress, we can state with confidence that the course set by the April Plenary Meeting received the active support of the Communists, of millions of working people.

The present stage, which is one of society's qualitative transformation, requires the Party and each of its organizations to make new efforts, to be principled in assessing their own work, and to show efficiency and dedication. The draft new edition of the Party Programme and the draft amendments in the Party Rules presented to the Congress proceed from the premise that the task of mobilizing all the factors of acceleration can only be carried out by a Party that has the interests of the people at heart, a Party having a scientifically substantiated perspective, asserting by its labour the confidence that the set targets would be attained.

The Party can resolve new problems successfully if it is itself in uninterrupted development, free of the "infallibility" complex, critically assesses the results that have been attained, and clearly sees what has to be done. The new requirements being made of cadres, of the entire style, methods, and character of work are dictated by the magnitude and complexity of the problems and the need to draw lessons from the past without compromise or reservations.

At present, comrades, we have to focus on the practical organization of our work and the placing and education of cadres, of the body of Party activists, and to take a fresh look at our entire work from the Party's point of view — at all levels, in all echelons. In this context, I should like to remind you of Lenin's words: "When the situation has changed and different problems have to be solved, we cannot look back and attempt to solve them by yesterday's methods. Don't try — you won't succeed!"

1. To work in a New Way, to Enhance the Role and Responsibility of Party Organizations

The purpose of restructuring Party work is that each Party organization — from republican to primary — should vigorously implement the course set by the April Plenary Meeting and live in an atmosphere of quest, of renewal of the forms and methods of its activity. This can only be done through the efforts of all the Communists, the utmost promotion of democracy within the Party itself, the application of the principle of collective leadership at all levels, the promotion of criticism and self-criticism, control, and a responsible attitude to the work at hand. It is only then that the spirit of novelty is generated, that inertness and stagnation become intolerable.

We feel just indignation about all sorts of shortcomings and those responsible for them — people who neglect their duties and are indifferent to society's interests: hack worker and idler, grabber and writer of anonymous letters, petty bureaucrat and bribe-taker. But they live and work in a concrete collective, town, or village, in a given organization and not some place away from us. Then who but the collective and the Communists should openly declare that in our working society each person is obliged to work conscientiously and abide strictly by the norms of socialist human association, which are the same for everybody? What and who prevents this?

This is where the task of enhancing the role of the Party organization rises to its full stature. It does not become us, the Communists, to put the blame on somebody else. If a Party organization lives a full-blooded life founded on relations of principle, if Communists are engaged in concrete matters and not in a chit-chat on general subjects, success is assured. It is not enough to see shortcomings and defects, to stigmatize them. It is necessary to do everything so that they should not exist. **There is no such thing as Communists' vanguard role in general: it is expressed in practical deeds.**

Party life that is healthy, businesslike, multiform in its concrete manifestations and concerns, characterized by openness and publicity of plans and decisions, by the humaneness and modesty of Communists — that is what we need today. We, the Communists, are looked upon as a model in everything — in work and behaviour. We have to live and work in such a way that the working person could say: "Yes, this is a real Communist." And the brighter and cleaner life is within the Party, the sooner we shall cope with the complex problems which are typical of the present time of change.

Guided by the decisions of the April and subsequent Plenary Meetings of the Central Committee and working boldly and perseveringly, many Party organizations have achieved good results. In defining the ways for advancement, the CPSU Central Committee relies chiefly on that experience, striving to make it common property. For example, the decisions on accelerating scientific and technological progress are based to a large extent on the innovatory approach to these matters in the Leningrad Party organization, and its experience underlies the drafting of the programmes for the intensification of science and production, and socio-economic planning. Party organizations in the Ukraine should be commended for creating scientific and technological complexes and engineering centres and for their productive work in effectively utilizing recycled resources. The measures to form a unified agro-industrial complex in the country underwent a preliminary trial in Georgia and Estonia.

Many examples could be given of a modern approach to work. A feel for the new, and active restructuring in accordance with the changing conditions are a characteristic of the Byelorussian, Latvian, Sverdlovsk, Chelyabinsk, Krasnodar, Omsk, Ulyanovsk, and other Party organizations. Evidence of this is also provided by many election meetings, conferences, and republican congresses. They were notable for their businesslike formulation of issues, the commitment of Communists to seeking untapped resources and ways of speeding up our progress, and exactingness in assessing the work of elective bodies.

But not everybody can see the need for restructuring, and not everywhere. There still are many organizations, as is also confirmed by the election campaign, in which one does not feel the proper frame of mind for a serious, self-critical analysis, for drawing practical conclusions. This is the effect of adherence to the old, the absence of a feel for the time, a propensity for excessive organization, the habit of speaking vaguely, and the fear of revealing the real state of affairs.

We shall not be able to move a single step forward if we do not learn to work in a new way, do not put an end to inertness and conservatism in any of their forms, if we lose the courage to assess the situation realistically and see it as it actually is. To make irresponsibility recede into the past, we have to make a rule of calling things by their names, of judging everything openly. It is about time to stop exercises in misplaced tact where there should be exactingness and honesty, a Party conscience. Nobody has the right to forget Lenin's stern warning: "False rhetoric and false boastfulness spell moral ruin and lead unfailingly to political extinction."

The consistent implementation of the **principle of collectivism** is a key condition for a healthy life in every Party organization. But in some organizations the role of plenary meetings and of the bureaus as collegiate bodies was downgraded, and the joint drafting of decisions was replaced by instructions issued by one individual, and this often led to gross errors. Such side-tracking from the norms of Party life was tolerated in the Central Committee of the Communist Party of Kirghizia. A principled assessment was given at the Congress of the Republic's Communist Party of the activities not only of the former First Secretary but also of those who connived at unscrupulousness and servility.

It is only strict compliance with and the utmost strengthening of the principle of collective leadership that can be a barrier to subjectivist excesses and create the conditions for the adoption of considered and substantiated decisions. A leader who understands this clearly has the right to count on long and productive work.

More urgently then before there is now the **need to promote criticism and self-criticism and step up the efforts to combat window-dressing.** From the recent past we know that where criticism and self-criticism are smothered, where talk about successes is substituted for a Party analysis of the actual situation, all Party activity is deformed and a situation of complacency, permissiveness, and impunity arises that leads to the most serious consequences. In the localities and even in the centre there appeared quite a few officials who are oversensitive to critical remarks levelled at them and who go so far as to harass people who come up with criticism.

The labour achievements of the people of Moscow are widely known. But one can say confidently that these accomplishments would have been much greater had the city Party organization not lost since some time ago the spirit of self-criticism and a healthy dissatisfaction with what had been achieved, had complacency not surfaced. As was noted at the city Party conference, the leadership of the City Committee had evaded decisions on complex problems while parading its successes. This is what generated complacency and was an impediment to making a principled evaluation of serious shortcomings.

Perhaps in their most glaring form negative processes stemming from an absence of criticism and self-criticism manifested themselves in Uzbekistan. Having lost touch with life the republic's former top leadership made it a rule to speak only of successes, paper over shortcomings, and respond irritably to any criticism. In the republican Party organization discipline slackened, and persons for whom the sole principle was lack of principles, their own well-being, and careerist considerations were in favour. Toadyism and unbridled laudation of those "senior in rank" became widespread. All this could not but affect the state of affairs. The situation in the economy and in the social sphere deteriorated markedly, machinations, embezzlement, and bribery thrived, and socialist legality was grossly transgressed.

It required intervention by the CPSU Central Committee to normalize the situation. The republic was given all-sided assistance. Many sectors of Party, governmental, and economic work were reinforced with cadres. These measures won the approval and active support of the Communists and the working people of Uzbekistan.

There is something else that causes concern. The shortcomings in the republic did not appear overnight, they piled up over the years, growing from small to big. Officials from all-Union bodies, including the Central Committee, went to Uzbekistan on many occasions and they must have noticed what was happening. Working people of the Republic wrote indignant letters to the central bodies about the malpractices. But these signals were not duly investigated.

The reason for this is that at some stage some republics, territories, regions, and cities were placed out of bounds to criticism. As a result, in the localities there began to appear districts, collective farms, state farms, industrial facilities, and so on that enjoyed a kind of immunity. From this we have to draw the firm conclusion that **in the Party there neither are nor should be organizations outside the pale of control and closed to criticism, there neither are nor should be leaders fenced off from Party responsibility**.

This applies equally to ministries, departments, and any enterprises and organizations. The CPSU Central Committee considers that the role of Party committees of ministries and departments must be enhanced significantly, that their role in restructuring the work of the management apparatus and of industries as a whole must be raised. An examination of the reports of the Party committees of some ministries in the Central Committee shows that they are still using their right of control very timidly and warily, that they are not catalysts of the new, of the struggle against departmentalism, paperwork, and red tape.

The Party provides political leadership and defines the general prospect for development. It formulates the main tasks in socio-economic and intellectual life, selects and places cadres, and exercises general control. As regards the ways and means of resolving specific economic and socio-cultural problems, wide freedom of choice is given to each management body and work collective, and managerial personnel.

In improving the forms and methods of leadership, the Party is emphatically against confusion the functions of Party committees with those of governmental and public bodies. This is not a simple question. In life it is sometimes hard to see the boundary beyond which Party control and the organization of the fulfilment of practical tasks become petty tutelage or even substitution for governmental and economic bodies. Needless to say, each situation requires a specific approach, and here much is determined by the political culture and maturity of leaders. The Party will endeavour to organize work so that everyone on his job will act professionally and energetically, unafraid to shoulder responsibility. Such is the principled Leninist decision on this question and we should abide strictly by it at all levels of Party activity.

2. For the Purity and Integrity of the Image of Party Member,
for a Principled Personnel Policy

Comrades,
The more consistently we draw the Party's huge creative potential

into the efforts to accelerate the development of Soviet society, the more tangible becomes the profound substantiation of the conclusion drawn by the April Plenary Meeting **about the necessity of enhancing the initiative and responsibility of cadres and about the importance of an untiring struggle for the purity and integrity of the image of Party member**.

The Communist Party is the political and moral vanguard. During the past five years it has admitted nearly 1,600,000 new members. Its roots in the working class, in all strata of society are growing increasingly stronger. In terms of per hundred new members there are 59 workers and 26 trained specialists working in various branches of the economy, while four-fifths of all those admitted are young people.

By and large, the Party's composition is formed and its ranks grow in accordance with the Rules, but as in any matter the process of admittance to the Party requires further improvement. Some organizations hasten the growth of the Party ranks to the detriment of their quality, and do not set high standards for new members. Our task is to show tireless concern for the purity of the Party ranks and dependably close the Party to uncommitted people, to those who join it out of careerist or other mercenary considerations.

We have to go on improving the ideological education of Communists and insist upon stricter compliance with Party discipline and unqualified fulfilment of the requirements set by the Rules. In each Party organization the Communists should themselves create an atmosphere of mutual exactingness that would rule out all possibility of anyone disregarding Party norms. In this context, we should support an disseminate the experience of many Party organizations in which communists report regularly to their comrades, and where character references to Party members are discussed and endorsed at Party meetings. This helps to give all Party members without exception a higher sense of responsibility to their organization.

We suffer quite a lot of damage because some Communists behave unworthily or commit acts that discredit them. Of late a number of senior officials have been discharged from their posts and expelled from the Party for various abuses. Some of them have been indicted. There have been such cases, for example, in the Alma-Ata, Chimkent, and some other regions as well as in some republics, and also in ministries and departments. Phenomena of this kind are, as a rule, generated by violations of Party principles in selecting and educating cadres, and in controlling their work. The Party will resolutely go on getting rid of all who discredit the name of Communist.

At this Congress I should like to say a few more words about **efficiency**. This is a question of principle. Any disparity between what is said and done hurts the main thing — the prestige of Party policy — and cannot be tolerated in any form. The Communist Party is a Party whose words are matched by deeds. This should be remembered by every leader, by every Communist. It is by the unity of words and deeds that the Soviet people will judge our work.

Important resolutions have been adopted and interesting ideas and recommendations have been put forward both in the centre and in the localities since the April Plenary Meeting. But if we were to analyse what of this has been introduced into life and been mirrored in work, it will be found that alongside unquestionable changes much has still got stuck on the way to practical utilization. No restructuring, no change can take place unless every communist, especially a leader, appreciates the immense significance of practical actions, which are the only vehicles that can move life forward and make labour more productive. Organizational work cannot be squandered on bombast and empty rhetoric at countless meetings and conferences.

And another thing. The Party must declare a determined and relentless war on bureaucratic practices. Vladimir Ilyich Lenin held that it was especially important to fight them at moments of change, during a transition from one system of management to another, where there is a need for maximum efficiency, speed, and energy. Burcaucracy is today a serious obstacle to the solution of our principal problem — the acceleration of the country's socio-economic development and the fundamental restructuring of the mechanism of economic management linked to that development. This is a troubling question and appropriate conclusions are required. Here it is important to bear in mind that bureaucratic distortions manifest themselves all the stronger where there is no efficiency, publicity, and control from below, where people are held less accountable for what they do.

Comrades, of late many new, energetic people who think in modern terms have been appointed to high positions. The Party will continue the practice of including experienced and young cadres in the leadership. More women are being promoted to leadership positions. There are now more of them in Party and local government bodies. The criteria for all promotions and changes are the same: political qualities, efficiency, ability, and actual achievements of the person

concerned and the attitude to people. I feel it is necessary to emphasize this also because some people have dropped the Party tradition of
maintaining constant contact with rank-and-file Communists, with
working people. This is what undermines the very essence of Party
work.

The person needed today to head each Party organization is one
who has close ties to the masses and is ideologically committed, thinks
in an innovative way, and is energetic. It is hardly necessary to remind
you that with the personality of a leader, of a Party leader in the first
place, people link all the advantages and shortcomings of the
concrete, actual life they live. The secretary of a district committee, a
city committee or a regional committee of the Party is the criterion by
which the rank-and-file worker forms an opinion of the Party
committee and of the Party as a whole.

Cadres devoted to the Party cause and heading the efforts to
implement its political line are our main and most precious asset. Party
activists, all Communists should master the great traditions of Bolshe-
vism and be brought up in the spirit of these traditions. In the Party, at
each level, a principled stand and Party comradeship should become
immutable norms. This is the only attitude that can ensure the Party's
moral health, which is the earnest of society's health.

3. To Reinforce Ideology's Link to Life and Enrich People's Intellectual World

Comrades,

"You cannot be an ideological leader without . . . theoretical work,
just as you cannot be one without directing this work to meet the needs
of the cause, and without spreading the results of this theory . . .. "
That is what Lenin taught us.

Marxism–Leninism is the greatest revolutionary world view. It
substantiated the most humane objective that humankind has ever set
itself — the creation of a just social system on earth. It indicates the
way to a scientific study of society's development as an integral process
that is law-governed in all its huge diversity and contradictoriness,
teaches to see the character and interaction of economic and political
forces, to select correct orientations, forms, and methods of struggle,
and to feel confident at all steep turns in history.

In all its work the CPSU proceeds from the premise that fidelity to
the Marxist–Leninist doctrine lies in creatively developing it on the

basis of the experience that has been accumulated. The intricate range of problems stemming from the present landmark character of the development of our society and of the world as a whole is in the focus of the Party's theoretical thinking. The many-sided tasks of acceleration and its interrelated aspects — political, economic, scientific, technological, social, cultural-intellectual, and psychological — require further in-depth and all-embracing analysis. We feel a pressing need for serious philosophical generalizations, well-founded economic and social forecasts, and profound historical researches.

We cannot escape the fact that our philosophy and economics, as indeed our social sciences as a whole, are, I would say, in a state that is some distance away from the imperatives of life. Besides, our economic planning bodies and other departments do not display the proper interest in carrying rational recommendations of social scientists into practice.

Time sets the question of the social sciences broadly tackling the concrete requirements of practice and demands that social scientists should be sensitive to the ongoing changes in life, keep new phenomena in sight, and draw conclusion that would correctly orient practice. Viability can only be claimed by those scientific schools that come from practice and return to it enriched with meaningful generalizations and constructive recommendations. Scholasticism, doctrinairism, and dogmatism have always been shackles for a genuine addition to knowledge. They lead to stagnation of thought, put a solid wall around science, keeping it away from life and inhibiting its development. Truth is acquired not by declarations and instructions, it is born in scientific discussion and debate and is verified in action. The Central Committee favours this way of developing our social sciences, a way that makes it possible to obtain significant results in theory and practice.

The atmosphere of creativity, which the Party is asserting in all areas of life, is particularly productive for the social sciences. We hope that it will be used actively by our economists and philosophers, lawyers an sociologists, historians and literary critics for a bold and innovative formulation of new problems and for their creative theoretical elaboration.

But in themselves ideas, however attractive, do not give shape automatically to a coherent and active world view if they are not coupled to the socio-political experience of the masses. **Socialist ideology draws its energy and effectiveness from the interaction of**

advanced ideas with the practice of building the new society.

The Party defines the basic directions of ideological work in the new edition of the CPSU Programme. They have been discussed at Plenary Meetings of the CPSU Central Committee and at the USSR Practical-Scientific Conference held in December 1984. I shall mention only a few them.

The most essential thing on which the entire weight of Party influence must be focused is that every person should understand the urgency and landmark character of the moment we are living in. Any of our plans would hang in the air if people are left indifferent, if we fail to awaken the labour and social vigour of the masses, their energy and initiative. **The prime condition for accelerating the country's socio-economic development is to turn society towards new tasks and draw upon the creative potential of the people, of every work collective for carrying them out.**

It is an indisputable fact that intelligent and truthful words exercise a tremendous influence. But their significance is multiplied a hundred-fold if they are coupled to political, economic, and social steps. This is the only way to get rid of tiresome edification and to fill calls and slogans with the breath of real life.

Divergence of words from reality dramatically devalues ideological efforts. No matter how much lectures we deliver on tact and how much we censure callousness and bureaucracy, this evaporates if a person encounters rudeness in offices, in the street, in a shop. No matter how many talks we may have on the culture of behaviour, they will be useless if they are not reinforced by efforts to achieve a high level of culture in production, association between people and human relations. No matter how many articles we may write about social justice, order, and discipline, they will remain unproductive if they are not accompanied by vigorous actions on the part of the work collective and by consistent enforcement of the law.

People should constantly see and feel the great truth of our ideology and the principled character of our policy. Work and the distribution of benefits should be so organized and the laws and principles of socialist human relationships so scrupulously observed that every Soviet citizen should have firm faith in our ideals and values. Dwellings, food supplies, the quality of consumer goods, and the level of health care — all this most directly affects the consciousness and sentiment of people. It is exactly from these positions that we should approach the entire spectrum of problems linked to the educational work of Party and government bodies, and mass organizations.

Exceedingly favourable social conditions are created for boosting the effectiveness of ideological work in the drive to speed up socio-economic development. But nobody should count on ideological, political, labour, and moral education being thereby simplified. It must always be borne in mind that however favourable it may be the present situation has its own contradictions and difficulties. No concession in its assessments should be allowed.

It is always a complex process to develop the social consciousness, but the distinctive character of the present stage has made many pressing problems particularly sharp. First, the very magnitude of the task of acceleration determines the social atmosphere, its character and specific features. As yet not everybody has proved to be prepared to understand and accept what is taking place. Second, and this must be emphasized, the slackening of socio-economic development was the outcome of serious blunders not only in economic management but also in ideological work.

It cannot be said that there were few words in this matter or that they were wrong. But in practice purposeful educational work was often replaced by artificial campaigns leading propaganda away from life with an adverse effect on the social climate. The sharpness of the contradictions in life was often ignored and there was no realism in assessing the actual state of affairs in the economy, as well as in the social and other spheres. Vestiges of the past invariably leave an imprint. They make themselves felt, being reflected in people's consciousness, actions, and behaviour. The lifestyle cannot be changed in the twinkling of an eye, and it is still harder to overcome inertia in thinking. Energetic efforts must be made here.

Policy yields the expected results when it is found on an accurate account of the interests of classes, social groups, and individuals. While this is true from the standpoint of administering society, it is even truer where ideology and education are concerned. Society consists of concrete people, who have concrete interests, their joys and sorrows, their notions about life, about the actual and sham values.

In this context I should like to say a few words about **work with individuals as a major form of education.** It cannot be said that it receives no attention, but in the ideological sphere the customary "gross" approach is a serious hindrance. The relevant statistics are indeed impressive. Tens and hundreds of thousands of propagandists, agitators, and lecturers on politics, the study circles and seminars, the newspapers and journals with circulations running into millions, and the audiences of millions at lectures. All this is commendable. But does not the living person disappear in this playing around with figures and this "coverage"? Do not ideological statistics blind us, on the one hand, to selfless working people meriting high recognition by society and, on the other, to exponents of anti-socialist morality? That is why maximum concreteness in education is so important.

An essential feature of ideological work today is that it is conducted in a situation marked by a sharp confrontation between socialist and bourgeois ideology. Bourgeois ideology is an ideology serving capital and the profits of monopolies, adventurism and social revenge, an ideology of a society that has no future. Its objectives are clear: to use any method to embellish capitalism, camouflage its intrinsic anti-humaneness and injustice, to impose its standards of life and culture; by every means to throw mud at socialism and misrepresent the essence of such values as democracy, freedom, equality, and social progress.

The psychological welfare unleashed by imperialism cannot be qualified otherwise than as a specific form of aggression, of information imperialism which infringes on the sovereignty, history, and culture of peoples. Moreover, it is direct political and psychological preparations for war, which, of course, have nothing in common with a real comparison of views or with a free exchange of ideas, about which they speak hypocritically in the West. There is no other way for evaluating actions, when people are taught to look upon any society uncongenial to imperialism through a gunsight.

Of course, there is no need to overestimate the influence of bour-geois propaganda. Soviet people are quite aware of the real value of the various forecasters and forecasts, they clearly see the actual aims of the subversive activities of the ruling monopoly forces. But we must not forget that psychological warfare is a struggle for the minds of people, for shaping their outlook and their social and intellectual bearings in life. We are contending with a skilful class adversary, whose political experience is diverse and centuries-old in terms of time. He has built up a mammoth mass propaganda machine equipped with sophisticated technical means and having a huge well-trained staff of haters of socialism.

The insidiousness and unscrupulousness of bourgeois propa-gandists must be countered with a high standard of professionalism on the part of our ideological workers, by the morality and culture of socialist society, by the openness of information, and by the incisive and creative character of our propaganda. We must be on the offensive in exposing ideological subversion and in bringing home truthful information about the actual achievements of socialism, about the socialist way of life.

We have built a world free of oppression and exploitation and a society of social unity and confidence. We, patriots of our homeland, will go on safeguarding it with all our strength, increasing its wealth, and fortifying its economic and moral might. The inner sources of Soviet patriotism are in the social system, in our humanistic ideology. True patriotism lies in an active civic stand. Socialism is a society with a high level of morality. One cannot be ideologically committed without being honest, conscientious, decent, and critical of oneself. Our education will be all the more productive, the more vigorously the ideals, principles and values of the new society are asserted. Struggle for the purity of life is the most effective way of promoting the effectiveness and social yield of ideological education and creating guarantees against the emergence of unhealthy phenomena.

To put it in a nutshell, comrades, whatever area of ideological work we take, life must be the starting point in everything. Stagnation is simply intolerable in such a vital, dynamic, and multifaceted matter as information, propaganda, artistic creativity, and amateur art activity, the work of clubs, theatres, libraries, and museums — in the entire sphere of ideological, political, labour, moral, and atheistic education.

In our day, which is dynamic and full of changes, the **role of the mass media** is growing significantly. The time that has passed since the April Central Committee Plenary Meeting has been a rigorous test for the whole of the Party's work in journalism. Editorial staffs have started vigorously tackling complex problems that are new in many respects. Newspapers, journals, and television programmes have begun to pulse with life, with all its achievements and contradictions; there is a more analytical approach, civic motivation, and sharpness in bringing problems to light and in concrete criticism of shortcomings and omissions. Many constructive recommendations have been offered on pressing economic, social, and ideological issues.

It is even more important today to make sure that the mass media are effective. The Central Committee sees them as an instrument of creation and of expression of the Party's general viewpoint, which is incompatible with departmentalism and parochialism. Everything dictated by principled considerations, by the interests of improving our work will continue to be supported by the Party. The work of the mass media becomes all the more productive, the more thoughtfulness and timeliness and the less pursuit after the casual and the sensational there are in it.

Our television and radio networks are developing rapidly, acquiring an up-to-date technical level. They have definitely entered our life as all-embracing media carrying information and propagating and asserting our moral values and culture. Changes for the better have clearly appeared here: television and radio programmes have become more diversified and interesting, and there is a visible aspiration to surmount established stereotypes, to take various interests of audiences into account more fully.

But can it be said that our mass media and propaganda are using all their opportunities? For the time being, no. There still is much dullness, inertia has not been overcome, and deafness to the new has not been cured. People are dissatisfied with the inadequate promptness in the reporting of news, with the superficial coverage of the effort to introduce all that is new and advanced into practice. Justified censure is evoked by the low standard of some literary works, television programmes, and films that lack not only ideological and aesthetic clarity but also elementary taste. There has to be a radical improvement of film distribution and of book and journal publishing. The leadership of the Ministry of Culture, the State Television and Radio Committee, the State Film Committee, the State Publishing Committee of the USSR, and the news agencies have to draw practical conclusions from the innumerable critical remarks from the public. The shortcomings are common, but the responsibility is specific, and this must be constantly in the minds of ideological cadres.

The Party sees the main objective of its **cultural policy** in giving the widest scope for identifying people's abilities and making their lives intellectually rich and many-sided. In working for radical changes for the better in this area as well, it is important to build up cultural-educational work in such a way as to fully satisfy people's cultural requirements and interests.

Society's moral health and the intellectual climate in which people live are in no small measure determined by the state of **literature and art**. While reflecting the birth of the new world, our literature has been active in helping to build it, moulding the citizen of that world — the patriot of his homeland and the internationalist in the true meaning of the word. It thereby correctly chose its place, its role in the efforts of the entire people. But this is also a criterion which the people and the Party use to assess the work of the writer and the artist, and which literature and Soviet art themselves use to approach their own tasks.

When the social need arises to form a conception of the time one lives in, especially a time of change, it always brings forward people for whom this becomes an inner necessity. We are living in such a time today. Neither the Party nor the people need showy verbosity on paper, petty dirty-linen-washing, time-serving, and utilitarianism. What society expects from the writer is artistic innovation and the truth of life, which has always been the essence of real art.

But truth is not an abstract concept. It is concrete. It lies in the achievements of the people and in the contradictions of society's development, in heroism and the succession of day-to-day work, in triumphs and failures, in other words, in life itself, with all its versatility, dramatism, and grandeur. Only a literature that is ideologically motivated, artistic, and committed to the people educates people to be honest, strong in spirit, and capable of shouldering the burden of their time.

Criticism and self-criticism are a natural principle of our society's life. Without them there can be no progress. It is time for literary and art criticism to shake off complacency and servility to rank, which erodes healthy morals, and to remember that criticism is a social duty and not a sphere serving an author's vanity and ambitions.

Our unions of creative workers have rich traditions, and they play a considerable role in the life of art and of the whole of society, for that matter. But even here changes are needed. The main result of their work is measured not by resolutions and meetings, but by talented and imaginative books, films, plays, paintings, and music which are needed by society and which can enrich the people's intellectual life. In this context, serious consideration should be given to suggestions by the public that **the standard for judging works nominated for distinguished prizes should be raised**.

Guidance of intellectual and cultural life is not a simple matter. It requires tact, an understanding of creative work, and most certainly a love of literature and art, and respect for talent. Here much depends upon the ability to propagate the Party's cultural policy, to implement it in life, on fairness in evaluations, and a well-wishing attitude to the creative work and quests of the writer, the composer, and the artist.

Ideological work is creative work. It offers no universal means that are suitable to all occasions; it requires constant quest and the ability to keep abreast of life. Today it is particularly important to have a profound understanding of the nature of present-day problems, a sound scientific world view, a principled stand, a high cultural level, and a sense of responsibility for work in any sector. **To raise society's level of maturity and build communism means steadfastly to enhance the maturity of the individual's consciousness and enrich his intellectual world**.

The Party thinks highly of the knowledge, experience, and dedication of its ideological activists. Here, at our Congress, a word of the highest appreciation must be said to the millions of Party members who have fulfilled and continue to fulfil honourably an extremely important Party assignment in one of the main sectors of its work. We must continue to assign to ideological work such comrades who by personal example have proved their commitment, are able to think analytically, and know how to hear out and talk with people, in short, highly trained in political and professional terms, and capable of successfully carrying out the new tasks of our time.

VI. THE RESULTS OF THE DISCUSSION OF THE NEW EDITION OF THE PARTY PROGRAMME AND OF THE AMENDMENTS TO THE PARTY RULES

Comrades, the Political Report of the CPSU Central Committee examines the Party's programme goals, its present-day economic and political strategies, the problems of improving inner-Party life, and the style and methods of work, that is, all that constitutes the core of the drafts of the new edition of the Programme and of the amendments to the CPSU Rules. Therefore, there is no need to set them forth here in detail. Let me only dwell on some of the points of principle, taking into account the results of the Party-wide and nation-wide discussion of the drafts of these documents.

What are these results? First of all, the conclusions and provisions of the CPSU Programme and Rules have met with widespread approval. The Communists and all Soviet people support the Party's policy of accelerating the country's socio-economic development and its Programme's clear orientation towards the communist perspective and the strengthening of world peace. They point out that the new historical tasks are based on in-depth analysis of the urgent problems of the development of society.

The new edition of the Programme has also evoked a wide response abroad. Progressives take note of its profoundly humanist character, its addressing itself to man, its passionate call for mutual understanding among nations and for ensuring a peaceful future to mankind. Our friends abroad are inspired by the Soviet Union's unremitting striving for lasting comradely relations and all-round co-operation with all the countries of the socialist world system and its firm support of the peoples' anti-imperalist struggle for peace, democracy, social progress, and the consolidation of independence. Many of the sober-minded public figures in bourgeois countries take note of the peaceful orientation of our Programme, of the CPSU line for disarmament and for normal, sound relations with all the countries.

The preparation and discussion of the pre-Congress documents have invigorated the Party's ideological and political work and furthered the social activity of millions of working people.

The drafts of the new edition of the Programme and of the Rules have been thoroughly discussed at meetings of primary Party organizations, at district, city, area, regional and territorial election conferences, and at congresses of the Communist parties of Union Republics. Since the beginning of the discussion, over six million letters were received in connection with the draft Programme alone. They came from workers, collective farmers, scientists, teachers, engineers, doctors, Army and Navy servicemen, Communists and non-Party people, veterans and young people. Assessing the new edition of the Programme as a document that meets the vital interests of the Soviet people, they made numerous proposals, and suggested additions and more precise wordings. I believe it would be useful to dwell on some of them.

Stressing the novelty of the draft under discussion, the authors of some of the letters suggest adopting it at the Congress as the fourth Party Programme. It will be recalled that the adoption of new Party programmes, initially the second and then the third, was necessitated by the fact that the goals set in the preceding Programme has been reached. In our case, the situation is different.

The Party's basic tasks of developing and consolidating socialism, of improving it in every way on a planned basis, and of ensuring Soviet society's further advance to communism, remain in force. The document submitted for your consideration reiterates the theoretical and political guidelines which have stood the test of time.

At the same time, much has changed in our life in the quarter of a century since the adoption of the third Party Programme. New historical experience has been accumulated. Not all of the estimates and conclusions turned out to be correct. The idea of translating the tasks of the full-scale building of communism into direct practical action has proved to be premature. Certain miscalculations were made, too, in fixing deadlines for the solution of a number of concrete problems. New problems related to improving socialism and accelerating its development, as well as certain questions of international politics, have come to the fore and become acute. All this has to be reflected in the Party's programme document.

Thus, the assessment of the submitted document as a new edition of the third Party Programme is justified in reality and is of fundamental importance. It affirms the main goals of the CPSU, the basic laws governing communist construction, and at the same time shows that the accumulated historical experience has been interpreted in a creative manner, and that the strategy and tactics have been elaborated in conformity with specificities of the present turning point.

The public has paid great attention to those provisions of the Programme which describe the stage of social development reached by the country and the goals yet to be attained through its implementation. Various opinions were expressed on this score. While some suggest that references to developed socialism should be completely removed from the Programme, others, on the contrary, believe that this should be dealt with at greater length.

The draft sets forth a well-balanced and realistic position on this issue. The main conclusions about modern socialist society confirm that our country has entered the stage of development socialism. We also show understanding for the task of building developed socialism set down in the programme documents of the fraternal parties of other socialist countries.

At the same time, it is proper to recall that the thesis on developed socialism has gained currency in our country as a reaction to the simplistic ideas about the ways and period of time for carrying out the tasks of communist construction. Subsequently, however, the accents in the interpretation of developed socialism were gradually shifted. Things were not infrequently reduced to just registering successes, while many of the urgent problems related to the switching over of the economy to intensification, to raising labour productivity, improving supplies to the population, and overcoming negative things were not given due attention. Willy-nilly, this was a peculiar vindication of sluggishness in solving outstanding problems. Today, when the Party has proclaimed and is pursuing the policy of accelerating socioeconomic development, this approach has become unacceptable.

The prevailing conditions compel us to focus theoretical and political thought not on recording what has been achieved, but on substantiating the ways and methods of accelerating socio-economic progress, on which depend qualitative changes in various spheres of life. An incalculably deeper approach is wanted in solving the cardinal issues of social progress. The strategy of the CPSU set out in the new edition of the Programme is centred on the need for change, for stepping up the dynamism of society's development. It is through socio-economic acceleration that our society is to attain new frontiers, whereupon the advantages of the socialist system will assert themselves to the fullest extent and the problems that we have inherited from the preceding stages will be resolved.

Divergent opinions have been expressed, too, concerning details of the Programme provisions. Some people hold that the Programme should be a still more concise document, a kind of brief declaration of the Party's intentions. Others favour a more detailed description of the parameters of economic and social development. Some letters contain proposals for a more precise chronology of the period that Soviet society will pass through in its advance to communism.

According to Lenin's principles of drafting programme documents and the traditions that have shaped up, the Programme should present a comprehensive picture of the modern world, the main tendencies and laws governing its development, and a clear, well-argued account of the aims which the Party is setting itself and which it is summoning the masses to achieve. At the same time, however, Lenin stressed that the Programme must be strictly scientific, based on absolutely established facts, and that it should be economically precise and should not promise more than can be attained. He called for maximum realism in characterizing the future society and in defining objectives. "We should be as cautious and accurate as possible", Lenin wrote. " . . . But if we advance the slightest claim to something that we cannot give, the power of our Programme will be weakened. It will be suspected that our Programme is only a fantasy."

It seems to me that the submitted edition of the Programme is meeting these demands. As for the chronological limits in which the Programme targets are to be attained, they do not seem to be needed. The faults of the past are a lesson for us. The only thing we can say definitely today is that the fulfilment of the present Programme goes beyond the end of the present century.

The tasks that we are to carry out in the next 15 years can be defined more specifically, and have been set out in the new edition of the Programme, and in greater detail in the Guidelines for the Economic and Social Development of the USSR until the Year 2000. And, of course, the 12th five-year plan, a big step in the economy's conversion to intensive development through the acceleration of scientific and technological progress, will occupy an important place in the fulfil-ment of our programme aims.

Many of the responses and letters received by the CPSU Central Committee Commission which drew up the new edition of the CPSU Programme are devoted to social policy. Soviet people approve and support measures aimed at enhancing the people's wellbeing, assert-ing social justice everywhere, and clearing our life of everything that is contrary to the principles of socialism. They make proposals that are aimed at ensuring an increasingly full and strick fulfilment of the principle of distributing benefits according to the quantity and quality of labour and at improving the social consumption funds; at tightening control over the measure of labour and the measure of consumption, at doing away firmly with unearned incomes and attempts at using public property for egoistic ends; at eliminating unjustified distinctions in the material remuneration of equal work in various branches of the economy, at doing away with any levelling of pay, etc. Some of these proposals are reflected in the draft. Others must be carefully examined by Party, government and economic bodies, accounted for in legislative acts and decisions, and in our practical work.

The provisions of the Programme concerning the development of the people's socialist self-government have aroused considerable interest during the countrywide discussion. Unanimous support is expressed for the all-round democratisation of socialist society and the maximum and effective enlistment of all the working people in running the economic, social and political processes. The concrete steps taken in this field have also been commended, and ideas expressed that the capacity of work collectives as the primary cell of immediate, direct democracy should be shown more clearly when dealing with the problems of improving the administration of the affairs of society and the state. These ideas have been taken into account.

Concern for enhancing the role of cultural and moral values in our society prompted suggestions that the education of Soviet people should proceed more distinctly in the spirit of communist ideals and ethical norms, and struggle against their antipodes. The Programme Commission saw fit to accept these proposals, so that the principles of lofty ideological commitment and morality should imbue the content of the provisions of the Party Programme still more fully.

About two million people expressed their ideas concerning the CPSU Rules. Having examined the results of the discussion, the Central Committee of the Party has deemed it essential to introduce in the draft Rules a number of substantive additions and clarifications aimed at heightening the vanguard role of the Communists, the capability of primary Party organizations, at extending inner-party democracy, and at ensuring unflagging control over the activity of every Party organization, every Party worker.

In support of the idea of making more exacting demands on Communists, some comrades suggest carrying out a purge to free the Party of those whose conduct and way of life contradict our norms and ideals. I do not think there is any need for a special campaign to purge the ranks of the CPSU. Our Party is a healthy organism: it is perfecting the style and methods of its work, is eradicating formalism, red tape, and conventionalism, and is discarding everything stagnant and conservative that interferes with our progress; in this way it is freeing itself of persons who have compromised themselves by their poor work and unworthy behaviour. The Party organizations will continue to carry out this work consistently, systematically, and unswervingly.

The new edition of the Programme and also the proposed changes in the Party Rules register and develop the Bolshevik principles of Party building, the style and methods of Party work and the behavioural ethics of Communists that were elaborated by Lenin and have been tried and tested in practice.

On the whole, comrades, the discussion of the CPSU Programme and Rules has been exceptionally fruitful. They have helped to amplify many ideas and propositions, to clarify formulations and to improve wordings. Allow me, on behalf of our Congress, to express profound gratitude to the Communists and all Soviet people for their businesslike and committed participation in discussing the pre-Congress documents.

It is the opinion of the Central Committee of the Party that the submitted drafts, enriched by the Party's and people's experience, correspond to the spirit of the times and to the demands of the period of history through which we are now living. They confirm our Party's fidelity to the great doctrine of Marxism–Leninism, they provide scientifically substantiated answers to fundamental questions of domestic and international affairs, and they give the Communists and all working people a clear perspective.

Comrades, those are the programme aims of our further development which have been submitted for the consideration of the 27th Congress.

What leads us to think that the outlined plans are feasible? Where is the guarantee that the policy of accelerating socio-economic progress is correct and will be carried out?

First and foremost, the fact that our plans rest on the firm foundation of Marxist–Leninist theory, that they are based on the inexhaustible riches of Lenin's ideas.

The CPSU draws its strength from the enormous potentialities of socialism, for the vigorous creative efforts of the masses. At crucial turning points in history the Leninist Party has no more than one occasion demonstrated its ability to find correct roads of progress, to inspire, rally and organize the many-million masses of working people. That was the case during the revolution, in the years of wartime trials, and in the difficult postwar period. We are confident this will be the case in future, too.

We count on the support of the working class because the Party's policy is their policy.

We count on the support of the peasantry because the Party's is their policy.

We count on the support of the people's intelligentsia because the Party's policy is their policy.

We count on the support of women, young people, veterans, all social groups and all the nations and nationalities of our Soviet homeland because the Party's policy expresses the hopes, interests and aspirations of the entire people.

We are convinced that all conscientious, honest-minded Soviet patriots support the Party's strategy of strengthening the might of our country, of making our life better, purer, more just.

Those are the powerful social forces that stand behind the CPSU. They follow it, they have faith in the Communist Party.

The surging tide of history is now speeding towards the shallows that divide the second and third millennia. What lies ahead, beyond the shallows? Let us not prophesy. We do know, however, that the plans we are putting forward today are daring, and that our daily affairs are permeated with the spirit of socialist ethics and justice. In this troubled age the aim of our social and, I would add, vital strategy consists in that people should cherish our planet, the skies above, and outer space, exploring it as the pioneers of a **peaceful** civilization, ridding life of nuclear nightmares and completely releasing all the finest qualities of Man, that unique inhabitant of the Universe, for constructive efforts only.

The Soviet people can be confident that the Party is fully aware of its responsibility for our country's future, for the durable peace on Earth, and for the correctness of the charted policy. Its practical implementation requires above all persistent work, unity of the Party and the people, and cohesive actions by all working people.

That is the only way we will be able to carry out the behests of the great Lenin — to move forward energetically and with a singleness of will. History has given us no other destiny. But what a wonderful destiny it is, comrades!

2.

Statement by the General Secretary of the Central Committee of the CPSU
Pravda, 16 January 1986

The new year, 1986, is now in its third week. This will be a crucial year, in fact, a turning-point in Soviet history, the year of the 27th Party Congress. The Congress will set the guidelines for the political, social, economic and cultural progress of Soviet society up to the year 2000. It will adopt a programme of accelerated peaceful construction.

The CPSU is gearing all its efforts to a continued improvement in the Soviet people's standards of living.

A radical change for the better is also needed on the international scene. The peoples of the Soviet Union and of the world as a whole are demanding and expecting that change.

Therefore, in the early days of this year the Politbureau of the Central Committee of the CPSU and Soviet Government resolved to put forward a series of far-reaching foreign policy initiatives on fundamental issues of principle. Their objective is to facilitate as much as possible a normalization of the international situation. They are dictated by the need to offset the negative confrontation trends that have been growing in the last few years, to clear the way for a de-escalation of the nuclear arms race on earth and for preventing its development in outer space, to lessen the risk of war in general, and to promote mutual trust as an essential component of relations between nations.

I

The most important of these initiatives is a concrete and accurately

110

scheduled programme for the complete elimination of nuclear weapons in the world.

The Soviet Union is proposing a plan of staged and consistent moves to initiate and complete the process of relieving the world of the burden of nuclear weapons within the coming 15 years, before the end of this century.

The 20th century has brought mankind the benefits of atomic energy. However, this great achievement of the human mind may turn into a tool for self-destruction of the human species.

Can this contradiction be resolved? Our answer is a confident yes. To find an effective way of abolishing nuclear weapons is a feasible task if handled without delay.

The Soviet Union is proposing a plan to begin in 1986 to free mankind from the threat of nuclear catastrophe. This is International Peace Year proclaimed by the United Nations, which is an additional political and moral stimulus. Here it is imperative to rise above national self-interest, tactical considerations, controversy and discord, which are all of negligible significance compared with the preservation of the chief advantage — peace and a secure future. Atomic energy should serve only peace — such is the principle consistently upheld by our socialist state in the past and today.

This country was the first to propose — as far back as 1946 — a ban on the production and use of atomic weapons and the first to use nuclear power for peaceful purposes for the benefit of mankind.

What is the Soviet view of a practical procedure for cutting nuclear arms — both delivery vehicles and war-heads — down to their complete elimination? Our proposals may be summed up as follows:

The first stage. During the coming five to eight years the Soviet Union and the United States shall cut by half their arsenals of nuclear weapons which have each other's territories within their firing range. The delivery vehicles they will retain in this class shall carry not more than 6000 charges on each side.

Needless to say, such cuts will be possible only if the Soviet Union and the United States reciprocally renounce the development, testing and deployment of strike space weapons. As the Soviet Union has repeatedly warned, strike space weapons, if developed, will dash any hopes of nuclear arms reduction on earth.

At this first stage, agreement will have to be reached and implemented on the complete elimination of Soviet and US intermediate-range missiles in the European zone — both ballistic and cruise missiles — as a first step on the way to ridding the European continent of nuclear weapons.

At the same time, the United States should assume an obligation to refrain from supplying its strategic missiles and intermediate-range missiles to other countries, while Britain and France should undertake not to build up their arsenals of corresponding nuclear weapons.

It is necessary to ensure from the outset that the Soviet Union and the United States agree on the termination of all nuclear tests and appeal to other states to join in such a moratorium at the earliest date.

If the first stage of nuclear disarmament should seem to concern only the Soviet Union and the United States, the reason is that it is precisely these powers that must set an example to other nuclear powers. We stated that unequivocally to US President Ronald Reagan during our meeting at Geneva.

The second stage. At this stage which should begin in 1990 at the latest and last for five to seven years, the other nuclear powers should gradually join in the disarmament process. At first they should assume a commitment to freeze all their nuclear arms and not to station any in foreign territories.

During this period the Soviet Union and the United States shall continue the reductions agreed upon at the first stage, as well as taking further steps to eliminate their intermediate-range nuclear weapons and freezing their tactical nuclear arms.

When the Soviet Union and the United States have completed the 50 per cent reduction of their corresponding armaments at the second stage, another radical step is to be taken: all the nuclear powers will abolish their tactical nuclear weapons, that is, those with a range of up to 1000 km.

Also at this stage the Soviet–American agreement on banning strike space weapons should be made multi-lateral through the close involvement of the leading industrial powers.

All nuclear powers are to terminate their nuclear weapons tests.

A ban should be imposed on developing non-nuclear armaments based on new physical principles whose overkill capacity is comparable to that of nuclear or other weapons of mass destruction.

The third stage is to begin not later than 1995 to complete the abolition of all remaining nuclear weapons. By 1999 no nuclear weapons will be left on earth. A universal agreement is to be worked out to prevent these weapons from ever being reproduced.

This implies the drawing up of special procedures for eliminating nuclear weapons, as well as for dismantling, re-equipping or destroying delivery vehicles. At the same time the parties involved will agree on the quantities of weapons to be eliminated at each stage, the sites of their destruction, etc.

Control over weapons subject to elimination or limitation is to be carried out by both national monitoring facilities and by inspection on the spot. The Soviet Union is prepared to negotiate any other supplementary measures of verification.

The adoption of the programme of nuclear disarmament we are proposing would indisputably exert a beneficial influence on the bilateral and multilateral talks in progress. It would map out clear-cut routes and reference points, set deadlines for reaching and implementing agreements and lend the negotiations clarity and singleness of purpose. Thereby the dangerous trend by which the pace of the arms race outstrips the productiveness of negotiations would be neutralized.

Thus, we are proposing entry to the third millennium without the burden of nuclear arms on a basis of mutually acceptable agreements with strict verification of compliance. If the US Administration is committed to the cause of the complete and universal elimination of nuclear weapons, as it has repeatedly declared, it has a practical opportunity to engage in this undertaking. Instead of spending the coming 10 to 15 years on developing new space weapons — highly dangerous to mankind — with the alleged aim of making nuclear weapons useless, is it not more sensible to begin abolishing these very weapons and eventually to reduce their stockpiles to naught? This is precisely the option proposed by the Soviet Union.

The Soviet Union appeals to all peoples and states, and to the nuclear powers in the first place, to support the programme of eliminating nuclear weapons by the year 2000. It is perfectly obvious to any unbiassed person that once this programme is implemented nobody will be the loser and everybody will be the winner. Indeed, it is a matter of vital importance to all mankind, and it can and must be settled by joint efforts. So the sooner this programme is translated into practical action, the safer life on this planet will become.

II

Guided by the same approach and by its desire to take another practical step forward in the context of the programme of nuclear disarmament, the Soviet Union has made an important decision.

We are extending by three months the unilateral moratorium on all nuclear explosions whose term expired on 31 December 1985. This moratorium will be further extended if the United States reciprocates by ending its own nuclear tests. We are again calling on the United States to join in this initiative, whose significance is obvious literally to everyone on earth.

Clearly, taking that decision was by no means a simple matter for us. The Soviet Union cannot endlessly exercise unilateral restraint in relation to nuclear tests. However, the stakes are too high, the extent of our responsibility is too great for us not to explore every opportunity to influence the position of others by our example.

All specialists, scientists, political leaders and military men agree that the halting of tests is a sure means of preventing the development of the more powerful nuclear weapons. This is indeed a task of first priority. A reduction of nuclear arsenals alone, without a ban on nuclear weapons tests, offers no way out of the dilemma of nuclear danger, because the remaining part can be modernized and the possibility of developing ever more sophisticated and lethal nuclear weapons, and of trying out their new varieties on testing sites is preserved.

Hence, the termination of tests is a practical step in the direction of abolishing nuclear weapons.

I would like to forestall certain objections. Possible references to difficulties of verification as an obstacle to imposing a moratorium on nuclear explosions are absolutely groundless. We declare unequivocally that verification is no problem with us. If the United States agrees to terminate all nuclear explosions on a reciprocal basis, effective verification of compliance with the moratorium will be secured by national monitoring facilities, as well as by means of international procedures, with inspection on the spot whenever necessary. We invite the United States to come to terms on this issue.

The Soviet Union is strongly in favour of developing the moratorium from a bilateral into a multi-lateral act. We favour a resumption of tripartite negotiations (between the USSR, the USA and the UK) on a general and complete prohibition of nuclear weapons tests. This could be done without delay, even this month. We are also prepared, without wasting any time, to begin multilateral talks on banning tests within the framework of the Geneva disarmament conference, with all nuclear powers taking part.

The non-aligned countries have proposed consultations with a view to extending the Moscow Treaty prohibiting nuclear weapons tests in the atmosphere, outer space and under water to include underground tests, which are not covered by this treaty. The Soviet Union agrees to this.

Since last summer we have been urging the United States to follow our example by ending nuclear tests.

In defiance of public protests and demands and of the wishes of the majority of the world's nations, Washington has so far failed to do this. By exploding ever new nuclear devices, the American side is continuing its chase after the vain dream of military superiority. This is a fruitless and dangerous policy, a policy unworthy of the level of civilization attained by modern society.

In view of the absence of a positive response from the United States the Soviet side would have been fully justified in resuming nuclear tests as of 1 January 1986. If one is to follow the customary "logic" of the arms race, that is evidently what should have been done.

The point is, however, that this logic, if one may call it so, should be resolutely discarded. We are making another attempt to do so. Otherwise the process of military rivalry will turn into an avalanche and any control of developments will become impossible. It is impermissible to resign oneself to the spontaneous growth of the arms race. This would mean behaviour contrary to common sense and to the human instinct for self-preservation. The situation demands bold new approaches, new political thinking and a keen awareness of responsibility for the destiny of nations.

The US Administration again has additional time at its disposal to examine our proposals for ending nuclear tests and give an affirmative answer to them. That is precisely what will be expected of Washington everywhere in the world.

The Soviet Union is appealing to the US President and Congress, to the American people. You have the opportunity to check the process of modernizing nuclear arms and developing new overkill weapons. It should not be missed. The Soviet proposals place the Soviet Union and the United States on an equal footing. They are not an attempt to cheat or outplay the opposing side. We propose taking the path of sensible, responsible decisions.

III

To implement the programme of reduction and elimination of

nuclear arsenals it is necessary to bring into action the entire existing system of negotiations and to ensure the highest efficiency of the disarmament mechanisms.

In the next few days Soviet–American talks on nuclear and space weapons will be resumed at Geneva.

During the meeting with President Ronald Reagan at Geneva in November of last year we had a frank discussion on the entire range of problems on the agenda of these talks; that is, on outer space, strategic offensive arms, intermediate-range nuclear weapons. It was decided to speed up the negotiations, and that agreement cannot remain a mere declaration.

The Soviet delegation at Geneva will be instructed to act in strict compliance with that agreement. We expect an equally constructive approach from the American side, on the issue of outer space, first and foremost. Outer space should be maintained as a preserve of peace and no strike weapons should be stationed there. Nor should they be developed at all. Let the most stringent verification procedures be established, including the opening of the relevant laboratories to inspection.

Mankind is at a responsible stage of the new space era. It is high time to discard the mentality of the Stone Age when the main concern was to provide oneself with a larger stick or a heavier stone. We are opposed to weapons in outer space. Our material and intellectual potential make it possible for the Soviet Union to develop any weapon if we are forced to do so. However, we are fully aware of our responsibility to present and future generations. It is our profound conviction that what is needed for entry into the third millennium is not a "star wars" programme but large-scale projects for the peaceful exploration of outer space by the combined efforts of all mankind. We propose taking practical steps to draw up and implement such projects. This is one of the most important ways of ensuring progress on the whole of our planet and of building a dependable system of security for all.

To prevent the arms race from escalating into outer space is to remove the major obstacle to drastic cuts in nuclear armaments. The Soviet proposal for a 50 per cent reduction in the corresponding nuclear armaments of the Soviet Union and the United States is on the negotiating table at Geneva, and is an important step towards the total abolition of nuclear weapons. Locking the door to a solution of the problem of outer space speaks of unwillingness to have the arms race ended on earth. This should be stated frankly for all to hear. It is no accident that advocates of the nuclear arms race are zealous champions of the "star wars" programme as well. These are the two aspects of one and the same policy hostile to the interests of humanity.

Now for the European aspect of the nuclear problem. Extremely great concern is being caused by the situation where, contrary to the arguments of common sense and the national interests of the peoples of Europe, the deployment of American first-strike missiles is being continued in some countries of Western Europe. This problem has been under discussion for many years now. In the meantime the conditions of security in Europe have been steadily deteriorating.

It is time this trend was halted and the Gordian knot cut. The Soviet Union has long been proposing that Europe be freed from both intermediate-range and tactical nuclear weapons. This proposal is still valid. As a first radical step in this direction we are proposing now, as I have said above, that all Soviet and American intermediate-range ballistic and cruise missiles in the European zone be abolished in the first stage of the programme we are putting forward.

The achievement of tangible practical results at the Geneva talks would give strong material substance to our proposed programme of complete elimination of nuclear weapons by the year 2000.

IV

Another task the Soviet Union regards as perfectly feasible is one of completely eliminating such barbarian tools of war as chemical weapons, also in this century.

The talks on chemical weapons now in progress within the framework of the Geneva disarmament conference have of late shown signs of making headway. These talks, however, have been dragged out intolerably. We are in favour of intensifying the talks to conclude an effective and verifiable international convention on banning chemical weapons and destroying existing stocks, as was agreed with the US President Ronald Reagan at Geneva.

In the matter of banning chemical weapons as well as in other questions of disarmament, all negotiators are requested to take a fresh view of developments. I wish to emphasize that the Soviet Union favours early and complete liquidation of these weapons and of the very industrial base for their manufacture. We are prepared to supply up-to-date information on the location of factories manufacturing chemical weapons and on the cessation of their production, to begin working out procedures for destroying the relevant productive base, and to commence the elimination of chemical weapons stocks shortly after the convention comes into force. All these measures would be implemented under strict control, including international verification on the spot.

Some intermediate steps would contribute to a radical solution of this problem. For instance, agreement could be reached on a multilateral basis on the non-transference of chemical weapons to whoever it may be, and on their non-deployment in the territories of foreign states. As far as the Soviet Union is concerned, it has always strictly abided by these principles in its practical policies. We call upon other states to follow this example and exercise the same restraints.

V

Along with the withdrawal of weapons of mass destruction from national arsenals, the Soviet Union is proposing that conventional armaments and armed forces should be subjected to agreed reductions.

Agreement reached at the Vienna talks might give a signal for taking steps in this direction. Now one can see a rough outline of a possible agreement on cutting Soviet and American troop strengths to be followed by a freeze on the levels of the armed forces of the opposing groupings in Central Europe. The Soviet Union and our Warsaw Treaty allies are determined to make the Vienna talks a success. If the opposing side really seeks the same, the year 1986 could become a milestone for the Vienna talks as well. We proceed from the assumption that possible agreement on troop reductions will naturally require reasonable verification. We are prepared for this. As for compliance with the commitment to freeze troop strength, the national monitoring facilities could be supplemented with permanent posts for control over whatever military contingents might enter the zone of reductions. Concerning that very important forum, the Stockholm conference on confidence-building measures, security and disarmament in Europe; this is called upon to erect barriers against the use of force and against secret preparations for war — be it on land, at sea or in the air. Possibilities for achieving this have now arisen.

In our opinion, it is imperative, especially in the current situation, to reduce the strength of troops involved in large-scale military exercises of which notification has to be made in compliance with the Helsinki Final Act.

It is time effective steps were taken at the conference to deal with outstanding problems. The most difficult bottleneck, as we know, is the issue of notifications about large-scale exercises of land, naval and air forces. Needless to say, these are serious problems which should be settled once and for all in the interest of promoting trust in Europe. If, however, efforts to find a comprehensive solution fail for the time being, why not search for a piecemeal solution? Let us, say, agree now on notifications about large-scale exercises of land and air forces and refer the question of naval activities to the next stage of the conference.

It is not fortuitous that many of the new Soviet initiatives are directly addressed to Europe. If a sharp turn were taken in favour of a peace policy, Europe could perform a special role that of rebuilding the edifice of détente.

Europe has the requisite, in many ways unique, experience for this. Suffice it to recall that the Helsinki Final Act was worked out by the joint efforts of the Europeans, the United States and Canada. If a concrete and tangible example is needed to illustrate new thinking and political psychology in approaching the problems of peace, co-operation and international trust, this historic document may serve as such in many respects.

VI

For the Soviet Union, as one of the biggest powers of Asia, guaranteed security in Asia is of vital significance. The Soviet programme of eliminating nuclear and chemical weapons by the end of this century is consonant with the sentiments of the peoples of the continent of Asia facing no less acute problems of peace and security than the peoples of Europe. It would be relevant to recall here that Japan's cities of Hiroshima and Nagasaki were made victims of atomic bombing, while Vietnam became an arena for the use of chemical weapons.

We greatly appreciate the constructive initiatives put forward by the socialist countries of Asia, by India and by other participants in the non-aligned movement. We attach great significance to the fact that both nuclear powers situated in the continent of Asia — the USSR and the PRC — have assumed a commitment not to use nuclear weapons first.

The implementation of our programme would radically improve

the situation in Asia, deliver the peoples in this part of the world, too, from the menace of nuclear and chemical warfare and lend a new dimension to the security of the region.

We regard our programme as a contribution to the search being carried on jointly with all the countries of Asia for a general, comprehensive approach to establishing a security system and lasting peace on this continent.

VII

Our new proposals are addressed to the whole world. A transition to active steps to end the arms race and secure arms reductions is an indispensable prerequisite also for solving such increasingly acute global problems as the pollution of the human environment, the need to discover new energy sources, and the fight against economic backwardness, famine and disease. The principle of armament instead of development, imposed by militarism, must be replaced by its reverse disarmament for development. The noose of the trillion-dollar debt which is now strangling dozens of countries and whole continents is a direct sequel to the arms race. The total of over 250 thousand million dollars pumped out of the developing countries each year is a sum practically equal to the enormous US military budget. This apparent coincidence is in essence far from accidental.

The Soviet Union wants every measure of arms limitation and reduction, every step towards liberation from the burden of nuclear weapons not only to give the peoples greater security but also to release more resources for improving their standards of living. Naturally, the peoples seeking to overcome their backwardness and attain the level of highly industrialized countries link their prospects of deliverance from the debtor dependence on imperialism that is exhausting their economies to arms limitation and abolition, cuts in military spending, and the regearing of resources to the purposes of social and economic development. This subject will undoubtedly be a focus of discussion at the international conference on disarmament and development to be held in Paris next summer.

The Soviet Union is opposed to making the implementation of measures in the disarmament field dependent on the so-called regional conflicts. Such a requirement conceals both an unwillingness to follow the path of disarmament and a striving to impose their domination on sovereign nations and to maintain an order that would continue the extremely inequitable conditions of existence of some countries at the expense of others, and the exploitation of their natural, manpower and intellectual resources to further the selfish imperial aims of individual states or aggressive coalitions. The Soviet Union has always opposed this and will continue to do so. It has always been and will be a consistent champion of the freedom of nations, peace, security, and of strengthening international law and order. Its aim is not fomenting regional conflicts but their settlement by collective efforts on the principles of justice; and the sooner, the better.

There is no shortage nowadays of declarations of allegiance to the cause of peace. However, there is a shortage of concrete steps to consolidate its foundations. Much too often talk of peace conceals a policy of preparations for war, a stake in force. Moreover, some statements delivered from authoritative platforms seem to be intended in effect to undermine what is in fact new and beneficial in international relations today, the "Geneva spirit". Its opponents do not confine themselves to declarations. Actions are also undertaken with the obvious purpose of fomenting hostility and mistrust, and reviving the opposite of détente — a situation of confrontation.

We reject this manner of acting and thinking. We want the year 1986 to be not simply a year of peace but also a symbol of peace and nuclear disarmament by the end of the 20th century. The complex of new Soviet foreign policy initiatives is designed to secure mankind's entry into the year 2000 under peaceful skies and with peaceful outer space, without fear of the menace of nuclear, chemical or any other destruction, and with firm confidence in its own survival and the continuation of the human species.

The new, resolute moves to defend peace and to normalize the entire international situation undertaken by the Soviet Union now are an expression of the substance and spirit of our home and foreign policies, and of their organic unity. This is a fundamental historical law, which was stressed by Vladimir Ilyich Lenin. The whole world can see that this country is raising still higher the banner of peace, freedom and humanism which the Great October Socialist Revolution raised aloft over this planet.

In the matter of preserving peace and delivering mankind from the menace of nuclear war nobody can be an indifferent onlooker. This is a matter for each and every one of us. The contribution of every state, large or small, socialist or capitalist, is important here. The contribution of every responsible political party, every public organization, every man and woman is important, too.

There is no task more urgent, noble and humane than that of uniting all efforts into a whole to achieve this lofty aim. This task must be accomplished by the people of our generation without shifting it onto the shoulders of our descendants. Such is the dictate of the times and, if you will, the burden of our historical responsibility for decisions and actions in the period left before the third millennium.

The course of peace and disarmament has been and will be the pivot of the foreign policy of the CPSU and the Soviet State. While actively pursuing this course, the Soviet Union is prepared for broad cooperation with all those who adhere to the positions of reason and good will and are aware of their responsibility for securing the future of mankind without wars, without arms.

3.

Speech in the British Parliament
18 December 1984

Ladies and gentlemen,

It is with great interest that we are becoming acquainted with your country, its rich history and ancient culture, its varied traditions which have taken shape over long centuries; its hard-working and talented people, who have given the world many outstanding thinkers, scientists, writers and artists well known in the Soviet Union.

The Soviet people remember the ties that linked our two nations in the most bloody of wars. They remember that more than forty years ago the British Prime Minister presented the citizens of Stalingrad with a sword of honour, which symbolized the close co-operation of the Soviet and British peoples in the anti-Hitler coalition.

In other words, whatever is good, useful and constructive that has been gained and preserved by our two countries and peoples in their relations in different historical periods should be, in our opinion, carefully preserved and carried into the future.

A delegation from the Supreme Soviet of the USSR visited here almost ten years ago. Since then serious changes have taken place in Soviet–British relations and in the international situation. This makes the need for such a meeting as today's all the more obvious.

Hardly anyone will deny the fact that the destinies of the nations of Europe are indivisible; they were such when Europe lived in peace and accord and when storm clouds swept low over its lands. Profoundly convinced of this, we have come to your country with the intention of discussing what can be done by our two countries and their parliaments to ameliorate Soviet–British relations and improve the international situation as a whole. How the future of mankind and relations between individual states and groups of countries will shape depends on the concrete steps that are undertaken or may be undertaken today on the problems of war and peace and international co-operation.

These questions were in the focus of our discussions with the Prime Minister Mrs Thatcher, the Foreign Secretary, Sir Geoffrey Howe, and other cabinet members. The exchange of opinion was business-like, frank and, in our view, useful. Now, speaking before the members of the British Parliament, I would like in the first place to express what we think important for improving the international situation and developing our bilateral relations.

It is well known that in the seventies Europe became the cradle of the policy of détente. At that time important lines of co-operation formed between the countries of Western Europe on the one hand and the Soviet Union and other socialist countries on the other. That process was joined by the United States and Canada who both signed the Helsinki Final Act.

At one time it became possible to stop the channels of proliferation of nuclear weapons. That was formalized in the relevant international Treaty on the Non-Proliferation of Nuclear Weapons, to which more than 100 states are party today. Nuclear weapons tests in the atmosphere, outer space and under water were ended and banned, and talks were in progress on a general and complete prohibition of such tests. As a result of Soviet–American agreements, definite limitations were imposed on strategic nuclear arms and anti-missile defence systems. Active measures were under way to seek possible means of scaling down the arms race in other directions — both weapons of mass destruction and in conventional arms. The political dialogue was gathering momentum. Trade relations, cultural, scientific and other exchanges became appreciably more active. Nobody can deny the obvious fact that in the years to détente people felt safer and had greater confidence in their future.

In short, a normalization of the international climate was in evidence. It was not based on concessions by one side to the other. It was an expression of realism based on consideration of the mutual interests of countries belonging to different social systems and a general awareness of the fact that one's own security cannot be founded on means that prejudice the security of others.

In other words, it was a victory for common sense and a realization of the fact that war is an unfit and unacceptable method of settling disputes and that in a nuclear war, as in arms race and confrontation, there can be no winners. It had become obvious that the Cold War was an abnormal state of relations constantly fraught with the risk of war. All this had laid the groundwork for the favourable trend of international events in the seventies. On this foundation the peaceful coexistence of states belonging to different social systems became more and more deeply and securely implanted in the entire system of international relations. We believe that today, too, no reasonable alternative to the policy of peaceful coexistence exists or can exist. I wish to lay strong emphasis on this fact.

One naturally wonders why there has been a new increase in the danger of war when it was possible at that time to lessen it. I shall not go into details. The Soviet viewpoint on this subject is well known. Nevertheless, I wish to say once again that the cause of that change for the worse — which is corroborated by facts — was a change in the policy of certain forces seeking to achieve military superiority and thereby gain the ability to dictate their will to others.

We in the Soviet Union well remember the statements and actions that created the climate of mistrust and hostility and led to a destabilization of the international situation. However, I am recalling this today without meaning to give offence to anybody.

We see our aim in deciding jointly — since nobody can do it alone — the most important problems which are essentially common to all of us: how to prevent war; how to check the arms race and proceed to disarmament; how to settle existing, and prevent potential, conflicts and crises; how to create a world situation that would allow every country to concentrate its attention and resources on solving its own problems (just name a country where no problems exist); how to pool efforts to deal with global problems — the fight against famine and disease, protection of the environment, provision of mankind with energy and raw material resources.

If Great Britain abides by this approach, we would be glad to cooperate with it. If the United States abides by the same approach and really puts its policy on the lines of peaceful co-operation, it, too, will find a dependable partner in us.

This is how we see the situation, and it is with these views that our parliamentary delegation has come to Britain.

If one agrees with the basic principles I have listed, the main question will still remain: how to solve the problems all of us consider important, how to prevent a further deterioration of the current dangerous situation and achieve a stable and secure situation in the world. In other words, how to lessen tensions, to clear the debris of Cold War and to revive détente, fruitful negotiations and co-operation.

For that, words alone are not enough (although they are also important in politics). Concrete action is necessary. A practical solution, if you will, to outstanding problems is required. As we see it, it is now important, as never before, for every country — its government, parliament, political and public circles — to be aware of its responsibility for the state of world affairs. We in the Soviet Union remember the horrors of the last war and clearly realize the catastrophic consequences of a future war; we are doing, and will do, our level best to live up to this great responsibility.

I will not list now all our foreign policy proposals and initiatives. I shall only say that they provide for as radical cuts in nuclear arms as possible (down to their complete elimination), as well as for cuts in conventional armaments, a ban on chemical weapons and the liquidation of stocks. We desire a broad dialogue and the development of mutually beneficial co-operation on a basis of equality in solving acute political problems, in the economic field, in science and technology, and in the area of cultural ties and exchanges.

When we speak of war and peace, we ought to keep it in mind that the character of modern weapons, nuclear weapons first and foremost, has changed the traditional concepts of these problems. Mankind is on the threshold of a new stage in the scientific and technological revolution, which will affect, in particular, the future development of military technology. Those who discourse on "limited" "short" or "protracted" nuclear wars are evidently still captives of the old-fashioned stereotypes of the time when war was a great tragedy but did not threaten mankind with extinction as it does today. The nuclear age inevitably dictates new political thinking. The most acute and urgent problem facing all people on earth today is the problem of averting nuclear war.

Our proposal for establishing definite rules of behaviour for the nuclear powers pursues the aim of averting the threat of nuclear war, finding a way to check the arms race, and to create a world situation where no nation would fear for its future. It will be recalled that the Soviet Union has already assumed a unilateral commitment not to use nuclear weapons first.

Such is our policy of principle. This is the starting point of all our proposals aimed at curbing the arms race and preventing war.

Guided by this principle, the Soviet Union has recently come forward with the initiative of holding talks with the United States on the full range of problems concerning nuclear and space weapons. On the basis of this initiative, agreement has been reached with the US Administration to open a completely new round of talks covering both the problem of the non-militarization of outer space and that of the reduction of strategic and intermediate-range nuclear weapons. All of these should be discussed and settled as interlinked problems. Prevention of a race in space weapons is of key significance. Should such a race be started, it would not only be dangerous of itself but it would also whip up the arms race in other directions. The Soviet Union is prepared to seek and elaborate the most radical solutions to all these problems which would assist progress towards a total ban on nuclear weapons and eventually their complete elimination. It is now up to the United States, in its turn, to take a realistic stance that would facilitate the success of the negotiations.

We know that all issues concerning a lessening of the risk of nuclear war are widely discussed in Great Britain and other countries of Western Europe. The questions of defence and security are, of course, an internal affair of the sovereign states. I can declare, however, that any concrete step in the direction of lessening the risk of nuclear war, in Europe in particular, will find a corresponding practical response on our part.

It is true, of course, that the Soviet Union and Great Britain often take different stances on major international problems. Neither of us is playing down this fact. Nevertheless, it is our profound conviction that under present conditions all countries and peoples need, as never before, a constructive dialogue, a search for solutions to key international problems, for areas of agreement that could lead to greater mutual trust and create an international climate free from the nuclear menace, hostility and suspicion, fear and hatred.

The Soviet Union has formulated its approach in clear and unambiguous terms: to end tensions, to settle differences and disputed problems not by force or threats but through negotiations taking account of each other's legitimate interests, to avoid interference in each other's internal affairs. I would put it this way: all must constantly learn to live together, adapting to the realities of the modern world constantly changing in accordance with its own laws.

The development of the world situation is largely influenced by the way relations take shape between states in Europe. I have already mentioned the favourable trends in these relations in the seventies, especially after the adoption of the Final Act of the all-European conference at Helsinki. This document remains to this day a life-giving source, feeding the trends towards mutual understanding and co-operation in Europe, and not only in Europe. We believe that this source should be protected against bombardment and blockage.

Indeed, good relations between European states are largely a guarantee of security and peace in the world as a whole. The peoples of Europe have paid a high price for understanding that under no circumstances should one connive with forces that to this day persist in their attempts to revise the territorial realities that took shape in Europe in the wake of the Second World War. These realities were borne of a joint victory. They are reflected and affirmed in the inter-allied agreements on the postwar order, in important bilateral negotiations between a number of states, and in the Helsinki Final Act. Allegiance to all this must constitute a solid obstacle in the way of those who would like to call in question the results of the Second World War and postwar development, the inviolability of the state frontiers in Europe. There is no room for any ambiguities here.

The Stockholm Conference could open definite prospects for strengthening peace in Europe. It has on its agenda, in particular, such an important proposal as one for concluding a treaty on the non-use of military force and supporting peaceful relations. Our approach is based on the principle that a combination of large-scale moves in the areas of politics and international law with confidence-building measures in the military field as an extension of the Helsinki Final Act would secure success at the Stockholm Conference and make its results a substantial contribution to strengthening European and international security.

I have listed just a few of the most vital problems whose solution would help put an end to the arms race and consolidate European and world security. I wish to emphasize again that the leadership of the Soviet Union are in favour of concrete and honest negotiations that would help make progress in solving, on a mutually acceptable basis, the problems involved in the limitation and reduction of armaments, especially nuclear weapons, right down to their complete elimination. We are prepared to meet our Western partners in negotiations halfway. Naturally, parity and equal security will have to be the basis for any arrangement. Needless to say, any move to achieve military superiority over the Soviet Union and its allies is unacceptable and would fail.

All of us are agreed that we live in a vulnerable, rather fragile but interconnected world. It is a world where coexistence is necessary, whether one wants it or not. Whatever divides us, we have the same planet to live on. Europe is our common home; and it is a home, not a "theatre of war".

The Soviet Union is in favour of normalizing relations between states. In politics and diplomacy there is always room enough for reasonable compromises, and a vast field for developing and strengthening mutual understanding and trust on a basis of similar or identical interests. It is the desire to cultivate this field that is needed. The Soviet Union and Great Britain, the Soviet and British peoples have such identical interests; the most important is the preservation of peace.

The history of Soviet–British relations is more than sixty years old, and it has its own unforgettable milestones. In the postwar period there were years of productive co-operation. There were also times of decline. And today our relations, which are not developing in a political vacuum but in the troubled atmosphere of a growing nuclear danger, are not on the upgrade and are far from what is desirable. It will be recalled that at one time Britain was the Soviet Union's leading trade partner. Today it is no higher than seventh or eighth. I cannot but agree with the opinion of those representatives of Britain's trade and industrial circles who believe that politics should help commerce and commerce should promote mutual understanding and trust. This is absolutely correct.

British MPs know that a number of British statesmen have held talks in Moscow this year. We have declared our willingness to develop Soviet–British relations actively and on a wide range of questions. If the British side takes the same stance, this development will become a fact. May I avail myself of this opportunity to reaffirm this viewpoint of the Soviet Union.

The foreign policy of every state is inseparable from its home affairs, social and economic aims and requirements. The main aim of our plans is to advance considerably the material and cultural levels of the life of our people.

Our Party and State are directing their chief efforts to further economic developments by raising the efficiency of production and re-gearing the economy on the lines of intensification. Acceleration of scientific and technological progress in industry and agriculture is the focus of our work. We are setting and tackling large-scale and long-term tasks designed for the period up to the year 2000, taking advantage of all the achievements of the scientific and technological revolution available to man.

The Soviet Union needs peace to accomplish these truly breath-taking development plans. This is our policy of principle which is not dependent on any political expendiency.

Great historical responsibility for the present and future of the world devolves today on its political leaders, legislators, on all those who shape the policies of states.

In view of this, the Supreme Soviet of the USSR, in its appeals of December 1982 and December 1983, clearly declared that the Soviet Union does not threaten the security of any country in the West or in the East. It desires to live at peace with all countries, to translate into reality the principles of peaceful coexistence of states belonging to different socio-political systems. The supreme legislative body of the USSR has expressed its willingness to make an effective contribution, jointly with the parliaments of other countries, to solving the most burning problem of today — that of saving mankind from nuclear catastrophe.

The world situation is truly complicated. The risk of war is one of today's realities. In the face of this grim reality I wish to emphasize this idea: let us look to the future and let us not forget the past. In other words, without forgetting what is good or bad, and learning lessons from both, let us concentrate all our efforts on opening new horizons for confident progress towards a world safer for all and truly secure.

Our delegation has been staying in Britain for a few days. We are grateful for the hospitality accorded us here and we hope that our visit, our new acquaintances and meetings will assist Soviet–British co-operation for the benefit of the peoples of our two countries, co-operation that will develop in the interest of mutual understanding and peace on earth.

May I avail myself of this opportunity to convey best wishes for prosperity, happiness and peace from the peoples of the Soviet Union to the people of Great Britain.

4.

On convening the regular 27th Congress of the CPSU and the problems involved
Report at the Plenary Meeting of the Central Committee of the CPSU
23 April 1985

Yesterday our Party, the Soviet people and the peoples of the socialist countries solemnly commemorated the 115th anniversary of the birth of Vladimir Ilyich Lenin. All the realities of life, the entire course of history, are conclusively corroborating the great truth of Lenin's doctrine. It has been and remains for us a guide to action, a source of inspiration, a dependable compass in mapping out the strategy and tactics of our advice.

Lenin taught communists to be guided in all matters by the interests of the working people, to make a thorough study of social life, to assess social phenomena realistically from class positions, and to be constantly engaged in a creative search for the best ways of accomplishing the ideals of communism.

Lenin and his great ideals are a model for our work and our plans, and today we live and work in accordance with Lenin's behests.

This Plenary Meeting is to discuss problems of great political significance: the convening of the regular 27th Party Congress and the tasks to be fulfilled in preparing and holding it.

In accordance with the Rules of CPSU, the Politbureau proposes to convene the next Party Congress on 25 February 1986. The Congress will have the following items on its agenda:

1. Report of the Central Committee of the CPSU and the tasks facing the Party.
2. Report of the Central Auditing Commission of the CPSU.
3. New edition of the Programme of the CPSU.
4. Amendments to the Rules of the CPSU.
5. Guidelines for the economic and Social development of the USSR in the period 1986-90 and up to the year 2000.
6. Election of the Party's governing bodies. The reports of the CPSU Central Committee and the Central Auditing Commission, as well as the report on the guidelines for economic and social development will be delivered from the rostrum and followed by a debate. As for the new edition of the Programme and amendments to the Rules of the CPSU, their essence may be described in the report of the CPSU Central Committee, obviating the need for separate reports.

It is contemplated to elect to the Congress one delegate from every 3670 communists, that is, a total of 5000 delegates. This will provide good representation of all the organizations of our Party and reflect its social and ethnic composition.

Over the nine months remaining before the Congress we have to analyse our record of work since the 26th Congress in comprehensive detail to define the prospects for further development; and to formulate the tasks to be carried out in the field of home and foreign policy. It is imperative to prepare the most important documents, especially such fundamental items as a new edition of the Programme and the guidelines for development in the coming five years and up to the end of the century, and to discuss them at a Plenary Meeting of the CPSU Central Committee, followed by a broad discussion within the Party and country. Great attention will have to be paid both to the reports and elections in Party organizations, in order to ensure high standards, and to completing the eleventh Five-Year Plan in exemplary fashion.

In short, this will be a time of tense and diverse activities, political, economic, organizing, ideological and theoretical.

Today we are reaffirming the continuity of the strategic line mapped out by the 26th Party Congress and the subsequent Plenary Meetings of the Central Committee. As Lenin viewed it, this continuity invariably implies steady advance, identifying and solving new problems and removing all obstacles to development. We are obliged to follow this Leninist tradition unfailingly, enriching and developing our Party policy and our general line of perfecting mature socialist society.

The forthcoming 27th Congress of the CPSU will indisputably become a milestone in the country's development. Its significance is determined by the paramount importance of the questions on the agenda, the character of the period under review, and the novelty and large scale of the tasks facing society. This lends a new dimension to all the Party's pre-Congress work, demanding a profound analysis of the current situation, bold decisions and vigorous actions.

The country has scored great achievements in all areas of social life. Profiting from the advantages of the new system, it has scaled the summits of economic and social progress within only a short historical time. The Soviet Union today has a powerful, diversified economy, and a large body of skilled workers, specialists and scientists. In many aspects of the development of production, science and technology we have a firm hold on leading positions in the world.

Profound changes have taken place in social life also. For the first time in history the working man has become master of his country and of his own destiny. The guaranteed right to work and remuneration, society's concern for man from birth to old age, broad access to intellectual culture, respect for the dignity and rights of the individual, a steady widening of the working people's involvement in management — all these are permanent values, inalienable features of the socialist way of life. They are the basic source of political stability, social optimism and confidence in the future.

The Soviet people are rightly proud of all this. However, life and its dynamic nature dictate the need for further changes and transformations in order to attain a new qualitative state of society in the broadest sense of the word. This means above all scientific and technological renovation of production and the achievement of the highest level of labour efficiency in the world. This means the perfection of social relations, primarily the economic ones, which means profound changes in the sphere of work and in the material and cultural conditions of people's lives. This implies more active functioning of the entire system of political and social institutions, a deepening of socialist democracy, and self-government by the people.

The development of Soviet society will be determined decisively by qualitative changes in the economy, its regearing onto lines of intensive growth, and all-round enhancement of its efficiency. It is precisely from these positions that one should assess the situation in the national economy and set the tasks for the future.

It is widely known that along with the successes achieved in the country's economic development unfavourable trends have appeared and quite a few difficulties have arisen in the last few years. Thanks to the Party's active efforts, since 1983 the operation of many sectors of the national economy has been improved and the situation has changed for the better. The difficulties, however, are far from having been overcome, and we shall have to put in a good deal of effort to lay a dependable basis for rapid progress.

What is the cause of the difficulties? The answer to this question is, as you know, of key significance to the Party.

Of course, the influence of a number of natural and external factors has had a part to play. However, the chief cause, as I see it, was failure to make a proper assessment of the changes in the objective conditions of the development of production and of the need to accelerate its intensification and revise methods of management, plus — which is particularly important — lack of persistence in working out and implementing large-scale measures in the economic field. We must be thoroughly aware of the situation and draw the most serious conclusions from it. The historical destiny of the country and the position of socialism in the modern world largely depend on how we shall manage affairs from now on. Taking advantage of the achievements of the scientific and technological revolution on a broad scale and bringing the forms of socialist management into conformity with present conditions and requirements, we must secure a substantial speed-up in social and economic progress. There is simply no alternative.

This determines the success of the cause of socialism and communism today, the enormous responsibility of the Party, its Central Committee and all party organizations in the current, crucially important period of history. We Communists are obliged to do everything we can to live up to this responsibility and to the great tasks dictated by the times.

The chief question now is: what ways and means are needed to accelerate the country's economic development. Discussing this question in the Politbureau, we agreed unanimously that realistic possibilities for this do exist. The task of substantially accelerating growth rates is perfectly feasible if we focus our efforts on intensifying the economy and stepping up the rates of scientific and technological progress, reorganizing management and planning, implementing the structural and investment policy, enhancing organization and discipline everywhere, and improving the style of work radically.

I think that this Plenary Meeting will support this conclusion. Relatively quick returns can be obtained by activating organizational, economic and social reserves and, above all, by galvanizing the human factor to ensure that everyone works at his job conscientiously and efficiently.

The great potential available here was discussed at a recent conference with workers, economic managers, specialists and scientists at the Central Committee. Speakers pointed out that whenever necessary work collectives and their managers do brace themselves and begin to work better, so much so that within a short space of time the productivity of labour is raised to a level sometimes comparable with the plan assignments for a full five years.

Such latent reserves exist at every factory and plant, on every construction site, and on every state and collective farm. Nobody knows them better than the work collectives themselves, their party organizations and economic managers. Hence, much depends on their attitude to the matter in hand, their activity and ability to encourage the interest of their personnel in making the most of all the possibilities of increasing production and advancing its efficiency.

An important aspect of the question of responsibility and discipline is punctual delivery of high-quality raw materials, fuel, components, railway wagons, etc. Those accountable for this work are known. A certain improvement in contractual discipline in the national economy has recently been in evidence. It should be reinforced by steadily stiffening demands on the execution of contractual obligations without any allowance for objective conditions.

Another reserve that should be handled resolutely is what can be released by a crackdown on extravagance and waste. The leading executives of many Ministries and enterprises seek to "wrest" from the State as much as they can in the form of capital investments, machine-tools and other equipment, raw materials and fuel. At the same time, they are often careless about its rational use. Equipment available is sometimes idle or used below capacity.

Let us look at what is going on in the field of capital construction. Many projects are taking an intolerably long time to complete. As a result, large material values are immobilized. Increases in productive capacity are delayed and the country fails to receive needed commodities on time.

The plan for commissioning basic productive capacities is not fulfilled satisfactorily. Much equipment awaiting instalment lies idle in the warehouses of industrial plants and factories and new building sites. Considerable direct losses are caused by careless transportation, storage and use of cement, coal, mineral fertilizer and timber, farm produce and foodstuffs.

It is time this extravagance were ended without delay. Persuasion alone is evidently insufficient; there has been more than enough of that. It is imperative to make firmer demands on specific persons, in particular through legislation, to secure the preservation and rational use of all material resources. Proper order should be introduced at every enterprise and construction site, on every collective and state farm, in every organization. Without this any rational economic management, any growth of economic efficiency is out of the question. The Party is laying prime emphasis on a major acceleration of scientific and technological progress as the main strategic line of intensifying the operation of the national economy and making better use of the potential accumulated. In June a special conference is to be held at the CPSU Central Committee to discuss this question. Today I would like to express my views on some matters of principle.

In the majority of sectors scientific and technological progress is running a sluggish course, which is, in effect, evolution mainly by way of improving existing manufacturing processes and partly by modernizing machines and equipment. Of course, these measures yield certain returns, but they are too small. We need revolutionary breakthroughs: a switch to technological systems based on fundamentally new principles, to last-generation technology that ensures the highest efficiency. This implies, in effect, a radical modernization of all sectors of the national economy on the basis of the most up-to-date achievements of science and technology.

The urgency of this problem also stems from the fact that in the past few years the country's productive apparatus has largely become obsolescent and the rate of renewal of main production facilities has declined. In the Twelfth Five-Year Plan top priority must be attached to a substantial increase in the rate of equipment replacement.

The engineering industry must make a decisive contribution to this progress. Its development should be high on the list of priorities, so that even during the Twelfth Five-Year Plan period its growth rates become 50–100 per cent higher than now. The main task is to change over quickly to the production of the new generations of machines and equipment needed to secure the introduction of advanced technological processes, to raise the productivity of labour many times over, to reduce materials consumption per unit product and to raise the rate of return on investment. High priority should also be assigned to advancing the standards of machine-tool building, speeding up the development of computer technology, instrument-making, electrical engineering and electronics as the catalysts of scientific and technological progress.

In the light of these tasks, erosion of the prestige of engineering work cannot be accepted as a matter of course. It would be incorrect to say that everything is all right here. We must elevate the function and prestige of foremen, engineers, designers, and technologists, to enhance the material and moral incentives for their work.

Acceleration of scientific and technological progress and growth of production efficiency are inseparably linked with resolute steps to improve product quality. Its discrepancy from modern technical, economic, aesthetic and other consumer requirements, and at times the obvious spoilage constitute, in fact, a plundering of material resources and a wasting of our people's labours. This is why an all-out effort to improve product quality must be the hub of our economic policy. Quality comes first — such is our slogan today. Having solved the problem of quality, we can solve the problem of quantity. This is the only dependable way of continuing to increase our effectiveness in meeting the country's demand for up-to-date technology and the population's growing demand for various consumer goods, and of overcoming shortages in the national economy.

Whatever question we may discuss, whatever aspect of the economy we may examine, the need for a radical improvement of management, of the economic mechanism as a whole appears critically important. We witnessed that again during a recent meeting with workers and economic executives at the CPSU Central Committee, as well as during a visit to the Likhachov Motor Works in Moscow. Participants in those meetings spoke with grave concern about difficulties in work caused by the inefficiency of the management system, petty regimentation, an exorbitant amount of paperwork and other distressing bottlenecks. There is only one way out of this situation: immediate and vigorous steps must be taken to deal with the whole range of management problems.

The concept of restructuring the economic mechanism has now

become clearer to us. While developing further the principle of centralism in pursuing strategic tasks, we should proceed boldly with widening the rights of enterprises, encouraging their independence and introducing the principle of profit-orientated performance, thus enhancing the responsibility and interest of work collectives in the end results of their labour.

The record of a large-scale experiment being carried on in this direction seems to be fairly good. However, it cannot satisfy us completely. We have come to a point where experimentation must be followed by setting up an integrated system of economic operation and management. This means commencing the practical reorganization of work and of the higher echelons of economic management, their orientation primarily on long-range socio-economic, scientific and technological tasks and a search for the most effective forms of integrating science with production.

The life of society makes ever more stringent demands on planning, which is the core of management. It is called upon to be an effective means of intensifying production, implementing progressive economic decisions, and securing balanced and dynamic growth of the economy. At the same time, the plans of production associations and individual enterprises should be freed from an excess of detail, making wider use of the economic factors which give free rein to initiative and enterprise.

It is time measures were taken to perfect the organizational structures of management, to abolish redundant divisions, to simplify the apparatus and to raise its efficiency. Another reason for this is the fact that certain echelons of management have become an obstacle to progress. It is essential to limit drastically the number of instructions, regulations and prescribed methods of work, which often arbitrarily misinterpret Party and government decisions and handicap the independence of enterprises.

Another step of great significance is to bring the principles of profit-orientated performance to the knowledge of all work teams and of every team member. This will make it possible to combine measures to perfect the system of management from above with developing the collective forms of organization and stimulation of labour from below, thereby enhancing the working people's activity.

It is no less important to enhance the responsibility of republican and local bodies for the management of economic, social and cultural development and for meeting the working people's requirements.

This, of course, demands further measures to widen the powers of the local bodies, to encourage their initiative and interest in developing production, utilizing resources and organizing all consumer services. Therefore, local bodies should be fully accountable for the solution of all problems within their terms of reference and must get rid of tendencies to rely on external assistance as early as possible.

The CPSU sees its supreme aim in accelerating the country's socio-economic progress; in advancing steadily, step by step, the well-being of the people, improving all aspects of their life; and in creating favourable conditions for the harmonious development of the individual. At the same time, it must consistently pursue the line of promoting social justice in the distribution of material and cultural benefits, reinforcing the impact of social factors on the development of the economy and the advancement of its efficiency.

This line enjoys the Soviet people's complete approval and support. The task now is to work out concrete and effective measures to rid the mechanism of distribution of wage levelling, unearned income whatever runs counter to the economic norms and the moral ideals of our society, to secure a direct relationship between the material position of every worker and every collective and the results of their labour. The Party will continue to wage a determined struggle against all negative phenomena alien to the socialist way of life and to our Communist morality.

At present, detailed work is under way to draw up a social programme, which the Party intends to submit to its 27th Congress. However, there are tasks that brook no delay and demand special attention.

This concerns above all the implementation of the Food Programme. Over the last few years favourable changes have been in evidence in the development of agriculture, and the supply of the population with various foodstuffs has improved appreciably. This, however, is far from enough. The collective and state farms and food-processing enterprises have the requisite capacities for a considerable increase in the output of foodstuffs. These capacities should be used rationally, and the potential available should be brought into full play.

Sometimes we witness attempts by local bodies to shift the burden of responsibility for food supplies and the provision of feed for livestock onto the central authority. Such practices are unacceptable. The task is to make full use of all reserves for increasing food production on collective and state farms and on the subsidiary farms of individuals and enterprises.

In short, work on fulfilling the Food Programme should be intensified and supplemented with effective measures to develop the processing facilities of the agroindustrial complex and bring them closer to collective and state farms. The Politbureau has given such instructions to the State Planning Committee of the USSR and the relevant Ministries, and they are required to fulfil them completely and with full awareness of their responsibility.

The management of the agroindustrial complex also requires further improvement. Far from everything has been done to this effect. Influenced by their departments' interests, district and regional production associations are often unable to secure due co-ordination in solving the problems involved in the comprehensive development of agriculture and the related industries. If we are firmly convinced that the land should be managed by one master and that the agroindustrial associations are fully responsible for fulfilling the Food Programme — which, I believe, is not called in question by anyone — it is imperative to implement measures that would permit management, planning and financing of the agroindustrial complex as an integrated whole at all levels. This is what we agreed upon at the Plenary Meeting of the CPSU Central Committee in May 1982.

Much remains to be done to meet more effectively the demand for industrial goods and services, to saturate the market with the necessary products, to improve the quality and widen the assortment of manufactured goods, to lend greater flexibility to the system of prices and to raise the efficiency of trade. These tasks are to be implemented under the integrated programme of developing consumer goods and services. This provides for a substantial increase in the production of high-quality clothes and footwear, modern goods for cultural and household use, and the development of diverse consumer services.

This programme is to be approved in the near future. At the same time, as you know, the CPSU Central Committee and the Council of Ministers of the USSR have already adopted resolutions on work to be performed in a number of directions under this Programme. This refers to increases in the production of footwear, the development of local industries, house repair and building services, and improvement of telephone services for the public. It is important to ensure that the Soviet people see changes for the better in the very near future.

We must pay attention to the shifts taking place in the structure of effective demand. The working people want to use more of their income for improving their housing, cultural and living conditions, for rest and recreation, tourism and other pursuits. Such requirements must be met more completely. This is advantageous for the State as well. The possibilities available here, however, are not utilized effectively. Take, for instance, such a concrete question as developing fruit and vegetable garden co-operatives. This is a very useful field of work, which evokes broad interest. However, it has so far failed to assume wide scope. The need for garden plots, cottages, building materials and farm implements is met only partly. The Politbureau has discussed this question in great detail and instructed the relevant bodies to take effective steps to meet the citizens' requests and remove unjustified barriers in this field.

Such spheres as health care and public education are assuming steadily growing importance in the life of society and of every individual, and hence in the Party's social policy. We have achieved much in their development and secured for all citizens equal access to these vital benefits. Today, however, we are confronted by new tasks in this field too.

From the standpoint of modern requirements the material and technological base of the health care system, the standards of medical services and the supply of medicines to the public need substantial improvement. The Politbureau has recently discussed the need for effective measures to this end. They should be envisaged in the Twelfth Five-Year Plan.

We have started a school reform whose significance for the country's future can hardly be overestimated. It is now imperative to display not just a formal but a meaningful approach to the tasks set in this area and to radically improve the standards of education and upbringing of the younger generations — their preparation for socially useful work.

There are quite a few other problems that should be carefully considered in order to find solutions. These are improvement of the material position of labour veterans, especially those who have long retired from their jobs; the living conditions of young families; mother and child care. And, of course, it is important to step up further the efforts to solve such social problems as housing, so as to provide every family with a separate flat or a comfortable house.

We should be as attentive as we can in all matters concerning the individual, his work, material well-being and leisure. This is a key question in our policy.

Now for the current affairs linked with the performance of the annual plan. We did not get off to a good start: in the first quarter the increment in industrial output was a mere two per cent. The lag was particularly pronounced in crude oil, metal, power and transport. The rates of growth of labour efficiency slowed down. The situation is no better with prime costs, profit, and other indicators. In April there was a certain improvement, but efforts should be stepped up to make up for the loss in the remaining eight months.

It should be frankly stated that this is not a simple task. However, we see only one way to cope with it: the 1985 plan must be fulfilled, and without any scaling down adjustments, for that matter. The socialist emulation drive and all organizational and political work should be orientated on this target.

The farmers are also facing responsible tasks. They are expected to produce the sort of high output results that will gladden everyone in the country.

Simultaneously, next year's annual plan and the Twelfth Five-Year Plan as a whole will have to be very competently drawn up. For this purpose it would be wise to bring the target figures and norms to the knowledge of Ministries and other government departments, production associations and individual enterprises in the very near future. This will enable planners to examine in detail the proposals of work collectives for mobilizing available reserves and — which is most important — the Twelfth Five-Year Plan will thus be started by a vigorous well-organized effort from the beginning of next year.

The great and complex tasks of the present period, which affect all aspects of our life, can be accomplished only by efforts relying on the creativity of the people, their intelligence, talent and work. We need to stir millions of working people to an all-out effort to fulfil these tasks; to encourage constantly the initiative and energy of the working class, the peasantry and the intelligentsia; to bring into play the inexhaustible potential available to socialist society; and to give more active support to all useful initiatives.

The Leninist Communist Party has always been and still is the vanguard of the people. It is called upon to lead the nationwide movement to accelerate the country's social and economic progress. This requires every Party organization and every Communist to be actively involved in the drive to attain our immediate and long-range goals.

The preparations for the Congress, and the forthcoming reviews of the year's record and elections should contribute effectively to raising the activity and responsibility of Communists, reinforcing the militancy of Party organizations, consolidating their ties with the masses and, in the final analysis, advancing the guiding role of the Party.

The annual review and election campaign will begin in primary Party organizations, which constitute the Party's main potential. Here Party policy is translated into practical actions. Our successes and failures, our possibilities and reserves are visible in salient relief at this level.

This is why it is crucially important for these Communist meetings to review their record in the Leninist way, avoiding false indealization and empty verbal contention; to gather every bit of their positive experience; to expose shortcomings fearlessly; and to identify possibilities and practical ways of increasing production, advancing economic efficiency and improving work in general.

It is the duty of Party committees to do their best to ensure that meetings at primary Party organizations are held in a businesslike atmosphere of criticism and self-criticism, and true Communist frankness, and discuss the painful problems in the life of the work collective and ways to remove whatever obstacles exist to efficient work. It is imperative to secure a situation where every Party member could take full advantage of the right laid down in the Party Rules to submit proposals and express remarks, so that no critical statement could be ignored.

The question of reinforcing order and discipline is particularly vital today. This is an urgent demand of the day, which the Soviet people interpret broadly, meaning order in the sphere of production and consumer services, in the social and everyday life of every work team, in every town and village. We are determined to do our level best to have this order firmly implanted in the country.

Development has shown the people's unanimous approval of the measures being taken to reinforce order and the tangible results of such measures. It should be frankly admitted, however, that in recent times attention to this major problem has lessened. Therefore, more stringent demands should be made, primarily on the leading executives of work collectives who are personally responsible for the maintenance of discipline. Not infrequently, leading managers of enterprises overlook violations of discipline by their subordinates in the hope that the latter will in turn overlook their own failings. We will not put up with such attitudes of mutual lenience.

There is yet another indispensable prerequisite for success in strengthening order and discipline.

Everyone must do his own work and conscientiously perform his direct duties. No substantial results can be achieved in any sphere of work as long as a Party functionary substitutes for an economic executive or an engineer for a courier, or when a scientist works at a vegetables store and a weaver on a farm. Unfortunately this is not infrequently the case. Of course, this situation has not developed overnight, but has arisen because of certain difficulties, so that it cannot be remedied in one day. However, it must be remedied. Only then shall we be able to get rid of irresponsibility and laxity.

More stringent demands should also be made on the general tone, businesslike conduct and exacting nature of the forthcoming district, town, regional, and territorial Party conferences and the congresses of the Communist Parties of the Union Republics. They should not, as happens sometimes, allow eulogies and compliments, or attempts to conceal the essence of matters under a smokescreen of general verbiage and to shift the blame for shortcomings onto objective circumstances or departmental bottlenecks.

We expect the leading cadres, members of the Central Committee, leading executives of Ministries and other government departments to take a direct part not only in Party conferences but also in meetings of primary Party organizations, and to do their utmost to help the pre-Congress collective discussion of Communist to be as constructive and critical as possible.

The main slogans of the day, which should be made the leitmotif of our pre-Congress meetings and all preparations for the 27th Party Congress, are creativity in work, unity of word and deed, initiative and responsibility, exactingness to oneself and one's colleagues. A Communist must be a model in these respects. Every Party member should be faced with stiffer demands on his attitude to public duty, his contribution to the fulfilment of Party decisions, and his honesty and moral integrity as a Communist. Indeed, a Communist is assessed by his deeds. Other criteria do not and cannot exist.

In the course of reviews and elections the governing Party bodies will be formed and reinforced with new replacements, and outstanding questions concerning cadres will be settled. The recent plenary meetings of Party committees have conclusively demonstrated the maturity of Party cadres. At the same time, they have reaffirmed once again the need for the strictest compliance with the Leninist principles of selection, placement and education of cadres. Where these principles are infringed, and the promotion of executives is motivated by their personal loyalties, servility and protectionism, then criticism and self-criticism inevitably subside, the ties with the masses weaken, and failures in work follow as a result.

The Politbureau deems it a matter of principle to continue the line of ensuring stability in Party leadership, with a correct combination of experienced and young executives. This, however, cannot be accompanied by a stalemate in the movement of cadres. In their letters to the Central Committee, Communists call attention to the fact that some leading functionaries who occupy one and the same post for a long time not infrequently cease to discern innovation and get used to shortcomings.

There is much food for thought here. Ways should be sought — and found — for more active movement by our leading cadres. Women and young and promising workers should be more boldly promoted to responsible posts.

There is yet another important conclusion suggested by the recent plenary meetings of Party committees: no Party organization and no executive should be left without supervision. In the last two years the First Secretaries of the Central Committees of the Communist Parties of many Union Republics, territorial and regional Party committees have reported on various questions at meetings of the Politbureau and the Secretariat of the CPSU Central Committee. The meetings also heard reports by the leaders of a number of primary Party organizations, district and town committees, various Ministries and other government departments. Such work should, of course, be actively continued in the Republics, territories and regions. This corresponds to the rules of work inside our Party.

Since I have touched upon the question of supervision, I would like to expand on this subject. Supervision and inspection are necessary, of course, and each inspection must be practically useful and beneficial to the progress of work. However, one can hardly justify repeated inspections on one and the same question, at times not important enough, or numerous commissions organized out of formal considerations, distracting personnel from their regular duties and creating an atmosphere of anxiety.

Review meetings, conferences and congresses make it possible to make a comprehensive assessment of the activities of elective Party bodies, to study in detail the content and methods of their work.

Emphasis should be placed above all on an analysis of how they are coping with the key problems in the life and work of productive collectives and their members, in the development of the economy and culture, and how they carry on their organizing work within the masses. It is imperative to pursue persistently the line of rendering daily practical aid to local Party organizations, encouraging business-like conduct and efficiency, reducing paperwork, opposing the armchair style of work, the tendency towards numerous hearings and conferences.

It should be frankly stated that much remains to be done to defeat these practices. This is evidenced by many examples. The CPSU Central Committee has recently heard the reports of the Kalinin and Tselinograd regional Party committees on the problems involved in developing the agroindustrial complex. Grave shortcomings were exposed in the Party guidance of economic management, in the placement of cadres and educational work and in the activities of the bureaux and secretaries of the regional Party committees. The main cause of shortcomings here was an uncritical attitude to the record of work, a tendency to exaggerate achievements, and a reluctance to admit negative facts. Therefore, appropriate steps had to be taken.

Adherence to old-fashioned approaches to guidance and a lack of self-criticism are also to be found among some leading executives or Ministries and other government departments. This is an impediment to efficient work. The realities of life dictate the need for a resolute improvement in work to bring it into line with the requirements of the current stage in society's development.

Today, simple executive obedience is not enough: steadily growing importance is assumed by such businesslike qualities as competence, a flair for innovation, initiative, courage and willingness to take on the burden of responsibility, an ability to formulate a task and secure its complete fulfilment, constant awareness of the political implications of economic work. And also, I would say, a desire to learn to work well.

Another important task in the review and election campaign is further reinforcement of the Party guidance of the Soviets, the trade unions, Young Communist League and other components of our political system; that is, guidance of all work in developing Soviet democracy.

One should always remember Lenin's idea that socialist democracy cannot be interpreted abstractly. It has always been and remains an instrument for developing the economy, stimulating the activity of the individual and promoting the communist education of the masses. This has always been and will remain the keynote of the Party's effort to deepen the democracy of the Soviet system.

The preparations for the 27th Party Congress, with the discussion of the drafts of Congress documents by the working people will indisputably stir the Soviet people to greater activity. The Party committees should display concern for securing publicity, for keeping open all the channels of communication with the masses. They should know if enough attention is paid to public opinion, critical remarks and statements and letters received from individuals. The CPSU Central Committee regards them as great assistance as a visible manifestation of the Soviet people's interest in the affairs of state.

The Central Committee has repeatedly discussed the tasks involved in the Party's political education and ideological work. Attention to this area of work is quite natural, and certain progress is in evidence here. I believe, however, that much remains to be done to secure a close link between ideological work and real life. Formalism and didacticism disrupt this link. Much harm is sometimes caused by empty phraseology and inability to speak the language of truth. At times it so happens that a listener hears what is discrepant from the hard facts. This is a serious question, not only educationally but politically as well.

Ideological and political education in all its forms should be very closely linked with the central task of our day — one of accelerating the country's social and economic development. This cannot be achieved without taking account of the sum total of the conditions of life within the country and the specific features of the international situation. As you know, these questions were on the agenda of the All-Union Scientific and Practical Conference in December of last year, which discussed progress in fulfilling the resolutions of the Plenary Meeting of the CPSU Central Committee of June 1983. It would be relevant to recall again today that in propaganda and ideological work in general deeds should prevail over words, however paradoxical it may seem to some persons.

I would like to touch specifically on the work of the mass media, ranging from the factory and district ones to the national organs. The press, radio and television are effective instruments for organizing and educating the masses and for shaping public opinion. In recent time there have been favourable changes in their operation. Real life, however, is making greater demands on them.

The mass media are called upon to make a profound analysis of events and phenomena, to raise serious problems and offer ways of solving them by providing meaningful, prompt and competent information. An intelligent word from the Party addressed to the people stimulates their thinking, encourages their initiative, and cultivates their intolerance to shortcomings. The effectiveness of the press, television and radio broadcasts grows when Party committees give them active assistance and support. These, of course, should always be timely and tangible. And it goes without saying that any attempt to suppress or ignore well-grounded criticism should be opposed by the Party from positions of principle.

Literature and the arts have a great role to play in enriching the cultural life of society with new values, in the ideological and moral advancement of Soviet citizens. The artistic intelligentsia — prose writers, poets, composers, artists, theatrical and film workers — enjoy high prestige and public recognition. This is their enormous responsibility to society. The finest achievements of Soviet literature and art have always been inseparably linked with the main affairs and concerns of the Party and the people. There is no doubt that the new tasks being implemented today will be vividly reflected in true-to-life artistic creation affirming the socialist way of life.

We are now on the threshold of the 40th anniversary of the great victory over fascism. Remembering the incredibly gigantic price paid for that victory by the Soviet people and other nations of the anti-Hitler coalition, and recalling again and again the tragedy that befell mankind, the Communist Party and Soviet Government see the main purpose of their foreign policy as averting a repetition of anything like that, let alone nuclear catastrophe.

The Soviet Union and our Party have always been and will remain faithful to the sacred memory of the immortal exploits of the nations which defeated fascism.

The Soviet Union declares again and again that it will steadfastly follow the Leninist course of peace and peaceful coexistence, which is determined by our social system, our morality and our world outlook. We are in favour of normal, correct and, if you will, civilized interstate relations based of full respect for the standards of international law. It should be made perfectly clear, however, that only if imperialism abandons attempts to settle the historic contest between the two social systems by force of arms will it be possible to maintain international relations on the lines of normal co-operation.

The close-knit community of socialist states, its economic and defence potential and united action of the international scene are an invincible force in the struggle for mankind's peaceful future. The attainment of military-strategic parity with the member states of the aggressive NATO alliance is a crucially important achievement of the fraternal socialist countries. This parity should be thoroughly preserved for the sake of peace. It is a dependable means of sobering the aggressive ambitions of imperialism.

As before we will spare no effort to provide the Soviet armed forces with whatever is necessary for dependable defence of this country and its allies so that no one will be able to take us by surprise.

Today mankind has an enormous potential for maintaining peace, with varied experience and a sufficiently broad historical and social outlook on the world to realize where a policy of aggression may lead it. This understanding unites the peace forces ever more closely, galvanizes the anti-war and anti-nuclear movements and stirs ever new progressive and democratic contingents to struggle against the menace of war. Small wonder, therefore, that Washington's selfish militaristic policy is arousing growing discontent and resistance in many countries. The Communist and Worker's parties, the trade unions and other mass public organizations are making a great contribution to the common cause of the struggle for peace.

No people on earth wants war. This means the existence of enormous reserves and possibilities for the pursuit of a policy of peace and progress. We must do everything to prevent the forces of militarism and aggression from prevailing in international relations.

We are convinced that a world war can be averted. However, experience has proved that the struggle to preserve peace and guarantee general security is a difficult cause which needs ever new efforts. Imperialism is guilty of perpetuating the troubled and dangerous international situation. Mankind is facing a choice: either a further build-up of tensions and confrontation or a constructive search for mutually acceptable agreements that would check the process of material preparations for nuclear conflict.

It is primarily the ruling circles of the United States of America that are to blame for the prevailing situation, and this has to be stated unequivocally. They continue to whip up the arms race and sabotage disarmament — a fact well known to the world community. On their initiative, new types of weapons of mass destruction are constantly being invented. Today attempts are being made to escalate the arms race into outer space. The hundreds of American war bases scattered all over the globe are also destabilizing the world situation.

The United States openly lays claim to a "right" of intervention anywhere, ignores and often directly infringes the interests of other countries and peoples, the traditions of international intercourse, effective treaties and agreements. It is constantly creating areas of conflict and war danger, stepping up tensions now in one, now in another region of the world. Today the United States is threatening to unleash its military power against the heroic people of Nicaragua in an attempt to deprive them of freedom and sovereignty, as it did in Grenada. Solidarity with the progressive and democratic forces, with the countries and peoples defending their freedom and independence against the onslaught of reaction is a matter of principle for us. Our line here is as clear as ever.

One need not have very keen political vision to see that in the last few years imperialism has stepped up its subversive activities and co-ordinated its operations against socialist states. This extends to all spheres — political, economic, ideological, and military. It has been repeatedly emphasized in documents of the fraternal Parties that imperialism is seeking to carry through social reaction on a broad front: in relation to the socialist community of nations and against the countries which have rid themselves of the colonial yoke, against the national liberation movements and the working people in the capitalist states.

US economic expansion is growing in scope and intensity. Manipulation of interest rates, plunder by multi-national corporations, political restrictions on trade, all sorts of boycotts and sanctions create an atmosphere of tension and mistrust in international economic relations, disorganizing world economy and trade and undermining their legal foundations. The exploitation of the developing countries is being intensified and the processes of their economic decolonization are being obstructed. Concentrating in its hands a growing amount of the financial and material resources of other countries, the United States directly or indirectly harnesses them for its own gigantic military programmes.

In this situation the idea of working out and implementing measures to normalize international economic relations and guarantee the economic security of states is attracting steadily growing interest in the world.

The complicated international situation and sharpened tensions make it incumbent upon us to attach high priority to problems of foreign policy, as we have previously done.

Another task of growing significance is the all-round development and enrichment of co-operation, extending comprehensive ties with the fraternal socialist countries, securing their close interaction in the political, economic, ideological, defence, and other fields, developing the organic harmony between the national and international interests of all member nations of the great community.

The fraternal countries have on the order of the day their joint work in implementing the resolutions of the top-level Economic Conference of the Comecon Member Nations held in July of last year. This is also dictated by the common interests of the community, the requirements of the social and economic development of each member state and the exigencies of the international situation.

The exchanges of opinion we had in the middle of March with the Party and government leaders of the Warsaw Treaty member states permits us to declare confidently that we are unanimous in our belief that as long as NATO exists the Warsaw Treaty Organization will play an important part in defending the positions of socialism in Europe and the world, serving as an effective instrument for averting nuclear war and strengthening international security.

The Soviet Union will continue its purposeful and persistent efforts to develop relations and co-operation with other socialist countries, including the People's Republic of China. Our stance on this subject is already well-known and remains unchanged.

We are strongly in favour of further expansion of our many-sided co-operation with Asian, African and Latin American countries. The CPSU and the Soviet State invariably supports the right of all nations to shape their own socio-economic systems in accordance with their own choice and to build their future free of outside interference. Attempts to deny this sovereign right to the peoples are hopeless and doomed to failure.

We invariably come out in favour of developing normal relations with capitalist countries on a basis of equality. Disputed problems and conflict situations must be settled by political means. This is our strong conviction.

The Politbureau proceeds from the assumption that the interstate documents of the period of détente, including the Helsinki Final Act, have not lost their significance. They are a model of how international relations can be built if one is guided by the principles of parity and equal security, the realities which have taken shape in the world; if one does not seek unilateral advantages but mutually acceptable decisions and agreements. On the tenth anniversary of the Conference on Security and Co-operation in Europe, it might be useful if the states signatory to the Helsinki Final Act once again expressed their will to reduce dangerous tensions, develop peaceful co-operation and constructive principles in international life.

The Soviet Union is in favour of fruitful and comprehensive economic, scientific and technical co-operation based on the principles of mutual benefit and ruling out any discrimination whatsoever. It is prepared to widen and deepen trade relations further, to develop new forms of economic ties based on the mutual self-interest of the parties concerned in jointly developing innovative scientific ideas, technology and processes, designing and building projects, and developing raw material resources.

Viewing the question from this angle, it is necessary to analyse the state of our foreign economic relations, to look into their essence and to take account of the long-term perspectives, Favourable opportunities are available here, notwithstanding international tensions. The approach to mutually beneficial economic ties and foreign commerce should be on a large scale and orientated toward the future.

We are in favour of broad, many-sided and mutually beneficial co-operation with the states of Western Europe, Japan and other capitalist countries.

Our willingness to improve relations with the United States, to our mutual benefit and without any attempt to infringe each other's lawful rights and interests, is already well known. Confrontation between the two powers is not fatally inevitable. Summing up both the positive and negative record of Soviet–American relations, one can say that the most reasonable option is a search for ways leading to a normalization of relations and the building of a bridge of co-operation from both sides.

Unfortunately, the complete first round of the Geneva talks warrants the conclusion that Washington is not steering its policy towards agreement with the Soviet Union. This is evidenced in particular by its refusal in general to discuss the problem of non-escalation of the arms race to outer space simultaneously with talks on the limitation and reduction of nuclear arms. Washington is thereby contravening the agreement reached in January on the interconnection of the three issues: the prevention of an arms race in outer space, the reduction of strategic nuclear arms, and the reduction of intermediate-range nuclear weapons in Europe.

One wonders why Washington has taken this stance. The answer is the continued ambition of certain circles in the United States to gain a position of world supremacy, first and foremost militarily. We have more than once pointed out to the American side the hopelessness of these ambitious plans. The Soviet Union, its friends and allies and all other states committed to peace — and peaceful co-operation, for that matter — do not recognize the right of any state or group of states to supremacy or to dictate their will to other countries and peoples.

For its part, the Soviet Union has never pursued such an aim in the past or the present.

We hope that the United States will correct its position. This will open up an opportunity to reach mutually acceptable agreements. We are prepared to come to terms on this issue.

This is evidenced by the Soviet proposal for both sides to impose a moratorium on developing space weapons, to be effective while the talks are in progress, and to freeze strategic nuclear arsenals. Pursuing this line, the Soviet Union has unilaterally announced a moratorium on deploying intermediate-range missiles and building up other counter measures in Europe. Throughout the whole world this decision was assessed as an important and constructive one contributing to success in negotiations.

It will be recalled that this was not the only constructive step on the part of the Soviet Union. Its unilateral commitment not to use nuclear weapons first has been in force since 1982.

A unilateral Soviet moratorium on first stationing of anti-satellite weapons in outer space has been effective since 1983. The US Administration has not responded to any of these initiatives with any gesture of good will. On the contrary, Soviet moves aimed at lessening the risk of war and achieving agreements are presented in a distorted light and their aims are called into question as deserving no trust. In short, our opponents are going out of their way to avoid taking positive reciprocal steps.

One cannot but be surprised at the haste with which the US Administration responds to our proposals with its standard and habitual "No!", which is clear evidence of its unwillingness to lead the matter to a reasonable settlement. I wish to say only one thing: the arms race and disarmament talks cannot be dovetailed; this is clear if one does not succumb to hypocrisy or intend to delude public opinion.

The Soviet Union will not contribute to this line, which must be known to those who are now engaged in political gambling rather than serious politics. We would like to see no repetition of the sad experience of earlier negotiations.

For its own part, the Soviet Union will persistently seek concrete, mutually acceptable agreements at Geneva, that would not only put an end to the arms race but also secure progress in the cause of disarmament. Today a political will to safeguard peace on earth and achieve a better future is more imperative than ever before.

Such are our tasks and the main guidelines of our home and foreign policies. They will indisputably be discussed in circumstantial detail at this Plenary Meeting, which is called upon to determine the character of the pre-Congress activities of the Party as a whole and of each of its organizations.

We need to conduct deliberations at this Plenary Meeting that could be summed up in Lenin's phrase as follows:

"Our tasks today are much clearer, more concrete and graphic to us than yesterday; we are not afraid to point out our mistakes openly so as to be able to remedy them. Now we will concentrate all the efforts of the Party on improving its organization, advancing the standards and content of its work, establishing closer ties with the masses, working out ever more correct and accurate tactics and strategy of the working class."[1]

The Party and the Soviet people are expecting us to make comprehensive and responsible decisions, and we are confident that they will be supported by the Communists and all working people. They will support them by their social interest, activity and work.

[1] V. I. Lenin, *Collected Works*, vol. 44, pp. 99–100

5.

Speech in Warsaw at a reception in honour of the participants in the top-level conference of Party and Government leaders of the Warsaw Treaty member countries
26 April 1985

Dear Comrade Jaruzelski!
Dear comrades and friends!

First of all, I wish to express on behalf of the Soviet delegation and all the participants in this meeting our heartfelt gratitude for the hospitality accorded by the leaders of the Polish United Workers' Party and the Polish State. We also convey our fraternal greetings to the citizens of the heroic and beautiful city of Warsaw and to all the working people of People's Poland, and wish them success in building socialism.

Here in Warsaw, the city which gave its name to our alliance, an act of historic significance has been performed today. The Treaty of Friendship, Co-operation and Mutual Assistance concluded thirty years ago has been prolonged. It has been prolonged, as Comrade Jaruzelski has said, with confidence that our alliance is vitally necessary to all its members in order to strengthen peace and the security of nations.

In Lenin's vivid words, a revolution must be capable of defending itself. For the peoples of our countries the Warsaw Treaty is a reliable defence of their revolutionary achievements. What has the Warsaw Treaty given all of us? It has guaranteed the possibility of peaceful constructive work. The inviolability of our borders is securely protected. A strong barrier has been erected in the way of the latter-day crusaders bent on overthrowing socialism and claiming world supremacy.

History has never known another alliance like ours, where relations are based on the complete equality and comradely mutual assistance of sovereign states. It is an alliance which is a community of nations in the true sense of the word. This alliance threatens no one and is wholly committed to the defence of peace. We are developing relations with countries with a different social system on the principle of peaceful coexistence, which is the sole reasonable basis, particularly in the nuclear age.

The Warsaw Treaty powers have come forward with important initiatives aimed at consolidating peace in Europe and promoting détente. Today's meeting has reaffirmed our common willingness to continue our collective search for ways to remove the menace of war and broaden international co-operation. We are in favour of taking the edge off the confrontation between the two military-political alliances, which would meet the interests of all the peoples on earth.

It was not the Soviet Union or any other socialist state that set the stage for the division of Europe and the postwar world. That was done by the founders of NATO, and it was only some six years later that our alliance came into being. Since then we have more than once expressed our readiness to disband the Warsaw Treaty Organization if NATO agrees to reciprocate. This position of principle remains fully valid. Unfortunately, the other side has never evinced a similar intention. On the contrary, new aggressive doctrines are being advanced and both nuclear and conventional armaments are being augmented before our very eyes. This compels us now to think of further measures to reinforce the Warsaw Treaty Organization.

Mankind is confronted by this alternative: either it will manage to check this perilous course of development or the risk of nuclear war will continue to grow. This risk is increased many times over by the US military plans for outer space. Whatever is said by their authors to justify themselves, the essence of these plans is clear: it is to gain a capability to deliver a first nuclear strike with impunity. Since the

United States and NATO flatly refuse to follow the Soviet Union's example and assume an obligation not to use nuclear weapons first, their intentions appear all the more dangerous.

The development of weapons for "star wars" is still in its initial stage. However, it is already causing alarm throughout the world, leading to a destabilization of the entire system of international relations and to a more acute political and military confrontation than exists today. This should not be forgotten by the initiators of this provocative venture or by those who are being persuaded to take part in it.

Our approach is different in principle: not to convert outer space into a new source of war danger, not to develop strike space weapons, but to destroy the existing anti-satellite systems. Simultaneously, we have proposed coming to terms on a radical reduction of nuclear weapons and eventually on their complete elimination.

A freeze on the nuclear potentials of both sides suggests itself as a simple and natural step to take in this situation. We hear the following objection: a freeze of this kind will perpetuate Soviet military superiority. Let me reply: first, such superiority does not exist. We have repeatedly proved this with the relevant figures at hand, and Washington could not disprove them in a single instance. Second, we have never said that we want just a freeze and would stop there. On the contrary, we insist that a freeze should be followed by a radical reduction of nuclear armaments.

We have already proposed that as a first step both sides should reduce their strategic offensive arms by a quarter. However, we would have no objection to more radical mutual reductions either. All these measures are possible unless an arms race begins in outer space, that is, if space remains a peaceful preserve.

The Soviet Union and other Warsaw powers are not seeking superiority either on earth or in outer space. We want no contest in building a higher nuclear fence, so to say. However, we will not allow military-strategic parity to be upset. This is the common, firm stand of all Warsaw Treaty nations. If preparations for "star wars" continue, we shall have no alternative but to take counter measures, including, of course, reinforcement and perfection of offensive nuclear arms.

The first round of Soviet–American talks on nuclear and space weapons which has just come to a close has shown that these talks are rough going. It is clear that success in the talks is possible only if the parties abide by the principle of parity and equal security and are in agreement that the ultimate aim of the talks is interconnected settlement of the issues under discussion.

As announced earlier, the Soviet Union has unilaterally suspended deployment of intermediate-range missiles and other counter measures in Europe. The moratorium was put into effect on 7 April. This step has been welcomed by the world public and by many sober-minded American and West European political leaders. We are entitled to expect that Washington and the capitals of other NATO powers will take a more serious and considered approach to the evaluation of our initiative and will for their part exercise restraint in the matter of deployment of American missiles in Western Europe. Indeed, reciprocity on this issue would help place the Geneva talks on course toward practical settlements and would contribute to the solution of more complicated problems.

The Warsaw Treaty has been in force for almost a third of a century, and throughout this time it has been generating constructive ideas aimed at promoting détente, limiting armaments and developing all-European co-operation. Its growing prestige in the field of international politics has a favourable impact on the general climate in the world. This is the outcome of our collective efforts, the contribution of each of its fraternal member countries.

On the eve of the 40th anniversary of the great victory over fascism we again recall the oath of the victorious powers over the graves and ruins of the Second World War: that war should never happen again! We remember that oath and the lessons of the war. One of the main lessons was the example of co-operation between the powers of the anti-Hitler coalition. Today we call upon all the states of Europe and other continents to rise above their differences, to become partners in the struggle against a new danger that threatens all mankind — the danger of nuclear annihilation.

Now that we have prolonged the Warsaw Treaty, we reaffirm our strong conviction that war can and must be prevented by joint efforts. Such is the will of the peoples of our countries. This is the aim of the policy of our Parties and governments, and of all the activities of the defensive alliance of the socialist states.

May the co-operation of our Parties and states, their unity and cohesion grow stronger on the principles of Marxism–Leninism and socialist internationalism!

May the fraternal alliance of the socialist countries united by the Warsaw Treaty flourish and grow stronger!

To the prosperity of socialist People's Poland, to the good health of Comrade Wojciech Jaruzclski and the other members of the Polish leadership, to all participants in this meeting!

To lasting peace on earth!

6.

The Immortal Exploit of the Soviet People. Report at the ceremonial meeting in the Kremlin Palace of Congresses commemorating the 40th anniversary of the Soviet people's victory in the Great Patriotic War 8 May 1985

Dear comrades! Friends! Ladies and gentlemen!

The four years of the war were long and hard years for our people; the road to victory was a difficult one. But finally there came the glorious day in May 1945 when the Soviet soldiers, all Soviet people, could proudly say: Our righteous cause has triumphed! The enemy has been routed! We are the victors!

The Soviet people and their valiant Armed Forces inflicted a devastating defeat on Nazi Germany, defended the freedom and independence of their country and brought liberation to the peoples of Europe. The rout of fascism and victorious conclusion of the war were epoch-making events of worldwide historic significance which opened up for rescued humanity new means of social progress and the prospect of a just and lasting peace on earth. Our victory has not receded into the past. It is a living victory crucial to the present and the future.

The Central Committee of the CPSU, the Presidium of the

Supreme Soviet of the USSR and the Soviet Government convey their heartfelt congratulations to the heroic Soviet people on the occasion of the 40th anniversary of the great victory. Our warmest greetings to you, dear countrymen and women!

On this day our motherland is paying a tribute of honour to the courage, valour and heroism of its sons and daughters, to all those who did their patriotic duty in the firing lines who did not spare themselves to bring victory nearer.

Our warmest greetings to you, veteran officers and men, partisans and members of the underground resistance! We admire your battle exploits in defence of the motherland, in the name of life on earth!

It is with dignity and honour that you bear the proud title of veterans of the Great Patriotic War, a title dear to all Soviet citizens.

Today the country is honouring the heroic work and unprecedented staunchness of the home front: those who forged the weapons of victory, smelted metal, grew crops; those who worked so hard for victory in the factories and coal mines, on the railways, in the fields and on the farms; in the research laboratories and design bureaux.

Our warm greetings to you, dear comrades! We honour and praise all those whose life and work in war time were dedicated to one sacred duty: "Everything for the war effort, everything for victory!"

The Soviet people feel infinite respect for and gratitude to the war and labour veterans. This country owes its victory to you, dear comrades, and it will never forget the exploits you performed in the years 1941–45 on the battlefields, and in unprecedentedly tense work on the home front.

Your splendid deeds are a model for educating new generations of Soviet people, who are learning from you lessons in courage, valour and staunchness, boundless loyalty to the Communist ideals, strong determination to overcome all obstacles and endure any hardship in response to the country's call.

Our people made great sacrifices in the name of victory. The war took a toll of over twenty million Soviet lives. Almost every Soviet family lost a member or a relative and was scorched by war. The pain of those losses and grief over the dead will never abate. Without their heroic lives, given for the motherland, victory would have been impossible.

The memory of the immortal exploits of those who led the way in attack, who threw themselves at fire-spitting machine-guns and silenced them with their own bodies, who rammed enemy planes in the air, who knocked out tanks, with hand grenades, who engaged the enemy in hand-to-hand fighting, who sank enemy ships and derailed enemy trains, who fought courageously on the underground front, who defied death on the battlefield, who were not subdued by torture or by Nazi dungeons and death camps will live forever in the flame of the torch at the Tomb of the Unknown Soldier, in majestic memorials and modest obelisks, in works of literature and the arts, in the hearts of the present generation and of our descendants.

May eternal glory invest the heroes who fell in fighting for the freedom and independence of our Soviet motherland.

Let us honour their memory with a minute of silence.

Many countries and peoples came out in a united front against the aggression of German fascism and Japanese militarism. The Soviet people remember with great appreciation the contribution of all its allies in the Second World War to the defeat of their common enemy and honour their combat services in the struggle for freedom, peace and justice.

I extend our heartfelt greetings to the foreign guests who have come to Moscow to commemorate together with the Soviet people the 40th anniversary of the great historic event that is dear to all honest people on our planet.

I

The last war went down in the history of our motherland as the Great Patriotic War. The Soviet people clearly realized that the destiny of their socialist country was being decided in that mortal combat — whether our people would be free or reduced to slavery, whether they would preserve their national state, languages and culture or would lose their all and sink into historical non-existence. The mortal danger hanging over the country and the enormous force of patriotism stirred the whole people to a sacred national war. The Soviet people drew their strength from the great Lenin's ideas. They were inspired by the heroic pages of our history, the people's struggle against foreign invaders. They rose to the defence of their motherland.

As regards its class essence, our war with Nazi Germany was the biggest military conflict between socialism and the strike forces of imperialism. The young Soviet State, which was not yet a quarter-century old at the time, was carrying out epoch-making social transformations. The new social system was revealing its constructive potentials ever more clearly. A period of peace was vitally necessary and the Party and the Soviet Government were doing their utmost to prevent war. Soviet foreign policy and diplomacy were orientated toward that end.

In the situation of growing danger of war the country was preparing to give the potential aggressor a fitting rebuff if attacked. The Party was educating the Soviet people in the spirit of vigilance, hatred of fascism and readiness for defence of the socialist state. It displayed a constant concern for supplying the armed forces with modern weapons and military equipment. The country's defence capability was being strengthened on the basis of the powerful industry built in the early Five-Year Plan years.

A great deal had been done toward defence before the war broke out. However, for various reasons, including lack of time, we had been unable to do everything that was necessary to complete our preparations.

The beginning of the war was disastrous for us. We were attacked by a ruthless and treacherous aggressor. The enemy had already tried out his war machine and harnessed to it the economy of the occupied countries of Europe. His total military-economic potential was twice that of the Soviet Union. The Nazis also had the advantage of a surprise attack. Some miscalculations on our part also contributed to our setbacks in the early period of the war.

The Red Army was retreating to the heart of the country, fighting back fiercely. That retreat to Moscow and Leningrad, to the Volga and the Caucasus was an incredibly bitter experience. The Nazi invasion brought in its wake unheard-of suffering, torture and privation for our people. We confronted some critical situations in the course of the fighting too. From its early days, however, the war revealed the powerful spirit and high morale of the people, generated by the entire tenor of life in socialist society, and a profound awareness of the fact that the country's destiny was in the hands of every Soviet citizen. In the most difficult times the people never lost their confidence in eventual victory or their faith in the Party and in the triumph of our righteous cause. The whole world was amazed and delighted by the staunchness of the Soviet officers and men and by the fortitude of our great people.

By the year 1941 the blitzkrieg plan drawn up by the Nazi High Command was already being frustrated by the heroic resistance the Nazi hordes had encountered on Soviet territory. The world remembers the inflexible courage of the defenders of the Brest Fortress, Moscow, Leningrad and Stalingrad, Kiev and Minsk, Odessa and Sevastopol, Novorosiisk and Kerch, Tula, Smolensk and Murmansk. Cities become heroic when their defenders are heroes. The war proved this conclusively. In fact, the Nazi casualties in officers and men on the defensive lines of Sevastopol alone were comparable to the total losses of the Wehrmacht in all theatres of war prior to its attack on the USSR. The Soviet Army was bleeding the enemy in fierce fighting, accumulating experience and strength and learning the art of warfare.

The country stood up to all its ordeals and turned the tide of hostilities. The Soviet forces defeated the Nazi hordes in the Battle of Moscow, Stalingrad and Leningrad and in the Battle of the Caucasus, and inflicted devastating blows on the enemy in the Battle of Kursk, in the Ukraine on the right bank of the Dnieper, in Byelorussia, in the Yassy-Kishinev and Vistula-Oder operations, and in the Battle of Berlin.

What was decisive to the victorious outcome of these battles, which were without precedent in history? What helped us to win the war that had begun so disastrously for us?

The mainspring of that victory lay in the nature of socialism, the Soviet way of life, the national character of the Great Patriotic War. As the greatest of trials, the war threw into salient relief and reaffirmed in practice the fact that the popular masses are the decisive force in history. Soviet citizens of different nationalities displayed heroism on a massive scale in battle and in work, defending their socialist motherland. They were united and heartened by the great Russian people, whose courage, endurance and unyielding fortitude were an inspiring model of indomitable will to victory.

Millions of people took part in the war, but in this unprecedented battle they were not a faceless mass. Their heroism strikingly expressed the lofty personal merits of the fighting men of the Great Patriotic War — from the private Alexander Matrosov to Marshal Georgy Zhukov.

The banners of our armed forces are invested with unfading glory. Born in the flames of the October Revolution, the Red Army was an army of the people. Soviet officers and men were distinguished by such lofty traits as utter dedication to the motherland, courage and fighting skill.They displayed their high moral principles vividly in mortal combat with the enemy. The enormous sacrifices made in the war and the atrocities perpetrated by the Nazis did not darken their minds with the blind thirst for revenge. When they entered Germany as victors, they did not extend their hatred of fascism to the German people. While fierce battles were still going on, Soviet servicemen started to help them restore the normal civilian way of life.

The great battles on a scale never witnessed in the history of war brought into play the rich talent of Soviet generals and military strategists. Hailing from the midst of the people and raised by the Party, they proved to be worthy heirs to the nation's finest traditions of the art of warfare. The battles with a strong and experienced enemy showed clearly the superiority of Soviet military doctrine and the skill of Soviet generals: their strategic foresight, creativity in planning operations, persistence and great energy in achieving their aims, their ability to combine the high morale and fighting spirit of officers and men with the formidable power of modern weaponry. The splendid names of the outstanding generals and strategists of the Great Patriotic War are known throughout the country. Our war veterans, our Armed Forces and all Soviet citizens are proud of them.

The national character of the war was vividly expressed in the formation of a two-million-strong force of people's volunteers, in the struggle of the resistance fighters in the Nazi-occupied areas and the wide scope of the guerrilla movement. Another front was opened by the partisans behind the frontline, in the enemy rear. More than a million fighters waged that guerrilla warfare. The earth was literally burning under the invaders' feet, and many of their divisions met their doom in those flames.

"War is a test of all the economic and organizing forces of each nation", Lenin has said.[1] The Soviet economy withstood that test excellently. The socialist organization of industry and agriculture conclusively proved its advantages.

In the most difficult situation and in a record time that seems incredible even today we evacuated to the heartland more than 1500 large plants, considerable material resources and values. By a year after the enemy attack on the Soviet Union more than two-thirds of its weapons and military equipment were being manufactured in its

---

[1] V. I. Lenin, *Collected Works*, vol. 39, p. 321.

eastern regions. The advantages of the socialist economy were strikingly manifest in its high efficiency. Though the Soviet Union's output of steel was roughly one-third and the output of coal slightly over one-fifth of those of Germany and the countries occupied by it, we produced almost twice as much military equipment as all of them put together.

The efficiency of the Soviet war economy was secured by the unchallenged authority of the state plan, strict discipline and responsibility for work performance, the initiative, inventiveness, innovative ideas and selfless efforts of the workers, collective farmers, engineers, designers and scientists, and the organizing skill of leading executives.

At the time of formidable danger the country was turned into what was effectively a closeknit military camp. The Soviet working class displayed unprecedented heroism and staunchness. At the most critical moments, workers' battalions joined the ranks of the regular fighting forces, and work in factory departments was not suspended even when the enemy was literally at the factory gates and bombs and shells were exploding nearby. By its high political awareness and organization the working class once again reaffirmed its role as the leading force in Soviet society and did everything that was necessary for victory.

The alliance of the working class and the peasantry, the socialist organization of agriculture — the collective farm system — withstood a test of strength in that war. Although the country's main granaries were seized by the enemy and there was a shortage of manpower and farm machinery, the farmers kept up steady supplies of foodstuffs to the army and the general population and of raw materials to industry. The collective farmers, the personnel of state farms and machine-and-tractor stations were all working to the best of their ability to help defeat the invaders and worthily fulfilled their patriotic duty to the motherland.

The Soviet intelligentsia drew its inspiration from the whole people's determination to rout the aggressor. Soviet scientists, designers and engineers, relying on their talent and hard work, developed new types of aircraft and tanks, artillery and mortars, and other weapons which were superior in their characteristics to whatever the enemy had at his disposal. Soviet weaponry was indeed a powerful tool of victory.

The hard-hitting lines of the daily press, and the vivid characters of war prose, patriotic songs, films, plays, poems and posters inspired the

Soviet people and fortified their spirit in their fierce battles with the invaders.

The people will always remember the heroic exploits of the Komsomols, young people of the "roaring forties" whose adolescence passed in war time. The invaders were given battle by a generation born after the October Revolution and raised under the socialist system. That generation had absorbed its revolutionary, collectivist moral principles and psychology in the years of childhood. It was a generation that did not falter but went bravely into the firing lines, endured all the ordeals of the war and proved that a country capable of raising such youth could not be defeated.

That fighting spirit was equally in evidence on the battlefields and on the home front. Young lads and girls, teenagers worked tirelessly in the factories and plants and on the fields of collective and state farms. It is customary to say that they were indefatigable. Of course, they were not, but they knew that their embattled motherland needed their work badly. And today millions of our countrymen and women cherish the memories of their wartime childhood and youth as a period of hard work for the noble cause upheld by their country.

We always feel deep gratitude, recalling the heroism of Soviet women. The face of war is too ugly for a woman, of course. However, defying the danger of death, women went into attack side by side with men, bravely fought the hateful invaders, tended the wounded servicemen and surrounded them with care and attention at field medical stations and hospitals. Millions of fighting men survived the war thanks to the courage and compassion of our women. The people will never forget the splendid record of Soviet women on the home front. They stood up bravely to all the hardship of wartime in everyday life, endured the pain of the loss of their near and dear ones, displaying great determination and preserving the warmth of love that never dies. We feel boundless admiration for the patriotic Soviet women and deep gratitude for what they did for the sake of victory.

Planning their aggression against the Soviet Union, the Nazis expected to instigate ethnic strife between its different nations and national minorities. These designs were frustrated by realities. Mankind knows no other example of a war that so closely united all the nations and national minorities of a country in resisting foreign aggression. That fraternal unity of nations forcefully demonstrated the wisdom and farsightedness of the Leninist policy on the national question, as a result of which the great socialist union remained as strong and unbreakable as ever.

The gigantic war effort in the various theatres of operations and on the home front was directed by the Party, its Central Committee and the State Defence Committee headed by the General Secretary of the CPSU Central Committee, Joseph Stalin.

The Party committees became the truly militant headquarters and political organizers of the masses. Everywhere — in the frontline trenches, in guerilla units, and in the underground — Party organizations were vigorously at work, and Party political instructors inspired fighting men with their impassioned calls for struggle and by their personal example. Pravda wrote in 1942:

"The figure of a helmeted political instructor in a camouflage cloak with a tommy-gun in hand leading the way in an attack with soldiers following him determined to defeat the Nazis and liberate their motherland will go down in the history of the Great Patriotic War as one of the most splendid examples of dedication to a noble cause."[1]

Communists volunteered to fight in the most dangerous and responsible sectors of the battlefront. Four out of every five Communists were with the troops or worked at defence plants in those years. Members of the Central Committee, the best Party cadres were assigned to work there. Three million Communists laid down their lives in fighting the Nazi invaders. More than five million new members joined the Party during those heroic years.

The Leninist Party became an embattled party forming a common force with the embattled people. At the most arduous stage of our history it was keenly aware of its enormous responsibility for the destiny of the motherland and led it to victory. In wartime the Party's moral and political prestige increased tremendously and the name of a Communist became a lofty symbol to any Soviet citizen. We members of the Leninist Party will always be proud of and cherish this prestige.

The factors that were decisive to winning the war were not only our superior weapons, our economy and political system. It was also a triumph of the ideals for which the revolution had been carried out, for which Soviet citizens had fought and died. It was a triumph for our ideology and moral principles expressing the lofty ideals of humanism and justice, a triumph over the fascist ideology of hatred of mankind.

The Soviet Army honourably performed its great mission of lib-

---

[1] *Pravda*, March 22 1942.

eration. It entered Nazi-enslaved Europe as an army of liberation and it fought bravely to put an end to the war and to fascism, so that the nations of Europe could live in conditions of lasting and dependable peace.

Celebrating Victory Day, we express our admiration for the valour of the officers and men of the allied armies of the United States, Great Britain and France. We will never forget the staunchness and courage of the Yugoslav people and their National Liberation Army. We admire the selfless struggle waged by the Polish people, who were never subdued by the invaders. The Polish Army and the Czechoslovak Army fought the Nazis shoulder to shoulder with Soviet forces both on Soviet territory and during the liberation of their own countries.

The guerrillas, members of the Resistance and, in the last stages of the war, the armies of Bulgaria and Romania and military units of Hungary also contributed to the defeat of the Nazis. The Albanian and Greek peoples put up a stubborn fight against the invaders. We also remember the struggle that the German Communists and all anti-fascists courageously waged, against overwhelming odds, with the Nazi regime.

The Soviet people admire the valour of the fighters of the Resistance movements. The Communist Parties of France, Italy, Norway, Denmark, Belgium, the Netherlands and other countries of Western Europe were in the vanguard of the Resistance. They stirred and united the peoples in a struggle against the Nazi tyranny, for their freedom and national independence. Many Communists laid their lives on the altar of victory. The French Communist Party went down in history as a party of martyrs.

The Soviet Union, scrupulously faithful to its alliance commitments in the Second World War, played an enormous part in the defeat of militarist Japan. We acted in close combat co-operation with the great Chinese people. The common enemy was also actively fought by the army of the Mongolian People's Republic. The patriotic forces of Vietnam, Korea and other Asian countries waged a stubborn struggle against the Japanese invaders.

Reviewing the events of that period, recalling the joint battle of the allied nations against their common enemy, we are proud to note that the outcome of the Second World War was decided on the Soviet–German front. The Nazi aggressor lost over 70 per cent of his troops and weapons here.

The Soviet people's heroic exploits in the Great Patriotic War are unforgettable. The war years mean much to us: the grief of losses and the joy of victory, the valour of Soviet fighting men in fierce battle and the grandeur and modesty of day-to-day work on the home front.

Our victory greatly enhanced the Soviet Union's international prestige. It stirred a wave of patriotic sentiment among the Soviet people. The victory has always been and will remain a source of inspiration from which to draw new energy to translate our constructive plans into reality, to increase the power and prosperity of the Union of Soviet Socialist Republics.

Our victory in the Great Patriotic War will never fade in our memory.

II

The greatest benefit that victory gave us is that we live and work in peace today. Our trial by war has proved that our socialist system is invincible and its vital forces inexhaustible.

Peacetime is making its own high demands on us and putting to a gruelling test our society's ability to secure steady growth of the economy, continued improvement of social relations, and amelioration of the working and living conditions of the people.

Casting our mind's eye over the last forty years, we can confidently declare that socialism has proved conclusively its enormous potentials and advantages in the sphere of peaceful development as well.

People of the older generation remember the terrible scenes of devastation in the areas liberated from the invaders: pock-marked fields, houses in ruins, blast furnaces blown up and coal mines abandoned. Almost 1700 large and small towns and 70,000 villages were in ruins. About 25 million people were left homeless. Industrial plants and farms ravaged by war numbered tens of thousands. The flames of war had consumed almost one-third of the country's national wealth created by the hard work of the people. But the most terrible loss was the deaths of millions of Soviet citizens — an irreplaceable loss that defies description.

Ill-wishers of socialism cherished the hope that the ravages of war inflicted on this country would doom it to backwardness and dependence on the West. However, they miscalculated again. The towns and villages, factories and plants, destroyed by the Nazis were raised from their ashes by the stubborn and selfless labours of the workers, the collective farmers and the intelligentsia. It took the Soviet Union a mere three years to regain the pre-war level of production in industry and five years in agriculture.

That was yet another heroic exploit, now in the field of construction, performed by the Soviet people in the difficult postwar years. This exploit threw into salient relief the capabilities of a people inspired by the majestic goals of socialist construction. Since then, this country has advanced very far in all directions of economic, social, political and cultural development. Soviet society today has a highly advanced economy. The country's national income has grown some sixteen-fold from the prewar level, and industrial output has grown by 24-fold. Soviet industry advanced twice as fast as that of the developed capitalist states. The USSR today is producing more pig iron and steel, crude oil and gas, cement and mineral fertilizer, machine-tools, tractors, and grain harvesting combines and many other goods than any other power in the world.

Radical changes have been effected in the structure and scientific and technological standards of production. New industries have been developed, such as the nuclear, aerospace, electronics and microbiological industries. Giant production complexes have sprung up or are in the process of formation in the central areas of the USSR, in the Urals, Siberia and the Far East, Central Asia and Transcaucasia — in practically every region of the country. A widely ramified network of power supply lines, oil and gas pipelines has been built in all areas. Canals, thousands of kilometres long, have been built to restore arid steppes to fertile agricultural areas, and marshland has been reclaimed for the cultivation of crops. The country's economic map has changed beyond recognition during the last few decades.

The main productive force of society, its constructive potential, has changed substantially. Today the Soviet Union has a large force of skilled and highly educated manpower. The occupational skills, general cultural standards and specialist qualifications of the workers and collective farmers have improved significantly. We have raised a large contingent of engineers and scientists. In the postwar period Soviet science and technology have more than once demonstrated spectacular achievements in the major areas of world-wide scientific and technological progress. The Soviet Union built the world's first atomic power plant and the first atom-powered ice-breaker, and launched the first artificial earth satellite. The Soviet citizen, Yuri Gagarin, was the first man to see the earth from a space orbit.

In Soviet society today the people's well-being is steadily growing. The rapid advance of the economy has enabled us, without relaxing our efforts to build up the economic potential, to begin a turn in the direction of more complete satisfaction of consumer demand and to achieve impressive results in the field of economic work as well. Real per capita income has increased more than six-fold from the prewar level. Housing construction has assumed enormous scope. The network of hospitals and polyclinics creches and kindergartens, and consumer services has widened appreciably.

Soviet society today has high popular educational and cultural standards and a rich cultural life. Whereas before the war only five out of every 100 workers employed on jobs requiring mainly physical work had higher or secondary education, today the number has grown to 82.

The Soviet citizen today has a broad cultural and political outlook and high intellectual interests.

In Soviet society today the biggest social problems have been settled. The whole system of social relations has reached a new level of maturity, and the alliance of the working class, the peasantry and the intelligentsia has grown stronger still. We have made further headway on the path of overcoming essential distinctions between town and village, physical and mental work. The rapid advance of nations and national minorities combines organically with their all-round consolidation. Every Soviet citizen has deeply implanted in his heart and mind a sense of identity with a common family — the Soviet people as a new social and international community, never known in history before.

Soviet society today is a society of genuine and real democracy where the dignity and rights of citizens are highly respected and their sense of responsibility is encouraged. The working people's involvement in the affairs of state and of their work collectives is broadening and becoming more efficient, and the system of socialist self-government of the people is being steadily perfected.

Forty years since its great victory the Soviet Union is a powerful and prosperous state, which is confidently blazing the trail to the Communist morrow.

Our achievements are truly spectacular. However, the dialectics of social development widen the historical horizons once one has achieved certain targets, and confront the people with more complicated and responsible tasks. Today we are confronted by such tasks. Their essence is the need to secure a new qualitative state of society — its economy, the system of socio-political relations and institutions, the sum total of the working conditions and the life of millions of Soviet citizens.

The April Plenary Meeting of the CPSU Central Committee held in 1985 discussed the most urgent problems of the day. The Party sees its main task today in securing a rapid increase in the socio-economic progress of Soviet society. This is dictated by developments both at home and abroad and refers primarily to the intensive and dynamic development of the economy based on the most up-to-date achievements of science and technology. This is the foundation that will enable us to secure continued improvement in the people's well-being, to strengthen the country's economic and defence potentials and to promote the progress of developed socialist society in all areas.

The chief criterion of economic development today is the achievement of high end results with the most rational use of resources. The prevailing economic situation should be seen from this viewpoint. We are obliged to advance to the frontiers of efficient productive work within a brief historical period, as well as to improve product quality and raise the efficiency of production in general. Such is the imperative demand of the day.

The main route towards this goal is scientific and technological progress. The way we solve the problems of acceleration in this area and of securing the effective and rapid introduction of scientific and technological achievements into the national economy will largely determine the rate of our development and the course of the economic contest against capitalism.

In short, the tasks facing Soviet society at the current new historical stage should be handled on an exceptionally wide scale. However, we have at our disposal ample possibilities for their successful accomplishment and will indisputably achieve the goals we have set.

We are confident that the advantages of the socialist system will serve Soviet society well in the new historical situation as well. For this, however, it is important to adopt urgent measures, which must be largely innovative, to bring the forms and methods of socialist economic management, economic and social planning into conformity with the present requirements and with the long-range perspective.

Our strategy of advancing management is based on Lenin's idea that "socialism must in its own way, by its own methods — let us say, in more concrete terms, by Soviet methods — implement this onward movement".[1] The economic mechanism should have forms and

[1] V. I. Lenin, *Collected Works*, vol. 36, p. 178.

structures that would give maximum stimulation to an increase in the efficiency of production and an improvement of quality indicators, and would set the tone for accelerating scientific and technological progress in general.

The guarantee of all our achievements is the creativity of the people. The working people's profound interest in and concern for the destiny of their socialist country, their labour enthusiasm and political activity have invariably given and are to today giving a powerful impetus to the accelerated progress of society and have always enabled us to overcome all obstacles and difficulties success-fully. It is important today to give as much scope as possible to the social initiative of the masses and to direct it into solving the cardinal problems involved in accelerating socio-economic development.

Nothing stimulates the working man to activity more than his confidence in the unfailing implementation of the principle of social justice. The Party will do everything to this end to erect a strong barrier against digressions from socialist principles and against all such negative phenomena, and to block all sources of unearned income while simultaneously enhancing the role of material and moral incentives to conscientious and efficient work. This would be the solution to many key socio-economic, political and ideological education problems, exciting the interest of millions of working people in achieving the targets facing us and giving a new stimulus to political awareness and organization.

Now that we have less and less time to go before the regular 27th CPSU Congress, the Central Committee is taking steps to bring the Party's political line into full harmony with the requirements of social development, the interests and aspirations of the mass of the working people. For this purpose the Party is constantly at work to improve its own style of operating and the forms in which Party and government leadership are conducted.

Today it is crucially important for us to be able, as Lenin taught us, to act, relying on our prestige, our energy, our greater experience, competence and talent. Let us not drown our plans in a torrent of words, assurances and promises, but actually do more in real terms, achieve better practical results, enhance our responsibility and adher-ence to principle, secure better team work, pay greater attention to the individual and attach greater significance to personal modesty. Such are the main criteria for assessment of all personnel, their ideological dedication and competence, and such is the essence of the Party's demands on style and methods of work.

The struggle to accelerate socio-economic development and to maintain firm and impartial enforcement of law and order, and the steps to improve organization and strengthen discipline are meeting with enthusiastic approval and full support on the part of Soviet citizens. The Central Committee of the CPSU, its Politbureau and the Soviet Government put a high value on the people's trust in Party policy and will do their utmost to live up to it.

The Party's policy is based on its profound faith in the creativity and talent of the Soviet people. A people who have defeated the enemy in open battle, endured the difficult years of postwar recovery and achieved outstanding success in developing their socialist motherland will certainly win victory in a new historical situation, and will give a worthy answer to any challenge posed by the times.

The Party has within its field of vision the tasks facing the country and ways of implementing them effectively, and is mobilizing the Soviet people in an all-time effort to secure a new powerful upsurge of the economy so as to continue improvement in the people's well-being. This is a worthy extension of the cause for which the Soviet people selflessly fought in the grim years of the war and struggled in the years of peaceful socialist construction.

III

Comrades! Going back in our minds and hearts today to the spring of Victory in 1945 we are naturally wondering whether the hopes of millions who fought for the peace and happiness of our own generation, our children and grandchildren, have come true.

Yes, they have come true. However, much still remains to be done to save our planet for us, the living generation and for succeeding generations, those who will come after us. The planet is mankind's common home; therefore, war should be banished from the life of society in general.

Forty years is not a short time by any standards. Time flies; those born after the Victory have reached the age of maturity, their children have come of age, and for the majority the Second World War is not an event of which they have first-hand experience. The war, however, has left an aftermath so severe that its results and lessons continue to affect the entire course and character of world development and the consciousness of men.

The Second World War had its seeds long before the first battles began to rage on the fields of Europe and in the vast spaces of the oceans. The ominous shadow of war hung over mankind at a time when some politicians failed — others were unwilling — to oppose the coming of the Nazis to power. Today we know more and better than we knew at the time who it was that helped the Nazi ruling clique to arm itself, to build up its aggressive potential, and to prepare for military adventures.

The attempts by the leading groups of monopoly capital to manipulate the expansion of German fascism and direct it toward the East was the extreme limit of political irresponsibility. The Munich deal will remain forever in the record of disgrace covering the names of those who so insistently prompted Hitler to attack the Soviet Union. One would have to suffer from a severe case of political sclerosis to forget this fact.

Today it is not so essential to know who of the bourgeois political leaders and statesmen of the thirties was sincerely deluded and who was guided by selfish class interest. History will not rephrase its verdict of guilty: "The Munich policy" of the Western powers and their connivance in Nazi aggression was a real tragedy for all the nations of Europe. The line of those who refused to come out in a united front in response to the Soviet Union's insistent appeals and to check the advance of the Nazi adventurers was truly criminal. History will never absolve them of their responsibility for the catastrophe that could have been prevented if the Western leaders of the day had not been blinded by their hatred of socialism.

Unfortunately, history repeats itself. And today, more than ever before, it is a question of vigilance in relation to the intrigues of those who are pushing the world towards the abyss — this time a nuclear abyss. One should clearly realize the source of the danger for mankind in our day. The Soviet Union is proclaiming this and just as emphatically as before the war is warning of the growing danger of war. We have to touch on this subject again because the malicious myth of the "Soviet war menace" which the Nazis used so vociferously is now in currency again.

Whatever efforts are being made to rewrite history, the peoples of the world know that it was precisely the Soviet Union that was the first to sound the alarm and warn the world of the imminent danger of fascism. It was precisely the Communists that offered a clear-cut programme of struggle against the brown plague when it was still in embryo. Finally, it was precisely the Soviet Union that came forward with a series of proposals aimed at curbing the aggressor. However, all these Soviet steps were then denounced as "Communist propaganda".

The Nazis and their allies had to occupy almost the whole of Western Europe, to seize Paris, to bomb London and to attack Pearl Harbour before the cynical hopes and hopeless plans of the Western politicians were shattered. The brilliant victories of the Red Army were needed before agreements with the Soviet State on co-operation in the struggle against fascism could assume material form.

The expansion of the Nazi danger compelled Western politicians to look at the world realistically. The entire experience of the anti-Hitler coalition proved indisputably that states belonging to opposite social systems could join their efforts in fighting a common enemy, find mutually acceptable solutions and operate effectively to achieve a common goal.

The Soviet Union has not forgotten the material aid the Allies gave. It is true, it was not as large as it is often claimed in the West, but we are thankful for this aid and regard it as a symbol of co-operation. The opening of the Second Front in Europe, however belated, was a substantial contribution to the common allied struggle.

The favourable atmosphere of co-operation between the countries of the coalition and a realistic view of the new world situation following the defeat of fascism were reflected in the postwar settlement and in the resolutions of the allied conferences at Teheran, Yalta and Potsdam. These decisions, as well as the UN Charter and other international agreements of those years are pervaded with the spirit of co-operation. They secured such a settlement of the complicated problems of the postwar order, including the territorial issues, that was in accord with the interests of long-awaited peace.

It would be relevant to recall this today when all the peoples of the world have one common enemy — the risk of nuclear war, and one fundamental task — to eliminate this danger.

Twice in this century the forces of imperialism have unleashed world wide, bloody wars, expecting in this way to achieve their class objectives, to consolidate their positions and to secure their selfish interests. History, however, has willed it differently. Small wonder, therefore, that the two wars that began as adventurist expeditions of an imperialism insolently convinced that it would be able to avoid retaliation and confident that international law was written by the invader's fist not only ended in the defeat of their direct initiators but triggered off a series of critical cataclysms in the very system generating war.

Defending the freedom and independence of their country the Soviet people was also implementing its great internationalist task of saving world civilization from fascism. As a result of its victory, the positions of the progressive democratic forces were fortified, which led to the triumph of a new social system in a number of countries of Europe and Asia. The first workers' and peasants' state was born on German soil, too. In the course of the people's struggle against Nazism and Japanese imperialism, a struggle which was closely linked with the aspirations of the masses for far-reaching social change, the force of attraction of socialist ideas visibly increased and the Communist Parties of many countries grew stronger and turned into powerful forces.

In the postwar years the world socialist system took shape and travelled a long way; the community of socialist states came into being. The new social system has become firmly established on earth and proved its viability. It has brought into play the creative potential of millions of people and made it possible to accomplish tasks on a historic scale within record time. Today socialism is a powerful world system which is exerting an enormous influence on the development of mankind and its future and is an irresistible factor of peace and a guarantee of the security of nations.

The member states of this great community have invaluable experience and a well-adjusted mechanism for co-ordinating their policies. They present a united front on international issues, consistently upholding the cause of peace and disarmament and the principles of peaceful coexistence. A special role in this area is played by the Warsaw Treaty Organization, its Political Consultative Committee and the united armed forces of the allied states. As long as the danger to peace and security exists, the member countries of the Warsaw Treaty Organization will continue to do whatever is necessary to safeguard themselves against any attack. This has been reaffirmed by the prolongation of the Warsaw Treaty by another term by a unanimous decision of all its members.

Profound transformations in the postwar world were caused by the collapse of the colonial system. Dozens of independent states have sprung up in place of former colonies and semi-colonies. In fact, their development has followed an irregular course and has had its ups and downs, its achievements and its tragedies. Indeed, the developing countries faced very difficult problems, both those inherited from the past and those generated by neocolonialist policies.

However, it is a fact that the colonial system has been almost completely uprooted and many young national states have a growing progressive role to play in world politics. Actively supported by the socialist countries they are waging a persistent struggle for a new and more equitable world economic order. The non-aligned movement has become an important factor in present-day international affairs.

As we see, the world map has changed radically over the 40 years since Victory Day.

The sphere of imperialist domination has narrowed drastically. Its possibilities for manoeuvre and for dictating its will to sovereign states and peoples with impunity have been lessened substantially. The alignment of forces within the capitalist world itself has also changed. The defeat inflicted in the Second World War on such a powerful predator as German imperialism, the defeat of the militarist Japan, and the weakening of the erstwhile powerful British and French rivals advanced US imperialism to the leading position in the capitalist world in all major areas — economic, financial and military. The claims to world supremacy laid by the US ruling class were partly due to the US being in fact the only large power which derived fabulous profits from the war.

Imperialist reaction which was dissatisfied with the social and international political results of the war attempted already in the early postwar years to achieve a historical *revanche* of a kind — to push back socialism and the other democratic forces from their positions. That strategy was directed against the Soviet Union and relied on the economic power and temporary atomic weapons monopoly of the United States. The US ruling elite regarded the latter as an instrument for military and political pressure against us and the other socialist countries, and for the intimidation of all nations.

Therefore, reviewing the results of the postwar decades, it would be wrong to perceive only those which we sincerely welcome and support. Unfortunately, many other developments are causing growing concern. Needless to say, today's world is quite unlike the world of the thirties, but far from all in the West have so far renounced attempts to talk to the Soviet Union in a language of threats.

The Cold War kindled by the war-like circles in the West was nothing but an attempt to revise the results of the Second World War and deprive the Soviet people — the world's progressive democratic forces — of the fruits of victory. In fact, these goals were never concealed. They were expressed in the ideology and policy of "throwing back socialism", "massive retaliation", "brinkmanship", etc. As a result, international trust was undermined and the possibilities for constructive co-operation between states initiated within the framework of the anti-Hitler coalition were greatly narrowed.

US militarism is the main culprit responsible for the threats of war that menaces mankind. US policy is steadily assuming a more war-like character and has become a permanently negative factor in international relations which we cannot ignore. The aggressive ambitions of the US ruling elite are manifested by its attempts to upset the military strategic balance — the foundation of international security, and escalate the arms race — in the nuclear field first and foremost, and in its dangerous plans for militarizing outer space. Barbarian doctrines and conceptions of using nuclear weapons are being worked out, and hundreds of war bases and other military installations have been established in all continents. A policy of state terrorism against Nicaragua is being pursued and an undeclared war is being waged against Afghanistan.

The United States is trying to impose on the international community its claims to an exceptional role and special pre-destination in history. These alone can explain its imperial claims to "zones of vital interests", a "right" to interfere in the internal affairs of foreign states, to "encourage" or "punish" sovereign countries and peoples as Washington wishes. Even its own political and legal commitments are violated by the US.

It would be relevant here to point out the increasing danger of West German revanchism which is being reanimated with the active participation of the present US leadership. The leaders of the seven leading capitalist powers who assembled at Bonn the other day marked the 40th anniversary of VE Day in their own way and challenged even the territorial and political realities in Europe which took shape in the wake of the defeat of Nazi Germany and postwar development. Some politicians are ready to go as far as pardoning the SS butchers, moreover, and even to honour them, which is an insult to mankind's memory of the millions who were shot dead, burned alive or poisoned in gas chambers.

Aware of the scope of the war menace and our responsibility for the destiny of peace we will not allow the military-strategic parity between the USSR and the USA, the Warsaw Treaty Organization and NATO to be upset. We will continue to pursue this policy because we have learned the lessons of history very well.

In short, the situation remains complicated, even dangerous, but we believe that realistic possibilities exist for curbing the forces of militarism. People throughout the world realize increasingly well that a world without wars and weapons is feasible. They are convinced that such a world can be built even in our day and that it is imperative to act vigorously and fight immediately to make it a reality.

This conviction is corroborated by the record of the policy of peaceful coexistence and the practical results achieved in the sphere of co-operation between states belonging to the two different systems. Such examples are not few. They induce ever broader masses of the peoples to oppose aggression and violence in international relations. There is a growing awareness of the fact that peace will be durable only if peaceful, constructive coexistence, and mutually beneficial co-operation of states regardless of their social system and based on equality become the supreme universal laws of international relations. There is no doubt that the anti-war movement will continue to grow, hampering the adventurist moves of aggressive forces ever more effectively.

The only reasonable way out today is by organizing active co-operation between all states in the interests of their common peaceful future, the establishment and development of international mechanisms and institutions that would enable us to find optimum relationships between the national interests and the interests of mankind.

We are calling on the various social and political forces to co-operate sincerely in a spirit of good will, in the name of peace. This is not a simple task, and it cannot be implemented overnight and demands a high degree of confidence in relations between countries. The trend of developments can take a sharp turn for the better if tangible success is achieved at the Soviet–American talks on nuclear and space weapons at Geneva. This is our firm conviction.

In this area the experience of the seventies is, in our view, truly inestimable. At that time good political, legal, moral and psychological foundations were laid for co-operation between states belonging to the two different systems in a new historical situation, in particular in such sensitive areas as the security of the two sides. The results, however, could have been even more significant if the West had displayed a more responsible attitude to the record of *détente*.

We are strongly in favour of reviving the process of *détente*. This, however, does not mean a simple reversal to what was achieved in the seventies. It is necessary to advance much further. In our view, détente is not the eventual aim of policy. It is an indispensable, but merely a transitional, stage from a world overloaded with arms to a dependable and comprehensive system of international security.

The Soviet Union is prepared to follow this road. The quest for any opportunity to help remove the risk of nuclear war should be the supreme duty of governments and responsible statesmen. I wish today, on the day of the anniversary, so memorable for all of us, to repeat again: the Soviet Union is resolutely in favour of a world without wars, a world without arms. We declare again and again: the outcome of the historic contest between the two systems cannot be decided by military means.

Our allegiance to the policy of peaceful coexistence is evidence of the strength of the new social system and of our faith in its historical possibilities. It is in the interests of all countries and nations, pervaded with the spirit of genuine humanism, the ideals of peace and freedom which inspired the Soviet people in the years of the last war.

To defend man's sacred right to life, to secure a lasting peace is our common duty to present and future generations and a tribute to the millions who laid down their lives for freedom and social progress.

Comrades! The great Soviet people, a people in uniform and workers' overalls, led by the Bolshevik Party was the main factor of Victory.

Celebrating Victory Day we honour the memory of the courageous sons and daughters of this country, who gave their lives for the sacred cause of defence of the motherland.

Celebrating Victory Day we praise the war and labour veterans, we praise Soviet man — a soldier and a worker, our heroic working class, the collective farmers and the people's intelligentsia.

Celebrating Victory Day we praise all the nations and national minorities united in the friendly family of nations — the Union of Soviet Socialist Republics.

Celebrating Victory Day we praise the Soviet soldier, our valiant armed forces.

Celebrating Victory Day we praise the Leninist Communist Party, the party of our victor nation.

May the memory of the exploit of the Soviet people in the Great Patriotic War live on in the centuries to come.

7.

Interview with the Press Trust
of India
18 May 1985

Question. In the light of your forthcoming meeting with Prime Minister Rajiv Gandhi, how would you assess the state and prospects of Soviet–Indian relations in the context of the struggle for peace and disarmament?

Answer. First of all, I wish to emphasize that in my country the leaders of India are invariably welcomed with special warmth. This is an expression of the Soviet people's sincere affection and respect for the great and friendly Indian people. Different generations of the Soviet people and the people of India have inscribed their own splendid pages in the history of our friendship, to which Jawaharlal Nehru and Indira Gandhi contributed so much.

Our attitude to India reflects the Soviet Union's high-principled and unvarying support for the struggle waged by peoples against imperialist oppression, for strengthening their independence and for social renovation. This policy was bequeathed to us by the great Lenin and we are dedicatedly faithful to it. It would be no exaggeration to say that we have inherited a unique, truly priceless heritage. "We are not only linked by relations between governments and not only by our political and economic co-operation: our relationship is a union of the warm hearts of two nations." This vivid and figurative phrase of Indira Gandhi is the best description of the level and entire diversity of our mutual relations.

I avail myself of this opportunity to pay tribute once again to the lucid memory of the outstanding daughter of the Indian people, whose name is inscribed in the history of Soviet–Indian friendship forever. The awarding of the international Lenin Prize "For Strengthening Peace Among Nations" is a recognition of her enormous contribution to the struggle for lasting peace, for friendship among nations.

An Indian proverb says that the shortest road is one on which people meet each other half-way. For decades our two peoples have been following such a road. This is why our relations have always been on the upgrade. We are satisfied with the high level, dynamic and many-sided character or our relations based on the Treaty of Peace, Friendship and Co-operation.

We highly appreciate India's contribution to the common efforts to preserve peace and prevent nuclear war. Leading the non-aligned movement today, a movement that has become a crucial factor in international relations, India is doing much to consolidate its unity and increase its favourable impact on the world climate.

Soviet–Indian friendship is an achievement of crucial importance not only for our two nations. It is an important factor of peace and stability in the present-day tense situation, and it is a model for fruitful co-operation between countries belonging to different social economic systems if they are guided by the ideals of peace, the principles of mutual respect and co-operation based on equality. We have an optimistic view of the prospect for Soviet–Indian relations. Already during our previous meeting with Prime Minister Rajiv Gandhi both sides reaffirmed their desire to have their co-operation further developed. I have no doubt that the forthcoming discussion on a wide range of problems in the area of both bilateral and international relations will lend a new dimension to our traditional ties and serve the interests of both the Soviet and the Indian peoples, as well as the interests of peace in Asia and the rest of the world.

Of course, it will be a pleasure for me personally to resume contacts with the Indian leader who enjoys profound respect in my country.

Question: The Soviet public has given its broad approval to the initiative of the heads of state and government of the six countries representing four continents which were put forward in their declarations of 1984 and 1985. How, in your opinion, could these initiatives be translated into reality?

Answer. We have a high opinion of these initiatives. The ideas expressed in the documents drawn up by the heads of the six countries and the Soviet initiatives follow the same lines. The eventual task of the declaration outline is the banishing of nuclear weapons from mankind's life, which is in full agreement with the aims of Soviet foreign policy.

Accepting the proposal for continued talks with the United States at Geneva we agreed that their aim was a ban on an arms race in outer space, an end to the arms race and a start on a radical reduction of nuclear weapons down to their eventual complete elimination.

As the leaders of the six expressed themselves one could, for a start, end the development, production and deployment of nuclear weapons, freeze nuclear arsenals and take steps to cut them down and prevent an escalation of the arms race to outer space, and conclude a treaty prohibiting nuclear tests completely.

We proposed as a first step to suspend a further build-up of armaments, so that the United States and the Soviet Union could comply throughout the period of the Geneva talks with a moratorium on development, including research and development, testing and deployment of strike space weapons, as well as imposing a freeze on strategic offensive arms and providing for a ban on deployment of American intermediate range missiles in Europe and on Soviet counter measures.

At the same time the Soviet Union, acting without delay has already announced unilaterally a moratorium to be effective until November of this year on deployment of intermediate-range missiles and suspending other counter measures in Europe. Faithful to its pledge, the Soviet Union is strictly abiding by the terms of this moratorium. We are entitled to hope for a more serious and considerate assessment of our initiative on the part of Washington and its NATO partners and for their restraint in the deployment of American missiles in Western Europe. Reciprocity on this issue would help put the Geneva talks on practical lines.

Finally, on the cessation of nuclear weapons tests. We have repeatedly called on the United States and the other nuclear powers to take this step. The Soviet Union has offered in the past and is offering now to nuclear weapons states to impose a moratorium on all nuclear explosions to be effective until the conclusion of a treaty on the general and complete prohibition of nuclear weapons tests. This could be enacted as of 6 August 1985, that is, from the day of the 40th anniversary of the tragic atomic bombing of Hiroshima, or even from an earlier date.

The Soviet Union is prepared for the immediate resumption of the talks on a complete prohibition of nuclear weapons tests which, as is known, were interrupted through the fault of the United States. It is time we gave effect to the Soviet–American treaties signed in 1974 and 1976 on the limitation of underground nuclear weapons tests and on underground nuclear explosions for peaceful purposes not yet ratified for which the Soviet Union is not to blame either.

Of course, the nuclear powers, primarily the Soviet Union and the United States bear the brunt of the responsibility for the destiny of peace. However, the Soviet Union has never viewed the world through the prism of Soviet–American relations. We are profoundly convinced that all states can and must be involved in a search for realistic solutions to outstanding problems, in lessening international tensions. The voice of millions of people in different countries in favour of effective steps to end the arms race and reduce the arms stockpiles, against attempts to use negotiations as a smokescreen for continuing this race, is of enormous significance.

Question: What could you say of the prospects of securing lasting peace and developing co-operation in Asia, in the area of the Indian Ocean in particular?

Answer: I wish to emphasize that we have a high opinion of India's contribution to consolidating peace and stability in Asia, and of its sober and well-balanced approach to the key problems of the region.

As far as the Soviet Union is concerned, it has always been and is today in favour of peace and security of nations and co-operation between the states of the continent on a basis of equality. This holds true of the Indian Ocean basin. We support the idea of converting this region into a zone of peace.

As is known, the United States has been opposing an international conference on this issue for a number of years now. The United States also unilaterally broke off Soviet–American talks on restriction of military activities in the Indian Ocean basin. In the meantime the United States is constantly building up its military presence there.

The Soviet Union has repeatedly declared its willingness to resume negotiations. The Soviet proposal put forward in the course of the Soviet–Indian top level meeting in 1982 is still valid. This proposal provides for abstention from any step likely to aggravate the situation in this region without waiting for the conference. This refers to all states whose ships sail in the Indian Ocean basin. What do we have in mind? Abstention from sending large naval fleets and from naval exercises, from expanding or modernizing the military bases of those non-coastal states which have them.

Today the calling of an international conference on this issue has become pivotal in the struggle for a zone of peace in the Indian Ocean. I wish to emphasize our desire to work together with the other states concerned to have this forum convened, so that the Indian Ocean could eventually become a sphere of the vital interests of its own coastal states rather than any other, and become a zone of peace rather than of tension and conflict.

In conclusion let me convey through your agency my best wishes for the happiness, prosperity and peace of the Indian people. We wish the government and all the citizens of India complete success in their efforts to consolidate further their national unity and cohesion, to promote the social progress and prosperity of your country.

In the course of the discussion following the presentation of Mr Gorbachov's replies to the questions of the Press Trust of India, the General Secretary said that Soviet leaders attached great significance to the forthcoming visit of Prime Minister Rajiv Gandhi and believed that it would become a significant event in the life of the two states and in developing relations between them. This is always the case: every visit by the leaders of our two countries, their every meeting has left an appreciable trace in Soviet–Indian relations. In this context we in the Soviet Union recall warmly and repectfully the visit paid to this country by the outstanding leaders of India, Jawaharlal Nehru and Indira Gandhi. We are confident that the visit of Prime Minister Rajiv Gandhi will be of much value to the continued development of Soviet–Indian co-operation and contribute to our joint struggle for lasting peace and greater international security. The Prime Minister and myself have already established good personal contacts, and we hope to make them stronger still.

Friendship with India, profound respect for its great people, its rich and ancient culture and its contributions to mankind's progress are all implanted in the hearts and minds of all Soviet citizens.

Friendship with India is also an active tradition of Soviet foreign policy over the last few decades. We proceed from the assumption that a united and strong India committed to peace is a necessary and indispensable component of the modern world.

I personally have an enormous interest in your country and I hope that the courteous invitation I have received from Prime Minister Rajiv Gandhi will enable me to visit India and meet its people when the right time comes.

Mikhail Gorbachov also answered other questions put by the PTI correspondent:

To a question about the factors which were in his opinion crucial to the successful progress of his work as a Party leader, Mikhail Gorbachov underscored that there was only one clue to this success: our Soviet socialist way of life, the conditions the socialist system provides for the education and development of the individual. The labour training received in a family of farmers, like the one received by millions of children of workers, peasants and members of the intelligentsia, a good education to which access is open to all in the Soviet Union, and the socio-political school of training at first in the ranks of the Komsomol and then in a Party organization are all factors typical of the Soviet way of life, which enable Soviet citizens to take an active part in a specified area of the country's development and in building a new life in general. Capable people exist in every country and among any people, but in our opinion the socialist system provides the best conditions for their development and for the socially useful expression of their abilities.

Some political leaders in the West, as SPK Gupta said, while pointing out the energy and dynamic policy of the Soviet Union express their apprehensions that the implementation of its plans in the field of foreign policy and the measures contemplated in the field of socio-economic development pose a growing danger to the West, the United States in particular. The correspondent asked Mikhail Gorbachov's opinion on this subject.

Mikhail Gorbachov said in response that such "apprehensions" should be left to the conscience of those Western leaders who express them. The leadership of our Party and state have of late been carrying out enormous work to secure an acceleration of the country's peaceful socio-economic development. We attempted to make a realistic assessment of the situation in various areas of economic life, consulted experts and discussed these questions with a wide range of working people in town and country. As a result, we formed a general idea of a programme whose implementations, as we believe, will secure the achievement of the goals the Party and people have set themselves. We hope to complete our work on drafting the guidelines of the strategy of our socio-economic development by the 27th Party Congress, and we are confident that our plans will obtain the approval of the Party and the Soviet people as a whole.

Since the Soviet Union is formulating great and far-reaching aims for peaceful development we naturally need a lasting peace, and we will do everything we can to preserve and consolidate peace on Earth. In this matter, as we are convinced, our interests are identical with those of all other countries — those of the socialist countries, the developed capitalist countries and the countries of Asia, Africa and Latin America which have thrown off the yoke of colonialism. Perhaps these plans will displease some groups of imperialists, who would like to sustain international tensions and go ahead with the arms race, using them for their narrow selfish ends. But this is a totally different matter. We believe that our policy accords with the interests of the Soviet people and the peoples of all other countries.

At the conclusion of the interview, the correspondent thanked Mikhail Gorbachov for his clear and conclusive answers to the questions put to him.

8.

Speech at a dinner at the Kremlin Grand Palace in honour of the Prime Minister of the Republic of India, Rajiv Gandhi 21 May 1985

Esteemed Mr Prime Minister!
Esteemed Mrs Gandhi!
Ladies and Gentlemen!

We are happy to welcome here in Moscow the Prime Minister of India and members of his entourage, representatives of a country which enjoys enormous respect in the Soviet Union. Meetings between Soviet and Indian leaders are invariably distinguished by warmth and cordiality, trust and understanding. They have a beneficial influence on relations between our two countries, on the situation in Asia and in the world as a whole.

Years and decades pass, generations change in our two countries, but relations of friendship and co-operation between the USSR and India are invariably on the upgrade. The reason is their development on a basis of equality and mutual respect, of an identity or similarity of the stands held by the two countries on the vital problems of today.

Our co-operation with India which has so many dimensions today is free from any pressure or from efforts to impose any terms on each other. The Soviet Union has consistently supported India at all stages of its struggle to consolidate its independence, has displayed and is displaying today effective solidarity with that great country, upholding its sovereignty, dignity, and its right to an independent road of development.

In any sphere of co-operation with India we share the best of what we have. We are profoundly satisfied with the fact that the economic ties between the USSR and India have contributed to the solution of important problems in its progress — key problems for each concrete historical period — be it the laying of foundations for heavy industry or establishing a fuel and energy complex. And today, the list of our joint projects contains those whose implementation will indisputably be an effective contribution to economic development and the strengthening of the defence capability of India on the threshold of a new age.

The high effectiveness and, I would say, the great potential of our scientific and technological ties are evidenced, in particular, by the successful space venture of a joint Soviet–Indian crew.

The wide and varied cultural exchanges between the two countries express their traditional mutual interests in each other's rich culture and their definite spiritual affinity.

However, the broad scope of our achievements should not make us blind to the great opportunities available for further progress. A desire to advance in this direction was expressed by both sides in the course of today's talks. We are in a good position to advance our co-operation to a new level of quality in many areas.

The efforts being made by the USSR and India to remove the risk of war and end the arms race have a special part to play in our co-operation. Nobody can ignore the fact that the friendship and co-operation between our countries are playing an increasingly beneficial role in the entire system of international relations. They are a model which helps to affirm the principles of peaceful coexistence and serves to strengthen the peace in the security of all nations. Our Treaty of Peace, Friendship and Co-operation effectively serves these aims as well.

All nations desire peace and progress, and none of them wants war. However, forces exist which pursue different aims. They are unwilling to reckon with the legitimate interests of others and with the political realities of the modern world. In a chase after the phantom of military superiority these forces have pushed the world to the threshold of another spiral in the arms race of unprecedented proportions which threatens to rise to a qualitatively new phase, whose processes may get out of hand.

What, for instance, can the world's nations gain from the much-vaunted "star wars" programme which Washington, for purposes of camouflage describes as its strategic defence initiative? This programme entails in the first place a significant growth in the danger of nuclear war. And, of course, this programme drastically lessens the chances for reaching agreement on disarmament issues. Enormous resources will be harnessed additionally to the arms race, in nuclear weapons in particular. These resources could be released and re-directed to serve the interests of mankind's peaceful development and help solve such vital problems as eradication of poverty and famine, disease and illiteracy.

The problem of preventing the militarization of outer space there-fore affects the interests of all countries and all nations; it leaves no one unaffected. Therefore, before it is too late, while an irreversible situation has not yet been created under a smokescreen of reassuring declarations, we believe that all states committed to peace should voice their protest against this new danger.

One of the realities of modern times is the entry into the world arena of dozens of states in Asia, Africa and Latin America which are seeking to rid themselves of the disastrous heritage of colonialism. The overwhelming majority of these states follow a policy of non-alignment. The emergence of the non-aligned movement and its conversion into a key factor in world politics is a legitimate phenom-enon today. This graphically illustrates the desire of the newly liber-ated peoples for co-operation between states on the basis of equality, for recognition of their lawful rights and interests by foreign nations, for exclusion from international affairs of any manifestation of domi-nation and dictation, or of claims to world supremacy.

In short, the newly liberated countries desire a situation in which they would not be regarded as sources of super-profits for foreign monopolies and they are opposed to the establishment of war bases and bridgeheads in their territories. One is obliged to understand these countries. When they are declared spheres of "vital interests" of some countries without asking their opinion, their own interests are of course completely ignored. Their interests are in effect regarded as non-existent.

There is no need to dwell at length on the great danger of conflicts flaring up in different regions on the world today. Taking a closer look at them one will easily see that these conflicts stem as a rule from the attempts of imperialist powers to interfere in the affairs of liberated

Plate 1. M. S. Gorbachov talking with builders and other workers at the Surgut.

Plate 2. Leningrad, 15 May. General Secretary of the CPSU Central Committee M. S. Gorbachov getting to know the life of the hero-city and the work of the Leningraders, visiting the Kirov Mill, famous for its revolutionary, fighting and labour traditions. In the rolling mill he had a frank conversation with a senior hand, I. Ya. Prokofyev, a veteran of the defence of Leningrad.

PLATE 3. On 20 September a large party of veteran stakhanovites, pioneers of all-union socialist competition, were invited to meet the Central Committee of the CPSU. They were greeted by M. S. Gorbachov, N. I. Ryzhkov, V. I. Dolgikh, B. N. Ponomaryov, L. N. Zaikov, M. V. Zimyanin, I. V. Kapitonov, V. N. Nikonov and K. V. Rusakov.

PLATE 4. Talking to students.

PLATE 5. Leningrad, 15 May. During his time in the hero-city, M. S. Gorbachov visited Victory Square, where he laid flowers on the monument to the heroic defenders of Leningrad and talked with workers living in the city.

PLATE 6. M. S. Gorbachov visiting the I. A. Likhachov factory, where he chatted with people at their workplaces and showed a detailed interest in working and living conditions.

PLATE 7. M. S. Gorbachov as a guest of a children's holiday camp.

PLATE 8. At the tomb of the Unknown Warrior in Kiev, M. S. Gorbachov observed a minute's silence
in honour of the Soviet citizens who laid down their lives in the Great Patriotic War for the liberty and
independence of the Soviet Motherland and placed a wreath on behalf of the Central Committee of
the CPSU.

PLATE 9. Moscow. On 13 November in the Kremlin M. S. Gorbachov received a delegation from the congress of laureates of the Nobel Peace Prize, which took place in Maastricht, Holland, on 25-27 October. The delegation was composed of George Wold (USA), Theo Knippenberg and Susana Gabriel (Netherlands) and Alois Englander – secretary of the Federation of Nobel Prize Laureates (Austria).

PLATE 10. Moscow. On 18 December in the Kremlin M. S. Gorbachov received the American co-chairman of the international movement "International Physicians for the Prevention of Nuclear War" Professor B. Lown. The Soviet co-chairman Academician E. I. Chazov also took part in the meeting.

PLATE 11. Geneva, 21 November 1985. At the closing ceremony of the meeting between General Secretary of the CPSU Central Committee and the President of the United States of America. M. S. Gorbachov and R. Reagan at the international press centre.

PLATE 12. On 13 March in the Kremlin M. S. Gorbachov held discussions with the Prime Minister of Great Britain, M. Thatcher. Also taking part were Member of the Politbureau of the CPSU Central Committee, First Vice-Chairman of the Council of Ministers of the USSR, and Minister for Foreign Affairs A. A. Gromyko and the Minister for Foreign and Commonwealth Affairs G. Howe.

PLATE 13. On 13 March in the Kremlin M. S. Gorbachov held discussions with the Prime Minister of Great Britain, M. Thatcher.

PLATE 14. Moscow. On 10 April in the Kremlin M. S. Gorbachov received the Speaker of the US House of Representatives T. O'Neill, head of the delegation from the House of Representatives invited by the Supreme Soviet of the USSR. Talks were held between M. S. Gorbachov and T. O'Neill; also taking part were the Chairman of the Council of the Supreme Soviet of the USSR L. N. Tolkunov and members of the US House of Representatives R. Michael, D. Rostenkovsky and S. Conte, together with the US Ambassador to the USSR, A. Hartman.

PLATE 15. Geneva, November 1985. M. S. Gorbachov and his wife R. M. Gorbachova, being welcomed at the Geneva Airport.

PLATE 16. The visit by M. S. Gorbachov to France. At Orly Airport M. S. Gorbachov meets F. Mitterand.

PLATE 17. General Secretary of the CPSU Central Committee, M. S. Gorbachov, and French President F. Mitterand at the joint press conference at the Elysée Palace.

PLATE 18. Geneva. On 19 November 1985 at their own request M. S. Gorbachov received a delegation of the leaders of the main anti-war movements in the USA. In the photograph, M. S. Gorbachov is talking with American proponents of peace. Centre (*left*) is former presidential candidate and prominent social activist, Jesse Jackson.

PLATE 19. During a meeting between M. S. Gorbachov and representatives of the leadership of the France–USSR Society.

PLATE 20. Moscow. On 22 May in the Kremlin the formal signing of the Soviet–Indian documents took place. They were signed by General Secretary of the CPSU Central Committee M. S. Gorbachov and the Prime Minister of the Republic of India, R. Gandhi. The photograph was taken after the ceremony.

PLATE 21. On 22 May in the Kremlin General Secretary of the CPSU Central Committee M. S. Gorbachov held talks with the Prime Minister of the Republic of India Rajiv Gandhi.

PLATE 22. On 14 March in the Kremlin General Secretary of the CPSU Central Committee M. S. Gorbachov received the President of the Republic of Finland, Mauno Koivisto, who had come to Moscow to attend the funeral of K. U. Chernenko. Also taking part in the discussion was Member of the Politbureau of the CPSU Central Committee, First Vice-Chairman of the Council of Ministers of the USSR and Minister for Foreign Affairs of the USSR, A. A. Gromyko.

countries in whatever form, and to subordinate them to their influence. This is the main reason for the emergence of so many seats of tension in the world rather than the so-called "rivalry between superpowers".

I believe, that steps to eradicate these seats of tension and to secure a peaceful settlement of conflicts in Asia, Africa and Latin America could be facilitated by the adoption by each permanent member of the UN Security Council of a commitment to strict observance in their relations with these countries of the principles of non-interference, non-use of force or threat of force and to avoid involving them in military blocs. The Soviet Union is prepared to assume such a commitment. This would be in full conformity with the principles of our foreign policy. The notion of *détente* was born in Europe. We are approaching the tenth anniversary of the day when a hisotric document was signed at Helsinki which summed up, as it were, whatever the nations imply by this meaningful word. Much of what was based on this foundation has been destroyed by the icy winds blowing from beyond the ocean. Much, however, has survived and struck firm root, and is bringing tangible benefits to the nations.

In Asia today, the problems of ensuring peace and security are perhaps no less painful and vital than in Europe and in certain areas they are perhaps more urgent. Small wonder, therefore, that over the past few years a number of important, constructive initiatives have been put forward on some aspects of the security of the Asian continent and its individual regions. The authors of these initiatives are socialist states and member states of the non-aligned movement. The USSR and India are among them.

The proposals mentioned above are on the agenda of international life. For instance, the proposal for converting the Indian Ocean into a zone of peace was supported by the UN General Assembly and the non-aligned movement at the recent New Delhi Conference, in particular. One should not underestimate the fact that both nuclear weapons powers situated on the Asian continent — the USSR and the PRC — have assumed an obligation not to use nuclear weapons first.

The question we are facing now is as follows: should we not, taking account of all these initiatives and of the experience of Europe to a certain extent, jointly consider some common comprehensive approach to the problem of security in Asia and, if possible to the pooling of efforts of Asian states in this direction? Of course, the road to this aim is a difficult one. It will be recalled, however, that the road to Helsinki was not smooth either. Apparently different methods may be applied here — bilateral talks, multilateral consultations — down to holding, in the future, an all-Asian conference to exchange opinion and jointly search for constructive solutions.

One thing seems indisputable: the peoples of Asia have a vital interest in maintaining peace and developing peaceful co-operation as much as the peoples of any other continent and they can do much to this end.

I believe that a highly important contribution to this purpose could be made by India, a great power which enjoys high prestige and great respect in the Asian countries and throughout the world.

We highly appreciate India's contribution to the cause of strengthening peace and international security, and to enhancing the role of the non-aligned movement in this matter.

The peoples will always remember the names of the great leaders of India, Jawaharlal Nehru and Indira Gandhi, as names linked inseparably both with the history of India and the history of the national liberation movement in all continents. They charted the political path on which India has gained impressive successes in its internal development and in consolidating its international positions. They have done much to establish and promote the non-aligned movement as a positive factor of crucial importance in the modern world.

The awarding to Indira Gandhi of the international Lenin Prize "For the Promotion of Peace among Nations" posthumously was an expression of the broad recognition of her outstanding service in the struggle for the preservation and consolidation of peace.

The Soviet people will always gratefully remember Jawaharlal Nehru and Indira Gandhi as staunch and consistent champions of close friendship and co-operation between our two countries. We highly appreciate, Mr Prime Minister, your determination to continue the cause of your famous predecessors. I can assure you that the leadership of the Soviet Union is determined to work actively to develop and strengthen further the friendly relations between the USSR and India. An independent India committed to peace will always meet with understanding and support in the Soviet Union.

Please accept our heartfelt wishes for good health and prosperity.

Let me propose a toast to the esteemed Prime Minister of the Republic of India, Rajiv Gandhi, Mrs Gandhi and all our Indian friends!

May the great people of India advance further on the path of success and prosperity!

May friendship and co-operation between our two countries grow stronger!

May lasting peace reign on Earth!

9.

Outer Space should Serve the Cause of Peace.
Reply to a message from the "Concerned Scientists' Union"
Pravda, 6 July 1985

Dear Mr Kendall,

I have received your message with an appeal for banning space weapons on behalf of the "Concerned Scientists' Union". I wish to tell you that I feel profound respect for the opinion of the eminent scientists who are more clearly aware than many others of the danger to mankind that would be entailed by an escalation of the arms race to outer space and its conversion into an arena of military rivalry.

The "Concerned Scientists' Union" demands, for good reason, that a clear-cut and irreversible political decision be taken to prevent the militarization of outer space and to leave it free for peaceful co-operation. Indeed, this problem requires a bold approach. The criteria of yesterday, narrow views of unilateral advantages and bene-fits — illusory views for that matter — are hardly applicable here. Now we need as never before a far-sighted policy based on a clear under-standing of the realities of the day and the dangers we shall inevitably face tomorrow if those who can and must take the right decision evade their responsibility today.

On behalf of the Soviet leadership I wish to declare unambiguously that the Soviet Union will not take a first step into outer space with arms in hand. We will apply every effort to persuade other countries, the United States first and foremost, to refrain from such a fatal step,

196

which would inevitably aggravate the risk of nuclear war and trigger off an uncontrollable arms race in all directions.

In pursuit of this goal the Soviet Union, as you evidently know, submitted to the United Nations a radical proposal — a draft treaty banning the use of force in outer space and from outer space in relation to earth. If the United States joined the vast majority of the UN member states which supported this initiative, the issue of space weapons could be settled once and for all.

At the Soviet–American talks on nuclear and space weapons at Geneva we are seeking to reach agreement on a total ban on development, testing and deployment of strike space systems. Such a ban would not only allow us to preserve outer space for peaceful exploration, research and scientific discovery but also initiate a process of drastic reduction and elimination on nuclear weapons.

We have more than once undertaken unilateral steps to set a good example for the United States to follow. The moratorium imposed by the Soviet Union on deployment of anti-satellite weapons in outer space has been effective for two years now, and it will remain in force as long as the other states refrain from such deployment. We submitted to Washington our proposal for both sides to cease completely their work on the development of new anti-satellite facilities and for the destruction of facilities already available to the USSR and the US, including those whose tests have not yet been completed. In the near future the moves of the American side will show which alternative is preferable to the US Administration.

Strategic stability and mutual trust would indisputably become stronger if the United States agreed, together with the USSR, to reaffirm in a binding form their allegiance to the terms of the Treaty on the Limitation of Anti-Missile Defence Systems without restriction as to time. The Soviet Union is not developing space strike weapons or broader scale anti-missile defence systems as the foundation for such defence and is strictly abiding by its commitments under the Treaty as a whole; in particular, it is unfailingly abiding by the spirit and letter of this document which is of major significance. We invite the US leadership to join us in this matter, to give up their plans of militarizing outer space, which would inevitably make the document — key link in the whole process of nuclear arms limitation — null and void.

The Soviet Union proceeds from the assumption that a practical settlement of the problems of preventing an arms race in outer space and ending the arms race on earth is possible if the two sides display the necessary political will and a sincere desire to achieve this historic goal. The Soviet Union does have this desire and this political will.

I wish the "Concerned Scientists' Union" and all its members success in their noble work for the benefit of peace and progress.

10.

Statement by the General Secretary of the CPSU Central Committee, Mikhail Gorbachov
Pravda, 30 July 1985

The continuing nuclear arms race is fraught with enormous dangers to the future of world civilization. It is causing growing tensions in the international arena and aggravating the risk of war, diverting colossal intellectual and material resources from constructive purposes.

Since the advent of the nuclear age, the Soviet Union has been carrying on a consistent and vigorous struggle to end the building up of nuclear arsenals, to curb military rivalry and to promote relations of mutual trust and peaceful co-operation among nations. This is the purpose of the Soviet Union's immense activities within the UN framework and in the multilateral and bilateral talks on arms limitation and reduction. The Soviet Union is not seeking military superiority; it is in favour of preserving the military balance at as low a level as possible.

In our view, termination of all nuclear weapons tests would be a major contribution to consolidating the strategic stability and peace on earth. It is an open secret that in the process of such tests new, even more lethal types of weapons of mass destruction are tested and perfected.

To provide favourable conditions for concluding an international treaty on the general and complete prohibition of nuclear weapons tests, the Soviet Union has repeatedly proposed to nuclear weapons countries to agree on a moratorium on all nuclear explosions starting from a date fixed by mutual agreement. Unfortunately, it has so far proved impossible to take this important step.

In order to facilitate termination of the dangerous contest in building up nuclear arsenals and to give a good example of good will the Soviet Union has taken a decision to end unilaterally all nuclear explosions as of 6 August this year. We call on the US Government to terminate nuclear explosions as of that date which is commemorated as Hiroshima Day throughout the world. Our moratorium is to be effective until 1 January 1986. It will be further extended, however, if the United States for its part refrains from holding nuclear explosions.

It is indisputable that a reciprocal Soviet–American moratorium on all nuclear explosions would set a good example to be followed by other states possessing nuclear weapons.

The Soviet Union expects that the United States will respond favourably to this initiative and halt its nuclear tests.

This would meet the hopes and aspirations of all nations.

11.

Message to Herr Willy Brandt, Chairman of the Social Democratic Party of Germany
Pravda, 12 August 1985

Dear Willy Brandt,

I share completely the assessment of the Moscow Treaty you gave in your letter. One of the fundamental documents of the postwar era, it has laid down the principles of developing relations between our two countries and has exerted a favourable influence on the entire complex of inter-state relations on the European continent, affirming the important principle of the inviolability of the borders of all states in Europe today and in the future. I would like to point out in this context that your personal contribution to its conclusion is well remembered in the Soviet Union.

The provisions of the Moscow Treaty have not lost their significance today. Moreover, as we see it, in the current aggravated international situation and in conditions of a growing risk of war any digression from these principles would run counter to the aim of ending the arms race and strengthening peace in Europe and the world.

As far as the Soviet Union is concerned, I wish to reaffirm the fact that our state, as in the past, remains a consistent champion of converting Europe into a continent of peace and mutually beneficial co-operation between all countries and peoples, including the USSR and the FRG, and is prepared to take practical steps to facilitate progress towards this noble objective.

12.

Interview with the Soviet News Agency TASS
Pravda, 14 August 1985

Question. What is your opinion of world reaction to the latest Soviet initiative: the imposing of a moratorium on nuclear explosions?

Answer. As far as the sentiments of the public at large are concerned, I believe we have full reason to say that the new initiative of the Soviet Union which has unilaterally halted all nuclear explosions and called on the United States to follow suit has met with enthusiastic approval throughout the world. In many countries — the United States, in particular — prominent statesmen, political and public figures are expressing themselves in favour of the idea of a moratorium on nuclear weapons tests and for other nuclear powers to follow the Soviet example. Our proposal implies a concrete and tangible measure. People hope that it will slow down the nuclear arms race and eventually bring it to a standstill.

I know that our initiative has not pleased everybody. Those in the West who have bound up their policy with a further escalation of the arms race, who are extracting great profits from it, are opposed to ending nuclear tests. They are opposing the moratorium because they are unwilling to have nuclear weapons manufacturing ended. They are obsessed with vain dreams of gaining military superiority, no matter how. At the same time they are circulating absurd fabrications about Soviet policy, in particular in connection with our declared moratorium on nuclear explosions.

That was an honest and open step on our part. We imposed the moratorium because we are profoundly convinced that practical steps should be taken to check the process of building up nuclear weapons and their further improvement. It was by no means our intention to place the US leadership in a quandary. The US President was notified in advance of our move in a message in which we proposed to the American side to do likewise. We would like the American leadership to give a positive response to our message. Public pronouncements of government officials in Washington on the question of the moratorium create the sad impression that the main problem that engages attention there now is a quest for a shrewd way to evade an answer. I would not be mistaken if I say that the world expects a different attitude.

Question. President Reagan said the other day that the United States could not agree to a moratorium on nuclear tests since it has not yet completed its nuclear programme. He alleged at the same time that the Soviet Union had completed an intensive series of nuclear explosions and could now therefore afford to have a break. Is that so?

Answer. Before taking the decision to end nuclear explosions unilaterally the Soviet leadership had examined this question thoroughly and comprehensively. It was not an easy decision to take. In order to impose a unilateral moratorium we had to break off the testing programme before it was completed.

It would be relevant to recall that before the declaration of the moratorium the Soviet Union had carried out practically as many nuclear explosions as the United States during this year. As for nuclear tests staged to date, the United States has on record a much larger number than the Soviet Union. This is known in the White House.

However, taking a decision to impose a unilateral moratorium the Soviet Union was guided not by arithmetic but by fundamental political considerations, its desire to contribute to ending the arms race and to induce the United States as well as other nuclear weapons states to follow suit. Our aim is a total and universal ban on nuclear weapons tests rather than taking time out before another explosion.

A view is being circulated that a moratorium on nuclear explosions would not meet the US interests. A moratorium, however, is an important step on the path towards ending further work to improve these lethal weapons. Moreover, the longer the period without tests, the faster the process of "obsolescence" of nuclear weapons stockpiles.

Finally, a moratorium creates the most favourable conditions for achieving agreement on ending nuclear tests and for advancement towards the eventual abolition of nuclear weapons in general.

One wonders what in this matter is discordant with the interests of the United States and the American people? This path is unacceptable only to those who rely on force, who are harbouring plans of developing ever new types of nuclear weapons on earth, who are seeking to escalate the arms race to outer space. How can this be reconciled with the genuine interests of strengthening peace and international security to which Washington has more than once declared its commitment?

The unwillingness to end nuclear tests is sometimes justified by references to the alleged "lag" of the United States in the area of nuclear weapons. This is nothing but idle talk. At one time there was talk of a "lag" in bombers, and later, in missiles. Each time, however, it turned out to be a deliberate lie, which was recognized in Washington later. In other words, talk of a "lag" is started up again whenever someone is seeking to achieve military superiority and lacks the genuine desire to find a solution to the problems of arms limitation. These are precisely the problems which must be solved by a political leadership and not with references to legends of the "Soviet menace" but with due regard to the real situation, the genuine security interests of the country concerned and the interests of international security.

Question. How do you see the problem of verification in the context of the proposals to end nuclear explosions?

Answer. The scientific and technological potential available to us, the United States and other countries, secures the requisite degree of confidence that a nuclear explosion, even with a low yield, will be identified and become known. Those who allege the contrary certainly know what the true answer is.

Unilateral steps to end nuclear explosions are not, of course, a final solution to the problem of complete general and complete termination of nuclear weapons tests. For this problem to be solved once and for all an international agreement is necessary. Besides the relevant obligations it would provide for a dependable system of verification measures, both national and international ones. In short, we are in favour of a verifiable termination of nuclear explosions, but we are opposed to substitution for an end to tests by their continuance in the presence of observers.

It will be recalled that the problem of general and complete prohibition of nuclear weapons tests is by no means a new one. A few years ago it was discussed in detail in the course of tripartite negotiations between the USSR, the United States and Britain. The problems of verification were examined in minute detail. The sides were close to a mutual understanding in many areas. The United States, however, broke off those negotiations because the limitations that were being planned would hamper the Pentagon's programmes.

We have more than once called upon the United States to resume negotiations, and today we are calling on it to halt nuclear weapons tests completely. It would be much easier to hold such talks and make them fruitful if the United States and the Soviet Union halted nuclear tests. The United States, however, is unwilling to return to the negotiating table. This means that the United States is unwilling to end nuclear tests or set up a dependable verification system. No other conclusion suggests itself.

It is sometimes argued that the question of ending nuclear weapons tests should be discussed at the disarmament Conference at Geneva. Well, we are prepared to discuss it there as well. At Geneva, however, the United States and other Western powers, have long been sabotaging such negotiations. Therefore, the question of where an end to nuclear weapons tests should be discussed is irrelevant. It is important to consider this problem seriously and without delay, having in mind, among other things, the forthcoming Soviet–American meeting.

Question. Can one, nevertheless, expect a positive settlement of the nuclear tests issue as you see it?

Answer. Yes, I think so. Although the current US attitude to our proposal does not give cause for optimism, we would not like to abandon all hope. The reason is this. The responsibility resting with the Soviet Union and the United States is too great for them to evade a settlement of major security problems.

What we are proposing is a realistic opportunity to check the continued build-up of nuclear arsenals and get down to work practically to solve the problem of their reduction and eventual abolition.

13.

Message to the Conference on the Record of Compliance with the Nuclear Weapons Non-Proliferation Treaty
Pravda, 28 August 1985

Dear Sirs,

I extend my greetings to the representatives of states signatory to the Treaty on the Non-Proliferation of Nuclear Weapons assembled at Geneva at a conference to discuss the record of compliance with this fundamental international agreement.

The Non-Proliferation Treaty worked out by the joint efforts of many states has proved its viability in practice. Since the time it was concluded no new nuclear weapons state has appeared in the world. For the number of its signatory states this is the broadest agreement in the field of arms limitation. The international regime of nuclear weapons non-proliferation which has emerged on its basis has become an effective instrument for peace.

Another important result of the conclusion of the Non-Proliferation Treaty is the favourable climate it has created for broad international co-operation in the peaceful uses of atomic energy, which is so indispensable for solving the problem of supplying mankind with energy and other major international problems of concern to all nations. The International Atomic Energy Agency has a good record of practical work to implement these tasks.

The Soviet Union is a determined supporter of the further expansion and deepening of such co-operation. It is important to ensure that atomic energy should indeed become available to all mankind and serve the interests of peace and construction alone.

Faithful to its commitments under the Treaty, the Soviet Union has been doing and will continue to do all in its power to prevent nuclear weapons proliferation, to check the arms race and to reverse it.

The Soviet Union has more than once taken unilateral steps, setting a model to others and facilitating thereby the efforts to reach agreements on the limitation and termination of the nuclear arms race. The Soviet Union has assumed an obligation not to use nuclear weapons first. If the nuclear powers which have not yet taken the same step followed suit, that would on the whole be tantamount to a general ban on the use of nuclear weapons.

The Soviet Union's moratorium on all nuclear explosions is further evidence of our desire to ease progress towards ending the nuclear arms race. It is indisputable that a mutual Soviet–American moratorium on nuclear explosions would provide favourable conditions for concluding an international treaty on the general and complete prohibition of nuclear weapons tests and contribute to a more extensive application of the provisions of the Treaty on the Non-Proliferation of Nuclear Weapons.

In the nuclear and space age the problem of curbing the nuclear arms race is inseparably bound up with that of preventing the use of outer space for military purposes. If outer space is placed at the service of war, this would sharply increase the nuclear menace. If, however, outer space is preserved peaceful and kept outside the sphere of military rivalry, this would make for progress towards a settlement of the full range of problems involved in the limitation and reduction of nuclear arsenals. At the same time, broad opportunities would be opened up for all-round international co-operation in various fields of human activity — both on earth and in outer space. This is the object of the Soviet Union's concrete proposals for international co-operation in the peaceful exploration of outer space, free from any weapons, to be discussed at the 40th session of the UN General Assembly.

In short, we are in favour of vigorous efforts in all directions to stop the arms race. As before, measures to prevent nuclear weapons proliferation certainly hold an important place in this area of work.

I wish the delegates to the conference full success in their efforts to promote the Treaty on the Non-Proliferation of Nuclear Weapons.

14.

Interview with the US
Time Magazine
28 August 1985

The US Time Magazine asked General Secretary Mikhail Gorbachov to grant an interview to the Director General of Time Inc. G. Grunwald, the Editor-in-Chief of Time Magazine R. Cave, the Deputy Editor-in-Chief R. Duncan, and the chief of the Time Moscow bureau J. Jackson. Mr. Gorbachov answered the questions from Time and had a discussion with the American journalists.

Question. Could you describe the current state of Soviet–American relations and the main events that determine them now?

Answer. If you had put this question a couple of months ago, I would have said that the situation in our relations was changing for the better, and that some hopes for positive shifts were now in evidence.

Today, however, to my profound regret, I can no longer say that.

We must see the hard facts for what they are. Despite the Geneva talks, which have just opened, and the agreement on a summit meeting, relations between our two countries are tending to deteriorate, the arms race is spiralling and the risk of war is not lessening. But what is causing all this? What is the matter, after all? My colleagues and I are exacting and self-critical enough in relation to our own activities, both at home and abroad. So we keep wondering if it is not our own actions are to blame.

But in that case, what are we to blame for? Indeed, in the current responsible situation Moscow is exercising restraint in its statements concerning the United States and refraining from anti-American

208

campaigns, let alone fomenting hostility towards your country. We deem it highly important not to undermine, even at times of political crisis, the Soviet people's traditional feelings of respect for the American people, which are, to the best of my knowledge, largely mutual.

Isn't it a really good thing that now that disarmament talks have resumed and preparations are under way for the first summit conference after an interval of six years we are persistently searching for ways to break the vicious circle and end the stalemate in the process of arms limitation? This is precisely the objective pursued, in particular by our moratorium on nuclear explosions, our appeal to the United States to join in and resume talks on a total ban on nuclear testing, as well as our proposals for peaceful co-operation and preventing an arms race in outer space. We are convinced that the way out of the present predicament should be sought by joint efforts.

We do not understand why our proposals have aroused such open discontent among high ranking US officials. It is known that they were dismissed as sheer propaganda.

Any person familiar, to whatever extent, with our proposals will easily see that they are motivated by very serious intentions rather than by an attempt to influence public opinion. All practical efforts to limit nuclear armaments have begun with a ban on testing; just recall the Treaty of 1963, which was the first long step along this road. Complete cessation of nuclear tests would halt the nuclear arms race in the most dangerous, qualitative, direction. In addition, it would be an effective contribution to preserving and reinforcing the nuclear weapons non-proliferation regime.

If everything we are doing for peace is really seen as nothing but propaganda, why not respond to it on the principle "an eye for an eye, a tooth for a tooth"? We have ended nuclear testing. You Americans would do well to respond in kind. In addition, you could deal us another propaganda blow, say, by halting development of one of your new strategic missiles. We would respond in kind again. And so on, and so forth. Who would be harmed, I would ask, by a contest in such "propaganda"? Of course, it could not substitute for a comprehensive arms limitation agreement, but it would indisputably be an important step in the direction of that agreement.

Alas, the US Administration has taken a different path. In response to our moratorium, though demonstrably in defiance of all others, it hastened to carry out the next nuclear explosion. And in response to our proposals for keeping outer space peaceful it took a decision to stage the first combat test of anti-satellite weapons. In addition, it launched another "hate campaign" against the Soviet Union.

What impression is produced by such steps? On the one hand, an impression of confusion and uncertainty in Washington. I can explain this only by one thing: a feeling of anxiety lest our initiatives disprove the allegation that the Soviet Union is a "focus of evil" and the source of danger to all, which is, in effect, the basis for the entire arms race policy. On the other hand, the impression of an inadequate sense of responsibility for the destiny of the world. And this, frankly speaking, faces us again and again with this question: is it possible in general to conduct affairs and develop rational relations between countries in such an atmosphere?

You have asked me to identify what is the main thing decisive to Soviet–American relations. I believe it is the indisputable fact that whether we like each other or not we can survive or perish only together. The main question we must pose to ourselves is whether we are finally prepared to recognize that there is no alternative to living in peace with each other, whether we are prepared to reorientate our way of thinking and acting from military to civilian lines. As they say in your country, to live and let live. We call it peaceful coexistence. As far as the Soviet Union is concerned, we say "yes" to this question.

Question. What, in your opinion, will be the results of your meeting at Geneva with President Ronald Reagan in November? What practical steps should the United States and the Soviet Union undertake to improve their bilateral relations?

Answer. I have in fact already listed the reasons why I regard the prospects of the Geneva summit with greater caution than at the time when we consented to it. Indeed, its results will largely depend on what is going on now.

Perhaps everybody will agree that the political atmosphere of negotiations is created in advance of them. Neither the President nor myself can ignore the public sentiments inside our countries, as well as the sentiments of our allies. In other words, today's actions largely determine the "scenarios" of the November discussions.

I must frankly admit that I am disappointed and worried by current developments. We are naturally concerned about the approach which, it seems to us, is beginning to take shape in Washington — in its practical policies and in the pronouncements made by top officials of the White House. This is a scenario of pressure, of attempts to drive us into a corner, to impute to us, as was done more than once in the past, all mortal sins ranging from the responsibility for unleashng the arms race to "aggression" in the Middle East, from human rights violations to some intrigues even within the Republic of South Africa. This is not a statesmanlike policy but a feverish witch-hunt.

We are prepared for a concrete and businesslike discussion and can present our own list of complaints. I want to assure the readers of *Time* that we have plenty we could say about the responsibility of the United States for the nuclear arms race, about its conduct in various regions of the world, its support for those who, in effect, resort to terrorism and about violations of human rights in the United States itself and in many countries close to it. I am wondering, however, whether it was worth our while to arrange a summit meeting on which our two peoples and the people of all continents pin their hopes for peace and a secure and tranquil life. Bad language is no help in a good venture.

I have a different conception of this important meeting. We in Moscow are naturally fully aware of the deep gulf separating us from our partners. Studying what has been said by US political leaders over the last few years, we could not ignore statements we disagree with, some of which speaking frankly, often aroused our indignation but at the same time we did not abandon the hope that points of contact and areas of common or similar interest could still be found. The reasons for such hopes do still exist. Take, for instance, the statements to the effect that a nuclear war cannot be waged and won, or that the United States is not seeking military superiority. In short, I hoped for an honest discussion, unaffected by prejudice and pervaded with a desire to find a way of retreat from the edge of the nuclear abyss. Not a discussion of threadbare political myths and stereotypes, which have become a bore to everyone, but real problems, the real interests of our two countries, our future, and the future of the entire world community.

By all indications, however, our partners are preparing for something else. It seems they are readying themselves for a match between political prize fighters and thinking up ways of deftly hitting the opponent in the most vulnerable spots and scoring more points. One is surprised by both the wording and content of some of their statements. Mr Macfarlane's recent "lecture" is an example in point. It contains not only the full "record of complaints" to be presented to us at Geneva but also what I would describe as a very peculiar interpretation of the forthcoming talks. As far as one can see, even the slightest progress towards agreement is made contingent on concessions from the Soviet Union. Concessions in all areas: armaments, regional problems, even in our internal affairs.

If those who make such statements mean what they say, Washington is obviously preparing for anything but the event agreed between us. The meeting at summit level is intended for talks on the basis of equality, not for signing an act of surrender . After all, we have not lost a war to America, not even a battle, and we owe it nothing whatsoever. Just as, by the way, the United States owes nothing to us.

If statements are not serious, then war-like rhetoric is all the more inappropriate. Why should one flex one's muscles and vociferate needlessly or apply methods of domestic political struggle to relations between two nuclear powers? Here the language of power politics is useless and dangerous. However, there is still some time to go before the summit and much can be done to make it constructive and useful, which, as I am sure you understand, depends on both sides.

Question. What is your opinion of the research programme of the strategic defence initiative in the context of Soviet–US relations? Do you see an opportunity for a mutual arrangement banning the development of such systems, and what kind of verification would be acceptable to the Soviet Union in such an event? What trend of developments do you foresee in other aspects of arms control, if such an arrangement fails to materialize?

Answer. Official Washington, in answering the critics of the so-called strategic defence intitiative, likes to invoke an argument that it probably thinks devastating — that the star wars programme is opposed by no one except the Russians. Hence it is a good and correct programme. However, if such logic prevails in the nuclear age, we have nothing to expect but a very gloomy future.

We have a different approach to this problem just as, I hope, many Americans have. We believe that in certain situations both sides are bound to lose. These are nuclear war, the arms race, and international tension. And conversely, there are situations in which both sides stand to win. These are peace and co-operation, equal security, and abolition of the menace of nuclear catastrophe.

As far as our assessment of the Star Wars project is concerned, we cannot take seriously the assertion to the effect that the SDI ensures invulnerability to nuclear attack and will thus render nuclear weapons useless. In the opinion of Soviet and, to the best of my knowledge, many American experts this is a vain dream, castles in the air. Moreover, even within the much more modest limits where the SDI is, in expert opinion, feasible as an antimissile defence system of limited effectiveness, it is extremely dangerous. This project would indisputably step up the arms race in all directions and increase the risk of war. Therefore, this project brings no good to you, and to all the people on earth.

We view what is called the SDI research programme from the same angle. First of all, we do not consider it a research programme as such. In our view, it is the first stage of a project to develop a new antimissile defence system, which was banned by the relevant treaty of 1972. Just think of its scope alone: it is planned to earmark 70 thousand million dollars for it in the coming few years. This is an incredibly large sum for fundamental research, as is pointed out, in particular, by American scientists. Indeed, in today's prices it is four times the cost of the Manhattan Project, the programme of developing the first atomic bomb, and more than twice the cost of the Apollo Project, which provided for a full decade of space exploration, including man's landing on the moon. Other facts, including the planned tests of strike space weapons systems, also indicate that it is not just a programme of fundamental research alone.

Therefore, the SDI programme as a whole and its so-called research part mean a new, even more dangerous round in the arms race, which will inevitably lead to a new crisis in Soviet–American relations. To ward off this danger, it is necessary to prevent an arms race in outer space, as the Soviet Foreign Minister and the US Secretary of State agreed in January. We are confident that an agreement to this effect is practicable and verifiable. I want to note that we trust the American side no more than they trust us, and hence we are equally interested in making every agreement subject to reliable verification.

If no such agreement is concluded, it will be impossible to reach agreement on nuclear arms limitations and reduction. The relationship between defensive and offensive armaments is so obvious that it needs no arguments to prove it. Thus, if the present US stand on space weapons is its final stand, then the Geneva talks have no meaning at all and this should be stated frankly.

Question. Since your election as General Secretary you have taken several steps to improve the state of the Soviet economy. Could you name some further steps you hope to undertake? What, in your opinion, are the main problems of the Soviet economy? What changes in the world economy could benefit the Soviet Union?

Answer. I shall begin with a look at history. There were problems that could not be blamed on us in any way. The Soviet Government had inherited a grim legacy from the old regime: a backward economy, strong survivals of feudalism, widespead illiteracy.

Add to that two devastating wars that laid waste a large part of the country, ruining or reducing to ashes much of what had been built by the hard work of the people. Some losses were irreplaceable: twenty million dead in the Second World War, millions wounded and crippled. It is forty years since then, but the bitter memories of the war are still alive among the people. To heal the bleeding sores in their hearts and on the face of their land the Soviet people needed peace more than anything else.

It was often predicted in the West that it would take the USSR fifty to a hundred years to recover from the ravages inflicted on it by the Nazi invasion. The Soviet people accomplished what seemed an impossible task and restored the economy in a record time. It is a fact, however, that wars and post-war economic recovery took a toll of at least two decades of our post-revolutionary history.

In a complicated situation, relying on the potentials of our system, we transformed the Soviet Union into one of the world's greatest economic powers. This is a vivid illustration of the viability and enormous advantages of socialism.

At the same time, there are difficulties of a different kind caused by our own mistakes and omissions. We are discussing them openly. We do not always work well enough, we have not yet learned to manage affairs the way required by the modern economy and our enormous potentials: our resources of raw materials and skilled manpower; our highly advanced science, particularly fundamental research; and, as we now see, the willingness and eagerness of the people to work better, more efficiently, more productively.

The times imperatively demand a drastic improvement in the state of economic affairs. This has given birth to the conception of accelerated socio-economic development. This is a task of top priority and crucial significance for us today. After comprehensive discussion we have outlined the ways to accomplish it. We intend to improve the efficiency of capital investments and to attach first priority to developing such key industries as general engineering, electrical engineering and electronics, power engineering, transport and others.

The industries of the agro-industrial complex, particularly farm produce-processing and storage facilities will also remain in the focus of our attention. In general, we will do whatever is necessary to meet the demand for high-quality foodstuffs more completely.

Improvement of the operation of the national economy will require further reinforcement of centralized management in the strategic sectors: a stricter subordination of industries, regions, and individual sectors of the economy to the interests of economic progress. However, we will simultaneously reinforce the democratic principles in management, widen the operational autonomy of production associations, factories and plants, collective and state farms, developing self-government at local level and encouraging initiative and enterprise, naturally, in the interests of society as a whole, not to its detriment.

In short, we are searching for the most rational methods of economic management. Large-scale economic experiments are being staged, with the object of creating a more efficient mechanism of management capable of speeding up drastically the rates of scientific and technological progress and improving the use of all resources. We are trying to employ in the implementation of this task all the levers of material and moral stimulation, such instruments as profit, price formation, credit and cost accounting. This constitutes the essence of our work to improve radically the entire system of planning and management.

At the same time, we rely upon other reserves for accelerating economic development. I have in mind reinforcement of discipline and order, and the stiffening of demands on all — from the rank-and-file worker to the government Minister, in the struggle against laxity and red tape, and in the cultivation of labour ethics and the promotion of social justice in all areas of the life of society.

So we have enough work and economic problems on our hands, but just name one country where they are non-existent! We are aware of our problems and we are confident of the potentialities of our social system and our country. I have recently visited various regions and met quite a few people — workers and peasants, engineers and scientists. What is characteristic of their attitude? The need for a breakthrough, the need for resolute steps to improve work is not only realized by the people but also demanded by them, and this is becoming a veritable dictate of the times.

I wish to emphasize that the attention we have been giving to the economy in recent time is not motivated by the intention to break records in the production of metal, oil, cement, machine-tools or other goods. Our main aim is to improve the life of the people. No other aim has greater value to us. In this year alone decisions have been taken to increase pay rates for a number of categories of public health personnel, research scientists, engineers and technicians; to improve material benefits for a large contingent of pensioners; to provide annually, free of charge, about a million subsidiary plots for gardening and making what you call a "second home". Many other steps are being planned, too. Their scope will naturally depend on successes in the economy. Positive signs have been seen here of late: the growth rates of industrial production and labour efficiency have been on the upgrade.

You have asked me what changes in the world economy could benefit the Soviet Union. First of all, an end to the arms race, though this is politics more than economics. We would prefer to spend every ruble that goes into defence today for civilian, peaceful needs. You in the United States, I presume, also have areas where you would prefer to invest the money being wasted on arms manufacturing today, not to speak of the problems generated by the budget deficit and the national debt. The problems of other countries should also be considered. Insisting on the need to end the arms race, we are also motivated by the idea that it is immoral to waste sums running to thousands of millions on manufacturing tools for exterminating man in a world where hundreds of millions of people are starving and are deprived of the bare necessities. All of us simply have no right to ignore the prevailing situation.

As far as the world economy itself is concerned, we believe that the Soviet Union and other countries would benefit from a stabilization of the general economic and monetary-financial situation, a just solution to the problem of foreign debts and progress towards a new economic order. And, of course, the lifting of discriminatory restrictions and all other obstacles to the development of world trade, and further deepening of the international division of labour, in which we and our allies are going to play a more active part. All the peoples on earth would benefit from such changes. For instance, establishing broad trade and economic relations between the Soviet Union and the United States would help create hundreds of thousands of jobs in your country.

Question. The Soviet Union is seeking to gain greater access to the high technology developed in the United States. How much is it needed by the Soviet Union and, most importantly, for what purposes? If the United States does not grant greater access to this technology, where are you going to get it?

Answer. The very wording of your question suggests reflection. Is there anyone, after all, who is not seeking to gain access to high technology today? All are seeking it, including the United States, the latter even more than anybody. I mean not only the illegal buying of licences and science-based commodities, or industrial espionage. The United States also resorts to its own specific methods. For instance, the "brain drain", not only from Western Europe but from the developing countries as well. Or take a look at the operations of the transnational corporations which lay their hands through their subsidiaries on scientific and technological achievements of other countries. Now attempts are in evidence to use the so-called Star Wars research programme for the same purposes.

As far as the Soviet Union is concerned, it is taking advantage of the achievements of foreign science and technology on a far smaller scale. However, we have never concealed our willingness to widen our participation in the international division of labour and develop scientific and technological co-operation, but we are going to this market not as beggars; we are not empty-handed.

Those who are spreading their story of the Soviet Union's alleged craving for American technology seem to have forgotten what our country is today. The Soviet Union has long become a great power in the field of science and technology, since winning technological independence after the Revolution. This enabled us to hold out in the Second World War, to launch a wide-scale programme of space exploration, to guarantee our dependable national defence and to develop successfully the country's productive forces as a whole. Incidentally, how is one to interpret this contradiction in American arguments? When arguments are needed to warrant military appropriations in the United States, they make a point of stressing the Soviet Union's fantastic achievements in technology. When a justification is sought for prohibitive measures, however, the Soviet Union is depicted as a backward village, trading with which — let alone co-operating with it — would be tantamount to undermining one's own "national security". Which of these statements is true? What is one supposed to take as credible?

We are frankly admitting our dissatisfaction with the scientific and technological standards of certain lines of products. However, we expect to achieve a speed-up in scientific and technological progress not by a "technology drain" from the United States to the Soviet Union but by introducng the most progressive ideas, discoveries and innovations of Soviet science into Soviet industry and agriculture, by more skilful use of our own scientific and technological potential. This is the clue to our plans and programmes.

At the same time, we have no intention of renouncing the additional advantages accruing from scientific and technological co-operation on a basis of equality with other countries, including the United States.

In the seventies this co-operation assumed fairly wide scope in power engineering — nuclear power engineering in particular, in chemistry and space exploration, in cardiology and oncology, and in other fields. It was mutually beneficial, which is known to American scientists as well as ours. Now this co-operation has been reduced to nil. We regret this fact, but I can assure you that we shall survive it. After all, the United States has no monopoly on scientific and technological achievements.

Aware of this fact, the United States is putting growing pressure on its allies to prevent their trading in science-based goods with us. Moreover, the United States has imposed an embargo on exporting some categories of such goods to Western Europe on the very same pretext of "national security", and more and more often bars West Europeans from its research laboratories and scientific symposia.

This is, of course, meant as a measure to disadvantage us. But not us alone, however. The United States is using the bogey of a "Soviet menace" ever more widely in its competitive struggle against its own allies in an effort to slow down their scientific and technological development and thereby undermine their competitive positions on the world market. These designs are increasingly obvious. I do not think, however, that other countries will resign themselves to the status of unequal partners who will have to give away their own technology and subsist on starvation rations themselves. This is on the whole a near-sighted and hopeless policy.

However, I would not like to finish our discussion on this pessimistic note. It is perfectly clear that if two such great powers as the United States and the Soviet Union, with their enormous scientific and technological potential, will co-operate in this sphere on an equal footing, this will benefit not only our two nations but the whole world as well.

I avail myself of this opportunity to convey to the readers of *Time* magazine my wishes for high achievements, a happy life and a peaceful future. On behalf of the Soviet leadership and the Soviet people I wish to tell all Americans the most important thing they must know about the Soviet Union: war will never come from our country; we will never unleash war.

M.S Gorbachov. I would like to express here a few ideas which, I believe, are of great significance for a correct understanding of the problems discussed in my text.

I must say that in recent times I have received quite a few requests for public statements and interviews from the mass media in various countries. Why have I decided to meet the request of *Time* magazine?

When I read your questions, I felt that their wording expressed definite concern about the character of relations taking shape between our two countries today. We do not often hear an expression of concern about these relations from representatives of American political and other circles. I reasoned that the character of the questions of *Time*, if I interpret it correctly, is very important in itself.

There is another reason, no less important. It is linked with our assessment of the situation prevailing in the world today. This is a complicated, tense and, I would even say, explosive situation. I will not speak here about the causes of this process. You know our viewpoint on this score. I would rather answer the question as to where all of us stand at the present time and what kind of a world we are living in. In so doing I do not intend to dramatize the situation at all. However, I intend to be frank with you, because much depends on its assessment by both sides. We believe that as far as the leaders of such powers as the United States and the Soviet Union are concerned, their analysis of the situation and their practical policies must be pervaded with a feeling of great responsibility to their own peoples and to all humanity.

The realities of our time are such that the development of science and technology may result in a perfectly new situation and trigger off a perfectly new stage in the arms race. I have tried to answer your question frankly, and I hope that you will not interpret my answers as just another barrage of "propaganda". Indeed, it is a hard fact that the United States and the Soviet Union already find it very difficult to come to terms and take any steps to meet each other halfway. So great is their mutual mistrust. If the arms race enters a new stage, if the most up-to-date achievements of science and technology are used for its purposes, is it not likely that one of the sides will be tempted to take advantage of its imagined superiority over the other side to free its own hands and take the fatal step? These are indeed highly responsible times.

For all the difficulties in our bilateral relations, certain limitations continue to operate today: the existence of a military-strategic parity which guarantees a definite degree of security to both sides, the Anti-missile Defence Treaty, the SALT2 Treaty, which is being practically observed by both sides, the Treaty banning nuclear tests in the three environments. These limitations do exist and have their influence on the situation. It is known, however, that efforts to undermine them are already in evidence; some forces are at work to lift these restrictions, which are obstructing an escalation of the arms race.

If all these restraining factors were removed from the scene, the contest in developing ever new types of weapons would assume unprecedented intensity. Indeed, any steps taken in this direction by one side would be followed by counter steps by the other side, as surely as the invention of a new poison is followed by the invention of an antidote. Such are the lessons of history, which should not be ignored.

Where should we find ourselves then?

I would put it this way: our time is running out; if we fail to act fast enough we may be late for the train. Such is the second motive for my consent to a *Time* interview.

All people want to live; nobody wants to die. Therefore the leaders of states must muster their political courage and check the growth of this menacing process. It is imperative to end the arms race, to begin disarmament and normalization of relations.

I have already had an occasion to state in a discussion with a delegation of the US Congress led by its speaker, O'Neill, which visited Moscow, that we are resolutely in favour of normalizing Soviet-American relations. Such is the stance of the Soviet leadership. We draw sober and realistic conclusions from the prevailing situation. It is an indisputable fact that not only do we appeal for the normalizing of the situation and improving of relations but we are also coming forward with very concrete proposals and taking practical steps in this direction. Naturally, we are expecting reciprocity from the American side.

Unfortunately, in response to all our attempts to break the vicious circle of the arms race and mutual distrust we hear only a negative answer: "No! No! No! Propaganda! Propaganda! Propaganda!" Really, serious political leaders should not behave like that in relation to their partners.

Nevertheless, we hope that the comments we have heard from Washington about the Soviet Union's latest steps, including our proposals designed to lend momentum to talks on the non-militarization of outer space, on strategic nuclear arms, on intermediate-range weapons and on our decision to end nuclear explosions etc. are not the final say of the US Administration. This is our fervent hope.

Gentlemen, I regard this part of our discussion, when we are looking each other in the face, as the most important one. We hope that your understanding of the situation which has taken shape in the world and in Soviet–American relations, and of our idea of what is to be done in this situation, will be clearly and conscientiously brought to the knowledge of the American public.

Our two countries simply cannot afford to allow the situation to grow into a full-scale confrontation. A lessening of tensions meets the genuine interests of the Soviet and American peoples. This must be translated into the language of realistic policy. We must check the arms race, begin disarmament and normalize Soviet–American relations. Indeed, it is time that relations between our two great nations were made consonant with their historic role. After all, the destiny of the world, the destiny of world civilization depends on these relations. We are prepared to work in this direction.

Another reason why the situation is deteriorating so sharply is the political atmosphere in Washington, which is being steadily aggravated, judging by the information available to us. Statements which are made there cannot but cause surprise and resentment.

The White House and other representatives of the US Administration give us to understand that any agreement with the Soviet Union on a limitation of the arms race is out of the question. They declare that the most one can expect is the acquaintance of Soviet and American leaders with each other and the drawing up of an agenda for discussions in the coming few years and even decades. That was the tone of the interview with such representatives of the US Administration as Armacost and Tower published a couple of days ago. In short, strenuous efforts are being made to forestall any possibility of agreements between the United States and the Soviet Union on ending the arms race and preventing the militarization of outer space. It is declared quite frankly in Washington that whatever the Soviet Union may undertake, the United States will go ahead with its programme of developing strike space weapons and anti-satellite systems. That is, indeed, something like hammering in nails, cutting off their heads and urging somebody else to pull them out with his teeth.

What is to be done in this situation? We must check this process. This will meet the interests of the Soviet Union and of the United States.

There have been many attempts in the past to exhaust the Soviet Union and bring it to its knees. All of them have failed, and any such attempts will come to nothing in the future.

As far as we are concerned, we are not declaring that the United States is an "evil empire". We know the United States and the American people for what they are, and we know what role they play in the world. We are in favour of a new and better stage in our mutual relations. However, if it comes to the qualitatively new spiral in the arms race, to which I have referred, this task will be far more difficult to implement, if — indeed — it will be possible at all. This is why we are calling on the United States to come to a serious agreement with us on strategic nuclear arms, on intermediate-range weapons and on the problems of outer space.

Now, I feel, I have said what matters most. Let me hand over to you the text of my answers to *Time*. I have signed it, so nobody can accuse you of publishing anonymous answers. You can see that its cover is green. There is no hint of the export of revolution here.

G. Grunwald. Mr General Secretary, we are happy to be here and have this interview. We are very glad that you have so generously alloted us time to convey your ideas related to this publication. We are also concerned about the state of Soviet–American relations, and this concern is shared by many.

You have spoken here about some persons in Washington who want to undermine relations with the Soviet Union. However, President Reagan has repeatedly stated that he feels no hostility towards the Soviet Union, desires to improve relations with it, and does not seek military superiority over your country. Do you accept these assurances? What is your general impression of President Reagan?

M.S. Gorbachov. I have touched on this subject in my written replies. We took note of some positive statements by the US President in 1983 and 1984 — his speech at the United Nations in particular. We took note of his statements to the effect that nuclear war is impermissible,

and that there would be no victors in nuclear war. This is very important. We also took note of his statement that the United States does not
seek military superiority over the Soviet Union. These and other positive
ideas in the President's pronouncements offer — it seems to us — an
opportunity jointly to take a look into the future and to overcome the
present negative trend in our relations. We believe that much can be
remedied by our mutual steps to meet each other halfway. This is why
we have agreed to a meeting with the President at Geneva. This is also
the reason for our sharp reactions to what is said in Washington in
connection with this meeting. As one American lady journalist said,
the American public is being persuaded to applaud the Geneva meeting even if it results in nothing but an exchange of ballet troupes.

We have serious intentions and are preparing serious proposals for
this meeting, no matter what is said by right-wing and other figures in
President Reagan's circle. If we did not hope for a positive outcome of
the meeting we would not have agreed to it. Such is our stance.

You have asked me about my personal view of the President. I have
never met him, and it is hard for me to tell what kind of person he is.
On the political plane, however, we proceed from the fact that the
President has been elected by the American people. The Soviet people
respect them, and we are prepared to do business with him.

G. Grunwald. Let me ask you a question concerning space weapons.
In your written replies to our questions and in the discussion with us
you have said that the Soviet Union is in favour of reaching agreement
in three areas: strategic offensive arms, intermediate-range nuclear
weapons and space weapons. However, comments reaching us from
Moscow create the impression that you leave no room for negotiation
on the problem of space weapons, since you insist on complete
cessation of all work on this type of weapon, beginning with research.
So I want to know if the Soviet Union is prepared to hold negotiations
on the problem of space weapons. As we know, you have also carried
out and are today doing wide-scale research in this area and you
evidently realize that this work cannot be stopped completely on the
basis of negotiations. It is only possible to come to terms on some
agreed levels or limits.

M.S. Gorbachov. It is indeed, a question of principle. If there is no
ban on the militarization of outer space and no prevention of an arms
race in outer space, there will be nothing to agree upon. This is our
firm view. It is based on our very careful assessment of the situation

and consideration of the security interests of both the Soviet Union and the United States. We are prepared to hold negotiations but not on space weapons, not on specific types of these weapons to be deployed in outer space but on measures to prevent an arms race in outer space.

The Soviet Union has proposed an agreement to be reached at Geneva on banning development, including research and development, testing and deployment of strike space weapons. It is mandatory to secure a ban on all stages of developing this new class of armaments. Indeed, research is part of the programme of developing space weapons. When we learn of outlays running to tens of thousand-million dollars for this research in the United States, we realize with perfect clarity the true intentions of those masterminding such programmes and the implications of the policy ensuing from them in relation to deploying weapons in outer space.

Speaking of research in the relevant field and the need to ban it, we do not have in mind fundamental science, of course. This kind of research is in progress and will evidently be pursued further. In the United States, however, research is conducted under assignments and contracts from the Defense Department up to a stage where mock-ups and test samples are bound to appear and where field trials and tests other than those in laboratories are indispensable. In short, this stage includes all that is necessary for the next stage of developing and manufacturing the relevant weapons systems.

When the United States inquires whether the relevant ban is verifiable we say "Yes, it is." At the stage I have just spoken of verification by means of national monitoring facilities is possible. If we can now read the licence plate numbers of motor vehicles from outer space we can certainly watch field tests outside laboratories. The main idea here is that if this research is stopped at its initial stage all interest in the subsequent stages of space weapons development will be lost. Who will indeed agree to make investments that will go to waste?

On the other hand, if tens of thousand-million dollars are spent on research, nobody will be willing to stop halfway. And when weapons are stationed in outer space, the process will get out of hand, and we shall find ourselves, as I have said, facing developments with unpredictable consequences.

In the meantime, the opposing side will not be sitting on their hands, you can be sure of that.

Arguments about pure research under the SDI programme are

basically intended to conceal the large-scale process of developing space weapons systems.

The US plans to test a second generation of anti-satellite systems are fraught with new dangers. We shall be forced to meet this new challenge effectively. It is in effect a question of testing some components of space-based anti-missile defence. In addition, we have to take account of Washington's negative attitude to our proposal for the US to join in our moratorium on nuclear explosions.

The US Administration has refused to end tests because these are needed for developing nuclear power sources for the laser systems of anti-missile defence. These are, in fact, components of a future space-based anti-missile defence system. What will happen if the programme is pursued on a full scale? The United States ought to give serious thought to the consequences of that.

Evidently, somebody in the United States has got the idea that now there is a good opportunity to gain an advantage over the Soviet Union and drive it into a corner. This is a delusion. Such efforts have failed in the past and will fail now. We will find an effective way to meet this challenge. Then, however, all negotiations will be buried, and I do not know when it will be possible to resume them. Perhaps this prospect satisfies the US military-industrial complex, but we at any rate are not going to work for it.

Our proposals meet the interests of both the Soviet people and the people of the United States. This is what is causing the greatest resentment of the mouthpieces of the military-industrial complex. There are many of them in the United States, in its government in particular, and we feel that, of course. I must say, however, that we have an enormous reserve of constructive initiative. We will continue to call on the US Administration to choose a different approach. This would open great opportunities for co-operation in solving the problems of strategic nuclear arms and intermediate-range weapons and would pave the way for effective efforts to improve relations between our two countries and to find a solution to other international problems.

I recall my recent visit to Dnepropetrovsk, where a worker asked me: "What is this Star Wars programme proposed by President Reagan? Won't the United States cheat us?" I told him this: "Don't you worry. We won't let them cheat us. But if our partners in negotiations show a willingness to seek mutually acceptable settlements we will do our best to that end."

I believe that our stance is humane and unselfish; it is fully consis-

tent with the interests of the Soviet Union and the United States —
and all other nations, for that matter.

Indeed, do you Americans have no other ways to spend your
money? We know you have your own problems demanding a solution.
Perhaps we are not as familiar with them as with our own problems,
but we do know that they exist.

R. Cave. I have two questions. Your words suggest concern about
certain events connected with statements and actions of the United
States during the last few weeks. I have in mind, in particular, the
announcement of the forthcoming test of an anti-satellite system, as
well as the very strange story of a chemical allegedly sprayed on
Americans in Moscow. Evidently, these two events cannot be viewed as
helpful to intensive preparations for the coming Soviet-American
summit. Were you surprised by these events? Have they caused grave
harm to the preparations for the summit?

M.S. Gorbachov. As far as preparations for the Geneva summit talks
are concerned, I can assure you that we are preparing for it seriously;
we attach enormous significance to this meeting and are pinning great
hopes on it. Occasionally, it is true, we can hear pronouncements from
our partners which indicate that in Washington the significance of this
meeting is being played down, and it is described as something like a
fact-finding visit intended to draw up the agenda of negotiations to be
held in the distant future. However, it would be too much of an
indulgence for the leaders of two such states as the Soviet Union and
the United States to go to Geneva only to shake hands and then
admire the sights of Lake Geneva and the Swiss Alps. At a time when
the international situation is so explosive as today that would be a
luxury we cannot afford.

In short, we are seriously preparing for this meeting and will work
to the best of our ability to make it yield tangible results in the context
of normalizing relations between the Soviet Union and the United
States.

R. Cave. This week the US ex-President Richard Nixon published
an article in a certain magazine. He writes, in particular, that agreements on arms limitation or reduction without a simultaneous agreement on mutual restraint in the political behaviour of states will fail to
make peace more secure. In short, Mr Nixon evidently believes that it
is not the problems of arms control but potential seats of tension in
relations between the Soviet Union and the United States that have
first priority. What do you think of that?

M.S. Gorbachov. It is interesting to learn Mr Nixon's viewpoint as you present it. As for the specific problems we shall discuss with President Reagan at Geneva, we are working on them, keeping in touch with the State Department and the White House. This process is continuing, I would not like to go into particulars.

The name of Mr Nixon calls up in my mind associations of a different kind. At one time, despite a complicated situation, we managed to find the ways and means of organizing co-operation with the US Administration headed by President Richard Nixon. Highly important decisions were taken at that time.

Just recall the sixties. The international situation was quite difficult at the time. However, in 1963 the Treaty banning nuclear tests in the three environments was concluded, which is a very important agreement effective to this day.

This belongs to history, but history is good when lessons are learned from it. Now it is necessary, too, to take a look at the situation from a position of responsibility and national interest and to find the avenues of approach to normalizing the situation and improving Soviet–American relations.

G. Grunwald. Let me ask you a personal question. You have initiated a new style of leadership in the Soviet Union. You often appear in public, mingle with people; in short, you are in the public eye. Do you like this style of work? What benefits does it bring?

M.S. Gorbachov. First, this is the style of work taught to us by Lenin. He often spoke of the need to live in the midst of the people, to heed their opinion, to understand their sentiments and translate their aspirations into practical policy. So the true initiator of this style is Lenin, and such people as him appear once in a century.

Second, this is not a new style with me. I followed it when I worked in the Stavropol territory and here in Moscow before I was elected to my present post. Many people in our country are working in this style. Perhaps now the press gives greater publicity and wider coverage to my visits and meetings with various people.

On the whole, we need this style of work. We are faced with problems that are fairly large, and they should be solved in a new way. In the last few years we have carried out an analysis of the current stage in our development, and it is necessary to bring our conclusions to the knowledge of the working people, to elicit their opinion, and then to submit them to the forthcoming congress of our Party.

So it is not so much a question of my likes or dislikes as of the need to work in this style if the policy we have planned is to yield practical results.

G. Grunwald. Another personal question. You are the initiator of very profound changes in Soviet society. In the course of this process many high-ranking persons have been replaced. This will evidently continue. Would you say people are afraid of you?

M.S. Gorbachov. I don't think so. What is being done in this country now has not been planned by me alone. This is a reflection of the common opinion of all our leadership. We are convinced that our steps are correct. These problems have come to a head and are demanding solution. The main conclusion one arrives at after meeting with the common people is that our proposals and practical steps have their whole-hearted support. What is more, a desire to advance at a still faster pace is manifest within the Party and among the people. We believe that boldness and determination must be combined with circumspection. We will continue to work in the spirit of high responsibility to the people. The people are requesting us to pursue a firm policy in which words are corroborated by deeds. So we are under strict control in this sense. The fact that we are now working in a situation of greater publicity lends a new dimension to our democracy. So the question about fear is irrelevant. On the contrary, people welcome our approach.

You shouldn't think, however, that I am trying to depict everything in rosy colours. The profound process now in evidence in the country demands a revision of traditional concepts, whoever may hold them. Naturally, this affects individuals, cadres and the methods of work of all. The replacement of some cadres does not mean that we are faced with a state of emergency. This is a natural process. It is a bad situation when the process stops.

So it is not a question of replacements reflecting a political struggle around the problems we are solving today. We believe that a new style of work is necessary to all and everywhere — to us, in the Republics and regions, and in every work collective. This, of course, will demand great efforts by the Party. Since the line we have chosen reflects the demands of the day the people give it their resolute support. This makes us confident that we are moving in the right direction.

In conclusion, I wish to express what may be called the key idea of our discussion. It is a truism that foreign policy is an extension of home policy. If we accept this, please consider this question: Since we are making such breathtaking plans at home, what situation would suit us best abroad? Think about it.

15.

Message to the Indian Institute for Analysis of the Non-aligned Movement
Pravda, 7 September 1985

Dear Sirs,

I sincerely thank the leadership of the Indian Institute for Analysis of the Non-aligned Movement for their warm and friendly message and their enthusiastic expression of support for the Soviet Union's peace initiatives in pursuing its foreign policy aimed at lessening international tensions and removing the risk of nuclear war.

It will be recalled that the Soviet Union, guided by a desire to provide favourable conditions for concluding an international treaty on the general and complete prohibition of nuclear weapons tests, has repeatedly invited states possessing nuclear weapons to agree on a moratorium on all nuclear explosions. Unfortunately, this has not been achieved for the time being. Our latest initiative on this issue has not pleased everybody in the West. The US Administration is showing no desire to follow the example of the Soviet Union, which has unilaterally suspended nuclear tests until the end of the year. Washington is going ahead with its policy of escalating the arms race and nuclear testing. We believe that if the United States joined in our initiative, our moratorium could be prolonged, and the prerequisites for a general solution to the problem of ending nuclear tests would be significantly improved.

I wish to emphasize that the Soviet Union has been persistently advocating the abolition of nuclear weapons ever since they were first developed. We are determined to continue consistently our search for ways to remove the risk of nuclear war and preserve peace on earth.

Practical measures in the field of disarmament would release enormous resources that could be harnessed to the needs of mankind's peaceful development, in particular, to solving such acute problems as poverty, famine, disease, and illiteracy, which have not yet been eradicated in many of the countries that were subjected to colonial exploitation and plunder until quite recently.

The Soviet people highly appreciate India's contribution to the struggle for peace and the security of nations. The voice of the 700-million peace-loving people of India is heeded in Asia and throughout the world. As the acknowledged leader of the non-aligned movement, India is doing much for its consolidation and development.

It is our profound conviction that the dynamically developing relations of friendship and co-operation between the Soviet Union and India, and their allegiance to peace are an important factor in averting the danger of thermonuclear war and in preserving life on earth.

16.

For a Peaceful, Free and Prosperous Future for Europe and All Other Continents. Speech at the French National Assembly
3 October 1985

Monsieur le Président!
Esteemed Deputies and Senators!
Ladies and Gentlemen!

I am happy to have this opportunity to speak in the French Parliament, and to meet you, the elected representatives of the French people. May I avail myself of this opportunity to thank the President of the French Republic for his courteous invitation to pay a visit to your country. It is the second day of the visit of our delegation, and we have had important meetings. We have started an exchange of views on vital problems in our bilateral relations and international affairs. Of course, it is too early to sum up the results of our talks with President François Mitterand of France and other French statesmen. It is already obvious, however, that both sides are determined to give a new impetus to the development of relations between our two countries and, taking account of the present realities, to bring our positions on international problems closer to each other.

Talking with the President of the Republic and speaking before you today I naturally want the people of France to understand more clearly the main line of Soviet foreign policy. Like the foreign policy of

231

any state it is motivated primarily by its domestic requirements.

Let me touch briefly on this question. I think you know what a long and difficult path our country has traversed in the years of Soviet government. We inherited from imperial Russia extreme economic backwardness. Three-quarters of the population was illiterate. However, within a brief space of time, in historical terms, the Soviet Union has grown into a mighty power, modern in every respect, with a high standard of popular culture. We have done away with unemployment, and secured for the population such social benefits as free housing, free medical care and free education. I shall list a few figures to illustrate the country's economic progress. During the postwar years alone our national income has increased over 16-fold and the output of industrial goods 24-fold. The real income of Soviet citizens has grown sixfold over the period. Our pride in our successes does not make us complacent. We can see that at the present stage the greater maturity of society is facing us with new tasks which are on a much wider scale and are largely new in content. We are clearly aware of the short-comings still existing in our work and of the bottlenecks and problems which are at times grave enough. The chief objective we are pursuing today may be expressed in this concise phrase: to accelerate society's social and economic progress.

For this purpose we must bring about a significant rise in the level of the scientific and technological base of the national economy and in the methods of management, as well as in man himself — his awareness, habits, and skills. In short, we are determined to achieve a new, qualitatively higher state of society.

Our main task today is to make the economy more efficient and more dynamic, and the life of the people culturally richer, fuller, more meaningful; to develop socialist self-government of the people.

It is easy to understand that the most important pre-requisites for achieving these aims are not only secure peace, but also a tranquil, normal international situation. These priorities determine our foreign policy, in which we naturally seek to take account as much as possible of the interests and requirements of other peoples — all the realities of the present epoch.

Our world, a world of many faces and contradictions, is rapidly approaching the end of the century and the present millenium. It abounds in complex problems of a political, economic and social character. The existence on our planet of two social systems, each of which is living and developing under its own laws has long become a reality.

However, we must be aware of still another reality. It is the fact that the mutual links and interdependence between countries and continents are steadily growing. This is an indispensable precondition of world economic development, of scientific and technological progress, of accelerating information exchange, conveyance of passengers and commodities overland and even via outer space. In short, of the entire development of human civilization.

Unfortunately, the achievements of civilization are by no means always beneficial to people. The achievements of science and technology are much too often actively used to develop tools of war for exterminating man, for perfecting and building up ever more lethal types of weaponry.

In this situation Hamlet's famous question "To be or not to be" is facing not an individual but the human species as a whole. It is growing into a global problem. There can be only one answer to it: mankind and civilization must survive at all costs. This, however, can be ensured only if people learn to live together, to coexist on this small planet, and to take heed of each other's interests, however difficult it may seem. This is what we call a policy of peaceful coexistence.

We are strong enough to give a devastating rebuff to any attempt to encroach on the security and peaceful work of our people. We believe, however, that the rightness of one's ideology, the advantages of the system chosen by each people of their own free will should be proved not by force of arms but by force of example. This is our unshakeable conviction.

I told the President yesterday about our understanding of the main axis of contradictions, the struggle between the two tendencies in world politics. We regard as highly dangerous the view, whatever is invoked to justify it, that the problems facing the international community can be settled by developing and stockpiling ever new and ever more destructive types of weapons — on the Earth and in outer space. We also regard as dangerous those moves that sustain and aggravate international tensions. They are high enough as it is. They are so high that it has now become extrememly difficult to agree not only on complicated issues that brook no delay but even on relatively simple problems. If we do not stop the tendencies at work now, we may be unable to overcome their monstrous momentum tomorrow. It would be even more difficult to negotiate any issues then.

This is why we regard it so important to stop — immediately, before it is too late — the "infernal machine" of the arms race, to begin arms reduction, to normalize the international situation, and to develop peaceful co-operation among nations. This would be in our mutual interest; it is our common task. None of us can afford to stay aloof.

As you may know, the Soviet Union is not only making appeals but is also taking steps in this direction.

We have unilaterally halted the deploy of intermediate-range miss-iles in Europe and called on the United States to reciprocate. We have halted all nuclear explosions and called on the United States to follow suit. We are naturally addressing this appeal to all the other nuclear powers as well.

The Soviet Union is proposing a reduction in the armed forces and armaments of both sides in Central Europe, beginning with cuts in Soviet and American troops. Moreover, we are prepared to reduce our troop strength by a larger quantity than the Americans.

As far as outer space is concerned, we are in favour of using it exclusively for peaceful purposes and we are insistently urging the other side to come to terms on this issue, since an escalation of the arms race to outer space would make a reduction of nuclear arsenals objectively impossible. As you know, we have submitted our proposal for international co-operation in the peaceful exploration of outer space for discussion at the United Nations.

Now I want to inform you of the new steps taken by the Soviet Union. They pursue the same aim: to check the pernicious process of the arms race, and to ward off the danger of war hanging over mankind.

First. The other day we addressed the US Administration with a proposal to agree on a total ban on strike space weapons by both sides and on a truly radical, 50 per cent reduction in nuclear weapons which have each other's territories within their striking range.

In other words, we are offering a practical solution to the very same tasks that were agreed upon by both sides early this year as the aims of the Geneva talks: not only to halt the arms race but also to effect drastic arms reductions and simultaneously to prevent an arms race in outer space.

It is hardly necessary to explain how much all these measures would strengthen strategic stability and mutual trust.

I can inform you that the Soviet delegation at Geneva has been instructed to table specific proposals on this issue and to give our partners detailed explanations.

I am dwelling on this subject at some length because quite a few different versions and false rumours about our proposals are circulating in the West and it is time this issue was made clear.

Second. About the intermediate-range nuclear weapons in Europe. To facilitate agreement on their speedy mutual reduction, which — so we are often told — is very much wanted in Western Europe, we deem it possible to conclude the relevant agreement separately, without linking it directly to the problem of space and strategic weapons. This way, we believe, may prove practicable.

In this context I think it important to explain our position on such issues as the place of the nuclear potentials of France and Britain in the European balance of strength. These potentials are rapidly growing and we cannot shut our eyes to this fact any longer. It was pointed out by the French side that France's nuclear forces are not subject to discussion without its participation. This is reasonable. From this it follows that it is time we started direct discussions on this subject and attempted to find an acceptable way out by joint efforts. The Soviet Union is prepared for such direct talks with France just as, naturally, with Britain as well.

I wish to emphasize at the same time that we will thoroughly take the security interests of France into consideration. Today, it seems to us, there is no question of the reduction of its armaments on the agenda.

Third. You know that we have declared a moratorium on deploying intermediate-range missiles in Europe. The Soviet Union now has 243 combat-ready SS-20 missiles in Europe. This number exactly corresponds to the level of June 1984, when additional deployment of our missiles was started in response to the deployment of American intermediate-range missiles in Europe.

The SS-20 missiles additionally deployed then have now been removed from combat duty and the stationary installations for deployment of these missiles will be dismantled in the coming two months. This is verifiable. At the same time, our counter-measures in relation to the territory of the US itself remain in force.

I also want to explain the meaning we attach in this case to the term "European zone". This is the zone of deployment of intermediate-range missiles capable of hitting targets in the territory of Western Europe.

It would be relevant to add to this that the old and very powerful SS-5 missiles have been completely removed from service, and the dismantling of SS-4 missiles is being continued. This means that the total number of intermediate-range missile carriers in the European part of the USSR is now significantly smaller than it was ten or even fifteen years ago. In this self-limitation where we are guided by the broader interests of European security. I believe that Europe now is entitled to expect a reciprocal step on the part of the United States — termination of further deployment of its intermediate-range missiles in the continent of Europe.

You can see what serious steps are being taken by the Soviet Union. In combination with our earlier moves our latest proposals constitute, it seems to us, a complex of constructive and realistic measures, whose implementation would mark a real turning-point in the development of international relations. That would be a fundamental change in favour of peace, security and co-operation among nations.

This is, if you will, our programme of defusing the explosive international situation threatening the peace of the world. We expect the West to meet us half-way in response to our proposals.

I wish to emphasize that the implementation of our programme would also mean substantial progress towards a goal so eagerly desired by, and so vital to, all the nations of the world: the prohibition and complete elimination of nuclear weapons, mankind's complete deliverance from the danger of nuclear war.

There can be no victors in a nuclear war; all responsible political leaders seem to be in agreement on this point. It is time a practical conclusion was drawn from this fact: the nuclear arms race should be ended. We believe that this demand will be supported by all honest, realistically-minded political forces and public leaders, all people to whom their country, their own lives, and the lives of their children and grandchildren are dear.

The task of imposing a total ban on chemical weapons and eliminating their stocks is assuming growing urgency.

At the Disarmament Conference at Geneva the Soviet Union is taking an active part in working out a convention on this subject. We are meeting our negotiating partners half-way on a number of substantial issues — on verification in particular. I am confident that we can very well come to terms on dependable verification.

Incidentally, the following idea suggests itself in this matter. Since we have managed to achieve an agreement on nuclear weapons non-proliferation, why not extend it to chemical weapons? That would accord with the general trend of efforts to secure a total ban upon them. The Soviet Union is prepared to take part in working out an international agreement on the non-proliferation of chemical weapons. We are ready to do our level best to help establish a zone free from chemical weapons in Central Europe.

Speaking here in Paris, in the heart of Western Europe, so to say, I wish to touch upon some essential problems of European security and the way we see them in the Soviet Union.

I shall begin with the most general problem. What is, in fact, security in Europe? It is the absence of war and the risk of war. The interconnection and intertwining of the destinies of nations are especially strikingly manifest in Europe, for all the difference between the social paths they have chosen. Because of the geographic destiny and over-abundance of weapons, Europe is more vulnerable than any other continent to an armed conflict, let alone nuclear war.

This means that the security of Europe cannot be guaranteed by military means, by force of arms. This is a perfectly new situation which demands a break with the traditional ways of thinking and behaving that have taken shape over the centuries, even over millennia of history. The human mind does not adapt to whatever is new at once. This holds true of everybody. We sense that, and we have begun a re-evaluation of many habitual concepts to bring them into full conformity with the new realities, in particular in the military field and, of course, in politics. We would like such re-evaluation also to be made in Western Europe and elsewhere.

For the time being, fear of inevitable retaliation remains an obstacle to war and the use of military force. It is clear to all, however, that a lasting peace cannot be built on the balance of terror alone. The problem boils down to a quest for an alternative to terror — or deterrence, in the military lingo.

We are witnessing attempts to find a way out of this predicament through reliance on new weapons to be used in the so-called "star-wars". This is a delusion, and a highly dangerous one at that. Speaking in general, it is naive to believe that a stronger shield and a sharper sword can provide a solution to the security problem, or can make the world a safer place for all. Security in Europe and the world as a whole can be assured only by peaceful co-existence, the easing of tensions, disarmament, greater mutual trust and wider international co-operation.

This requires long and persistent efforts to clear the debris of the mutual suspicion, mistrust and prejudice accumulated over decades.

However, there is no other way to survival. Any long path is begun with the first few steps, which are sometimes especially difficult to take. We realize this fact, and we want to make this task easier to ourselves and to you. This is the motive of the aforementioned proposals.

This also refers to the Stockholm Conference discussing the important problem of confidence-building measures in the military field. As it seems to us, an outline of future agreements is gradually coming into view there. They provide for making the principle of the non-use of force as concrete and effective as possible. They comprise a certain range of confidence-building measures in the military field which are safeguards of their own kind against misinterpretation of the other side's moves in conditions of acute military confrontation. A number of states, primarily neutral states, have proposed agreeing on mutual exchanges of annual plans of military exercises, subject to notification. We are prepared to come to terms on this issue, hoping that it would help overcome suspicion and hamper secret preparations for war.

Ideas of setting up nuclear-free zones in various parts of the world, including our own continent — in Northern Europe and in the Balkans — are steadily gaining wide popularity. We support these ideas and are prepared to share in the relevant guarantees where necessary. We regard as useful the idea of establishing a corridor free from nuclear weapons on both sides of the line separating the two military-political alliances. We also believe that states which have no nuclear weapons in their own arsenals or in their territories are entitled to dependable international-law guarantees of their security, guarantees against nuclear attack.

Many aspects of all European co-operation are formulated in the Helsinki Final Act. We believe that it is an important achievement, and that the Act has retained its full significance to date. In the days when the tenth anniversary of the Helsinki accords was commemorated, all participants in the all European process expressed themselves in favour of its continuation. The Soviet Union is prepared to take the most active part in this process. Each European country has contributed a share of its national experience to it. This is the common property of the peoples of Europe, and it should be preserved and augmented by joint efforts.

The political climate in Europe depends largely on how the economic ties develop between East and West. An innovative approach is needed in this area as well. The tasks facing every country today in connection with industrial, technological and scientific progress can be facilitated considerably by an efficient international division of labour. We in the Soviet Union are prepared, in particular, for quests for new forms of co-operation and joint projects. This, of course, should be based on the principles of mutual benefit, equality, and good faith in business relations.

We deem it useful to have more effective business ties between Comecon and the EEC. The Comecon member countries have come forward with a constructive initiative in this direction, which seems to have met with a favourable response. It is important to see that it yields concrete results. At the same time, as declared earlier, to the extent that the EEC countries come out as a "political entity" we are prepared to seek common ground with them on specific international problems. This could be done in a variety of forms, including parliamentary ties, in particular with members of the European Parliament.

Unless the efforts of all European countries are pooled, it will be impossible to solve effectively such an acute problem as the preservation and improvement of the environment on the continent of Europe. In many of its areas, speaking figuratively, the earth is scorched, the sky is pouring out acid rain, if not a rain of soot, and is invisible behind the screen of smoke. The European rivers and seas are in a sorry state. At one time all of us evidently acted without sufficient foresight and generated problems that are simply unamenable to solution within a national framework. This is indeed an area in which all should become aware of the common destiny of our continent.

Much could be done in the vast area called "humanitarian".

Preservation by joint efforts of the cultural values of the past, cultural exchange, which mutually enriches the nations of Europe — one of the cradles of mankind's intellectual culture — is this not a field deserving keen attention? We are awaiting with interest such an extraordinary event as the cultural forum due to open in Budapest in a few days from now. This sphere also comprises an expansion of information on each other's life, encouragement of feelings of friendship and mutual respect. Mutual study of each other's languages is highly important from this point of view. Broad exchanges of schoolchildren, students and teachers are a promising field of co-operation too. It is important, moreover, for the younger generations to have the right ideas of one another if they are to build a peaceful Europe.

Another task of crucial significance is to pool our efforts to fight diseases, both old and new.

The Soviet Union attaches very serious significance to guaranteed human rights. This problem, however, should be free from hypocrisy and falsehoods and attempts to interfere in the internal affairs of foreign nations. Europe today is faced by such problems as the plight of migrant workers, mixed marriages and family reunion. We are in favour of approaching such problems in a positive and humane spirit with complete respect for the sovereign rights of all states.

Ladies and gentlemen! I believe that in the present situation it is crucially important not to allow the extension — as the medieval fanatics did — of ideological differences into inter-state relations. Stability in these relations, making them less vulnerable to political expediency, will strengthen stability in Europe as a whole.

We do not believe, for instance, that an everlasting taboo has been imposed on the possibility of setting up some form of contacts between the Warsaw Treaty and the North Atlantic alliance as organizations, let alone the overcoming of the division of Europe into opposing blocs in a more or less foreseeable future. As you know, we and our allies are offering precisely this. Even in a situation where two such blocs exist it is possible, in our view, to establish a modus vivendi that would take the edge off the present confrontation.

And, of course, today it is more important than ever before to develop an intensive political dialogue between East and West, to take advantage of all its time-tested forms, such as regular meetings at various levels, including, of course, the summit level, political consultations, and broad scientific and cultural exchanges.

We regard the development of parliamentary ties as a highly important matter as well. I wish to place strong emphasis on this point before this audience. I mean, of course, the development of parliamentary ties with France in particular. Deputies of the National Assembly and the Senate of France may rest assured that they would be welcome guests in Moscow. I declare this formally on behalf of the Supreme Soviet of the USSR.

Such are the general outlines of our ideas on how it is practically possible to normalize the situation on our continent and to enhance the role of Europe in overcoming the current phase of confrontation.

I shall add one more thing. Now it is more imperative than ever before to co-operate actively to eradicate seats of conflict and tension existing in various regions. One example of such co-operation is the fact that the Soviet Union and France, despite their affiliation with opposing military-political alliances, have much in common in their approach to a number of regional problems and situations existing today. Take for instance, the situations in the Middle East, Central America, Southern Africa, and other areas. Our contacts with French leaders are good evidence to this effect.

Proposing an expansion of goodneighbourly relations and co-operation with Western Europe, we by no means intend to play down the significance of a possible contribution to these affairs on the part of Canada, which is a member of NATO and a signatory to the Helsinki Final Act. Nor does our policy have any anti-American orientation.

Since there is much speculation on this subject, I would like to dwell on it in greater detail. The allegation to the effect that by improving our relations with Western Europe we are seeking to drive a wedge between it and the United States, to instigate a quarrel between them, is absurd. First, we are willing to maintain good relations not only with Western Europe but with the United States as well. And also with China, Japan, and other countries. We are not pursuing a Metternich policy of "balance of power", of provoking quarrels between states, of knocking together blocs and counter-blocs, of creating "axes" or "triangles" but a policy of global *détente*, promoting world security and developing worldwide international co-operation. Second, we are realists, and hence we realize the strength of the ties — historical, political and economic — linking Western Europe with the United States.

Esteemed Deputies! Mankind's most brilliant minds have warned of the dangers posed by the lagging of his mentality behind the rapid changes in reality. This is a fact of critical importance in our day. Man is already taking the first steps towards the distant galaxies, but how much still remains to be done on earth! No people and no state is capable of solving the existing problems on its own. However, the old burden of dissociation, confrontation, and mistrust does not let them unite in a common family.

I know that many in this audience are opposed to our views and our ideology. As a realist I am not trying to convert anybody to our faith. Individuals and peoples adopt a philosophy in their own way, through agonizing experience, after they have accepted it in their minds and hearts. For all the difference between our political and philosophic views our ideals and values, we ought to remember the main thing: all of us are guardians of the flame of life handed down to us by the past generations.

Each of them had its own mission, and each of them enriched world civilization in its own way. The titans of the Renaissance and the Great French Revolution, the heroes of the October Revolution in Russia, the heroes of the victory over fascism and the heroes of the Resistance — all of them fulfilled their duty to history.

But what about our generation? It has made great discoveries but it has also found "recipes" for the self-destruction of the human species. On the threshold of the third millenium it is our duty to burn the black book of nuclear "alchemy". May the twenty-first century become the first century of life without the menace of a worldwide holocaust.

We will perform that mission if we combine our efforts. The Soviet Union is prepared to make its contribution to securing a peaceful, free and prosperous future of Europe and all the other continents. We will spare nothing to achieve that future.

17.

Statement at a press conference held jointly with the French President François Mitterand, at the Elysée Palace 4 October 1985

The press conference was opened by President Mitterand. The next speaker was Mikhail Gorbachov. The following is his statement and replies during question time.

Monsieur le Président!

I feel I can take over from you. I would like to explain again why we have come to France. We in the Soviet Union believe that the current situation in the world has reached a point of development where responsible decisions and responsible actions are necessary, primarily on the part of the countries whose influence in the world is great enough. I have in mind the Soviet Union, the United States, France, Britain and other countries. The realities of today's world are such that we can build a better and safer world, secure progress and normalize the international situation if we embrace all this as our common cause.

For all the difference between our political systems, ideologies and world outlooks, all of us are facing the need to seek ways towards a world of trust, mutual understanding and co-operation. We are in favour of a dialogue. The Soviet leadership, at any rate, believe this is dictated by common sense.

For the Soviet Union, France is an important partner in any discussion of such problems. First, this is based on traditions. These traditions sustain our relations today: I think they will sustain them in the future as well. Speaking of traditions, I have in mind not only political contacts at government level. I have in mind primarily what has united our peoples for decades and for centuries. This is the solid ground on which Russia and France, the Soviet Union and France have always been able to meet at the most difficult periods of human history to discuss the most acute and vital problems and search for a solution to such problems. That was our motive for accepting President Mitterand's invitation to visit France. I thank you again for your cordial hospitality.

I shall add to what you have said about the fact — before and during this visit, which is now coming to an end — that our two countries were and remain within their own socio-political systems, each with its own ideology and membership of a military-political alliance, with which it was affiliated yesterday and will be affiliated tomorrow. Neither I myself nor *Monsieur le Président* had any intention to convert the other to his own faith in the course of our discussions. But does our affiliation with different systems and military-political alliances detract from the significance of the dialogue between the Soviet Union and France, between the General Secretary and the President

I believe that in a certain sense this even has its advantages. What the President has told you about our discussions and meeting held in these days — and I have had three meetings with the President face to face, not to speak of our discussions with other French political leaders — confirms this conclusion. It is highly important that the President is of the same mind. Each in his own situation, the leaders of the Soviet Union and France have been able to rise above the existing differences and analyze the processes taking place in the world, to compare notes and exchange opinions regarding the contributions the Soviet Union and France could make toward bringing about a change for the better in world developments and in the international situation. I think this is evidence of the great sense of responsibility for the destiny of the world on the part of the Soviet leadership and the leadership of France. This, I believe, is important for carrying on a dialogue and outlining ways of joint or parallel actions to normalize the world situation.

On the whole we have a high opinion of the discussions we have held with President Mitterand and other statesmen and political leaders of France in the last few days. These have been meaningful and constructive discussions. They were frank and marked with a spirit of mutual respect and good will.

Monsieur le Président has already touched upon the problems we discussed. Our discussions focused on the most burning problems of the present explosive international situation. We have understandable disagreement on a number of specific issues. However, the discussions brought to light our common understanding of the need to do whatever is possible to normalize the situation and remove the danger hanging over our people, and to facilitate a turn of developments from confrontation to a relaxation of tensions. Our meetings have convinced me that the French President holds the same view.

Monsieur le Président has remarked that the word *détente* figured in our discussions, but not because we were reminiscing of the past. This, I would say, was a lesson learned in the process of *détente*. I will not touch on the reasons why this process was slowed down and to a certain extent undermined. All of us felt an urgent necessity to return to *détente*, if one is to base his judgement on important criteria and regard the problems of preserving peace with a keen sense of responsibility. In this context the realistic possibility of a return to *détente* was mentioned here and in the course of our discussions on *détente*.

The main issue in our discussions was the practical ways of ending the current unprecedented arms race. While we have been staying in Paris, we have informed the President, the National Assembly, the public, and the people of France of our proposals submitted to the US leadership, which are already on the agenda of the Geneva talks. These problems are worrying not only the leaders of France and the Soviet Union, but also all the nations, all sober-minded political leaders, all those who have not gone crazy about the arms race, confrontation, and hostility.

I will not repeat our new proposals now. You know them. I would only like to say that after our exchange of opinions, which was fairly detailed, the French leaders and *Monsieur le Président* personally expressed their understanding of the importance of our proposals and their constructive potential. In these proposals we gave substance to what the Soviet leadership has been proclaiming during the last few months. The Soviet Union is prepared to effect drastic reductions in nuclear weapons, provided strike space weapons are not admitted to outer space. This is the gist of the problem. This approach is in accord with the understanding reached by the Soviet

Foreign Minister with the Secretary of State last January.

Our partners at the Geneva talks asked us a few weeks and months ago: what about your radical proposals? Such information reached our ears. Now, however, we hear the following from the same sources: why are you pressing your proposals so hard?

This reminds me of the tale of Khoja Nasreddin. When he was riding on a donkey through Bokhara, strangers joked: why should an old donkey carry a young ass? But when he hauled the donkey on his back and carried it himself, they mocked him.

We believe that it is time practical steps were taken. Why? Because we have come to a point where it is no longer enough to say: yes, we are for a better world; yes, we shall normalize the international situation. If this is not followed by practical steps, then we call it political demagogy, deception of the people.

In addition to the measures the Soviet Union took earlier unilaterally, we have put forward new radical proposals to lend a constructive spirit to the Geneva talks. We realize perhaps better than anybody, no less clearly than the Americans at any rate, what will happen to the world, if the arms race is not stopped now. This realization adds to our responsibility.

With the situation as tense as it is, a new spiral of the arms race, this time in outer space, would call into question the very possibility of negotiations. How, indeed, could we approach them in such an event? This should be realized by all. Incidentally, the press should also be up to the mark in realizing the gravity of the situation in present-day international affairs. You journalists work not only for your editors and those who finance your publications; your first duty is your service of the people. The general demand, as we understand and feel it in the Soviet Union, is that we should stop and think at last, to take a look around to see where we are, and to take practical steps in the right direction. This is a simple formula, a simple plan, but we believe that is the way to follow by all who have a sense of responsibility for the destiny of their own people and the destinies of other peoples. It is a proposal to begin a constructive search. We are prepared for it.

What I know of the results of the meeting of the Soviet Foreign Minister with the US President Reagan and State Secretary Schultz gives some reason for hope. What we heard from them was not the typical stereotyped "No! It's propaganda!"

I feel that sober, realistic ideas are taking shape in US public opinion, within political circles and in Congress. It is naturally hard for me to predict the moves of the United States. We hope, however, that at Geneva, where the next round of talks has got under way with our proposals on the agenda, and at our forthcoming conference with President Reagan the United States will approach this problem in a spirit of high responsibility. In this sense I share Monsieur Mitterand's opinion that there are problems directly concerning the Soviet Union and the United States and that the process of talks should be brought out of its deadlock and directed towards a normalization.

We in the Soviet Union are firmly determined to help improve the world situation.

At our talks in Paris we also discussed the problem of intermediate-range missiles. We want to bring this problem out of its present state, which is hard to handle. We are discussing this problem with the American side at Geneva as well. It is a fact that Pershing and cruise missiles are being deployed in Western Europe.

As an extension of our stand we have tabled new proposals concerning intermediate-range missiles. We believe, as I have stated to Monsieur Mitterand, that a new situation is being created thereby. In general, we have not listed and are not going to list the French nuclear forces on the "Soviet–American record".

Now we say that it would be useful to discuss this problem with France, as well as with Britain. We have an opportunity to begin an exchange of opinion with France, which may develop into negotiations at some stage.

We are not raising the question of reducing the nuclear potential of France and ending the implementation of its military programmes. This is a matter for France to decide. As we realize, France will approach this question from its own position, taking account of all the processes occurring in the world. We say this, however: let us begin a dialogue, let us examine this problem in the context of other problems. It may be possible to have some mobile equivalent for the relevant nuclear forces. At any rate, this would be the first step. We have already had a detailed exchange of opinion on this subject with Monsieur Mitterand. As I understand it, the President is not averse to a further exchange of views on this problem. We are also in favour of this.

We have sent a similar proposal to Mrs Margaret Thatcher through our Ambassador in London.

We have also explained the essence and significance of the unilateral step we have just taken, as a result of which the number of Soviet SS-20 missiles in the European zone is not larger than what we had in June of last year. The SS-20s additionally deployed have been taken out of commission, and their launching pads and related install-ations will be dismantled in the coming two months. Whoever wants to make sure of that can take photos if he likes. It is rumoured that we are going to haul these missiles to Asia. This is malicious gossip. Whenever the Soviet Union agrees on something, it always plays fair.

In Asia we have as many missiles as necessary to counterbalance the relevant US potential in that region — no more and no less. Unless the United States builds it up, we will keep that level. If the situation changes for the better, however, we will respond in kind.

The President and I have devoted a lot of time to the problems of European security. In this area we have a record of efforts made jointly with France. As you know, this record has enabled us to gain a substantial potential for co-operation that could be used to sustain the European process based on the Helsinki accords and lend it a new dimension.

Speaking in the National Assembly yesterday, I set out our stance on this whole range of problems. There is no need to reiterate it. The essence of the matter, it seems to me, is the continued allegiance of both sides — the Soviet Union and France — to the cause of develop-ing and deepening the all-European process, as the President has again stated now. We, like France, are in favour of implementing the provisions of the Helsinki Final Act in all its parts, and I am profoundly convinced that a normalization of the situation on the European continent would be of enormous significance for the rest of the world as well. The military-political alliances are in direct contact in Europe. Its peoples have learned important lessons from their own history. The Helsinki Conference has provided the legal basis for further progress along the path of co-operation and security.

At one time the Soviet Union and France were the initiators of the Stockholm Conference. I believe it is time the conference took resol-ute steps to work out agreements. Incidentally, in our opinion, which is shared by France, opportunities for stepping up the quest for mutually acceptable decisions are available here.

In our discussions with President Mitterand we paid due attention to a number of regional problems and existing seats of tension. We have mutual understanding in our assessment of some of them. On some other problems we have areas of disagreement in both analysis and approach. We are in agreement, however, on the need to stamp out these trouble spots by political means with full respect for the independence and sovereignty of each country. Within the framework of this exchange of opinion we have touched upon the situation in Southern Africa, the Middle East and Central America, and upon other problems.

We came to Paris with a desire to give a new impetus to Franco-Soviet bilateral relations. As I have learned, the President's stance agrees with our desire. The results of the discussion of these problems warrant hope for a more active political dialogue and more intensive economic co-operation and trade between the Soviet Union and France.

It is a pleasure to know that in the last few years the rate of growth of our economic ties and trade has accelerated: they have in fact doubled. However, their level today is far below the possibilities available to our two countries. Therefore, we have agreed to intensify our efforts, to encourage greater initiative to our relations in the sphere of trade and economic co-operation. An agreement has just been signed on these questions.

Quite a few concrete and interesting projects have come to light, some of them on a large scale. We welcome them. We believe that this will also contribute to normalizing the general situation.

As I have emphasized in the foregoing, we have agreed to develop our political dialogue. On behalf of the Presidium of the Supreme Soviet of the USSR I have invited the President to pay a visit to our country. He will be a welcome guest in the Soviet Union. If intervals between visits became shorter, there would perhaps be fewer outstanding problems. We have also discussed the following idea. There is a nuclear fusion project called Tocamac, in which the Soviet Union, France, the United States, Japan and other countries have been involved. It may be interesting to find out whether this project could be brought to completion by joint efforts in the present situation, so that our research could be geared to a practical effort to obtain a truly inexhaustible source of energy. This is a fascinating idea. It would be announced at the right time, because it is a peaceful idea, while there are other ideas being pushed in other directions. As our experts have told me, there is a realistic hope for implementing our project.

On the whole, the results of our talks are, in our view, favourable, even impressive. They are beneficial to the Soviet and French peoples and meet the broader interests of European and world security.

In conclusion, I shall avail myself of this opportunity to express our gratitude to President Mitterand, the government, political and public leaders of France, and all Frenchmen and women whom we have met during our visit here for their hospitality, their feelings of friendship and respect for our country and the entire Soviet people.

General Secretary Mikhail Gorbachov then answered correspondents' questions.

Question (French TV network "Antenne-2")

General Secretary, you have said that the Soviet Union cannot shut its eyes to the development of French nuclear forces. Do you want the level of French nuclear forces not to increase at all or to increase within moderate limits? In other words, do you think that the modernization of French nuclear forces should be discussed with the Soviet Union?

M. S. Gorbachov. I believe I have expressed myself quite unequivocally on this subject. We propose opening a direct exchange of views. All specific issues can be discussed in the process.

Question (Italian newspaper "*Secolo XIX*")

General Secretary, as I understand it, you have announced the dismantling of all Soviet SS-20 missiles over 243 units. I would like to know if you would confirm this. As far as a separate agreement on intermediate-range missiles in Europe is concerned, do you think it possible to find the basis for such an agreement in what was called the "forest promenade agreement" in 1982?

M. S. Gorbachov. I confirm that now a total of 243 missiles are in combat readiness in the European zone. This is exactly as many as in June 1982. The other missiles have been removed, and the stationary launching installations will be dismantled in the coming two months.

Our counter-measures related directly to US territory remain in force. As for the further process of talks on intermediate-range missiles, we have proposed a separate agreement on this type of weapon to intensify this process and lend it a realistic direction. Simultaneously we have proposed a direct exchange of views with France and Britain. In our opinion, this will enable practical steps to be taken. We are prepared to meet our partners half-way; I have in mind the United States and, as far as French and British missiles are concerned, France and Britain.

Question (BBC Television)

General Secretary, my question concerns the Soviet Union's relations with Mrs Thatcher. Why, in your opinion, should the British Prime Minister take a different stand from France on the problems of its own intermediate-range nuclear forces? Second, have you resigned yourself to the decision of Mrs Thatcher's government to expel Soviet diplomats?

M. S. Gorbachov. Concerning your first question, I think that until now Britain's stand on intermediate-range missiles has been shaping in a different situation. Today I invite the French President — I have already done so — and Mrs Thatcher to take a new approach in view of the radical proposals made by the Soviet Union. Indeed, this is a radical change in the situation. A new situation naturally demands a new approach. I agree with President Mitterand — and it would be strange if we had started to discuss this question only yesterday, and had opened negotiations and reached agreement today.

I remember, however, that Monsieur Mitterand, in particular, during his last visit to Moscow, when he was explaining his stand on the French nuclear forces, said that France is committed to the quest for peace and the disarmament process. In his opinion, now the Soviet Union and the United States should make their contributions in the first place, which by no means rules out France's joining in this process at some stage. Now a new situation is emerging and new opportunities are opening up. It was natural for me to invite the President to exchange views on this situation.

Concerning your second question. Every Embassy in the country of accreditation has instructions from its government to study the processes occurring there, to submit the relevant information to forestall whatever may be unpredictable in mutual relations and international problems. I believe that this information is a natural process. It embraces all countries. Whenever someone wants to poison relations or interfere with their normalization, whenever signs of an international dialogue or a relaxation appear, some forces immediately come on the scene and act in accordance with their social aims. They are always on the alert. These may be called "rapid deployment forces" for provoking a deterioration in the international situation. As for those who have involved Mrs Thatcher in this affair, when all Soviet personnel are indiscriminately labelled as spies, I do not know where they belong.

We proceed from the assumption that the Soviet Union is not interested in relations with Britain any more than Britain is interested in relations with the Soviet Union. I repeat that we are in favour of relations and a political dialogue, as well as economic relations with Britain, our long-standing partner. I believe my answer is exhaustive enough.

Question (GDR television)

Comrade Gorbachov, since the end of the Second World War the Soviet Union has put forward, I think more than 100 proposals aimed at strengthening peace and achieving disarmament. Are they still valid?

M. S. Gorbachov. It would indeed be not bad to return to some former good proposals, for instance, the one for general and complete disarmament, which has been little by little driven into some corner, and is now in the position of a Cinderella. This, however, is a fundamental problem. Indeed, if this proposal had been heeded in good time, I am sure we would not have found ourselves in the present world situation. All our proposals of this kind, which were made with a view to the future rather than as a reaction to some current situation, are still valid.

Question (Dutch television)

General Secretary, could you give the number of SS-20 missiles in all Soviet territory? You know that the Dutch government is to take a decision on American missiles on 1 November.

M. S. Gorbachov. Your leadership has been informed of our steps, and it has time to reflect on our proposals. As for information about the number and types of missiles, I think my answer would take too much time, all the more so as I spoke of Europe and the entire European zone, which extends very far, even beyond the limits of the Urals, up the eightieth meridian. I believe this is enough for the Netherlands.

Question (Radio Israel)

You insisted on the need for practical steps to be taken for solving the problems of the seats of regional conflicts. As far as the Middle East is concerned, wouldn't one of the Soviet Union's practical steps be a resumption of diplomatic relations with the State of Israel? If not, why not?

M. S. Gorbachov. You can feel from the reaction of this audience that

I may even not need to reply to your question in view of the obvious-
ness of my answer. But I will give you a reply. The situation in the
Middle East is grave, and the President has already said so. This is
causing concern in both the Soviet Union and France. We shall
exchange opinion with the French leadership in search of a better
solution to this problem. The Israeli leadership are pursuing a near-
sighted policy, if they are seeking to promote their national interests
by separate deals. They may bring only temporary success, but the
problem needs a radical settlement. The Soviet Union has invariably
taken part in the efforts to secure a radical settlement and normalize
the entire situation in the Middle East. The Soviet Union is determined to work in this direction in the spirit of high responsibility, to
prevent the situation in this region getting out of hand. It is imperative
to seek political avenues of approach to a settlement. Some quarters
are opposed to the Soviet Union's involvement. However, the Soviet
presence in the Middle East is an objective factor, and we are not
renouncing our role there. We are in favour of collective efforts, and I
share the French President's idea to this effect.

As for restoring diplomatic relations with Israel, I believe that the
earlier the Middle East situation returns to normal, the earlier it will be
possible to start examining this problem. There will be no obstacles to
us in that case. The Soviet Union took part in founding the State of
Israel, and we recognize the sovereignty of this state, and its right to
life and security. However, there is a wide difference between the idea
of security as the Israeli ruling circles interpret it and our idea of
security.

Question (American CBS television company)
Why not allow all Jews to emigrate from the Soviet Union, if they so
desire? Could you say how many political prisoners are held in the
Soviet Union?

M. S. Gorbachov. I have answered these questions in my interview
with French television. I have nothing to add.

Question (French TF-1 television company)
You said in your yesterday's speech that the world economy and
technological progress demand an exchange of persons and ideas. Is it
planned to open the Soviet Union's door wider in the near future and
allow Soviet citizens freely to come to the West and people from the
West to come to the Soviet Union?

M. S. Gorbachov. We believe that the Helsinki process covers all problems, including humanitarian problems and exchanges of ideas, information and tourists. We give our full support to all this.

I believe that as the situation steadily improves, contacts will grow wider. On the other hand, the wider the contacts, the faster the situation will improve. Anyway, when visits are not linked with attempts to use them for provocative political aims the door to our country is wide open to all. I shall give an example: a group of Americans from different towns of the United States made a sight-seeing trip on two steamboats along the full length of the Volga. I learned of that when they had come back home and were sharing their impressions of their travel. They said that whatever they had previously known of the Soviet Union had come from brainwashing. But what they saw in the Soviet Union — the people and the Soviet way of life — convinced them that these people were very much like themselves and had the same aims, thoughts, friendliness and aspirations. Therefore, if certain centres do not use the channels of human intercourse to introduce what poisons relations and do not interfere in our internal affairs, the Soviet Union would favour the development of exchanges on a basis of equality. The Soviet Union, however, cannot be talked to like some dozens of other states and governments, which are treated as nonentities. The Soviet Union can put anybody in his place, if necessary.

Question (The French "Europa-1" broadcasting company)

General Secretary, whenever we see you, we always receive good news from the Soviet Union. I would like to ask you what you have told the President about Sakharov, Shcharansky and Nudel.

M. S. Gorbachov. Whenever it is a matter of family reunion, mixed marriages and other humanitarian questions, it is examined by competent authorities with due attention. This is what I told the President.

Question (Radio Canada)

General Secretary, is it possible for the Soviet Union to avenge itself in Lebanon or protect its citizens, or does it find itself just as helpless as Western countries?

M. S. Gorbachov. I believe there is no reason to talk of helplessness. The influence of the Soviet Union and other countries, including France, is enormous in all cases, in this matter in particular. I can only say that we are strongly opposed to terrorist methods. They are unacceptable. We have expressed ourselves in categorical terms on this subject, and are now using all means at our disposal to find a solution to this problem. I think that whoever resorts to terrorism will fail to achieve his ends.

Question (GDR radio)

I also have a question to the General Secretary of the CPSU Central Committee. You have spoken much here in Paris about the non-militarization of outer space. As for peaceful co-operation in outer space, are there any new concrete plans of joint space ventures like the one three years ago?

M. S. Gorbachov. Yes, we will continue co-operation with France in these directions. We have a good record of experience in this area. We have even considered the idea of another joint space flight. We have exchanged views on this subject with the French President. We are committed to the idea of peaceful uses and exploration of outer space. Great successes can be achieved here. I believe you know of our proposals to this effect submitted to the United Nations. It may be useful to set up an organization with headquarters in Paris and launch a joint programme of peaceful exploration of outer space.

Question (The American ABC television company)

General Secretary, in your statement this morning you hinted at elements of political demagogy in the American reaction to your proposal for arms reductions. Were you referring to President Reagan? If so, does this not contradict your statements to *Time* magazine on the need to soften rhetoric in the period of preparations for the Geneva meeting?

M. S. Gorbachov. Now I wish to reaffirm everything I said in the *Time* interview. I would like to point out at once that my remark was based on information available. In my view, it would be irresponsible to create the impression of an exchange of propaganda fire between us. As far as Mr Reagan's position is concerned, I just said that we sensed for the first time — as Foreign Minister Eduard Shevardnadze told me — a serious attitude to our proposals on the part of the President and those who took part in the discussion. I mean Mr Schultz, Mr Macfarlane and others. We hope this will be so in practice. We have no intention to prejudice the security of the United States. We have no such plans. We have no intention to outplay the United States, and expect reciprocity on its part.

Question (French journalist)

President and General Secretary, have you identified any areas of agreement in your positions on the Middle East? If so, what are they?

M. S. Gorbachov. Monsieur le Président has spoken about that. We are prepared to take part in international, collective searches for ways to normalize the Middle East situation. I welcome such efforts.

Question (*The Guardian*, London)

Do you make the problems of strategic arms reduction contingent on a US consent to call off its space weapons development programme or do you regard these questions as interdependent? How much are you inclined to come to terms with President Reagan during the Geneva meeting?

M. S. Gorbachov. I think we should not anticipate the results of the Geneva meeting at this press conference. This is a serious matter, after all. We and, I hope, the American side realize this fact and are preparing for it accordingly. As for the specific part of your question, I shall say the following: we believe that we must agree on the non-militarization of outer space and on a radical reduction of strategic nuclear arms on earth.

Question (BBC)

General Secretary, President Mitterand has said that he is not prepared to open negotiations on intermediate-range missiles with the Soviet Union. Why?

M. S. Gorbachov. I don't know what gave you that impression. I have said that step by step we are maintaining the momentum of this process, make it more dynamic, and break out of the deadlock, and that opportunities are opening up for contacts with the Americans, as well as with France and Britain.

Question (journalist from Lebanon)

The Middle East capitals are looking forward with hope and concern to your meeting with President Reagan. They are apprehensive of its possible consequences. What is the place of this region in your order of priorities? What would be your reaction if the US delegation refused to discuss with you the destiny of this region which the United States regards as its backyard? We know your high-principled stand on the question of the Arab lands occupied by Israel, but what would be your practical stand if Syria resorted to arms again?

M. S. Gorbachov. Whatever happens in the Middle East concerns us.

We have never stood aloof from the search for a just settlement in the Middle East. This implies that foreign troops should be withdrawn from the occupied territories, that the Palestinian problem should be settled on the basis of self-determination, that the integrity and peaceful development of Lebanon, and the lawful rights of the Israeli people and the State of Israel should be guaranteed. It is in this direction that the search for a settlement should be pursued.

I believe that other approaches — by way of making separate deals and by-passing manoeuvres — can lead only to some provisional settlement but will fail to solve the problem as a whole and secure a lasting peace in the Middle East. Therefore, collective efforts are necessary in search of truly realistic ways out of this situation. What the Americans regard as a sphere of their "vital interests", as you say, is irrelevant. They declare their "vital interests" here and there. Let them think over this formula.

Incidentally, this is one of the causes of misunderstanding and conflict. If spheres of someone's "vital interests" are declared everywhere in the world, what will be left for the other people? For the world's two hundred states? The status of vassals perhaps? This is at variance with the principle of the development of nations on the basis of equality, the right of every people to sovereignty, to self determination. Indeed, this process often runs a painful course.

We do not conceal our stand. When the people of a country take the road of progressive reform, seek to plan their own independent policy, to form their own outlook in the spiritual sphere and to establish their own economic institutions, we welcome them. We take sides with these people.

However, as soon as we announce this, we can hear the invariable cry "Hand of Moscow!"

International relations are maintained in a changing and diverse world as regards political, cultural and economic development and different stages of progress. We must take every step in the spirit of awareness of our high responsibility. Imperial ambitions cannot be tolerated. This holds true of all powers, including the Soviet Union. We have never permitted and will not permit them.

18.

Message to the Special Session of the UN General Assembly commemorating the 25th anniversary of the Declaration granting independence to the Colonial Countries and Peoples
Pravda, 17 October 1985

Dear Sirs,

I extend my greetings to the high-ranking representatives of the member states of the United Nations who have assembled in New York for a special session of the UN General Assembly on the occasion of the 25th anniversary of the adoption of the Declaration Granting Independence to the Colonial Countries and Peoples.

The Soviet people are extremely pleased to recall that this Declaration, which has become an international anti-colonial manifesto of its own kind, was adopted in 1960 by the 15th session of the UN General Assembly on the Soviet Union's initiative.

Worked out by the collective efforts of many states, this Declaration has contributed to the cohesion of the freedom-loving forces of all continents and to mobilizing them for determined action to abolish the disgraceful system of colonialism, to secure the rights of the peoples to self-determination and independence, and their right to shape their own future in freedom, without foreign interference.

Within a historically brief space of time the colonial empires were overthrown, and dozens of newly-independent states of Asia, Africa,

Latin America, and Oceania joined the United Nations as fully-fledged members. The growing role played by these states on the international scene is a reality today.

However, the aims formulated in the Declaration have not yet been completely achieved. The United Nations cannot reconcile itself to the fact that the peoples of some twenty colonial and dependent territories are still denied their lawful right to freedom and independence. Seeking to preserve their domination of these territories, the imperialist powers are imposing various kinds of neo-colonial status on them and are converting them into military-strategic strongholds and bridgeheads for their own aggression. This is vividly illustrated, for example, by the annexionist moves in relation to the trust territory of the Pacific islands.

In southern Africa the racist regime of Pretoria, supported by its Western patrons, is attempting to perpetuate the colonial-racist system. Ignoring the resolutions of the UN and the demands of the world public, the racists of the Republic of South Africa are continuing their criminal policy of apartheid, refusing to grant independence to the people of Namibia, and perpetrating acts of aggression against neighbouring African states.

The policy of colonialism in any form and manifestation, including racism and apartheid is incompatible with the UN Charter and the Declaration on decolonization. The conscience of honest people throughout the world cannot tolerate the preservation of seats of colonialism on this planet.

It is the duty of the United Nations to take urgent steps to have the Declaration implemented in full, so that all colonial peoples and trust territories may acquire geniune political and economic independence and occupy their rightful place in the international community of states.

It is the duty of the United Nations to contribute in every way to accelerating the process of decolonization in the economic field, and to restructuring international economic relations on a just and democratic basis. The United Nations ought to voice its protest against the exploitation of the developing countries by multi-national monopolies, against the plunder of the natural resources of these countries, and against strangling them with a noose of debts, supporting their actions against "cultural", "informational" and other forms of neo-colonialism.

Success in implementing these important tasks is dependent to a decisive extent on progress in the cause of strengthening world peace and international security, bringing to a halt the wasteful arms race and returning to the policy of *détente*.

The Soviet Union is determined to continue its vigorous efforts to have the Declaration on Granting Independence to the Colonial Countries and Peoples implemented in full and without delay, and to contribute actively to the United Nations' efforts to abolish colonialism, racism and apartheid for good and all.

19.

Speech at a meeting with a delegation of the Nobel Prize Laureates' Congress
Pravda, 14 November 1985

Ladies and Gentlemen!

It was a pleasure to receive a message signed by eminent scientists, laureates of the Nobel Prize. I wish to tell you at once that the Soviet leadership regard this message as a document of enormous significance for all mankind. Its appeal to the two great powers to secure a change for the better in international affairs, to end the arms race and to prevent the military uses of outer space is in complete harmony with the sentiments prevailing in our country and the practical intentions of our leadership.

It would be no exaggeration to describe our time as a turning-point. Mankind has now reached a point which requires great wisdom in decisions, a sense of balance, restraint in actions, and consideration not only of the national interests of one's country but of the interests of the entire world community. I believe it is this idea that motivates the initiative of the Nobel Prize laureates.

We in the Soviet Union believe that no task is more urgent and crucial today than one of putting a stop to all the means of further stockpiling of nuclear weapons, their increasingly sophisticated types in particular, while simultaneously blocking the entry to outer space by weapons of any kind. This accords with the views and proposals we shall take to the Soviet–American meeting in a few days.

Our approach to this meeting is frank and honest. We are preparing to come to Geneva with a clear awareness of the responsibility resting on the leaders of all states, especially the Soviet Union and the United States. We are going to Geneva for serious and productive work and, I must say, our hands are not empty.

The Soviet Union wants the meeting to contribute practically to solving the central problems of our time, those of strengthening international peace and security, normalizing relations between the Soviet Union and the United States, ending the arms race and preventing its escalation to outer space.

We are profoundly convinced that it is particularly important for every thinking person to be fully aware of his personal responsibility for averting the danger of war.

Scientists, who are perhaps more clearly aware than anybody of the disastrous consequences of a nuclear war, should voice their protest against war, be it on earth or a "star war". This is how I view your message. We in the Soviet Union admire the humanistic tradition of genuine scientists, who have invariably taken an active stand on the problem of war and peace. That tradition was pioneered by Niels Bohr, Albert Einstein, and Frederic Joliot-Curie.

Our day is truly the "Golden Age" of science. The boundaries of knowledge are expanding unusually rapidly. In all directions — from the microcosm to outer space — the human mind is exploring the depths and mysteries of nature that only recently seemed impenetrable. The use of the fruits of knowledge to the full would make it possible to enrich man's material and spiritual life with a new quality.

Is it not a monstrous paradox of the twentieth century that the achievements of science should be used to develop weapons of mass destruction that threaten the human species with total extinction?

The problem of war and peace has been brought into the foreground by the objective course of developments. Scientists, with their prestige and expert opinions, can and must play a great role in awakening people's consciousness and stirring them to resolute action to stop and reverse the arms race and achieve arms reductions.

It is correctly emphasized in your message that today courage is needed not in preparation for war but in efforts to achieve peace. This is especially true now that the arms race has reached a critical point. The development of military technology has already made the problem of arms control extremely difficult. We have come close to a point beyond which the situation in general may get out of hand.

The question whether strike weapons will or will not be deployed in outer space is a critical one, the answer to which will pre-determine world developments for many years. Indeed, what kind of peaceful future and what kind of strategic stability can be said to exist at all when in addition to missiles poised for attack in underground silos and in the depths of the ocean another mortal danger will face mankind from outer space

Try to imagine what the world would look like in such an event, say in ten or twenty years from now. Waves of various types of strike weapons would be passing over the heads of all the inhabitants of this planet, everywhere — from the limits of the atmosphere, a hundred kilometres high, to stationary earth orbits.

The Soviet people, who have lived for forty years within an encirclement of American "forward-based" weapons, are resolute in their denunciation of the very idea of their deployment in outer space; they abhor the prospect of having them over their heads, over their homes.

One may wonder how such deployment will be regarded by the plain Americans, who are not yet accustomed to living with foreign weapons along their borders, either on the earth or in the sky. I believe that the tensions in relations between our two countries will reach a very high pitch, unprecedented even by today's standards, and that these tensions will be even less amenable to control.

The militarization of outer space will be an oppressive psychological burden to the inhabitants of all countries and will create an atmosphere of general instability and uncertainty.

One may ask why such steps are being planned at all. It would be relevant, too, to ask this question: Is the very fact of stationing weapons by some state in outer space over the territories of other states not a violation of national sovereignty?

In their letters, Soviet citizens often ask how the Soviet Union will act if the United States, ignoring all protests, starts developing, testing and deploying a multi-stage antimissile defence system. We have already pointed out that the Soviet Union will find an effective answer to that challenge corresponding to our view of the need to maintain strategic balance and stability. In such an event, however, there will be another spiral in the arms race.

As we know, there have been no weapons in outer space up to the present. If they did appear, it would be extremely difficult to remove them. And it would be absurd to expect that the development of strike space weapons will result in the abolition of nuclear weapons on earth. The history of the advent of new types of weapons and the existing realities provide conclusive evidence to the contrary.

Is there in general any logic in the argument that in order to disarm it is necessary to arm oneself to the teeth first? In other words, why make missiles to destroy missiles when there is another way, more dependable and safer and, what is most important, leading directly to the desired goal — the negotiation of agreements on the reduction and eventual complete elimination of the existing missiles?

It is clear that the latter way is the only reasonable one from all points of view and is consistent with elementary common sense. We are in favour of this way.

You know that the Soviet Union has proposed a fifty per cent cut in the nuclear weapons delivery vehicles of the Soviet Union and the United States capable of reaching targets in each other's territories. We have halted all nuclear weapons tests. We are also carrying out a unilateral reduction of intermediate-range missiles in Europe. We are prepared to conclude a non-aggression treaty, to agree on the establishment of zones free from nuclear and chemical weapons.

All our steps, like many of the proposals on the agenda of the negotiations — collectively and individually make it possible to bring about a significant improvement in the international situation, to lessen the risk of nuclear war and to pave the way towards complete nuclear disarmament. We realize perfectly well that life constantly exposed to the threat of nuclear war is a cheerless prospect for mankind.

What alternative is offered by the "strategic defence initiative"? We are firmly convinced, that it is only an unlimited and mutually accelerated race in the so-called "defensive" and "offensive" weapons.

I have more than once given a political characterization of the "strategic defence initiative". I will not re-emphasize its clearly imperial ambition to try to achieve superiority, both military and technological, over other states.

I shall touch upon another aspect. It is claimed that the "strategic defence initiative" will secure a breakthrough in the technological field. But even if one presumes that its implementation will accelerate scientific and technological progress, there is the question of the price that will have to be paid for this. It is perfectly clear that the price will be the development of suicidal tools of destruction. Growing numbers of people realize that, in the United States in particular.

We are in favour of a fundamentally different way of accelerating progress in the field of science and technology; we are for technological competition and constructive co-operation in conditions of lasting and just peace.

And is it not true to say that outer space itself is an exceptionally promising area for international co-operation? Today we have just started to explore it in the interest of science and man's practical activity. How much has indeed been achieved in record time! The first artificial earth satellite, the first man in outer space, the first man on the Moon, the landings on Venus and Mars, a beautiful map of Venus.

But these are just the first few steps. The exploration of the limitless expanses of outer space must become a common cause of different states.

We have submitted to the United Nations a comprehensive programme for peaceful co-operation in outer space. The Soviet Union has proposed setting up a world space organization to co-ordinate efforts in this venture on a worldwide scale.

There are fundamental research and interplanetary space probes to Mars for instance, in such a programme.

There are the applications of the results of space exploration in the fields of biology, medicine, materials study, weather forecasting, the study of the climate and the natural environment, the development of global satellite communications systems and the remote-control probing of the Earth, and exploration of the Oceans.

Finally, there are the joint development of new space technology and its use for the benefit of all nations, including large orbital research stations, various manned spaceships, and — in the long-term perspective — the industrialization of near-earth space.

Naturally, we are prepared to develop peaceful co-operation in outer space also on a bilateral basis with those states which have an interest in it. This refers in full measure to the United States as well.

You certainly remember the link-up of the "Soyuz" and "Apollo" spaceships, which fascinated the whole world. Some such work is being done now, too: Soviet and American scientists are involved in a joint exploration of Venus and the Halle comet within the framework of the international "Vega" project, and the Soviet Union is co-operating with other countries in a space search and rescue service.

This, however, is but a tiny part of what could be accomplished by joint efforts. It is unreasonable to miss such opportunities.

By all indications, the American public, scientists and members of Congress are showing great interest in a resumption of co-operation, and concrete projects are being put forward to this end. We are prepared to examine serious proposals of this kind.

Both military programmes and civilian projects in space, including research and development, are costly ventures. This is yet another reason why peaceful co-operation is the preferable alternative.

Research on thermonuclear fusion is another promising area of international co-operation. This is bound to give mankind a practically inexhaustible source of energy, a man-made Sun of its own kind.

It is widely known that the idea of controlled thermonuclear reaction was first expressed by Academician I. V. Kurchatov in his famous lecture in Britain as far back as 1956, when he acquainted the international scientific community with works of Soviet physicists.

The project for an international experimental thermonuclear reactor "Tocamac" has been under development in Vienna since 1978 on the Soviet Union's intitiative, with scientists of a number of West European countries, as well as the United States and Japan, taking part.

Today there is good reason to say that it is technologically feasible to build such a reactor, so specialists believe, in the not too distant future, before the year 2000 at any rate.

During our recent visit to Paris we shared our ideas with the French President, François Mitterand. He took a favourable view of our proposal. We deem it important, even indispensable, to pool the efforts of all interested states to solve the problem of nuclear fusion, which will in turn resolve one of the most vital global problems facing mankind today — the energy shortage.

In the modern world there are quite a few urgent tasks that demand co-ordination and co-operation of effort to implement them. I would like to emphasize once again that the Soviet Union is a staunch and consistent champion of co-operation on the broadest scale, of pooling the efforts of different states in the use of the achievements of scientific and technological progress exclusively for the benefit of peace and progress. I can assure you that the Soviet Union is prepared to develop such co-operation in the spirit of good will.

I wish you success in your fruitful scientific activities and in your noble efforts to uphold the cause of peace and achieve a world without arms, without wars.

20.

Press Conference at Geneva
21 November 1985

On 21 November the General Secretary of the CPSU Central Committee, Mikhail Gorbachov, gave a press conference at the Soviet press centre in Geneva for journalists covering the Soviet–American talks.

Addressing the representatives of the mass media, Mikhail Gorbachov said:

Our talks with the US President, the first in the last six and a half years have just come to a close. This is indisputably a significant event in international affairs. The significance of this meeting becomes clearer, having in mind not only Soviet–American relations but the entire system of international relations, which is now going through a particularly difficult period.

First a couple of words about what preceded the Geneva meeting. It had been impatiently awaited throughout the world. People pinned on it their hopes for a normalization of the world situation and an easing of international tensions. Some, it is true, expressed their doubts as to whether the confrontation had gone too far for any arrangement to be possible at all. There were in fact such apprehensions, you know that as well as I do.

As far as the Soviet Union is concerned, we were clearly aware of the real situation and did not harbour even the faintest illusions about American policy. We realize how far the militarization of the economy and political thinking had gone in that country.

We understood only too well, however, that the world situation was too dangerous for us to ignore even the slightest chance to remedy it and advance in the direction of more secure and lasting peace.

In the preliminary period, a few months before the meeting, we had already begun paving the way, so to say, to creating a favourable climate for the summit. Last summer we unilaterally ended nuclear explosions and expressed our willingness to resume negotiations immediately on the complete termination of nuclear testing. We also reaffirmed our unilateral moratorium on the testing of anti-satellite weapons, and, as you know, submitted proposals for radical reductions of nuclear arsenals. Our proposal for preventing an escalation of the arms race into outer space was followed by our proposals for broad international co-operation in the peaceful uses and exploration of outer space for the benefit of all nations.

I repeat that we had been doing our utmost to lay the groundwork for mutual understanding and to normalize the political atmosphere even before the meeting. On the eve of the Geneva summit the Political Consultative Committee of the Warsaw Treaty member states held a session in Sofia at which the socialist countries took a strong stand in defence of peace, in favour of a relaxation of international tensions and of co-operation and against the arms race and confrontation in favour of the normalization of the international situation in the interest of all the peoples of the world.

Although these steps, which were dictated by our awareness of responsibility for the destiny of the world, failed to elicit a favourable response from our partners at the forthcoming Geneva negotiations, we firmly adhered to our constructive stand. We deemed it necessary to attempt to check the dangerous trend of developments by conclusive arguments, by our own example, and by appeals to common sense. The complexity of the international situation made it clear to us that a direct discussion with the US President was indispensable. The great role played by the Soviet Union and the United States in the world today naturally entails the great responsibility of these states and their political leaders. Our conclusion was as follows: it is time that both sides confronted by the threat of wholesale nuclear destruction, learned to live together. The Soviet people and, I am profoundly convinced, the American people, too, have a vital interest in such coexistence. It is vital also to all the nations of the world.

We were aware — and we remain aware today — of the sentiments of the people of all countries in favour of peace, their desire not only to preserve peace but also to normalize the situation, to achieve real success in the struggle to end the arms race. This growing movement for peace is of enormous significance. Two important conclusions can be drawn from it.

On the one hand, our efforts for peace were inspired by our awareness that they answered the hopes and aspirations of the mass of the people of the world, regardless of where they live and of their political views, religious faith and traditions. On the other hand, this awareness imposed great obligations upon us, primarily that of responsibility.

What is the characteristic of the present stage in the development of the international situation? To put it briefly, it is the growing responsibility for the destiny of the world. The people have realized this enormous responsibility, and they are acting in forms accessible to them.

It follows that this situation and this responsibility should motivate the policy of states and the practical moves of political leaders. The absence of a policy adequate to the exigencies felt by all the peoples of the world cannot be replaced by various means of propaganda camouflage. The people have learned to understand quickly what is what, and to put everything in its proper place.

This is my profound conviction. I, and my colleagues in the Soviet Union's political leadership, interpret the situation precisely in this way and have focused our attention in a constructive direction, on a search for ways towards a better and more tranquil world.

I have been greatly impressed by the letters I have received from the Soviet Union, the United States, Australia, Europe, Asia and Africa. These letters have come from men, women and children and from war veterans. It is important to emphasize that the youth of the world has also voiced its opinion in these letters. Those to whom the future belongs and who are now taking an independent path in life are assuming responsibility for the destiny of the world.

Now for the meeting itself. Quite a lot of time during the summit was taken up by my private discussions with President Reagan. A short time ago, bidding a farewell to the US President, we counted the number of such private discussions.

We agreed on the figure five or six. These discussions lasted for an hour, as a rule: sometimes longer. This is not simply arithmetic. Our discussions were frank, prolonged and heated — at certain moments extremely heated. Nevertheless it seems to me that they were productive to a certain extent. Of course, much more time than planned was spent on them. I would say that they took up most of the time in the last two days.

This enabled us to discuss a wide range of problems face to face. We discussed issues in a political language, frank and straightforward, and I believe this fact was of great, even decisive significance.

It was primarily at these discussions, as well as the plenary meetings and broad exchanges between all members of the delegations and experts at corresponding levels who came from the Soviet and American sides — people enjoying prestige in the two countries and the rest of the world — that made it possible to handle a lot of work in a matter of only two days.

We submitted to the President our considerations and our assessments of the situation in the world. The starting point of our analysis was as follows: over the last few decades cardinal changes have taken place in the world, which demand a new approach, a fresh view of many things in foreign policy. The present international situation is characterized by a highly important distinction which we and the United States should take into account in our foreign policies. I have in mind the following. Under present conditions, it is not only a matter of confrontation between the two social systems, but a matter of choice between survival and mutual destruction.

In other words, the problems of war and peace, the problems of survival have been placed in the focus of world politics by the objective course of world development. I wish to emphasize that I intentionally use the word "survival" not to dramatize the situation and foment fears, but to make all of us feel keenly and realize clearly the realities of today's world.

The problem of war and peace is the most vital top priority problem, which affects the interests of all the inhabitants of this planet. I re-emphasize that it has become the focus of world politics. We cannot avoid the quest for solutions to this vital problem. This is our firm conviction. Such is the will of the Soviet people and such is the will of the American people, of all peoples. This is the first thing.

Second, we called the attention of the American side again to the following circumstance, which I have already mentioned. This circumstance is so important, and we attach so much significance to it, that we decided to point it out again at the Geneva meeting. It is the fact that if today it is already very difficult for us to begin a productive dialogue and negotiations on the problems of ending the arms race and achieving nuclear disarmament, it will be even more difficult to do so tomorrow.

That is why a meeting and a responsible dialogue were necessary.

We have all come to a point at which we must stop, take a look around and decide what to do next in the world on the basis of its realities and a broad approach to a definition of national interests. In the course of our discussions I tried to understand the position of the US Administration on the cardinal problem, the problem of war and peace.

All of us have read a lot on this subject. You journalists have also said quite a lot on this score. For those in decision-making positions, however, it is important to understand the initial point where the partner's policy is shaped, the initial background of the foreign policy pursued by the present US Administration. Much effort was needed to assess all this information in a spirit of responsibility, without bias, so as to find an answer to this highly important question.

This analysis proved that for all the difference between the approaches of the two sides and their assessments made in the course of this serious and important work, which had to be done if we were to come to the summit with our hands full, we have, it seems to me, a common point of departure for improving Soviet–American relations: this is an understanding that nuclear war is impermissible and that there can be no victors in such a war. This idea has been more than once expressed by both Soviet and American sides. Hence the conclusion that the key problem in relations between the two countries at the current stage is the problem of security. We are resolutely in favour of reaching agreements to guarantee equal security for the two sides.

We believe that it is precisely on this basis that it will be possible to secure the consistent growth of mutual trust, and a general normalization of the political atmosphere, in which one can hope for developing a political dialogue, and fruitful discussion of economic and humanitarian problems and the problems of contacts and information exchange. This is the key to preserving life on earth, to changing the political atmosphere in favour of good will.

We have told the President that we have not sought and will not seek military superiority over the United States. Moreover, I have expressed more than once in private discussions and at plenary meetings our profound conviction that a situation in which the United States felt less secure than the Soviet Union would be disadvantageous to us, because it would generate mistrust and instability. We expect a similar approach on the part of the United States in matters concerning the security of our country. At the same time we have told the President that we would never allow the United States to gain military superiority over the Soviet Union. I think this is a logical way to view this question. Both sides should get used to strategic parity as a natural state of Soviet–American relations. If a discussion is to be fruitful, it should be focused primarily on mutual efforts to reduce the level of this parity. In other words, realistic measures should be carried out to reduce nuclear armaments on a basis of reciprocity. This is a worthy field of activity for the leaders of such great powers as the Soviet Union and the United States, and for other leaders of states, for that matter, because it is our common problem.

This, however, logically suggests the next conclusion of principle. None of us — neither the United States, nor the Soviet Union — should do anything to open the door to an arms race in new spheres, specifically, in outer space. If the way to outer space were opened for weapons, the scope of military rivalry would grow immeasurably and the arms race would become irreversible and get out of hand, which is something that can be predicted with certainty. In such an event each side would always feel that it is losing in some area and would certainly engage in a feverish search for ever new ways of meeting the challenge. This would step up the arms race not only in outer space, but on earth as well, because a response should not necessarily be confined to the same sphere. A response should simply be effective.

This is the logic I followed in my conversations with the President. If such a situation took shape then, I repeat, the possibility of agreement on any limitation of military rivalry and the arms race would be highly problematic. I want to go back to what I said before: We have come to a definite limit today. If one fails to ponder in a spirit of responsibility on the steps to be taken, one may draw mistaken conclusions and take political steps that will entail grave consequences for all nations.

Of course, the differences between our two countries will continue. Their rivalry will also be there. However, this rivalry should be kept within limits and not extend beyond what is permissible or lead to military confrontation. Let each of the social systems prove its advantages by example.

We are well aware of the weak and strong sides of American society and other advanced countries. We know of their achievements and their potentials. Naturally, we are more familiar with our own potentials, our latent possibilities in particular. In short, we are in favour of a contest with the United States, an active contest at that. History itself, rather than theoretical conjectures and arguments has confirmed the viability of the policy of peaceful coexistence.

Much in relations between the Soviet Union and the United States depends on the way each side views the surrounding world. Here, as we see it, it is highly important to have a clear understanding of the historical realities and take them into consideration in planning policy. I have in mind both the Soviet and the American leadership.

Today's world is a many-multifaceted community of sovereign countries and peoples who have their specific interests, ambitions, policies, traditions and aspirations. Many of them have only recently become independent. They are taking their first steps in incredibly difficult conditions inherited from colonialism and foreign dependence. Once they have achieved political independence, they seek to secure economic independence. They know that they have natural resources and manpower, that is, the necessities to give them a better life if the relevant work processes are rationally organized. These countries occupy enormous continents. The desire of every nation to take advantage of its sovereign rights in the political, economic and social spheres is quite natural.

Whether this policy is welcomed or detested by foreign powers, it reflects the internal processes occurring in each country, the interests of the people who alone enjoy sovereign rights. These include the right to choose a path of development, a system to live under, methods and forms of work, and the right to choose allies. This is the birthright of every nation. If this right is challenged, I do not know how international relations can be maintained at all.

When I was in Britain in December of last year a phrase of Palmerston came to mind. I remembered it from the time I studied international relations at the Moscow University Department of Law. Palmerston said that Britain has neither eternal friends nor eternal enemies, but only eternal interests. I told Mrs Margaret Thatcher that I was in agreement with that. But if Palmerston and you, the present political leader of Britain, admit that you have such interests, you must admit that other peoples and other countries also have their own interests.

When about two hundred states are acting on the international scene, and each of them pursues its own interests, to what extent can they be successful? This depends on consideration of the interests of others on the basis of co-operation. We reject the idea that the whole world is the property of whoever claims title to it. We have always stated this — ten years ago and today, and we will say this tomorrow. We have no dual policy to pursue. We are pursuing an honest and open policy. We have always followed and will continue to follow this line.

Tension, conflicts in individual regions and even wars between different states in various parts of the world have their roots in the past and in the present socio-economic conditions of these countries and regions. It would be wrong and very dangerous to depict all these seats of contradictions as the product of rivalry between East and West. I have said this to the President and the American delegation.

If today, for instance, Mexico, Brazil and a number of other countries are unable to repay their debts or even pay interest on them, one can imagine the gravity of the processes taking place in those countries. This may inflame the situation and trigger off an explosion. Will the "hand of Moscow" be again cited as the culprit? One should not so irresponsibly pronounce such judgements on such problems for the whole world to hear. Such banalities may be accepted in some quarters, but they are impermissible at such conferences as ours. Therefore, we agreed from the start not to mouth banalities to each other. Quite a few of them had been said during the preparations for the summit. It was a spirited battle, and not without your aid as journalists.

Of course, the Soviet Union and the United States are two mighty powers with global interests, with their own friends and allies. They have their own priorities in foreign policy. The Soviet leadership, however, sees in this fact not a source of confrontation but rather a reason for a specially high sense of responsibility by the Soviet Union and the United States and their leaders for the destiny of the world. This is our view of the situation. Naturally, we may disagree on the state of affairs in a specific area of the world. Our assessments may be different and often contradictory, particularly in regard to specific events or the causes of specific conflicts. We are not opposed in principle to discussing specific regional problems in the context of the search for ways to facilitate their settlement. We stated this and agreed with the President to go ahead with our joint efforts, which was reflected in the joint declaration issued at the end of the talks. At the same time we repeatedly emphasized — and I want to say this now — that no interference in the internal affairs of foreign states should be allowed. This is our conception of Soviet–American relations which we brought to the summit meeting and set out to the President and all members of the American delegation. It was presented in a more extended form, but I have described its essence here.

We believe that an improvement in Soviet–American relations is perfectly feasible. Many problems have accumulated and there is, I would say, a lot of debris to be cleared. The Soviet leadership has the political will to do this. However, it should be undertaken jointly with the American side. As we know, when geologists or miners are trapped underground and find themselves in a critical situation, rescue teams advance towards each other to save lives.

Efforts to save our relations from growing tensions, preventing their progress towards confrontation and channelling them towards normalization, should be carried out jointly. We are willing to make such efforts, and I have told the US President that it would be a grave mistake on our part if we missed this chance and failed to change Soviet–American relations in the direction of normalization, which would mean an improvement of the world situation as a whole.

We would like now to return to the main question, which was crucial to the Geneva talks. At every meeting and in every private conference the problems of war and peace and the verification of disarmament were the main items on the agenda. This was the pivot of the Geneva meeting. We explained to the American side that the Star Wars programme would not only give an added impetus to the race in all types of weapons, but it would also put an end to all restraints. In reply we heard arguments about the allegedly defensive character of the wide-scale anti missile defence system with space-based components. We heard the following argument: what will you say to your people after Geneva if you refuse to undertake cuts in offensive weapons? We had an answer to this question and I repeat it here: This is wrong. We are prepared for a radical reduction of nuclear arsenals provided the door is shut securely on an arms race escalation to outer space. Under this condition we are prepared to carry out the first stage on the basis of a 50 per cent reduction in nuclear armaments and then, inviting other nuclear powers to follow suit, to proceed along the line of radical reduction.

There is a definite positive reaction to SDI in a definite part of the world, perhaps even among some political leaders and within journalistic circles. SDI is allegedly a defensive weapon, a sort of shield. This is absolutely wrong. Indeed, mountains of weapons have already been stockpiled, the arms race is spiralling, and we are unable to cope with this process, take it under control, check or reverse it, while in such a situation, complicated as it is, the United States is proposing to open a contest in outer space. Who can guarantee, then, that we shall be able to organize any productive negotiations at all? I believe that no sober-minded person can guarantee that. The American side is unwilling to recognize that SDI implies deployment of weapons in outer space. These weapons — both American and Soviet — will fly in waves overhead. All of us will watch the bristling sky and expect something to fall on our heads at any moment. Let us imagine — and we said this to the American side — the consequences of an accidental collision in outer space. Let us say something has fallen off a missile, so that its head continues to fly on while its vehicle part collides with some space weapons complex. Alarm signals will come on, which may be interpreted as an attempt by the other side — no matter which — to destroy the opponent's weapons. All the computers will be activated, and in such a situation the political leaders will be unable to undertake any sensible move. Well, shall we become captives to such a situation? Quite a few similar scenes can be imagined. I told the US President that we feel that this idea fascinated him as a man, and that to a certain extent we could understand him. However, we could not understand his position as a political leader responsible for the policy of such a powerful state and its security. We hope that after our discussions, the American side will analyze everything that we stated on this subject in a spirit of due responsibility.

As we see it, it became obvious at the meeting that the Americans disliked our logic; but we, for our part, failed to see any logic in their arguments. We were told to believe the promise that if the Americans happened to be the first to implement SDI, they would share their success with the Soviet Union. I then said: Mr. President, I call on you to trust us: We have already declared that we will not use nuclear weapons first and we will not attack the United States. Why do you intend, while preserving the entire offensive potential on earth and under water, to escalate the arms race to outer space? Don't you trust us? We see that you don't. But why should we trust you more than you trust us? All the more so as we have good reason not to trust you, since we propose that both sides should not introduce weapons into outer space, but devote themselves to disarmament on earth. This is understandable to everyone.

On the whole, we would like to hope that this is not the last word from the American side. Our discussions with the President were circumstantial and we listened attentively to each other's arguments and put them all on record. If the United States has the will and determination to think again and size up all the lethal aspects and consequences of the Star Wars programme, the way will be open for a constructive solution to the problems of international security and the ending of the arms race. When I speak of this I have in mind the problems of verification as well. Many speculative arguments are heaped up over this problem and the Soviet Union's stand is deliberately distorted. It is true, however, that the Soviet Union is open to verification. If agreement is reached on banning the deployment of weapons in outer space, we would be prepared to open our laboratories on a basis of reciprocity for verification of compliance with such an agreement. What we are offered is this: let us open our laboratories and see how the arms race is getting on in outer space. This is a naive offer and its starting point is defective and unacceptable.

If the American side also ends all nuclear weapons tests and we conclude an agreement to this effect there will be no problems on our part in matters of verification, including on an international basis.

If both sides agree to cut nuclear armaments by fifty per cent, it would of course be necessary to verify the process of reduction, in which we are by no means less interested than the Americans are.

I want to say a couple of words about the following. At this stage differences in attitudes came to light in relation to a fifty per cent cut in nuclear arsenals. We have amendments to offer on the American draft and the Americans have suggestions concerning our drafts. However, we do not wish to dramatize these differences and are prepared to seek mutually acceptable solutions. Unless an arms race starts in outer space, of course. The proposals of the two sides provide the basis for a search for mutually acceptable decisions. Compromise deals are possible here, and it will take some time before the situation becomes clear. We are prepared to seek these solutions, proceeding from the fundamental principle that we do not seek military superiority and are in favour of parity of security.

During the meeting we exchanged our views on humanitarian problems. The result was the relevant agreements listed in our joint communique. It will be recalled that we agreed on some aspects of bilateral Soviet–American relations, on an expansion of links in the scientific and cultural fields, as well as in the fields of education and information. The exchange of students, TV programmes, and sports delegations will be widened. An understanding has been reached in principle to conclude an agreement on air travel. I am informed that this problem was settled yesterday.

I wish to call your attention to our decision to make a joint appeal to a number of other states for co-operation in the field of nuclear fusion research. This is a fascinating idea. If translated into reality, it will open a new chapter in a highly important area and provide mankind with what is, in effect, an inexhaustible source of energy. This is a good field for joint activities. It will require enormous efforts on the part of scientists and engineers, and new solutions in technology and processes, all of which will maintain the momentum of technological progress and the development of new processes.

From the viewpoint of the political results and consequences of this meeting it is important, it seems to me, to take another factor into account. We evidenced the great political effect of the summit. It brought to light and stimulated the interest of the world public in the problems of Soviet–American relations, the dangers of the arms race, and the necessity to normalize the international situation.

I would like to mention a few episodes in this context. The day before yesterday our mission was visited by a group of leaders of the US peace movement, led by Jesse Jackson, an eminent political figure. I wish to tell you that we regard them as worthy and respected citizens representing millions of Americans who signed the appeal to President Reagan and myself, wishing us success and expressing specific suggestions concerning ways to strengthen peace, including a call for an end to nuclear testing. American war veterans who participated in the Soviet–American link-up on the Elbe also came to Geneva, and respresentatives of many public organizations of other countries — children's organizations in particular — also stopped here in the last few days. At my request they were received by the Soviet delegation. Those were exciting meetings. We constantly sensed the powerful support and solidarity of our socialist allies and the non-aligned countries. Even before our meeting, the leaders of six states — India, Mexico, Argentina, Tanzania, Greece and Sweden — addressed us with a proposal to freeze all types of nuclear weapons. We are highly appreciative of their initiative. A large group of Nobel Prize laureates put forth proposals which I was ready to sign immediately except for one. This expressed a wish or maybe a demand that we should not leave Geneva without coming to terms. It would be risky to consent to that condition. One might not be able to go back home for a long time. Now, however, I think differently. I would probably sign this condition, too.

Ladies and gentlemen! Comrades! At the turning points of history moments of truth may be as indispensable as air for breathing. The international situation has become much too dangerous because of the spiralling arms race, and too many falsehoods on this subject are circulated with the aim of intimidating the common people. It is really necessary to dispel this fog and to put words to the test of deeds. For this it is best to resort to direct conversations which are usually implied by a summit meeting, especially having in mind our two States and taking account of their role and responsibility in the world. Here a discussion of problems is put on a new plane where it is impossible to evade hard facts. Thus, speaking of the general results of the meeting, it would hardly be correct to make a straightforward assessment. Of course, it would have been far better if we had come to terms at Geneva on the main, vital problem, one of ending the arms race. This, unfortunately, has failed to happen.

The American side has proved, for the time being, unprepared to make important decisions. I believe, however, that on the whole this process could not have been settled in a matter of two days even if it had followed the right lines. We have a mechanism at our disposal for implementing such processes. At the same time, the meeting was too important to be viewed in oversimplified terms. It has enabled us to see more clearly the nature of our differences, and to remove — I hope — some biased assessments concerning the Soviet Union and policy of its leadership, as well as some of the other prejudices that had accumulated over the years. This may have a favourable impact on further trends of development. Trust cannot be restored overnight. It is not an easy process. We accepted, with understanding, the American President's assurances that the United States is not seeking superiority and is revolted by the idea of nuclear war. It is our sincere desire to see these declarations reaffirmed by practical moves.

We would like to regard this meeting as the beginning of a dialogue with the object of securing changes for the better, both in Soviet–American relations and in the world in general. In this sense I could describe the summit as a meeting that has laid the groundwork for further progress.

Such, in general outline, is our assessment of the results and significance of the Geneva meeting. This gives me a good reason to look to the future with optimism now that we are taking leave of the hospitable city of Geneva. Common sense must triumph. Goodbye until we meet again.

Mikhail Gorbachov's statement was followed by question time.

Question (BBC, Britain).

General Secretary, what is your view of the prospects for developing Soviet–American relations and international situation as a whole following the Geneva summit?

Answer. I have an optimistic view of the future. If all of us continue to act in the spirit of responsibility in Soviet–American relations and in international relations in general, which was sensed — however slightly — at the Geneva meeting, we shall certainly find the right answers to the most burning problems and the most effective avenues of approach to their solution. This is my profound conviction.

Question (Soviet television)

You have spoken of the need for a new approach in present-day international relations — even a new thinking. What is the essence of this new approach and new thinking, as you see it?

Answer Yes, I am convinced that a new policy is needed at the present stage of international relations characterized by great interconnection and interdependence of states.

We believe that a new approach makes it incumbent on the modern policy of any state to proceed from the realities of the modern world. This is the main prerequisite for making the foreign policy of states constructive. This is precisely what will lead to an improvement in the world situation.

The problem of war and peace is in the focus of all world politics. This is a matter of special concern to all nations.

In all countries — in the developed capitalist countries, the socialist and the developing countries — there are economic problems, social problems and ecological problems. They can be more successfully and effectively settled on the basis of co-operation and mutual under-standing. What is needed is a dialogue, an expansion of co-operation and collective efforts.

Take, for instance, the problems of the developing world. One cannot stay aloof from them. So a new policy consistent with reality is obliging all of us to seek answers to the problems of this community of states aspiring towards a better life.

The main question now — I am reiterating it — is the need to find out what is to be done to check the arms race. Public realization of this necessity is steadily growing. If this overall problem is not solved, all our other hopes, plans and actions may be frustrated.

I am convinced that no progress is possible, if we stick to old approaches confined to self-interest, although this is presented as defence of national interests. A new policy is needed to meet the demands of the present stage, taking account of the realities advanced to the foreground by the course of world developments.

Question (US NBC television company)

During the Second World War the United States and the Soviet Union jointly fought and defeated fascism. In view of your discussions with President Reagan, do you believe that the Soviet Union and the United States can become allies in the fight against famine in Africa, against international terrorism, against environmental pollution, against cancer and other diseases?

Answer. I am thankful to you for recalling an important period in our common history. We remember it and will never allow it to fade from our memory. I believe that the Geneva meeting provides opportunities for promoting broad co-operation between our two countries and peoples. And when I say "between our countries and peoples" I do not oversimplify the situation.

I know the gulf of differences dividing us and I take account of the actual state of Soviet–American relations. I am convinced, however, that co-operation is possible between us. This includes, among other things, co-operation on the problems you listed in your question. I will not dwell upon the details of these problems now.

We can release enormous resources for aid to the developing countries. Today a huge number of people, half of them children, are famished or undernourished in Latin America alone. A cut in the world's military spending by a mere five or ten per cent would make possible a solution to this problem.

So the problem deserves careful consideration.

I welcome your question and I say "yes" to it. This does not mean, however, that there are not certain differences of nuance in our approach to the problems you have mentioned.

Question (US NBC television company)

You have said that you were disappointed by President Reagan's answer on the SDI issue. After this meeting as much weaponry has remained in the world as was before it. Can you say, however, that the world has become a safer place after Geneva? If so, how?

Answer. I venture to assert that although there is as much weaponry today as there was before Geneva the world has become a safer place to live in. At any rate, so it seems to me, and the meeting itself and its results are a definite contribution to greater security because this summit is the beginning of a road towards dialogue, towards understanding, that is, towards what contributes to greater security. Geneva is yielding a good political effect in this context.

Question (newspaper *Pravda*)

What practical steps could the Soviet Union and the United States take to secure an early end to the arms race?

Answer. Although I devoted all my statement to this question I think I should say once again: it's time we stopped. If we prevent an extension of the arms race into outer space, our proposals and what the American side has proposed will enable us to make headway and search for compromise deals, and achieve parity at a lower level. There is a good mechanism for this: the Geneva negotiations.

I would like to add to this that we hope that the US Administration has not yet said its last word concerning a ban on all nuclear weapons tests. The whole world wants this ban. The American side still has time to think over the situation. A positive decision would be a great step that would stimulate the process of limitation and termination of the arms race. I believe that this process would also be facilitated by further political dialogue between the leadership of the Soviet Union and that of the United States. We have agreed to widen it and I hope that the participation of the leaders of our two countries in this political dialogue will help curtail the arms race.

And another thing. What is on the agenda of the Geneva talks, that is, the aims and subject of these talks, is a matter for all nations. Responsible political leaders, the leaders of states first and foremost, must take a firm constructive stand on this issue. That would be of enormous significance.

I believe that the vast majority of political leaders are in favour of speeding up the search for a settlement at Geneva, and finding ways to end the arms race and begin disarmament.

Question (GDR television)

What, in your opinion, are the most important results of the Geneva summit? And another question: What is the significance of political dialogue at top level?

Answer. In answering your question I would first of all emphasize that the Geneva meeting is an important stage in Soviet–American relations. It has set the stage for the search for ways to normalize and develop them in all directions. If these quests continue in further joint efforts by both sides, they will make for an improvement in the world situation. This is, I would say, the political outcome of the meeting.

The Geneva summit focused on problems of vital concern to all nations of the world. The joint declaration of the leaders of the Soviet Union and the United States to the effect that nuclear war is impermissible and should never be unleashed, that they are not seeking to gain military superiority and will give a new impetus to the Geneva talks — this in itself is of enormous significance if consistently implemented through practical steps.

Now for the second question. I believe that the summit meeting has proved that we should maintain a political dialogue which enables us to compare our positions, to understand each other better, and on this basis to look for mutually acceptable solutions to vital modern problems.

Question (The newspaper *Mattino*, Italy)

The Soviet Union suffered great material and human casualties in the Second World War. Nevertheless, do you not think that now, forty years after the end of the war, the Soviet Union could contribute to reunification of the two Germany states?

Answer. I believe this question was discussed in great detail at the Helsinki Conference. The Helsinki process and the Final Act, signed by all European states, as well as the United States and Canada, is our common achievement. The Helsinki process deserves our support and our efforts to encourage it in every way. It is precisely the results of the Helsinki Conference that provide the answer to your question.

Question (Radio Switzerland)

You have emphasized the deep gulf between the Soviet and US positions on Star Wars. Will it not interfere with the progress of the Geneva talks?

Answer. I will not repeat myself. I can describe our stance in a couple of words. At the Geneva talks we follow a constructive line. We shall seek solutions to halt the arms race, and to achieve a radical cut in nuclear arms in order, as one of the next stages, to approach the abolition of nuclear weapons in earnest, with all nuclear powers involved. We firmly believe that this is quite feasible if the door to an arms race in outer space is firmly held shut.

Question (Associated Press)

You said that the President is personally committed to the Star Wars programme and that you discussed SDI in detail. How did he take your arguments? What were his reactions? Do you think it possible to end the deadlock on this issue?

Answer. I believe that the American side has full reason to think over whatever we said at the meeting. We hope for an understanding of our arguments. Their meaning, as we see it, is in accord with the spirit of the January understanding. This means that following upon the Geneva talks we must take the road of radical cuts in nuclear armaments, provided an arms race in outer space is banned.

We formulated this objective jointly at an earlier date. The US President has declared that SDI is a shield. I hope we have conclusively proved that in fact it is a space weapon that can be used against missiles, satellites, and targets on earth. It is a new type of weapon. Through it a new sphere will be opened in the arms race. This is unacceptable. It would complicate the whole situation and make progress at the Geneva talks problematic in general.

Therefore, I value the fact that the US President and the General Secretary of the CPSU jointly emphasized that the Geneva talks would be accelerated on the basis of the January understanding. Now this point of view has been confirmed not only by the Ministers of Foreign Affairs, but by the leaders of the two countries as well. We regard this as a definite signal and as a sign of hope.

Question (BBC, Britain)

If the sides fail to agree on preventing an arms race in outer space, will the Soviet Union be able to compete against American technology in this area or it will lag behind the United States?

Answer. You have touched upon a very interesting question. I attempted to explain to the President in a frank and straightforward discussion that, as it seems to me, much in American policy in relation to the USSR is based on delusions. On the one hand, it is hoped that the arms race and its escalation will exhaust the Soviet Union economically, undermine its influence in the world and thus free the hands of the United States. History has put such prophets to shame — even at a time when our society had a far smaller potential than today's, and smaller possibilities in general. Today, however, they are enormous. So delusions on this score only hamper the conduct of a realistic policy.

On the other hand, there were also delusions in the area of military plans. Attempts were made to outstrip us. Intercontinental ballistic missiles were put into regular service. This was followed by a Soviet response. After a slight delay, it is true, but it did follow. Then multiple nuclear warheads came on the scene. A Soviet response followed. We have always been able to meet any challenge.

Today, it seems to me, the illusions lingering in US military circles have been adopted to a certain extent by the political circles; by the President in particular. It is only a likelihood, of course, so I am not positive about it, but we do have such an impression.

It is evidently believed in the United States that it now has a definite edge on the Soviet Union in certain types of technology, computers and electronics. So again a desire has arisen to seize on this "edge" and achieve military superiority. President Johnson's well known phrase to the effect that the nations that will rule outer space will rule the earth is again in current usage. Someone is evidently itching for a fight and is being consumed by ambition for world supremacy.

It is the old ambition of days of yore. The world has changed very much since then.

Thus, speaking of the so called technological edge which is to be realized through SDI and thus create a predicament for the Soviet Union, I must give this answer: this is just another delusion. We will meet this challenge.

I told the President frankly the following: "You must bear in mind that you are not dealing with country bumpkins."

If the President feels so committed to SDI it is easy to see why we deemed it our duty to study the Star Wars programme in detail and analyse it.

And so we examined this problem. All the more so as the American side is making something like an offer: let us see, let us examine, let us discuss not the issue of preventing the militarization of outer space, but what kind of weapons to take to outer space. We are against this. We are against an arms race in outer space.

We also analysed another aspect of the problem: let us assume the Americans will not accept our arguments, will fail to appreciate our good will and our appeal to seek a way out of this situation by ending the arms race and reducing existing nuclear arsenals — that is, if the United States goes ahead with its former policy. We will certainly make an adequate response to it. At the same time the Soviet leadership gave the relevant assignments to the institutions and scientists concerned and now we can say that our response will be effective, less costly, and more practical; that is, it will take us less time to meet the challenge.

But our political choice is different. It is our desire to induce the United States to examine the situation carefully and to pursue a realistic policy based on common sense and taking account of the sentiments and aspirations of the common people, rather than aggravating the most crucial problem in international relations.

Question (Czechoslovak television and the newspaper *Rude Pravo*)

What are the practical fields where you see opportunities for developing Soviet–American relations after your meeting with President Reagan?

Answer. I believe that the political dialogue will go on and grow wider. It will be carried on at different levels. We have agreed to exchange visits. This should be welcomed in itself. We shall have additional opportunities to develop our bilateral co-operation in the spheres agreed upon. Obviously, we shall continue and widen our consultations in examining regional problems and the situation in various parts of the world.

Finally, we proceed from an assumption that mutual interest in improving relations — and I know this with certainty — is preserved in the Soviet Union and within the US business community. If matters keep going in this direction, we shall be able to widen the scope of co-operation in the economic field as well. We are prepared to invite the US business community to participate in implementing our large scale projects. We have great plans on our hands. We are doing much with the West Europeans to widen the framework of our economic co-operation. We welcome such developments.

I expressed to the President my idea that we should not underestimate economic relations between the two countries. The reason is not that we cannot survive without the United States or the other way around. We can survive quite well and I hope America will too. This, however, is the material basis for political relations, for normalizing them and creating an atmosphere of trust.

Speaking frankly, economic ties involve mutual inter-dependence, which influences the settlement of political problems later.

I believe that a further expansion of economic ties would meet the interests of both the Soviet Union and the United States. You need not think, however, that we are begging for it.

Question (the newspaper *An-Nahar Arab Report*, Lebanon)
Speaking of regional problems, did you discuss the situation in the Middle East, and the situation in Lebanon in particular? What is your forecast regarding this situation after the summit meeting?

Answer. In the course of the meeting we touched on the situation in such regions as Central America, the Middle East and Africa. However, we devoted practically all of our time to discussing the fundamental aspects of these questions. We agreed to continue political consultations and widen the framework of co-operation on regional problems.

Question (the writer, J. Semyonov)
Comrade Gorbachov, you have spoken of the need to learn to live together. My experience as an author tells me that since the notorious time of McCarthy, the film industry and television of the United States have been painting Soviet citizens as monsters. Do you not believe that now, after the meeting at Geneva, it would be highly important for the United States to revise its biased ideas of the Soviet people and take a more objective view of them as a partner of the American people?

Answer. I can tell you this, Comrade Semyonov. Do not put all problems on the shoulders of the political leaders. We have agreed on an expansion of cultural exchanges, which include motion pictures, so you can meet and come to terms with each other. You must act in the spirit of Geneva, that is, help improve Soviet–American relations.

21.

Report at the 4th Session of the 11th Supreme Soviet of the USSR
Pravda, 28 November 1985

Comrade deputies!

The key problems of the home and foreign policies of the Soviet State have been submitted to the present session of the Supreme Soviet of the USSR.

The laws on the State Plan for the Economic and Social Development of the USSR and the State Budget for 1986 adopted by this session are of enormous significance to this country, to its present and future, to each work collective and each Soviet family. The coming year 1986 is not only the first year of the 12th Five-Year Plan, but it also opens a qualitatively new chapter in the development of Soviet society.

The plan for 1986 reflects the Party's strategic line of accelerating the country's socio-economic progress. It provides for faster growth rates of the national income, production of farm and industrial goods and labour efficiency. The effectiveness of use of material resources will grow. First priority is attached to the development of the industries called upon to secure rapid scientific and technological progress and improve product quality.

Measures have been outlined to accelerate reconstruction, renewal, and modernization of production, and to improve management and the economic mechanism. Further improvement of public welfare is contemplated.

It is important for all of us constantly to keep the specifics of the plan for 1986 in our field of vision.

Already in the first year of the Five-Year Plan an accurate pace should be set for the entire five-year period. In view of this, the development rates of the national economy in 1986 have been set to secure fulfilment of the assignments of the Five-Year Plan as a whole. These rates will be gradually raised in the coming few years. This will enable us to avoid a situation like the one which was in evidence in the last Five-Year Plan period, where reduced indicators were set for the first few years, while the bulk of the increment was shifted towards later years. What negative results followed such practices is well known.

Another distinction of the plan is a maximum consideration given to the need to speed up scientific and technological progress. Guided by the instructions of the June Conference at the CPSU Central Committee, the plan incorporates in the first place assignments for accelerating scientific and technological progress envisaged in the resolutions on developing the key research trends in science and technology in individual sectors of the national economy. Simultaneously the traditional principles of planning have been largely revised. The plan provides for the first time for major summary indicators to assess scientific and technological progress in individual industries and its efficiency. These indicators are set to stimulate more active practical work by the Ministries, production associations and enterprises to secure an advance to the frontiers of science and technology.

The next distinct feature of the plan for 1986 is its orientation on a practical transition to intensive methods of economic work. This is dictated by the realities of life and the fairly complex situation in the area of manpower and material resources, the exhaustion of the main extensive factors of economic growth. Next year we must achieve an increment in production based as much as possible on saved resources. In other words, saving in practical terms is becoming the main source of resource supply for securing all increments in production. This is evidenced by the following figures. In the next year 97 per cent of the increment in national income will be secured by increased labour productivity, while metal consumption in the national income will be reduced by 2.7 per cent and power consumption by 3 per cent.

And, finally, there is a broad transition to new methods of economic management which have proved their efficiency. From January 1986 industry will be manufacturing more than half of the total products at enterprises operating under new conditions.

On the whole, the line mapped out is certainly right. Now we have to implement it in the process of further detailing of plans in industries, republics, territories and regions, at production associations and smaller enterprises and, naturally, in daily practical work.

This aspect should be emphasized specifically because many executives in central bodies and at local level, in particular in economic planning bodies, have not yet realized the full importance of the assessment and settlement of the country's economic, social and financial problems in a new way.

The present session is taking place in a highly responsible pre-Congress period. The April Plenary Meeting of the CPSU Central Committee charted a policy of accelerating the socio-economic development of society and initiated substantial changes in approach to the solution of economic and political problems. The Plenary Meeting set a new tone for all the activities of the Party, government, and local Soviet organizations, and of all Soviet cadres and work collectives.

For the areas of domestic and international affairs the Party's political line has been reflected completely in the fundamental theoretical and political documents which will be submitted to the 27th Congress of the CPSU, in the drafts of a new edition of the CPSU Programme, and in the amendments to the Party Rules, and the Guidelines for the Economic and Social Development of the USSR in the period 1986-1990 and up to 2000.

The first results of the Party's discussions with the people testify that the documents submitted for their consideration give them profound satisfaction. Their active support for the Party's strategic line — support by word and deed — is the source of our optimism, and our confidence in the correctness of the chosen path and the feasibility of our plans.

As you know, the Central Committee of the Party and the Soviet Government have recently taken a series of important steps to accelerate the re-orientation of the economy on the lines of intensive development, to raise the efficiency of the economic management on a nation-wide scale. Practical measures are being implemented further to promote law and order, labour discipline, discipline in government work, strict economy and the campaign against drunkenness and alcoholism. In other words, the great and intense work launched in all spheres of social life is already yielding its first fruits.

The innovative approach in our life today has stirred the enthusiasm of the Soviet people and stimulated their creativity. It has proved once again the existence of enormous latent reserves and potentials in the socialist system.

Now we can confidently say that a change for the better is already in evidence. The growth rates of production are rising and other economic indicators are improving. Despite some setbacks in a number of economic sectors in the early days of the year, the Soviet people have remedied the situation and brought the economy close to its targets. Positive shifts are taking place in the agrarian sector of the country as well.

Credit for these achievements is due to the heroic working class, which is sparing no effort or energy to overcome the difficulties and do its utmost to fulfil the plans. These achievements are also due to the intense work of the collective farmers, and all the workers of the agro-industrial complex. They are also based on the creative ideas of scientists, engineers and the people's intelligentsia. Many important initiatives have been pioneered by young Soviet citizens who are coping with difficult and complicated tasks boldly and vigorously, and are actively supporting the changes taking place in society, linking them with their own future.

We also link these changes with more active work done by our Party, local government and trade union bodies and cadres.

In short, very much is being done. However, it would be a mistake to overestimate our achievements, and this would be contrary to our traditions. We have taken only the first step along a complicated and arduous road demanding a creative approach to the tasks that life poses — purposefulness, discipline and selflessness. We have enormous reserves and potentials and we will have to do a good deal of work to bring them into play to the best advantage. This should be done in all avenues and areas of economic, social and cultural development. It refers primarily to areas where the situation remains complex and the lag is being overcome slowly.

Today, in the final stretch of the Five-Year Plan, hard work is needed to begin confident and dynamic progress from next year, to secure the attainment of our targets, and provide the prerequisites for a further qualitative change in modernizing the country's productive forces.

The 1986 plan graphically demonstrates the peaceful character of our work. All our foreign policy goals and the international policy of the Soviet State in general are closely linked with the peaceful orientation of domestic policy.

The foreign policy goals formulated at the April Plenary Meeting of the Central Committee CPSU are a concrete expression of the Soviet Union's Leninist foreign policy today. The Plenary Meeting emphasized the need to intensify all aspects of the Soviet Union's efforts for peace along the broadest front of international relations. The meeting appealed for an all-out effort to prevent militarism and aggression from prevailing over the forces of peace and emphasized the urgency of ending the arms race and beginning disarmament. It took a stand in favour of developing balanced, correct and civilized relations between states, as well as widening and deepening mutually beneficial economic exchanges.

These Plenary Meeting guidelines were dictated by the times, the distinctive features of the prevailing situation and the requirements of the socialist policy of peace and progress. In its estimates the Politbureau of the Central Committee proceeded from the assumption that the continuing arms race entails a growing unpredictability of events. The possible militarization of outer space lends a new dimension to the arms race and inevitably leads to the obsolescence of the very concept of strategic stability, which is the basis of the maintenance of peace in the nuclear age. It would entail a situation where decisions of principle, irreversible in regard of their possible consequences, would be taken in effect by electronic computers without the participation of the human mind and the political will, and without taking account of the moral and ethical criteria. Such developments could lead to general catastrophe even if it were triggered by an error or a technical hitch in a highly sophisticated computerized system.

In other words, world developments have come to a critical limit, where highly responsible decisions are needed and where inaction or delay are criminal because the very existence of civilization and life itself are at stake. This is why we deem it necessary, as in the past, to take whatever steps are needed to break the vicious circle of the arms race, and to seize every chance to turn the tide of events in the direction of improvement. The problem is extremely acute and well defined: it is imperative to rise above narrow national interests and realize the collective responsibility of all states in the face of mortal danger to the human community on the threshold of the third millenium.

That is precisely the approach we have been instructed to apply in implementing Soviet foreign policy by the April Plenary Meeting of the Central Committee. This approach is in complete accord with the interests of the Soviet people and the peoples of other socialist states and, as we have witnessed, it is welcomed also in other countries of the world. In a brief but eventful period the Soviet Union has sought to co-operate in the interest of peace with a broad range of states. We have invariably proceeded from the assumption that this period of dangerous tensions can be ended only by the efforts of all countries, large and small.

Over the past few months the political and economic ties of the countries belonging to the socialist community have become much more active and more profound. Long-term programmes have been drawn up for co-operation in the economic, scientific and technological fields. A mechanism of operational ties has been established and the co-ordination of foreign policies is becoming more effective. The meetings of the leaders of the fraternal countries in Moscow, Warsaw, Sofia, and Prague are milestones on the road of further cohesion of the socialist community. Our ties with all the socialist states are developing and growing stronger.

Co-operation with states which have recently liberated themselves from colonial oppression and are now members of the non-aligned movement is steadily growing, too. Important steps have been taken to develop relations with many of these countries. This is a factor of enormous significance in the violent ocean of present-day international relations, a factor operating in favour of peace, equality, freedom and the independence of nations.

The Soviet Union is making strenuous efforts to improve its ties with capitalist states. I will emphasize specifically the recent Franco-Soviet conference in Paris, which undertook effective steps to further Franco-Soviet bilateral co-operation, promote European and world security, and facilitate a return to *détente*.

We will continue to prosecute our foreign policy on a comprehensive basis, maintaining stable and durable bilateral relations with all countries. The realities of the modern world, however, impose on some states — by virtue of their military, economic, scientific and technological potential and their international prestige — a special responsibility for the character of world developments, their course and consequences. I wish to emphasize that this is a responsibility, not a privilege but a duty, which has been imposed by history on the Soviet Union and the United States. Viewed from this angle the Soviet–

American summit held last week was, in the estimation of the Central Committee's Politbureau, an important event not only in our bilateral relations but in world politics as a whole. I have already discussed my first impressions of the talks with the US President at a press conference at Geneva. The communique of the meeting — a joint declaration — is also known to you.

Speaking before the Supreme Soviet of the USSR today, I would like to evaluate the results and significance of the Geneva summit in the context of the present-day situation, taking account of the record of the past and the prospects for the future and with a view to the tasks we are to accomplish.

I must tell you in the first place that the road towards the Geneva dialogue had been long and arduous for a variety of reasons. The US Administration which had come into office in the early eighties frankly set course for a confrontation and rejected the very possibility of Soviet–American relations developing favourably. I believe everybody remembers the vehement anti-Soviet rhetoric of those years, and the power politics visible in the conduct of the American ruling circles.

The efforts made for years by the two sides to provide the necessary modicum of trust in these relations were buried in oblivion and almost all ties of bilateral co-operation were severed. The very concept of *détente* was declared prejudicial to the interests of the United States.

Seeking to achieve military superiority over the USSR, the US Administration embarked on a programme of nuclear rearmament of the United States and arms modernization in other fields. In Western Europe, American first-strike missiles were deployed. That created a situation of great military and political unpredictability, with all the risks of war involved.

Finally, the Star Wars project, the so-called Strategic Defence Initiative, came on the scene. This idea literally captivated Washington, which did not give much thought to the fatal consequences that would inevitably follow its implementation. The plan to invade outer space with armaments is extremely dangerous to all nations of the world, without exception.

However, we also knew that US policy was bound to collide with reality. That is what has in fact happened. The Soviet Union and its allies have declared for all the world to hear that they would not allow military superiority to be gained over them.

There was confusion even among US allies faced by such blatant contempt for their security interests and by Washington's determination to stake everything on a chase after the chimera of military superiority. This policy has caused serious doubts in the United States itself. The announcement of plans for the preparations for Star Wars sounded as a veritable alarm signal throughout the world.

Those who believed that their policy of confrontation would be decisive for international development have miscalculated: I should add in this context that their dreams of world supremacy are basically defective both in what concerns their goals and in what concerns their means. As plans for *perpetuum mobile* are generated by ignorance of the elementary laws of nature, so imperial ambitions are generated by concepts of the modern world far distant from reality.

The Soviet Union combined its firm rebuff to the US policy of upsetting the military strategic balance with large-scale peace initiatives and excercised restraint and a constructive approach in handling the central problem of peace and security.

We have clearly shown by our numerous initiatives what we are trying to achieve in the world arena, calling on the United States and its allies to join in our efforts. These actions by the Soviet Union have been welcomed by the world public and by the governments of many countries.

Washington was compelled to back down and manoeuvre under the impact of these factors. Declarations by the US Administration sounded notes of an apparent commitment to peace. They were not corroborated by deeds, but their very appearance was symptomatic.

Early in this year agreement was reached on our initiative on new talks between the Soviet Union and the United States on the full range of space and nuclear weapons, with the object of preventing an arms race in outer space and ending the arms race on earth.

The atmosphere of Soviet–American relations and the US conduct on the international scene showed signs of change which were taken into account in examining the problem of a possible summit meeting.

Taking that decision we firmly abided by the principle that the talks should focus on the problems crucial to our relations and the world situation — the problems of security. At the same time we took into consideration the political and strategic realities in Europe and the world, the opinion of our friends and allies, the positions of the governments and public circles of many countries, and their persistent appeals to the Soviet Union to do its utmost to bring about a top level meeting. We realized how many hopes were pinned on this summit throughout the world and took practical steps to help normalize the international climate and make it more favourable to the forthcoming meeting.

At the Geneva talks on nuclear and space weapons we advanced concrete and radical proposals. What is their essence?

We proposed in the first place a total ban on space strike weapons. We made this proposal, because an arms race in outer space and even the deployment of only anti-missile systems in near-earth space will not strengthen the security of any state. Under cover of a space shield the nuclear means of attack will become even more dangerous.

The development of strike space weapons could play havoc with the present strategic balance, trigger off a feverish arms race in all directions and undermine one of the main barriers against it — the Anti-Missile Defence Treaty. As a result, mistrust in relations between countries would grow and their security would be greatly damaged.

Further, along with a total ban on strike space weapons we proposed a fifty per cent reduction in all nuclear armaments available to the USSR and the United States capable of reaching each other's territories. The total number of nuclear charges on each side was to be limited to 6000. These are indeed radical cuts involving thousands of nuclear charges.

This approach is fair. It covers the weapons that maintain the strategic balance and allows assessment of real nuclear danger to each side, regardless of where and how nuclear charges are to be delivered to their territories — by missile or plane, from their own territories or from those of their allies.

We regard a reduction in the Soviet and American nuclear arsenals by fifty per cent as only a first step. We are prepared to go as far as the complete abolition of nuclear weapons, with other nuclear powers, of course, taking part.

Naturally, the nuclear arms race is causing grave concern among European nations. We understand this concern quite well. Europe is bristling with nuclear weapons. The Soviet Union is in favour of the complete deliverance of Europe from nuclear weapons, both medium-range and tactical. However, the United States and its NATO partners would not agree. Then we proposed interim decisions for a start, to be followed by further reductions. We are convinced that these proposals meet the hopes of the European nations for lessening the risk of nuclear war and for greater security in Europe.

I wish to emphasize one point of principle: in all the three areas of the talks — outer space, strategic offensive arms, and intermediate-range nuclear weapons — we have proposed nothing to the United States that would prejudice its security. Moreover, our proposals make it possible to find a solution to the problems the American side has raised to the rank of "special concerns".

For instance, there is much talk about Soviet intercontinental ballistic missiles. Our proposals provide for a cut in the number of ICBMs and a limit to the proportion of warheads in the total number of nuclear charges. Or take another example. In the West there has been much clamour about Soviet SS-20 missiles. We propose a substantial cut in their number in the context of a solution to the problem of intermediate-range nuclear weapons in Europe.

The nuclear forces of Britain and France are presented as an obstacle to a settlement. It is claimed that they cannot be discussed at Soviet–American talks. Well, we are prepared to seek a solution in this area as well. We propose a direct exchange of opinion with these countries regarding their nuclear weapons.

The Soviet proposals have met with a broad and favourable response throughout the world. They are backed by the prestige of the Warsaw Treaty member states which are unanimously in favour of our constructive initiative. Our approach is shared in many ways by the joint declarations of the leaders of six countries — Argentina, Mexico, Tanzania, India, Sweden and Greece. The Soviet initiative has been received with hope and approval by Communist and Workers' Parties, large public organizations in different countries and continents, scientists of worldwide renown, prominent political and military leaders. It has been welcomed by the majority of the parties of the Socialist International.

I have not included the thousands of letters I received from Soviet and foreign nationals on the eve of the Geneva summit and while it was in progress. I avail myself of this opportunity to thank them for their good wishes, their advice and support, their profound and sincere concern for the preservation of peace.

On the eve of the summit the Americans had come forward with their counter-proposals. This fact is positive in itself. One of our numerous initiatives was reciprocated. The press has written at length on the essence of these counter-proposals. I will not repeat their contents. I will only say that they are half-hearted and largely unfair proposals. They are based on a one-sided approach and clearly dictated by ambitions for military superiority by the United States and NATO as a whole.

What matters most is the absence in the US proposals of a ban on developing strike space weapons. On the contrary, their development is to be made legal. The stand taken by the American side on the issue of Star Wars is the main obstacle to agreement on arms control. This is not only our opinion. The governments of France, Denmark, Norway, Greece, the Netherlands, Canada and Australia have refused to be involved in research on the so-called Strategic Defence Initiative. On the eve of the Geneva summit the UN General Assembly passed a resolution urging the leaders of the Soviet Union and the United States to work out effective agreements aimed at averting an arms race in outer space and ending the arms race on earth. Only the United States and a few of its allies chose to deny support to this clear appeal from the world community. This fact needs no comment, as they say.

It may be relevant to recall that powerful political forces in the United States went out of their way to frustrate the summit or at least to emasculate its content and reduce its significance to nil. I believe that many still remember such events as the testing of an anti-satellite system, the appearance of the battleship Iowa armed with long-range cruise missiles in the Baltic, the hasty deployment of Pershing missiles in the Federal Republic of Germany, the decision to manufacture binary chemical weapons and, finally, the adoption of a new record military budget.

Moreover, the President was already on his way to Geneva when we learned of a letter from the US Secretary of Defense urging him not to agree to any arrangements with the Soviet Union that would confirm the treaties on the limitation of strategic arms and on anti-missile defence. In other words, the United States would retain full freedom of action in all directions of the arms race both on earth and in outer space.

The matter, however, was not limited to the Pentagon alone. We also took note of the "mandate" of its own kind given to the US President by the American Right-wing extremists represented by their ideological headquarters "The Heritage Trust". The President was exhorted to continue the arms race, not to give the Soviet Union a chance to regear its resources to socio-economic programmes, and to make efforts to oust the USSR from international politics. These gentlemen went as far as to request the US Administration to force the Soviet Union to revise its system and its Constitution. These are familiar motifs. All of us have heard them more than once before. In short, there were quite a few attacks against us.

Nevertheless, we voted in favour of a meeting with the US President. Our motive was a desire to check the dangerous trends of developments in the world; we had no right to ignore the slightest chance of that. We realized that if we failed to open a frank dialogue now, it would be a hundred times more difficult to do so tomorrow, and perhaps it would be too late.

There is no doubt that the differences between us are truly enormous. In today's world, however, the interrelationship and interdependence between us are just as great. The gravity of the situation leaves no alternative for the leaders of the Soviet Union and the United States and their peoples to learning the great art of peaceful co-existence.

At the very first face to face discussion with the President — and such private sessions were many during the meeting at Geneva — it was stated frankly that the Soviet delegation had come to seek a solution to the most burning problem now in the focus of international affairs, the problem of preventing nuclear war and checking the arms race. As I told the President, this was the main purpose of our meeting that would determine its results.

I want to emphasize that the Geneva talks were at times quite heated and frank to the utmost. It is impossible to outsmart each other in this situation or hide under a smokescreen of political and propaganda cliches, because too much depends on the pivotal problems of war and peace.

In the course of the meeting the American side stubbornly insisted on the need to implement its SDI programme. We were told that it was a programme for developing defensive facilities which had nothing in common with weaponry. We were also told that these facilities would help stabilize the situation and do away with nuclear weapons in general. We were even offered an exchange of these facilities in some foreseeable future and the opening of laboratories to each other's inspection.

We frankly told the President of our disagreement with such ideas. We analysed all these questions thoroughly and arrived at a definite conclusion. Space weapons are not defensive at all. They can generate a dangerous illusion that a first nuclear strike can be delivered from behind a space shield, while a retaliation can be prevented or weakened at any rate. Besides, what guarantees can be given that space weapons would not be used to attack targets on earth? All the evidence available indicates that the US anti-missile space system in conceived not as a shield but as part of an integrated offensive complex.

Naturally, we cannot agree with the assertion that the space facilities envisaged in the SDI programme are not weapons. Nor can we trust the assurances that the United States would share with us what it managed to develop in this area.

If laboratories are to be opened, this should be done only for verification of compliance with a ban on developing strike space weapons, rather than for their legalization.

We are told of a desire to end the fear of missiles, to achieve the abolition of nuclear weapons in general. Such a desire should be welcomed and it completely accords with our own policy goals. However, it is much more practical to eliminate these weapons without developing strike space systems for this purpose. Why waste tens and hundreds of thousand-million dollars to build up stockpiles of space weapons in addition to nuclear ones? What is the significance of that?

I asked the President whether the US leadership seriously believed that if American space weapons were developed we would reduce our strategic potential and help the United States weaken it with our own hands? One should not expect that. The opposite would take place. To restore the balance the Soviet Union would be compelled to raise the efficiency, accuracy and power of its weapons to be able to neutralize, if necessary, the electronic space machine of Star Wars developed by the Americans.

Would the Americans indeed feel safer if our weapons were added to the echelons of space weapons Washington is planning to deploy in outer space? Indeed, the United States cannot hope for a monopoly on outer space. All this does not look serious, to say the least.

However, the US Administration still feels the temptation to explore the possibility of gaining military superiority. By initiating an arms race in outer space now, they are expecting to beat us in electronics and computers. As it has more than once been the case in the past, we will meet this challenge. It would be an effective, sufficiently quick and perhaps less costly response than the American programme. That we also declared to the President in all frankness.

I believe that a real improvement in our relations, meeting the interests of the Soviet Union and the United States and the interests of the world's nations, demands a new approach, a fresh look at many things and, what matters most, the political will of the leadership in both countries. The Soviet Union feels no hostility towards the United States and respects the American people, and I made a point of this at

Geneva. Our policy is not motivated by a desire to infringe US national interests. Moreover, I should say that we would not like, for instance, the strategic balance to be upset in our favour. The reason is simple: that situation would increase suspicions on the other side and the instability of the general situation.

Developments demand that our two countries should get used to strategic parity as a natural state. We must form a common understanding of what level of armaments on each side may be considered relatively sufficient for reliable defence. We are convinced that the level of such sufficiency is much lower than what is practically available to the Soviet Union and the United States today. This means that effective practical steps to limit and reduce armaments are quite possible. These measures would not undermine but, on the contrary, would strengthen the security of both the Soviet Union and the United States and increase the entire strategic stability in the world.

What can I say about other problems discussed at the meeting?

I shall start with the problem of regional conflicts. Both sides expressed their concern about the persistence of such trouble spots. And small wonder. Such conflicts are dangerous, especially in view of the threat of their expansion in the nuclear age.

However, our approaches to the causes and ways of settling such conflicts are not only different, but in fact diametrically opposed. The United States, accustomed to thinking in terms of "spheres of interests", reduces all these problems to a rivalry between East and West. In our day, however, it is a relapse into imperial mentality, a thinking that denies to the majority of nations the right to independent thought and decision making.

The deep-seated sources of such conflicts are diverse and partly rooted in history. But they stem mainly from the social and economic conditions facing the newly independent countries. It is not fortuitous, of course, that when speaking of the problems of regional conflicts the United States keeps silent about the atrocities of the apartheid system in the Republic of South Africa, the agression of that country against its African neighbours, the wars waged by American puppets in Central America and South-East Asia, Israel's aggression in the Middle East, and many other things. Washington is trying to put on the same footing the lawful governments of states following the path of national liberation and social progress, on the one hand, and counter-revolution on the other.

Needless to say, we could not accept that interpretation. We told the

President that we are in favour of a recognition of the inalienable right of every people to freedom and independence, and to a free choice of the system to live under. We are opposed to violations of such rights, to foreign interference in internal affairs; we are for the triumph of freedom, not tyranny. We have always been and will be on the side of the peoples, defending their independence. This is our policy of principle.

The President touched on the issue of Afghanistan. In this context it was again reaffirmed that the Soviet Union consistently advocated a political settlement of the situation around Afghanistan. We want friendly, neighbouring Afghanistan to continue to be an independent nonaligned state, and a policy of guaranteed non-interference in the affairs of Afghanistan to be established. The question of the withdrawal of Soviet troops from that country would thereby be settled. The Soviet Union and the government of Afghanistan are a hundred per cent in favour. If anyone is interfering with an early solution to this problem, it is above all the United States, which is financing, supporting, and arming counter-revolutionary gangs and frustrating efforts to normalize the situation.

Problems of bilateral relations were discussed in fairly great detail during the talks. Some improvement which has been in evidence in this area of late has now been reinforced with concrete agreements on exchanges and ties in the fields of science, education and culture, and on a resumption of air travel between our two countries.

Needless to say, it would be much easier to bring into play the full potential available here in a situation where work will be started to settle the security problems vital to our relations. If co-operation is to be effective it should be on an equal basis, without any discrimination or preconditions, without any attempts to interfere in the internal affairs of the other side. We have taken a strong and consistent stand on this issue.

How is one to assess the main results of the Geneva meeting?

The summit was indisputably a significant event. Straightforward, clear and constructive discussions are very useful, just as a chance to compare our positions is a good opportunity, too. Indeed, too many explosive and pressing problems have accumulated, and these problems have to be discussed seriously to end the stalemate in our relations.

We value the personal contacts we have established with the US President. A dialogue between top leaders invariably adds an element of truth to relations between states. It is important that such a dialogue has been held at all, since in the present complicated situation it is a factor of stability in itself.

However, we are realists and we should frankly say that we have failed to find solutions to the key problems involved in ending the arms race. The unwillingness of the US leadership to renounce the Star Wars programme precluded the Geneva summit from producing concrete arrangements on practical disarmament and primarily on the central problem of nuclear and space weapons. The stockpiles of weapons on both sides have not diminished as a result of the Geneva summit and the arms race is going on. This, of course, is causing disappointment.

The Soviet Union and the United States are divided as before by wide differences on a number of other problems of principle regarding the world situation and developments in individual regions However, we by no means intend to play down the significance of the accords reached at Geneva.

I will recall the most important of them. This is primarily our common understanding expressed in our joint declaration that nuclear war must never be allowed to happen and that there would be no victors in such a war, as well as the commitment of the Soviet Union and the United States to build their relations on the basis of this indisputable fact, refraining from attempts to gain military superiority.

We believe that this understanding, reached jointly at the top level, should serve practically as the basis of the foreign policies of the two states. As long as it is admitted that nuclear war cannot be an instrument for achieving any rational aims whatsoever, the stimulus to its prevention, cessation of development and testing of weapons of mass destruction, and complete abolition of the existing stockpiles of nuclear weapons must be stronger still. It is absolutely impermissible to initiate new directions in the arms race. Of course, a joint declaration is not a treaty, but it is a binding commitment of principle on the part of the leaders of the two countries.

Further, the Soviet Union and the United States clearly reaffirmed their commitment to contribute in every way to improving the effectiveness of the control of the non proliferation of nuclear weapons and agreed on joint practical steps in this direction. In the present troubled international situation this is of fairly great significance for maintaining stability in the world and lessening the risk of nuclear war.

The joint declaration of the two leaders in favour of a total and universal prohibition and destruction of such barbarian tools of war as chemical weapons is also of fundamental significance. It is to be hoped that in its practical policy the United States will act in accordance with this important accord.

The agreement between the leadership of the Soviet Union and the United States, jointly with other states participating in the Stockholm Conference, to contribute to its early success also extends far beyond the framework of Soviet–American relations. This would involve the adoption of a document including concrete commitments on the non-use of force and mutually acceptable confidence-building measures.

It is gratifying to know that a number of useful agreements were reached in the course of the meeting in many areas of bilateral co-operation between the Soviet Union and the United States. I believe they will provide a good basis for enhancing trust between our two countries and peoples if, of course, the agreements are observed accurately and steps are taken to develop whatever good elements are available in them rather than to search for artificial pretexts to frustrate them.

I would like to mention specifically the significance of the agreements reached in Geneva on further political contacts between the Soviet Union and the United States, including new top-level meetings.

Thus, we are entitled to proclaim that the general balance of the Geneva talks is favourable.

The achievement of this hopeful result was indisputably facilitated to a decisive extent by the Soviet Union's constructive and consistent policy. At the same time, it would be unfair in relation to the American side not to commend certain elements of realism in its position, which were helpful to a number of settlements.

Of course, the true significance of whatever useful accords were reached at Geneva can be expressed in practical moves alone. I wish to declare in this context that the Soviet Union is determined to keep up the tempo and take further steps in the spirit of honest co-operation with the United States towards an end to the arms race and a general improvement of the international situation. We expect reciprocity on the part of the United States. Then, I am confident, the work done at Geneva would yield good fruits.

Such is our assessment of the summit and its role in international relations. I am pleased to tell you that this assessment is shared by our allies. The fraternal socialist countries, which was clearly evidenced by the conference of the leaders of the Warsaw treaty member states held in Prague immediately after the Soviet–American top-level talks.

The participants in the Prague meeting emphasized that the situation remained, of course, fairly complex. Efforts to normalize it are being continued, but the conditions for this work are improving, which is already obvious today. The Geneva summit is an important component of our long-term and closely coordinated joint efforts aimed at securing peace.

It is natural to pose the question: what is to be done next in view of the results of the Soviet–American dialogue at Geneva?

As I have said above, we attach great significance to the accord we have reached at Geneva on holding new Soviet–American talks at summit level. I wish to emphasize that our approach to this question is not a formal one. The very fact of another summit between the two leaders is important but it is its results that matter most. Our peoples will expect practical progress along the path mapped out at Geneva. This is precisely what we will work for. Preparations for the next Soviet–American summit should be started now, in the sphere of practical policy first and foremost.

Not to frustrate future arrangements, both sides, we are convinced, should abstain from actions likely to undermine what was reached at Geneva. They should refrain from acts that would block negotiations and erode the effective limitations on the arms race. This implies, in particular, honest and faithful compliance with the Treaty on the Limitation of Anti-Missile Defence Systems, as well as further mutual observance of the relevant provisions of the SALT-2 treaty by the two sides.

The main thing, of course, is the need to provide the requisite conditions for a real end to the arms race and to take practical steps to curtail the existing nuclear arsenals.

Is this possible in principle? We are firmly convinced that it is. It is true that there is a wide difference between our proposals and the American proposals for nuclear arms reductions. However, we do not want to dramatize this circumstance. Compromise deals are possible and we are prepared to search for them.

There is no doubt that such a development would help provide a solution to the problems of reliable verification in which the Soviet Union has a direct interest. One cannot rely on promises here, all the more so as it is a question of disarmament and national defence.

However, for all these problems to be settled it is absolutely impera-tive to shut the door securely on weapons to outer space. Without this a radical cut in nuclear arms is impossible. I declare this with a full awareness of my responsibility on behalf of the people and their supreme governmental body.

Agreement is feasible if the interests of both sides are taken into consideration. The stubbon desire of the American side to go ahead with developing space weapons can have only one result: frustration of the efforts to end the nuclear arms race. Needless to say, such an outcome would cause bitter disillusion among the world's nations, including, I am sure, the American people.

Today there is a realistic chance to lessen the risk of nuclear war drastically and then to make it impossible altogether. It would be a fatal mistake to miss this chance. We hope that what the American side stated about SDI at Geneva is not its last word.

We agreed with President Reagan to instruct our delegations at the Geneva talks on nuclear and space weapons to accelerate negotiations on the basis of the January accord between the two countries. Thus, the two sides have reaffirmed at top level that an arms race in outer space should be prevented and this problem should be settled in the context of nuclear arms reduction. The Soviet Union will make efforts to this end. We are calling on the United States to join us. By fulfilling our joint obligations we shall live up to the hopes of the nations of the world.

The problem of ending nuclear tests assumes added urgency as time goes by. The primary reason is that such a cessation would terminate work on developing new types of nuclear weapons and improving existing types. The next reason: in the absence of tests and renewal the process of obsolescence of nuclear weapons would tend to gain momentum. Finally, the last reason: it is no longer tolerable to have nuclear explosions of which there have been hundreds, cripple our beautiful earth, increasing our concern about the conditions of life that succeeding generations will face on this planet.

For that reason the Soviet Union announced a moratorium on all types of nuclear explosions to be effective until 1 January 1986 and is prepared to prolong this moratorium if the United States reciprocates. We are expecting from the US Administration a concrete and positive decision that would have a favourable im-pact on the entire situation, largely change it and strengthen trust between our two countries. We raised this question with the US President at the Geneva summit.

There was no answer. Indeed, there are no reasonable arguments against a ban on nuclear testing. Sometimes allusions to difficulties of verification are made. The Soviet Union, however, has clearly demonstrated the possibility of such verification by means of national monitoring facilities. This year we detected an underground nuclear explosion of very little power carried out in the United States without a prior announcement.

We are prepared to discuss the possibility of establishing international control. In this context proposals put forward in the message of the six states merit attention. They offered to set up special monitoring stations in their national territories to verify compliance with an agreement on ending nuclear tests.

The whole world is clamouring for a ban on nuclear testing. The UN General Assembly has just passed a resolution appealing for this step. Only three countries — the United States, Britain and France — voted against. This is very regrettable.

There is still time, however, and I believe that the leaders of the United States and the other nuclear powers will take advantage of this opportunity, motivated by the interests of peace, and live up to their responsibility. It will be recalled that our moratorium remains in force, and we hope that the discussion of this problem at this session of the Supreme Soviet of the USSR will be interpreted as an urgent appeal for an effective and prompt prohibition of all nuclear tests.

On the whole, the Soviet Union is proposing an all-embracing complex of measures designed to block all the channels of the arms race, be it in outer space or on earth, be it in nuclear, chemical or conventional armaments. Our concrete proposals to this effect are known; they were made in Vienna, at Geneva and in Stockholm. They are still valid and as urgent as ever.

Europe should be discussed separately. The task of preventing a further rise in military confrontation is pressing as never before in this area. Europe is our common home, where geography and history have blended into a common whole the destinies of dozens of countries and peoples. The Europeans can protect their home and make it more comfortable and safer only by collective efforts, following the sensible rules of international intercourse and co-operation.

We are aware of the fact that Europe, which has given the world so much in culture, science, technology and progressive social thought is capable of setting a model for solving the most complicated problems of present-day international affairs. The basis for this was laid at Helsinki ten years ago. It is our profound conviction that the whole world, including the United States, will eventually stand to gain from positive development of the European situation. We have worked hard and are determined to make a thorough further effort to have the principles and policy of *détente* implanted on the European continent, which has witnessed so many wars; for the debris of the past to be cleared and the consequences of the confrontation of the last two years to be done away with for good and all.

I would like to say a couple of words on trade and economic ties. The business community in many countries of the West desire to set up broader economic ties with the Soviet Union. I have heard on many occasions of this willingness to be involved in joint large-scale projects and major deals from very influential members of this community. I believe that political leaders trying to limit this natural desire of business co-operation in the hope of punishing whoever they consider a culprit and causing harm to a partner are simply not sensible enough. Such a policy has long outlived its time. It is much more useful to apply efforts to a difference cause to ensure that trade, scientific and technological exchanges strengthen the material basis for accord and trust.

In the struggle for lasting peace and co-operation among nations in Europe and on the other continents we will continue to act in close co-operation with our Warsaw Treaty allies, all members of the socialist community of nations. The member states of the Warsaw Treaty Organization would under no circumstances agree to anything that may jeopardize the security of their peoples. They will increasingly pool their efforts within the COMECON framework to accelerate their scientific and technological progress and then social and economic development.

The relations of co-operation with the non-aligned movement, including all-round co-operation with the Republic of India, is of enormous significance for normalizing international relations in general. We feel profound respect for the people and leadership of India.

The Soviet leadership attaches great significance to the Asian and Pacific regions. The Soviet Union has its longest borders in Asia; here we have loyal friends and dependable allies — from neighbouring Mongolia to socialist Vietnam. It is extremely important to ensure that this region should not be a source of tension or a sphere of military confrontation. We are in favour of a broadening political dialogue between all Asian states in the interests of peace, good-neighbourly relations, mutual trust, and co-operation.

We welcome the stand of the People's Republic of China, which is opposed to the militarization of outer space, and its declaration on the renunciation of first use of nuclear weapons.

We are in favour of improving relations with Japan and are confident that this improvement is practicable. This conclusion follows from the simple fact that our two countries are neighbours. The removal of the risk of nuclear war is a vital task in which the Soviet Union and Japan have an equal interest.

We have relations of co-operation based on equality with many states of Latin America. Africa, and the Middle East. The Soviet Union is determined to make consistent efforts to develop these relations. We value particularly highly the ties developed with socialist-oriented countries of different continents.

Today, the nations of the world face a great many problems that can be solved only by joint efforts in conditions of peace. A few decades ago people were hardly worried by any grave ecological problems. Already our generation, however, is witnessing a mass-scale destruction of forests, the extinction of animal species, the pollution of rivers and lakes and an expansion of deserts. What will the world be like for succeeding generations? Will they be able to live in the world if the rapacious destruction of nature is not stopped, and if the economic, technological and scientific achievements of today are used not to sustain the existence and development of man and his natural environment, but to improve the tools of war? Take the power problem. For the time being, we live mostly at the expense of the earth's entrails. What is close to the surface, however, has been nearly exhausted, and the continued use of these resources is increasingly costly and difficult. What is more, this source of power is not everlasting.

The growing gulf between a handful of highly developed capitalist countries and the developing countries which make up the vast majority plagued by poverty, famine, and frustration is also fraught with dangerous cataclysms. The gulf between these world poles is yawning and relations are becoming increasingly antagonistic. This cannot be otherwise unless the developed capitalist countries revise their selfish policy. Mankind can settle all these problems if its power and reason are united in a common endeavour. New summits in the development of civilization will become accessible then.

Militarism is hostile to the peoples. The arms race whipped up by the thirst for gain that is consuming the military industrial complex is reckless and senseless. It is detrimental to the vital interests of all countries and peoples. This is why we say a firm "No" whenever we are invited to join in extending the arms race to outer space instead of destroying nuclear weapons. We answer "No" because such a step would mean another instance of insane extravagance. We say "No" because this would mean an aggravation of the danger hanging over the world. We say "No" because the realities of life demand not a contest in armaments, but joint actions for the benefit of peace.

The Soviet Union is resolutely in favour of developing international relations in this direction.

On the Soviet Union's initiative work has got under way amongst scientists from different countries taking part on the Tocomac nuclear fusion reactor, which offers a radical solution to the energy problem. As evidenced by scientists a "man-made sun", an inexhaustible source of thermonuclear energy, can be created before the end of this century. We are pleased to acknowledge that at the Geneva summit we agreed to have this important work continued.

The Soviet Union has submitted to the United Nations a comprehensive programme of peaceful co-operation in outer space, a proposal to set up a worldwide space organization to co-ordinate the efforts of different countries in space research and exploration. The potentialities for this are truly limitless. These include fundamental scientific research and the application of its results in geology, medicine, materials study, and the study of the climate and the natural environment. There is the developing of global satellite communication systems and long-distance probing of the earth. There are, finally, the development and use of new space technology in the interests of all nations, in particular large orbital research stations, various manned ships and, in the long term, the industrialization of near-earth outer space. Such is the realistic alternative to the Star Wars plans which is oriented on mankind's peaceful future.

The Soviet Union is one of the most active initiators of the international convention on the economic use of the world's Ocean resources. The fulfilment of this task is also of enormous significance for sustaining the progress of human civilization, for widening and multiplying the possibilities available to human society today.

We are offering the whole world, the capitalist states in particular, a wide scale, long-term and comprehensive programme of mutually beneficial co-operation, taking advantage of the new opportunities offered to mankind by the era of the scientific and technological revolution. Co-operation between such states as the Soviet Union and the United States could play an important part in implementing this programme.

Our policy is clear: it is a policy of peace and co-operation.

The success of our foreign policy stems from the intrinsic nature of the socialist system. The Communist Party is well aware of the people's unanimous support for its home and foreign policies and values it highly. This support is manifest in the daily practical work of millions upon millions of working people. The achievements in the national economy are not only an economic but also a most important moral and political success, which is evidence of the correctness of the policy we have adopted.

We have important and difficult work lying ahead. "Difficulty," the great Lenin said, "is not impossibility. What is important is confidence in the correct choice of the path, and this confidence multiplies revolutionary energy and revolutionary enthusiasm a hundred-fold. . . ." The Party and the Soviet people do have this confidence, which multiplies our strength.

We are confident that every Communist, every worker, peasant, engineer, and scientist, every work collective, will do their duty, motivated by an awareness of their great responsibility to their country.

We are confident that every Soviet citizen will do his utmost to have the 1986 plan successfully fulfilled and overfulfilled; that this country will become still richer and mightier; and that the cause of peace on earth will grow stronger and will triumph.

22.

Speech at a Kremlin dinner for the participants in the regular Annual Meeting of the American–Soviet Trade and Economic Council
10 December 1985

Ladies and Gentlemen!
Comrades!

I am pleased to welcome to the Kremlin the participants in the regular annual meeting of the American–Soviet Trade and Economic Council. We much appreciate the great work the Council has been doing for over ten years, contributing to the development of contacts between American firms and Soviet foreign trade organizations. We value this work all the more since we know that these were not easy years.

I also address my greetings to the US Secretary of Commerce, Mr Malcolm Baldridge, who has arrived to attend this meeting. We welcome his presence here.

This meeting shows once again that co-operation between individuals, peoples, and states belonging to different social systems and holding different ideological positions is perfectly feasible, and today, I would say, it is indispensable.

Whether we like each other or not, we shall have to live on this planet together. Therefore, the most vital task facing us, as I stated during and after the Geneva meeting, is to learn to get along with each other. Since this is to be for a long time, we must learn to live like good, civilized neighbours.

This involves the question of trade, economic, scientific and technological ties between the United States and the Soviet Union and between East and West in general. We regard these ties primarily from the political angle. First, the main problem in our relations — the problem of war and peace — is decided in the field of politics. All other aspects of our relations, including trade and economic ties, should be subordinated to this problem. Second, our two countries are economic giants capable of living and developing without any trade with each other.

That is actually what is taking place today. You can make your own judgement. In the turnover of Soviet trade the United States, the world's biggest trading nation, holds thirteenth place — far below Finland, Belgium and Austria. In the turnover of US trade the Soviet Union ranks sixteenth. American imports from the Soviet Union are roughly equivalent in volume to those from the Republic of the Ivory Coast.

I see no economic tragedy in this fact. You can survive without us and we can survive without you, especially as there are quite a few other trading partners in the world.

But is this normal politically? My answer is a resolute "No!". In this dangerous world we simply cannot afford to ignore such important factors for stabilizing relations as trade, economic, scientific and technological ties. If we want to have really durable and stable relations capable of securing lasting peace, business relations must also be developed to strengthen their basis.

In our age every country and every people, large and small, regards its independence as its most valuable asset and defends it by every means at its disposal. Nevertheless, all of us are witnessing the growing interdependence of states. This is an objective result of the development of the modern world economy and, at the same time, an important factor of international stability. We must welcome such interdependence. It may become a powerful stimulus to building stable and normal, as well as friendly relations.

We are well aware of the complexity of the tasks facing us. I know that among you there are leading executives of firms holding a prominent place in the American armaments business. I should say quite frankly that we believe that this business is exerting a dangerous influence on politics. In fact, it is not only our point of view; the very concept of the military-industrial complex was formulated not by Marxists but by a conservative Republican, the US President Dwight Eisenhower, who warned the American people of the negative role this complex can play.

I am not saying this to rebuke our guests who have contracts with the Pentagon. They have come to Moscow, and we welcome this fact. It seems to me to be evidence of the common sense of some representatives of the armaments business. I presume that some of them, just like the US business community as a whole, are naturally worried by the economic and financial implications for the United States of its exorbitant military spending, as well as the lopsided development of its economy caused by its militarization.

As far as the Soviet leadership is concerned, we are profoundly convinced that an end to the arms race would meet the genuine vital interests of the Soviet Union and the United States. If, of course, one looks into the essence of the problem instead of seeking only the transient advantages accruing from a specific contract.

To learn to live in peace, in which, as I think, we have a common prevalent interest, means more than simply refraining from war. A full-blooded life, unlike a vegetative life in fear of a new escalation of the danger of war, implies developing many-sided relations and co-operation, in the field of commerce in particular.

Another reason why I regard the development of trade and economic ties between our two countries as a political problem is the fact that the chief obstacles in their way are political rather than economic.

The first such obstacle is the denial of the so-called "most favoured nation" treatment to the Soviet Union. This term misleads some persons into believing that this treatment means charity on the part of the United States towards the partner concerned. American businessmen, however, know perfectly well that this is wrong. In fact, most favoured nation treatment is no more than the absence of discrimination primarily in customs tarriffs. According to my information, about 120 countries enjoy this treatment from the United States.

The Soviet Union is denied this treatment, so that obstacles are erected to the export of many Soviet commodities to the United States. This deprives us of the dollar earnings needed for purchasing American commodities. Indeed, we cannot go on earning foreign exchange, say, in Western Europe for an indefinite period and spending it in the United States; our trade partners would not understand this.

Second, it is the obstacles to credits that we encounter in the United

States. You businessmen, wise from experience, hardly need my arguments to realize that truly efficient trade is impossible without credits.

The third obstacle is the so-called "export control", that is, an embargo on the export of many lines of commodities on the pretext that they may help the military industries in the USSR and thereby cause harm to US security interests. Speculations on this subject are especially numerous.

I wish to say first of all that the allegation that the Soviet Union's defence potential is almost completely based on imported Western technology and cannot develop without it is nonsense. Those who allege this simply forget or want their listeners to forget that the Soviet Union is a country with advanced science and high technology, outstanding scientists and engineers, and highly skilled workers.

Naturally, like any other country we rely on our own and world achievements in science and technology, and on world production experience, in our civilian and military production. This is an inevitable reality of life and the United States itself is a case in point. It is common knowledge that the decisive role in developing, say, nuclear weapons was played not by American science and scientists but by European — including Russian — scientists.

One should forget neither the real facts of today nor the lessons of history. Let me recall some of them in the interest of eliciting the truth.

It is a fact, for instance, that the theory of jet propulsion on which missile technology is based was invented and developed by the great Russian scientist Tsiolkovsky; that the idea of multi-stage rockets and the first experimental rockets appeared in Russia; and finally that the first artificial earth satellite was put into orbit by the Soviet Union. I do not need to remind you of the first man in outer space.

Very much can be said about the contributions of Russian and Soviet scientists, from Mendeleyev to the present day the progress of modern chemistry. I shall mention only the fact that since 1950 half of the transuranium elements have been discovered by Soviet scientists.

Another indisputable fact is the enormous and largely decisive contribution of Soviet scientists to developing the theory of chain reactions, the theory of light and radio waves, and the discovery of the laser. Modern aerodynamics, cryogenics and ultra-high pressure, and almost every kind of metallurgical processes in our day are all unimaginable without the research done by Soviet scientists.

However, we do not proclaim that American corporations are using technology stolen from the Soviet Union.

We are interested, just as you are, in developing scientific and technological exchanges and co-operation. This is a normal and legitimate interest. I would like everyone in the United States to understand that we will not agree to become a market for obsolescent goods and will buy only what is up to the highest world standard. If the United States persists in its current policy, we will manufacture what we need ourselves or buy it from other countries.

There is yet another obstacle to the development of our trade and economic exchanges: this is the policy of boycotts, embargoes, "punishment" violations of commercial contracts, which has become a matter of course with the United States. You all know the results: the Soviet Union has not sustained much damage, but the commercial reputation of American business and thus its competitive power have been seriously undermined on the Soviet market. Our economic executives have lost confidence in their American partners. Hence they more and more frequently give preference to others.

This has been the case with big orders for pipe-laying equipment, for plant and equipment for the Novolipetsk metallurgical complex, and for an aluminium plant in Siberia. As for the import of oil and gas drilling and prospecting equipment, the US share in our purchases has dropped to less than half of one per cent. You are more familiar with the world market situation than I am, so you know, in particular, that competition on the world market is expected to stiffen in the foreseeable future.

I shall be perfectly frank with you: until these obstacles are removed, there will be no normal wide-scale development of Soviet–American trade and other economic ties. We regret this fact, but we will not beg the United States for anything.

If these political barriers are lifted, then, I am confident, broad prospects will open before us. We are not your competitors on the world or domestic market; here the Americans have more problems with their allies than with us. We can become your natural partners and, I can assure you, honest and dependable partners.

For that, of course, you and we would have to do a good deal of work. We could make a better study of each other's markets and improve the mechanism of economic co-operation. I know that we are not guiltless in this respect either. The Soviet Government's attitude to our foreign trade organizations is critical enough. In our view, new forms of production, scientific and technological co-operation are possible.

We are now doing very great work in this area, jointly with other socialist countries. We regard deepening economic integration with them as a task of high priority. We will also widen trade and other forms of economic co-operation with Western Europe and Japan, as well as with the developing countries

We would like our economic relations with the United States not to remain outside the sphere of this process — both for the political reasons I have mentioned and for economic reasons. We have very great plans for developing our economy, science and technology. We would like to make the most of the additional possibilities offered by international co-operation, with the United States in particular. This may include large long-term projects, as well as a host of medium-sized and even small deals that may interest giants, as well as small and middle business. If the situation is normalized and a solid political and treaty-law basis is laid for developing trade and economic relations, we shall find what things to buy from you and what to sell you.

We could invite American companies and firms to take part in our programmes of further developing the power sector of the economy. We could consider partnership of American companies and firms in our great work to modernize radically our machine-tool, building and other engineering industries. Interested American firms might join in our efforts to develop the agro-industrial complex, the chemical and petrochemical industries, the production of systems of machines and facilities for intensive processes on crop and livestock farms.

However, a political good will is necessary for all such projects to materialize. Economic relations should be developed on a long-term basis. There is a need for guarantees that political winds will not begin to erode business relations again.

Now let me return to politics. It is only three weeks from this meeting of the American–Soviet Trade and Economic Council to the Soviet–American talks at Geneva. This accounts for its special significance. As I understand it, its aim is to analyse potentialities for Soviet–American economic co-operation and search for what should be done to meet the broader interests of the Soviet and American peoples.

An understanding of the fact that the current state of Soviet–American relations is unsatisfactory and dangerous was the main thing that led President Reagan and me to the Geneva talks. I am confident that the US President, just like me, had sensed that millions of men, women and even children in our two countries — and the rest of the world, for that matter — were looking to Geneva in those days with hope and concern.

That, I should tell you frankly, was not an easy experience. But neither of us deemed it possible to evade this enormous burden of human anxieties and hopes.

In view of the difficulties of the road to the Geneva summit, it may be considered a definite success. That, however, was only the first step. Every next step will require still greater efforts, still greater willingness to listen, a desire and an ability to understand and co-operate with each other. And, most important of all, a willingness to learn the difficult art of reaching agreement on an equal and mutually acceptable basis, without which we would never be able to solve serious problems.

In other words, we have entered a crucially important period, where words, intentions, and political declarations should be translated into concrete decisions and actions. This implies, as you can understand, decisions and actions that could contribute to a normalization of Soviet–American relations and to a general improvement in the world political climate.

Many representatives of the American business community are known for their great enterprise, a gift for innovation, an ability to find latent potentials for growth. Today, I am convinced that the best, truly rich opportunities of this kind should be sought, not on the road of destruction and death but on the road of peace and joint endeavour in the name of mutually beneficial co-operation between all countries and peoples, based on equality. This is the demand of life itself, and the advantages of this approach are indisputable.

I wish the Council every success in its useful activities.

23.

Discussion with Mr B. Lown, American Co-chairman of the "World Physicians for the Prevention of Nuclear War" movement
18 December 1985

On 18 December the General Secretary of the CPSU Central Committee, M. S. Gorbachov received at the Kremlin Professor B. Lown, American Co-chairman of the "World Physicians for the Prevention of Nuclear War" movement. Taking part in the discussion that followed was Academician E. I. Chazov, Soviet Co-chairman of the movement.

In the course of the discussion Professor Lown described the activities of the movement affiliating more than 145,000 physicians and medical workers from over fifty countries. The movement is making a substantial contribution to lessening the risk of nuclear war by studying the possible medico-biological after-effects of nuclear war and making its findings available to the public and to political leaders and governments.

The programme advanced by the movement calls for a freeze, reduction and abolition of nuclear weapons, a ban on testing, a renunciation of first use of nuclear weapons, non-escalation of the arms race to outer space and broad-scale international peaceful co-operation.

Professor Lown emphasized the crucial significance of involving the mass of the people in a discussion of the problems of ending the arms race and removing the danger of nuclear war. The voice of the peoples should be heeded and should influence the decisions of governments.

Professor Lown expressed his great appreciation of the Soviet Union's peace initiatives; in particular, its moratorium on all nuclear explosions, effective as of 6 August of this year. An appeal for such a moratorium was made in the message of the 5th international congress of the physicians movement, addressed to M. S. Gorbachov and to the US President, Ronald Reagan, in the summer of this year. The cessation of nuclear explosions, Professor Lown said, is consistent with the aspirations of all nations.

M. S. Gorbachov congratulated Professor Lown and Academician Chazov on the occasion of the awarding of the 1985 Nobel Peace Prize to the "World Physicians for the Prevention of Nuclear War" movement. Mr Gorbachov said in particular:

"In the Soviet Union the activities of this movement and its socially significant mission of aid are regarded with great respect and sympathy. Today it holds a well-deserved, prestigious place in the worldwide anti-war movement. Physicians disclose the ugly truth which should be known to all the people on earth, so what cannot be undone should not happen. In this sense the Hippocratic oath obliging physicians to protect their patients against whatever may threaten their lives has truly assumed a new dimension in the nuclear age.

The message of the 5th Congress of the physicians' international movement addressed to the General Secretary of the CPSU Central Committee and the US President is pervaded with an eager desire to safeguard all the inhabitants of the earth against the fatal consequences of nuclear catastrophe.

The human mind is not always capable of comprehending in good time changes on a historical scale. This is a grave failing which is especially dangerous today when the threat of wholesale nuclear destruction has come to the threshold of every home and every family. Therefore, the voice of the people and their public organizations in defence of peace is assuming still greater significance today. This is an expression of what may be called mankind's instinct for self-preservation.

Peace based on nuclear deterrence is a shaky peace. It is impossible to make it stable by building up armaments, either on earth or in outer space. Nobody has yet invented a more dependable and effective model of relations between states than *détente* and co-operation in conditions of peace and mutual security. A lessening of the level of military confrontation between them would reinforce the framework of these relations and make them stable and dependable.

These were precisely the motives for our consent to the Soviet–

American summit at Geneva. That meeting set the stage for normalizing Soviet–American relations and created the prerequisites for a general improvement in the international situation.

However, we are also witnessing a different trend of developments: the reactionary warlike circles in the United States who at one time went out of their way to frustrate the Geneva meeting are now attacking its results. A broad campaign has been mounted against normalizing relations with the Soviet Union and strengthening mutual trust in Soviet–American relations on which the two sides agreed at Geneva. The press, television and cinema are being used actively to foment mistrust and hostility towards the Soviet Union and Soviet citizens. Some persons in the United States are evidently disgruntled by the fact that the negotiators at the Geneva meeting expressed themselves in favour of greater mutual understanding between our two nations. By all indications, the notorious "hawks" are firmly determined to prevent the Geneva accords from being implemented, to thwart the next Soviet–American summit or at least to play down its significance. It is regrettable that the latest public pronouncements of US statesmen are hardly consistent with the "Geneva spirit", too.

As far as the Soviet Union is concerned, its policy is clear and consistent. The Soviet Union is prepared to contribute its equal share to building the structure of lasting mutual security and peaceful co-operation with the United States. However, we expect reciprocity from the US leadership. We extended our hand to the United States at Geneva. We are prepared to go over from a contest in armaments to disarmament, from confrontation to co-operation. "Co-operation, not confrontation!" was the motto of the recent international congress of the physicians movement. This is a slogan good for all. Indeed, co-operation today is indispensable for the progress of civilization and for our common survival.

The Soviet Union will go as far as necessary towards the complete abolition of nuclear weapons and the final removal of the risk of nuclear war. We are in favour of securing practical guarantees of man's fundamental right — the right to life. We are in favour of immediately imposing a freeze on nuclear weapons, a total and permanent ban on their testing and the most effective verification procedures. The only condition we make is reciprocity.

We proposed to the United States a radical, 50 per cent reduction of the strategic nuclear arsenals as a long practical step towards general nuclear disarmament. Naturally, this is provided a total ban is imposed on strike space weapons; that is, if the United States gives up its Star Wars programme, which can only undermine all efforts towards the abolition of nuclear weapons and escalate the arms race to enormous proportions. As is justly pointed out in the message of the physicians movement, this would sharply increase the danger of a global nuclear conflict.

This is realized by practically the whole world today. A total of 151 states, in fact, all the members of the United Nations except the United States, have just voted for the UN General Assembly's resolution on preventing an arms race in outer space.

M. S. Gorbachov dwelt in detail on the problem of ending nuclear weapons tests, which has been urged emphatically by the physicians movement, with conclusive arguments at its disposal. The Soviet Union's moratorium on all nuclear explosions, effective as of 6 August of this year, has been welcomed throughout the world. We have taken this step motivated by a sincere desire to break the vicious circle — to check the endless improvement of nuclear weapons and practically to immobilize their arsenals. I spoke in this vein with President Reagan at Geneva. Unfortunately, the United States has not yet followed our example.

In reply to Professor Lown, M. S. Gorbachov said: We are prepared to prolong the Soviet moratorium on nuclear explosions if the United States reciprocates. We are urging the US Administration to take this step. There is a unique chance to make the moratorium mutual and extend it beyond 1 January. It would be unreasonable, to say the least, to miss this chance of paving the way towards a final treaty ban on all nuclear weapons tests. The solution to this problem is in the hands of the US Administration.

Professor Lown is right: the peoples are awaiting an immediate cessation and prohibition of nuclear weapons testing. This is evidenced in particular by the UN General Assembly's resolution adopted the other day practically unanimously. Only three members — the United States, Britain, and France — voted against it.

In conclusion, M. S. Gorbachov wished his visitors and all members of the "World Physicians for the Prevention of Nuclear War" movement fresh success in their noble and useful work.

24.

Speech at a Kremlin assembly of the heads of diplomatic missions accredited to the USSR
27 December 1985

Ladies and gentlemen!

On the eve of the New Year I wish to convey my heartfelt greetings to the heads of diplomatic missions accredited to the Soviet Union assembled here in the Kremlin.

I welcome the representatives of socialist states, with which we are linked by bonds of fraternal friendship and close co-operation in implementing the programmes of socialist and communist construction, in accelerating the social and economic progress of our societies and in our joint struggle for lasting peace on earth.

I welcome the representatives of states which have liberated themselves from colonial oppression, taken the road of independent development and joined the non-aligned movement. We have established relations of sincere friendship, mutual respect and many-sided co-operation with these states. We regard the growing role played by the non-aligned states on the international scene as a good historical omen.

I welcome the representatives of a different, capitalist, system present in this audience — the states of North America, Western Europe, the Far East and other regions which belong to what in modern political terminology is called the West. The Soviet Union consistently seeks to develop relations with these countries on the principles of peaceful coexistence and mutually beneficial co-operation based on equality. We are well aware of the fact that the prospects for world peace depend to a significant extent on our relations with this group of states, and we approach this problem in an awareness of our high responsibility.

We have come to a threshold which does not mean just a calendar change of the years but has a much more profound meaning.

The year 1985 has seen many events of great historic significance. Some of them were fraught with new, formidable dangers to mankind; others offered hope. Which of these two trends of events will prevail in the coming year, 1986; whether it will be a year of practical action to strengthen peace and the security of nations, to develop their peaceful intercourse and co-operation, or whether the danger of nuclear catastrophe which hangs over this planet will become even more formidable depends on the efforts of the men — governments, statesmen and political leaders, and the world public at large.

The dangers are obvious. The continued reckless arms race and the stubborn attempts by militarist circles to extend it into outer space. The flagrant violations of the sovereignty and independence of a number of states; foreign interference in the internal affairs of nations. It is obvious, however, that these processes are meeting with stiffening resistance everywhere in the world. And, I would add, they are factors heightening the responsibility of all countries and peoples for the destiny of universal peace.

Every people and every country, large, medium-sized, or small, can contribute a share of their national experience to the cause of peace and international co-operation. This has been reaffirmed by the session of the UN General Assembly which has just come to an end. It has adopted practically unanimously a number of highly important resolutions, in particular, on the prevention of an arms race in outer space and on ending nuclear weapons testing.

As far as the Soviet leadership are concerned, we are optimists in our convictions; we believe in mankind's better future and we are determined to make vigorous efforts in this direction.

In recent times there has been an exchange of signals between East and West which offers some hope or, to be more cautious, a gleam of hope for advance towards mutually acceptable decisions.

As a result of the Soviet–American summit at Geneva, as is now widely recognized, a certain general amelioration of the international climate is taking place. Definite points of contact have appeared, or rather have a chance to appear, on the problems of nuclear and space arms negotiations. Progress will depend primarily on how much of the accord reached at the Geneva summit will be put into practice. This progress is decisive to making the year 1986 justify the hopes of the peoples for the prevention of an arms race in outer space and for ending the arms race on earth.

The constructive efforts of a number of states are bringing into relief an outline of possible agreements at the Stockholm Conference on Confidence-building Measures and Security in Europe. All its participants must do a good deal of work, as we see it, if the Stockholm Conference is to achieve favourable results before the next all-European conference begins in the autumn of next year.

At the Vienna talks on troop and arms reductions in Central Europe the negotiating sides have shown more desire to take account of each other's interests and concern. We are now studying carefully the latest proposals by our Western partners.

The participants in the Geneva Disarmament Conference seem to have become better aware of the urgent need to ban chemical weapons, to end all nuclear tests, and to renounce the use of force in outer space. However, more effort will be required before full accord is reached. The Soviet Union is prepared to go the full length of its part of the way towards balanced agreements.

The problem of nuclear explosions is rivetting the attention of statesmen and the public at large. They have been shaking the earth for several decades. It is time an end were put to them. We are convinced that this is practicable.

We are calling on the United States, as we have done before, to follow the Soviet Union's good example and end all nuclear explosions. If the two greatest powers took a joint stand on this issue, so vital to all mankind, it would be a step of truly enormous significance.

Speaking to this respected audience of diplomatic representatives, I am addressing all governments and peoples with this appeal: let us do whatever is necessary to make the year 1986 go down in history as the year of the ending of all nuclear explosions; as the year when people showed enough common sense to rise above their narrow selfish interests and stop crippling their own planet.

Since those evading a solution to this problem often refer to the alleged difficulties of verification in order to justify their stalling tactics, I wish to state emphatically that the problem of verification will not be a stumbling block as far as the Soviet Union is concerned. The Soviet Union is prepared to take the most radical steps to ensure control over the ending of nuclear tests, right down to on-the-spot inspection.

The Soviet Union, which knows the meaning of a treacherous attack from its own bitter experience, is as interested in reliable and strict verification as anybody is. In today's international situation, with its deficit of mutual trust, verification measures are indispensable. Whether it is verification using national monitoring facilities or international verification procedures, it should necessarily mean control over compliance with concrete agreements.

The Soviet leadership are prepared to negotiate on a reasonable and fair basis and expect a realistic and sensible approach from their partners. The grounds for the coming talks should be planted with good seed because only good seed can sprout well in spring and yield a bumper crop in the autumn.

There is yet another large and pressing problem. The Soviet Union very much wants to see substantial progress in 1986 in the cause of political settlement in the Middle East, in Central America, around Afghanistan, in Southern Africa and in the Persian Gulf region. We are prepared to search jointly with other countries for just settlements and to share in the relevant guarantees where necessary.

Efforts to stamp out seats of tension or to prevent their growth in any event are hampered by the habit of looking at conflict situations through the prism of political or ideological confrontation between East and West. It is myopic and dangerous to base policy on misguided concepts. Conflicts germinate on local social, economic and political soil. Hence they should be settled without infringing the legitimate interests of the peoples or their right to choose without foreign interference the way of life they want to lead, and their right to defend their choice.

I wish to emphasize in conclusion the great importance of the work of diplomatic representatives at this dangerous time. The decisions taken by the leaders of their countries depend to a fairly great extent on the completeness and dependability of their assessments and information. It would be no exaggeration to say that trust in relations between states begins with their Ambassadors. I should add that we demand complete objectivity and unprejudiced assessments from our Ambassadors.

On the other hand, we want you to be well informed about developments in the Soviet Union and not in its capital alone. The Soviet authorities will continue to accord foreign Ambassadors hospitality and to assist them in this work. We have nothing to conceal: the Soviet people and the Soviet leadership have only peaceful plans and peaceful intentions.

You know, of course, of the significance of the forthcoming 27th Congress of the CPSU for the life of our Party and country. Many of you, I hope, are familiar with the theoretical and political documents to be discussed at the Congress: the new edition of the CPSU Programme, the amendments to the Party Rules, the Guidelines for the Economic and Social Development of the USSR for 1986–1990 and in the period up to 2000. In many areas we are looking still further ahead, into the third millennium.

What kind of a period it will be largely depends on the generations alive today.

The burden of responsibility resting on all of us today is truly colossal. We must all take advantage of the existing opportunity to reduce armaments, to prevent the formidable danger threatening mankind from outer space, and to make our beautiful world a safer place to live in.

On behalf of all my countrymen and women, who are celebrating the New Year in an atmosphere of enthusiasm and creativity, I convey my wishes for peace and prosperity to the peoples of your countries and the peoples of the whole world. I wish success and a happy life to you and your families, members of your Embassy staffs, representatives of foreign trade organizations, banks and firms, journalists and technical specialists, teachers and students; in short, all your countrymen and women living and working in the Soviet Union.

25.

New Year's message to the people of the United States of America
Pravda, 2 January 1986

Dear citizens of the United States of America!

I see a good omen in the way we are entering the new year proclaimed Peace Year. We are entering it with a direct exchange of messages — President Reagan's message to the Soviet people and my message to you.

This is, in my view, a hopeful sign of changes, however slight, for the better in our relations. These few minutes during which I shall be speaking to you seem to me a meaningful symbol of our mutual desire to meet each other halfway, a process started by your President and myself at Geneva. We were delegated by our two nations to discuss progress in this direction. They want the constructive Soviet–American dialogue not to be broken off and to bring about tangible results.

Facing you today, I wish to tell you that the Soviet people are committed to peace as the supreme value equal to the blessing of life. The idea of peace is an idea we have suffered for, and it has become implanted in our flesh and blood with the pain of wounds that cannot be healed and the bitterness of irreplaceable losses. There is no family and no home in my country where the memory of their near and dear ones, who perished in the flames of war, is not alive. In that war the Soviet and American peoples were allies fighting in the same ranks.

I am recalling this now because our common desire for peace

328

has roots in the past and hence a historical record of experience from which we can draw inspiration for our joint work for the future.

Your numerous letters and my discussions with representatives of your country — Senators, congressmen, scientists, businessmen and statesmen — have convinced me that it is realized in the United States, too, that war between our two countries should never happen, that a conflict between us would be a great tragedy.

The senselessness of efforts to strengthen security with new types of weaponry is one of the realities of the modern world. Today every next step in the arms race aggravates the danger and risk of war for either side and for mankind as a whole.

The realities of life loudly and persistently call upon us to take the road of cutting the nuclear arsenals and preserving outer space in peace. This is on the agenda of our talks at Geneva, and we very much hope they will be crowned with success in the new year.

In our efforts for peace we should be guided by our awareness of the fact that today, as history has willed it, our two countries bear the enormous burden of responsibility to their own people and to all other nations for the preservation of life on earth. It is our duty to give mankind a firm prospect for peace, the prospect of entering the third millennium without fear of the future. Let us undertake the task of ending the danger hanging over mankind. Let us not shift this burden onto the shoulders of our children.

We shall hardly be able to achieve this goal unless we begin to collect, bit by bit, the most valuable capital there is — trust between states and peoples. It is imperative to begin getting rid of mistrust in Soviet–American relations.

I believe that one of the main results of my meeting with President Reagan is the fact that we, as leaders and on a purely human plane, took the first steps towards overcoming mistrust and brought into play the factor of confidence. We are still divided by a broad and high barrier, but we saw at Geneva that it is not insurmountable. To surmount it will take a heroic effort. The Soviet people are prepared to make it for the sake of world peace.

I recall the title of John Steinbeck's wonderful novel *The Winter of our Discontent*. Rewording it slightly, we may call the present time the winter of our hope. May this winter and all the seasons of this and later years give us hope for the better future we can make real by our joint efforts. I can assure you that we will do our utmost to make this hope come true.

For the Soviet people the year 1986 opens a new chapter in our plans of construction. These are peaceful plans and we have made them known to the whole world.

A Happy New year to all of you. I wish health, peace and happiness to every American family.

26.

Reply to a message from
K. Livingstone, leader of the
Greater London Council
Pravda, 3 January 1986

Dear Mr Livingstone,

I have carefully read your message, which is characterized by an awareness of the need to take urgent steps to deliver the peoples of the world from the nuclear menace. The concern of your countrymen and women about the dangerous world developments is fully shared in the Soviet Union.

Mankind is living through a critical period in its history. It has to make a choice between survival and wholesale destruction. Today, as never before, all political leaders who have a mandate from the people to make their life secure are required to be capable of a broad approach to statesmanship, of rising above narrow selfish interests, of realizing the complete collective and individual responsibility of states for the destiny of the world.

Pursuing its clear and consistent policy of peace, the Soviet Union is doing its utmost to bar the way for weapons to outer space, to achieve first a radical reduction of nuclear armaments and, eventually, their complete abolition. The Soviet Union has already undertaken practical steps in the direction you describe as necessary in your message. The Soviet Union has assumed a commitment not to use nuclear weapons first and imposed a unilateral moratorium on all nuclear explosions, which can be converted into a mutual moratorium if the US Administration follows suit.

We are in favour of an immediate freeze on nuclear arsenals, a total and permanent ban on nuclear weapons tests, with the most effective verification procedures. We are prepared to resume tripartite negotiations in the immediate future so as to find — jointly with representatives of the United States and Britain — a mutually acceptable solution to this problem.

You also know that the Soviet Union has proposed a 50 per cent reduction in the relevant nuclear forces of the USSR and the USA. Naturally, the Geneva talks can make progress provided a total ban is imposed on strike space weapons. In other words, this progress demands a renunciation of the Star Wars project which, if implemented, would play havoc with the strategic balance and trigger off a new uncontrollable spiral in the arms race. We are sorry to see that the governmental circles in Britain and some of the other close allies of the United States have not yet become fully aware of the disastrous consequences of involvement in the Star Wars project.

I have pleasant recollections of my visit to your country a year ago and my numerous meetings on British soil. I understand the desire of the British to preserve their traditions and historical heritage, to augment their achievements in various fields and to hand all of this down to their descendants safe and intact. The people of other countries of Europe, the Soviet Union and throughout the world, for that matter, show similar concern for the future. Small wonder, therefore, that the peoples are worried at seeing the growing stockpiles of deadly weapons standing in the way of implementing these noble and humane tasks. Indeed, even the relatively small British Isles are now bristling with nuclear arms which, it should be stated bluntly, do not make anybody's life more secure.

Measures to ensure the non-proliferation of nuclear weapons and set up nuclear-free zones in various regions of the world have an important part to play in efforts to narrow the sphere of nuclear war preparations. Proclaiming individual territories and towns free from nuclear weapons is a step in the same direction. We regard this as evidence of the peoples' awareness of their responsibility for the destiny of peace and their determination to act in ways accessible to them. The edifice of peace is made up of numerous bricks. Capital for *détente* is collected bit by bit. It is gratifying to see that the movement of municipal and other organizations in support of nuclear-free zones is increasing and growing stronger. In our view, such zones are not a product of wishful thinking or an idealistic daydream but a positive phenomenon in international affairs, reflecting the common people's longing for peace, co-operation and *détente*.

In our attitude to nuclear-free zones we make no exception for any state affiliated or not affiliated with a military alliance. We make only one condition; if a country has renounced nuclear weapons and has none of them in its territory, we give it firm and effective guarantees. For instance, if Great Britain fully renounced possession of nuclear weapons and closed down foreign nuclear bases in its territory, the Soviet Union would give it guarantees that Soviet nuclear weapons would be neither targeted on nor used against British territory. Such guarantees could be formalized by an official agreement, taking into account all the relevant aspects of the military balance.

We greatly appreciate the efforts of the Greater London Council and of hundreds of other municipal councils in dozens of countries of the world to contribute to the common efforts of the peoples to avert the risk of nuclear war and to revive an atmosphere of trust and mutual understanding in relations between states.

I wish you renewed success in your noble work for the benefit of world peace, and all the best in the new year.

27.

Message to the Congress of Scientists and Cultural Workers for a Peaceful Future for Earth
Pravda, 17 January 1986

Ladies and Gentlemen!

I convey my greetings to your Congress of Scientists and Cultural Workers for a Peaceful Future for Earth.

Your Congress opens, so to say, a calendar of important initiatives which are bound to be numerous in 1986, proclaimed International Peace Year by the United Nations. It is significant that you have assembled in Warsaw, a city whose past reminds one of the horrors of the last war and whose modern image is symbolic of man's irresistible will towards construction and peace.

Mankind is faced today with many complicated and difficult national, regional and global problems. None of them, however, is more urgent than the task of removing the nuclear menace — checking the arms race on earth, preventing its escalation into outer space — and preserving civilization.

The Soviet–American summit at Geneva has generated hopes for an improvement in the international situation and greater general security. To make these hopes come true, however, both sides must comply honestly with the accords reached at Geneva. The Geneva process should be taken further in order to determine the future course of world developments; this is demanded by all the peoples and is really imperative.

I can assure Congress delegates that the Soviet Union will continue to do its best to curb the arms race, to have it ended on earth and to

334

prevent its extension to outer space. This is the object of our far-reaching steps, our plans and proposals for meeting the interests of the further progress of all mankind. Our choice is not military rivalry but all-embracing international co-operation in all areas, including science and culture.

Seeking to facilitate as much as possible both a radical improvement in the international situation and the efforts to deliver mankind once and for all from the danger of nuclear catastrophe and the use of other barbarian weapons of mass destruction, the Soviet Union has come forward with a peace initiative of historic significance addressed to the United States and other nuclear powers, and to all governments and peoples of the world.

We invite them to agree on a programme for the complete elimination of nuclear weapons throughout the world during the coming fifteen years, before the end of the 20th century, and propose a concrete plan of staged, practical steps leading to this end, under strict international control. We are convinced that this is a perfectly realistic prospect provided that the plans for developing strike space weapons are renounced. Atoms for peace, space for peace — such is the essence of our programme.

We also propose the total elimination, before the end of the century, of all chemical weapons, their stocks and the industrial facilities for their production, also under stringent international control, including international verification on the spot.

We propose a ban on developing non-nuclear arms based on new physical principles and comparable in their overkill potential with nuclear and other weapons of mass destruction.

We also consider it possible to reach eventual practical agreements on mutual troop and arms reductions in Central Europe — at the Vienna talks, and on the non-use of force and confidence-building measures — at the Stockholm Conference.

To reaffirm once again the earnestness and sincerity of our intentions and our willingness to undertake — as early as possible — practical efforts to strengthen peace and deliver mankind from the threat of nuclear war, the Soviet Union has resolved to extend its moratorium on nuclear explosions by another three months and has called on the United States and other nuclear powers to do the same.

In short, the Soviet Union has proposed a concrete programme of measures to achieve the aim to which your Congress is dedicated: a peaceful future for the earth. We call on all peace forces in the world to support this programme.

We are convinced that mankind's intellectual potential must serve to augment material and cultural wealth rather than to develop new types of lethal weapons of global destruction. Not preparations for Star Wars but peaceful co-operation between states — such is our idea of what mankind's approach to the problem of outer space must be. A peaceful outer space is a key prerequisite for banishing war from the life of the human race.

The power of the struggle for peace is based on words of truth about the disastrous consequences of a nuclear conflict, should it not be prevented. The delegates of your Congress — prestigious representatives of the scientific community and the cultural world — can play a significant part in making this truth known to all, in making broad sections of the public realize their humane duty of active participation in the struggle for a truly lasting peace.

I wish your Congress success in its work for the common cause vital to all — the triumph of lasting peace on earth.

28.

Interview with the newspaper
L'Humanité
4 February 1986

The leading newspaper of the French Communist Party, L'Humanité, requested an interview with the General Secretary of the CPSU Central Committee.

On 4 February M. S. Gorbachov received Monsieur Roland Leroy, member of the Politbureau of the FCP, Political Director of L'Humanité; Gerard Streiff, L'Humanité correspondent in Moscow, and José Fort chief of the international desk of L'Humanité.

M. S. Gorbachov's replies are published below.

Question. Mr Gorbachov, I thank you for consenting to answer *L'Humanité's* questions. The fact that you are the General Secretary of the Central Committee of the Communist Party of the Soviet Union lends special authority to your answers about life in the Soviet Union, which is a matter of interest to French men and women, who are constantly subjected to the influence of hostile attacks against your country. Hence our first question. There is much talk nowadays about the Soviet Union's entry into a stage of development as important as the one ushered in by the October Revolution. Does this mean that a new revolution is under way?

Answer. No, certainly not. I believe it would be wrong to phrase the question this way. In my view, it would be more correct to say that today, in the eighties, we have resolved to boost the progress of the cause initiated by the Bolshevik Party almost 70 years ago.

The October Revolution was a turning point in the thousand-year history of our state, and for its significance and consequences for the

SW—M*

development of all mankind it was without precedent. However, it is not enough to carry out a revolution; it is necessary to defend it, to translate the working man's ideas of equality and justice and his social and moral ideals into reality. In other words, it is necessary to build a new society capable of ensuring a life worthy of human beings.

All this has required of our people and our Party an enormous amount of work, truly heroic exploits and sometimes sacrifices. The Civil War, the war against Nazi Germany, the deep-going transformations in the rural areas, the construction of a powerful industry, the eradication of the illiteracy of the bulk of the people, a radical social and cultural restructuring of society, the formation of fundamentally new interethnic relations — these are but a few of the most illustrious pages of our history, which is, in fact, very short.

We take pride in this history and, our pride is the source of Soviet patriotism. If we had not held our ground but suffered a defeat at least in one of the above-listed areas, whatever goals were pursued by the October Revolution would have been called into question. Each of these accomplishments in itself can be rightly called a truly revolutionary achievement.

This also holds true of the tasks being implemented today. They are complicated and highly important at the same time. If we fail to cope with them, we shall depreciate whatever we have achieved at the cost of enormous efforts in the past and we will make our own future more difficult. Perhaps the most difficult and most indispensable for every Soviet Communist and for the Party as a whole, for that matter, is the need to understand and to feel the challenge of the present epoch and to meet this challenge effectively.

This is a dual challenge.

On the one hand, Soviet society has entered a new stage of its history. Its essence may be described as follows: the requirements of the development of productive forces, the requirements of the people and the requirements of the individual have raised the question of the radical revision and improvement of many aspects of production relations, methods of economic work, and the methods, forms and style of Party and government direction; that is, of policy. It is a question of involving ever broader masses of the people in handling the affairs of society, of mobilizing the creative potential of the people and their experience to accomplish tasks that are increasingly sophisticated, that is, the continued development and enrichment of our socialist democracy.

We have been aware for quite some time of the need for change. The essence of what is being done in the country today, first and foremost in the Party, is a resolute effort to accelerate the socio-economic and intellectual development of Soviet society, having recourse to all available resources for this purpose. This is, of course, a revolutionary task.

On the other hand, the challenge of our epoch stems from the fact that human civilization has regretfully created very effective instruments of self-destruction. For a disaster to happen one need not even commit an unprecedented act of folly or a crime. It is enough to act in the same way as people have acted for thousands of years in settling international disputes, relying on arms and military force and using them if necessary. All these traditions which are thousands of years old should now be ruthlessly demolished and we should denounce them without hesitation. Otherwise, the problem of mankind's survival may prove insoluble. In the nuclear age one cannot live — for a long time at any rate — with the psychology, habits and rules of conduct of the Stone Age. Indeed, is this steep turn in international relations and in foreign policy ideas and practices not a profoundly revolutionary task? In my opinion, it is such a task. The Soviet Union as the first country to have carried out a socialist revolution is clearly aware of its great responsibility and its duty to help implement this task by every means at its disposal.

Speaking in general, we regard our programme of practical action, which will be discussed and adopted by the 27th Congress of the CPSU, from all points of view as a programme of a truly revolutionary character and scope.

Question. What are the key prospects for developing the Soviet economy in the coming 10–15 years? What effect will it have on the well-being of the people?

Answer. The prospects will depend on how effectively we shall deal with the problems facing us. In other words, on how well and skilfully we shall work. I should frankly admit that these are not simple problems. We have objective difficulties, like an unfavourable demographic situation and the arms race that has been imposed upon us. These are the greatest of our difficulties. Some difficulties may be attributed to our own faults. Their elimination has been delayed and so they have grown worse.

Today we have to do a very great deal within record time — to bring about a radical improvement in planning, management and material incentives, and to accelerate scientific and technological progress. On this basis the efficiency and qualitative performance of the economy should be improved and product quality advanced to a higher level. In the coming fifteen years we intend to double the country's productive potential and to make a substantial change in the very image of the economy and the character of work, and to re-structure the way of life of the people.

You have asked me how these measures will affect the well-being of the people. I should say that it is for the benefit of the people that we are taking all these steps. I have in mind both the quantity and quality of work, that is, the areas of consumption and services, housing, medicare and education, social security, access to cultural benefits, environmental protection, general improvement of towns and villages, leisure time, and many other things. I will not conceal from you that in many of these spheres the state of affairs is far from what we would like it to be. The fact is that our difficult history did not allow us to give due attention to these spheres. Part of the fault has been ours; it was the conservatism, inability or occasionally simple irresponsibility of executives, whole departments and organizations. If you read our newspapers you know of the sharp criticism being levied upon many executives, including some in very high positions. Now we have taken resolute steps to remedy the situation. This will naturally require time and quite great efforts. I am confident, however, that we shall achieve important improvements in all these areas. Of course, all of us would like to see results as soon as possible.

Among the most urgent problems is the need to fill the market with goods of high quality and in a broad variety. The goods should be both new and traditional, expensive and cheap, goods for young people and for older people; in short, they should meet all tastes and demands — within reasonable limits, of course. We regard this problem as one of exceptional significance.

Question. Are there still queues in the Soviet Union?

Answer. Yes, especially for high-quality goods, the demand for which is not completely satisfied.

I want to point out at the same time that not all ways of solving this problem are open to us. If, in the West, the demand for some commodity is higher than the supply, the price is raised. We very rarely do this, in relation to consumer goods in mass demand, at any rate. As a result, we have shortages, and shortages entail queues. I am saying all this to explain the problem, not to justify the existing shortcomings. Shortcomings — and we firmly insist on this — should not be justified, but eliminated. For this purpose we have now started serious efforts to restructure the economy and all economic mechanisms.

Question. Are the Soviet citizens entitled and able to "oppose" the actions of the "patrons" of their enterprises? Can they not only oppose, but also revise their decisions?

Answer. If you have in mind as "patrons" the managers and management — we have no private owners, and no private ownership. In the early years of Soviet government a complete mechanism was already established to protect the working people's rights: strict labour laws, broad trade union rights, Party and local government control. The rights of the working people and work collectives have been widened appreciably in the last two years. Practically all important decisions are now prepared and adopted with the participation of rank-and-file workers, after discussion with them. This refers, for instance, to the draft plans for the economic and social development of enterprises.

A couple of words about the trade unions. They conclude collective agreements with the management and exercise control over compliance with labour laws. If they find that violations committed by the management, such as dismissals without justification, irregularities in wages, salaries, provision of housing, etc., they are empowered to "oppose" digressions from the law and, what is more, very effectively, too. They may even demand the dismissal of the executive responsible. This really does happen from time to time.

However, this matter also has a different aspect. Not only the management and the trade union, but the work collective as a whole, must make definite demands on rank-and-file personnel regarding discipline, conscientious work, and behaviour during the work process. This is done, as a rule, with the full support of the workers. A work collective has a vested interest in the good work of each member. This interest is also shared by all the workers, since their earnings, working conditions and social benefits are dependent on good work.

Question. Is unemployment the inevitable price of modernizing production?

Answer. In the conditions of a planned economy orientated on the complete satisfaction of the social demand there is no such link between unemployment and modernization. Even if some radical improvement in technology obviates the need for a certain specialism, we are obliged and able to foresee this and take steps to secure retraining or to start new areas of production. This is what we do in real life. Moreover, since the modernization of enterprises is accompanied by their expansion, as a rule, the question of creating new jobs is settled at the enterprises affected. For the time being this is an almost academic question for us. The prime reason is the fact that we are plagued not by a surplus, but by a shortage of manpower. Frankly speaking, there is another reason too. We have so far carried out modernization at a slow rate, even in areas where it was knocking on the door. Whatever it may be, the Party takes account of the social aspect of modernization and believes it a matter of extreme significance to take this into consideration in drawing up plans for the country's economic development.

Question. Is the Communist Party in the USSR a "driving belt" in relation to the state? What meaning is attached today to the expression "to make policy" in your country?

Answer. In our society the Communist Party is the vanguard of the people. This Party status is legalized in the Constitution. The Party is not a symbol, but a real and constantly working political organization which has within its ranks almost twenty million active representatives of the workers, peasants and intelligentsia. It is a democratic organization which elects its governing bodies and leaders and makes them strictly accountable. Now we are seeking to strengthen these democratic principles in the life and work of the Party and to enhance the activities of all Party collectives. As we see it, this is one of the most effective instruments for widening democracy and involving millions of people in handling production, and social and political affairs. I believe that at the forthcoming Congress problems concerning the work of the Party under present conditions will have a conspicuous place on the agenda.

The Party is called upon to map out the strategy and tactics of building the new society, and to implement a rational policy in the placement of cadres and in the ideological education of the people. Party committees at all levels, including the Central Committee, are the bodies that give political direction. The Party is vitally interested in the active work of all the components of our political system. It supports and assists the local Soviets, the trade unions, the Young Communist League and other mass organizations and provides the requisite conditions for each of them to perform its functions efficiently.

You have asked me what meaning we attach to the expression

"make policy". I should tell you that we do not use this expression. We say: plan a policy, formulate a policy, pursue a policy. In my view, this is a more accurate way to express the essence of the matter, as we interpret it at any rate.

The planning of policy, for which the Party is responsible in the first place, as I have mentioned above, begins with a study of the objective situation, the precise requirements of society, and the sentiments of the masses (public opinion, which is analysed by the Party and taken fully into consideration). On this basis political decisions are shaped after due discussion. This process is not simple, of course, and it runs different courses according to the character of the tasks to be implemented. Not infrequently the adoption of a decision is preceded by broad discussion, at times on a nationwide scale. This implies, of course, a comparison of points of view on specific problems and a struggle between different viewpoints. This is the case, for instance with drafts of Five-Year Plans. There was a nationwide discussion of the new draft Constitution, labour and housing laws, the educational reform and, recently, the law on combating drunkenness and alcoholism. At the same time the main component of the political process is the implementation of decisions. No policy is possible without this. If you followed the discussion held throughout the country after the April 1985 Plenary Meeting of the CPSU Central Committee, you will certainly have noticed the special significance we attached to the correlation between words and deeds.

We are waging a determined struggle for such correlation. We criticize those who fail to live up to their commitments. We expose them to public censure and disciplinary penalties.

Question. Not infrequently we hear that Soviet young people are not interested in politics and are socially passive. Is this true?

Answer. This is claimed by those who wish us ill in the West. But I should say bluntly that it is wishful thinking. We have no reason to complain about our young people. They are remarkable, on the whole, for their high civic awareness and their profound interest in the affairs of society, and their keen interest in matters of home and foreign policy; young people are working well at factories, at plants and on collective farms, and the record of students at institutions of higher learning and of young servicemen is quite good. Young people volunteer of their own free will and with enthusiasm to work in the most difficult places — at the biggest construction projects in Siberia, in the Far North and in the Far East of the country. Today 1.5 million young volunteers are working on these building projects. In short, I cannot agree with the allegation that the Soviet young people are indifferent and passive. We have full political confidence in our younger generation.

This does not mean, of course, that problems and questions are non-existent in this area. They do exist. We were seriously worried, for instance, to learn that alcoholism had become widespread among a certain section of young people. Parasitic and consumer mentality, poor taste, narrow intellectual interests and inadequate knowledge of their cultural heritage are other phenomena still manifest on some occasions. We are well aware of them and naturally never cease to give them close attention. This is a broad field of activity for members of the Young Communist League. It is an old truism that a good example is more effective than the most eloquent words. I believe that all the measures now being taken in the country and Party will be very useful in the education of youngsters.

Question. There is talk about the persecution of Jews in the USSR and about political prisoners and censorship. Some names are mentioned too, for instance Sakharov. What can you say on the subject?

Answer. I shall begin with Soviet Jews. This question has become a component in an unbridled anti-Soviet campaign, a veritable psychological war against the USSR. In this country, the propagandism of anti-Semitism, like all other forms of racial discrimination, is forbidden by law as a criminal offence. In the Soviet Union some offences which are fairly often in evidence in the United States and even in France, like other Western countries, are impossible. These include acts of hooliganism against Jewish graves, and the activities of the neo-nazi organizations, which foment hatred of the Jews in the press and on the radio. Jews in the Soviet Union are just as free and equal as citizens of any other ethnic origin. They take an active part in social and state affairs. Books, magazines and newspapers are printed in Yiddish and synagogues are functioning. In my view, the constant attention of anti-Communist and Zionist propaganda to the fate of the Jews in the Soviet Union is hypocrisy motivated by far-reaching political goals and purposes which have nothing in common with the genuine interests of Soviet citizens of Jewish ethnic origin.

I believe that in civilized society there should be no room for anti-Semitism, Zionism or any other manifestations of nationalism, chauvinism and racism in general. The problem of exterminating these evils on a global scale is a matter of urgency. In the Republic of South Africa the racists are perpetrating bloody atrocities against the black majority of the population. In Western Europe pogroms and discrimination against Africans, Indians, Turks and immigrants from other Asian countries have become more frequent. In the United States racism has also mounted a counter-offensive in the last few years. The Arab people of Palestine are still deprived of their native lands, as they have been for so many years and for reasons known to all.

Now about political prisoners. We have none. Just as we do not persecute citizens for their convictions. Convictions are not a criminal offence in the USSR.

However, any state is obliged to protect itself against those who are undermining it, calling for its subversion or destruction or who collect intelligence for foreign secret services. In our laws these offences are qualified as high treason and crimes against the state. I have been informed that a little over two hundred persons are serving time in jail for all kinds of such offences in the Soviet Union.

Now for Sakharov. I have already had an occasion to answer a similar question, so I shall be brief. As we all know, he committed illegal actions. This has been more than once reported in the press. Measures taken against him are consistent with Soviet law.

The actual state of affairs is as follows. Sakharov lives in Gorky. His conditions are normal and he is doing scientific research. He remains a full member of the USSR Academy of Sciences. His state of health, as far as I know, is normal.

His wife has recently left this country for medical treatment. As for Sakharov himself, he is familiar, as he was before, with highly important state secrets and cannot therefore be allowed to travel abroad.

Now about censorship. We have it. Its task is to prevent the publication of state and military secrets in the press, war propaganda, propaganda of violence, cruelty, humiliation of individuals and pornography. The selection of works for publication, their editing and abridgement are a matter for the mass media and book publishers, their editors and editorial boards. I can add only one thing: censorship of this kind exists in every country in one form or another. In your country, for instance, owners of newspapers and publishing concerns or hired editors define what is and what is not to be printed. Slander or the divulging of state secrets is a criminal offence. In the United States there is a widespread practice of confiscating books from school libraries under pressure from reactionary elements. As announced at the latest Congress of the Pen Club, books by such authors as Dostoyevsky and Hemingway even Dickens not to speak of the Diaries of Anna Frank have been confiscated. Such are the hard facts.

It is to be regretted that in France and in the West, in general, people are unfamiliar with the Soviet press, television and radio programmes. Freedom of speech, freedom of criticism is very broad in the Soviet Union. Discussions in progress in the country are open and at times very heated. This is especially evident now, on the eve of the Congress. Frankly speaking, I regard as hypocritical the vociferous campaign being waged with the object of proving that the Soviet Union (and, by implication, socialism in general) is a society in which uniformity, conformity, official unanimity and other similar things are prevalent.

In our society an active stand in life, and a struggle against injustice, violations of legality and public morals are a norm of behaviour laid down in the Constitution, which proclaims criticism as a right available to every citizen. Moreover, whoever interferes with criticism, and they are often called "jammers of criticism" in this country, are actually in conflict with the law. For such offences an executive at any level may be arraigned for trial. The Soviet press, radio and television may not yet be perfect, but on the whole they are a broad and free mouthpiece of popular public opinion.

Question. One of the questions often asked in various circles in the West is this: have the revivals of Stalinism been uprooted in the Soviet Union?

Answer. Stalinism is a term invented by opponents of Communism and is widely used to denigrate the Soviet Union and socialism as a whole.

Since the 20th Party Congress raised the question of overcoming the cult of Stalin and the CPSU Central Committee adopted a resolution on this problem, thirty years have passed. I must say frankly that those were not easy decisions for our Party. That was a test for Party principledness, for loyalty to Leninism.

I believe that we withstood that test well and drew the right conclusions from the past. This refers to the life of the Party itself and of Soviet society as a whole. We regard as our major task the continued development of intra-party democracy, like socialist democracy in general, with a reinforcement of the principles of collective leadership and expansion of publicity. The Party and its Central Committee require persons elected to key posts to be modest and to cultivate intolerance of sycophancy and flattery among Communists. We attach and will continue to attach enormous significance to safeguarding and reinforcing socialist legality and will constantly keep law enforcement bodies under strict supervision. All these are important directions of the political work being pursued by the Party today. This work and all affairs of our life today provide a conclusive answer to your question.

Question. What effect will the processes occurring in your country now have on the state of culture in the USSR which, incidentally, is poorly known in the West?

Answer. Indeed, our cultural affairs are really poorly known in the West. Speaking frankly, this fact is used in the West to cram the public with falsehoods and to distort the actual situation.

Now the Soviet Union is a scene of unimaginable cultural upsurge. We have many outstanding authors, poets, composers, artists, actors and art directors, in opera, ballet, drama and the cinema. They are remarkable not only by domestic but also by world standards. Literature and the arts in the Soviet Union are available not to a handful of connoisseurs and patrons, but to the mass of the people. In the Soviet union classical and modern poetry and prose, both Soviet and foreign, — including, of course, those of France — are published in print-runs never witnessed elsewhere. Perhaps the most remarkable achievement of Soviet culture is the broad development of folk art.

I believe, therefore, that the changes taking place in our social life will indisputably affect Soviet culture and have a favourable impact upon it.

We have all that is needed for its further rapid and all-round progress: a high educational standard of the masses; splendid traditions of profound respect for, interest in, and attraction to cultural values; broad access to the entire wealth and variety of the multi-national culture of this country; and, finally, the policy of the Party, which regards the encouragement of the intellectual life of society as a task of high priority. We are also thinking now of steps to reinforce the material basis of culture, the intellectual sphere as a whole.

Question. Now let me go over to international problems. Can the American plans of Star Wars lead to war? Can you notice after the Geneva summit any new symptoms of a resumption of *détente* in international relations?

Answer. You have put two questions simultaneously.

First, about the American Star Wars programme. It is our profound conviction that this programme really does increase the risk of war and at a certain stage will even make it probable. The reasons for this conclusion have been discussed more than once and in adequate detail. I would like to point out only one aspect of the problem. Although the whole plan for Star Wars is to be completed decades from now and only a handful of "enthusiasts" believe that it is feasible, it may entail very grave consequences, even in the near future, if the United States persists in this matter. By implementing the Star Wars programme, Washington, in effect, is deliberately taking steps to frustrate the talks in progress and to cancel all existing agreements on arms limitation. In such an event the Soviet Union and the United States, their allies and the whole world would find themselves in the coming few years faced with an absolutely uncontrollable arms race, strategic chaos, dangerous instability, general insecurity and fear, with all the growing risk of catastrophe involved. This, I repeat is a danger threatening not our great-grandchildren, but ourselves, all of us, the whole of humanity.

Why should we run such risks? I presume that President Reagan has implicit faith in the "salutary" mission of Star Wars as a respite. If, however, an end to the nuclear threat is pivotal to the whole problem, why should the United States not agree in principle to the latest Soviet proposals. Indeed, they provide for a shorter, direct, cheap and, most important of all, safe way towards the removal of the danger of war — the complete elimination of nuclear weapons. I emphasize that this a safer way. Indeed, the way towards this goal proposed now by the United States is hopeless; nuclear weapons, contrary to the allegations of Star Wars champions, will not have time enough to become obsolescent; on the contrary they will be perfected. Developments may reach a point where they will become so sophisticated that all decisions will have to be entrusted to electronic computers and automatic devices. Thus, human civilization will be made a hostage to machines and hence to technical failures and hitches. How dangerous it is has again been shown by the recent tragedy of the American space shuttle Challenger, which was dependable, multiple-tested and tried out within the widest limits possible today in general.

I am confident that this is perfectly well realized in Washington, that every "believer" in this surrealistic plan of deliverance from the nuclear menace is faced by at least ten cynics who have in mind something by no means the same as what is evidently the dream of President Reagan. Some of them, evidently realizing that an "inpenetrable shield" is not feasible, are ready to accept a smaller option, a limited anti-missile defence system, which, in combination with forces for delivering a preemptive strike at the forces of retaliation of the other side would make the possibility of nuclear aggression with impunity real enough. Others simply want to line their pockets. Still others want to involve the USSR in a space race and undermine its economy. And there are also those who want to increase the technological lead of the United States on Western Europe and thus make it dependent on its senior partner, and so on and so forth.

Thus, you can see that the question of Star Wars is a very broad one. It contains a collision not only between two viewpoints on this concrete programme, but also two different approaches, two different concepts of security.

The American concept is one of guaranteed security, primarily through reliance on military-technological facilities, in the case under review on new super-weapons, a technological trick that would help end the nuclear stalemate. Despite the very vague and ridiculously untrustworthy statements about a willingness to share this "miracle technology" when the time comes with other countries, including the Soviet Union, the United States intends to get out of the stalemate alone so as to achieve absolute security for itself and to place all others in a situation of absolute insecurity.

The Soviet concept is one of guaranteed equal security for all by cutting armaments and effecting disarmament, down to complete elimination of all kinds of weapons of mass destruction. Indeed, in our day the security of the USSR is inconceivable without the security of the United States, the security of the Warsaw Treaty member nations and of the NATO powers. Universal security is impossible without mutual security.

In answering your question, I wish to single out the problem of delivering Europe from nuclear weapons, primarily intermediate-range missiles, which are seriously undermining European security. In this area we are entitled to expect realism and common sense, in British and, of course, French policies.

Advocates of nuclear armaments are circulating the argument that their abolition will leave the West "defenceless" in the face of a Soviet "superiority" in the so-called conventional armaments. I will not argue now as to whether such "superiority" is or is not real. The main point is different: our proposals provide for a cut in these armaments just as reinforcement of confidence-building measures. We have not proposed an end to nuclear weapons for the purpose of simply escalating the arms race to other spheres, which will in time become no less dangerous.

We realize that the implementation of our concept of security requires enormous effort, stubborn struggle and the renunciation of millennia-old traditions, as I have stated above. However, the world simply cannot afford to live and act in the old way, when the risk of nuclear war is so real.

Is a world without arms and without wars possible in general? I would answer this question with a counter question: is it possible to preserve human civilization while pursuing a steadily accelerating arms race, building up tensions and balancing on the increasingly precarious brink of war?

Are there any new symptoms of a resumption of *détente* in international relations following the Geneva summit? To my mind one must be cautious in one's assessment. Indeed, some signs and symptoms have of late been in evidence. It is not only a matter of certain shifts in the area of Soviet–American relations, because these shifts are limited, confined to the periphery and do not relate to vital problems. But a certain change in the political atmosphere can already be sensed. This has revived, among the people of many countries, hopes for and faith in the possibility of a return to *détente*, ending the reckless and insane arms race and developing normal and peaceful international co-operation. This is something real and politically substantial.

The changing political atmosphere is helping us, helping the Soviet Union to approach our work in planning new proposals and new initiatives more boldly and more resolutely. I am sometimes asked whether the Soviet Union believes that the present US Administration, as well as the governments of some of its allies, will accept such new Soviet proposals as, for instance, a total ban on nuclear explosions, phased elimination of nuclear weapons in Europe and everywhere in the world, prevention of an arms race in outer space, etc.

This is a legitimate question. However, national policy, particularly in the nuclear age, cannot be planned in accordance with the principle: do you trust your partner in general, or not? A policy must be based on a realistic foundation in keeping with the alignment of forces in the international arena, the demands of the day, the interests of one's own nation and of other nations, and the need for universal peace. Once this is so, the Soviet Union as a socialist state is simply obliged to offer the world a radical and realistic alternative to nuclear war, to meet the interests of all nations with a programme for solving the problems facing mankind. Such proposals give us a "glimpse of truth" of its own kind. They compel our partners in negotiations to show their hands, to show which aims their policy really pursues. When we proposed a moratorium on nuclear explosions, we were told: you are very shrewd. This year you staged more tests (which, incidentally, was not true) and now you ask the United States to halt them. In fact, it is now seven months since we stopped testing, so the United States can no longer use this pretext for refusal. Then control and verification were invoked as exonerating arguments. We expressed our willingness to allow any verification procedure. So this pretext also proved ineffectual. What is left then? Is it only the US determination to continue the arms race at all costs?

The Decree on Peace, written by Lenin, which was incidentally the first decree of the newly-born Soviet government, expressed the strong determination of the first socialist state in history to pursue its policy, to act ". . .openly before the whole people", to address its proposals "to governments and peoples", ". . .to have the peoples intervene in the problems of war and peace". Submitting the draft of this decree to the Congress of Soviets, Lenin said: "We are fighting against the fraud of governments which pay lip service to peace and justice while in reality waging predatory wars of conquest". At the same time, he said, having in mind the Soviet Republic's relations with the capitalist powers: "We cannot and must not give governments a chance to conceal themselves behind our intractability and conceal from the peoples the fact that they are being sent to a slaughter-house . . . an ultimatum will ease the position of our enemy. We, for our part, will show all the terms to the people. We face all governments with our terms and let them give an answer to their own peoples."

Such is the high-principled Communist presentation of this problem. It is not fortuitous that I recalled these words and principles of Lenin's. There is a striking similarity between today's situation and the situation which prevailed at that time. In 1917, when the First World War was at its height, the main problem was: what is to be done to end the bloodshed as early as possible, a bloodshed imposed on the peoples by imperialist governments? Lenin and the Party resolved that the most effective way was to appeal not only to governments, but also to the people. Today the peoples of the world have been drawn into the arms race and a nuclear rivalry which threatens them with even more terrible slaughter. It is natural that we should be making painstaking efforts to solve these problems with the governments of the West and be constantly appealing to the peoples, to which our policy is addressed.

Question. Is there any reason to expect an end to the war in Afghanistan in the near future, and hence the withdrawal of Soviet troops from that country?

Answer. We desire that very much, and we will work to this end to the best of our ability. And we know that the government of Afghanistan is of the same mind. It is prepared to advance a long way towards a settlement of the complex problems involved in the country's internal development and is taking vigorous steps to invite various political forces in the centre and in the provinces to contribute to the normalization of daily life. These include representatives of tribes, the clergy, the intellectuals and the business community. At the same time, there are problems whose solution does not depend on the government of Afghanistan. Among the foreign forces who have an interest in its continuation and expansion are Pakistan and the United States, which provoked this conflict by their interference. Western Europe can also influence developments here. I believe that if the situation in and around Afghanistan were soberly assessed there, and if their own interests — the interests of general peace — were also soberly assessed, then ways of assisting a solution to the problem would certainly be found.

Question. Can Soviet–French relations be improved, and what should be done to this effect?

Answer. Of course, they can. I would even say they *must* be improved. The Soviet Union is in favour of broad co-operation with France and of friendship between the Soviet and French peoples. The differences between the USSR and France are by no means an obstacle to their accord and co-operation. This is our firm and long-term position of principle. We regard the improvement of mutual understanding and co-operation between the Soviet Union and France as important for what constitutes the vital interests of our two countries — the consolidation of peace in Europe and throughout the world, and normalization of the international situation.

To give a new impetus to Franco–Soviet relations was also the purpose of the top-level meeting in Paris in the autumn of last year. Some successes have been scored in recent time. We believe, however, that great opportunities have remained unused. We would like to hope that our two countries will be active partners in solving such problems of historic scope and the curbing of the arms race and the complete abolition of nuclear weapons, and other types of weapons of mass destruction, and the prevention of developing strike space weapons.

The Soviet Union and France, with their large scientific, technological and intellectual potentials and their record of experience in maintaining good-neighbourly relations, could jointly set a good model of co-operation in the field of science and technology. At the same time this could be helpful to solving the problem of unemployment in France, along with the continued development of trade and economic relations.

Franco–Soviet relations have been based historically on the traditional mutual sympathy and respect of the two peoples for one another. We fail to understand, therefore, the current stubborn desire in some quarters in your country to arouse hostility and mistrust of the Soviet Union among the French people and to create a false image of the Soviet Union and its policy. We are thankful to the French Communists and to *L'Humanité* for their opposition to anti-Sovietism and their support of truthful information about the Soviet Union and socialism. We regard this as one of the important forms of solidarity between the FCP and the CPSU.

The Communist movement derives its strength from this solidarity, which is solidarity in action, the solidarity of all its constituent parties, which are equal, independent and determined to implement their different tasks in their different conditions. They are united by their joint struggle in defence of the interests of the labouring masses, for peace and socialism.

In conclusion I wish to convey my heartfelt greetings and good wishes to the readers of *L'Humanité*, the French Communists and all the working people of France.

M. S. Gorbachov and R. Leroy then had a discussion which passed in a cordial and comradely atmosphere.

R. Leroy. I wish to thank you for your frank and straightforward replies to our questions. The subjects you have discussed are of great interest to the French people, who have not enough objective information. I must unfortunately acknowledge that the French mass media are pursuing a clearly anti-Soviet line. This holds true of most of them.

M. S. Gorbachov. Whenever they meet us, representatives of different circles of France, including the President, make declarations about the traditional friendly character of Franco–Soviet relations and recall that their roots go deep into history. At the same time they emphasize that they desire to preserve such relations and lend a new dimension to them. Our stand is identical. We are in favour of maintaining our traditional friendly ties with France and we are doing our level best to help develop good Franco–Soviet relations. On this background we find it hard to understand why the campaign of hostility towards the USSR has assumed such wide scope.

Or take, for instance, the recent expulsion from France of several Soviet Embassy officials on the alleged pretext of their illegal activities. We see that the ghost of "Soviet spies" is haunting France again. This, of course, is a groundless step undertaken under a fabricated pretext. Suffice it to say, for instance, that one of those accused of "illegal contacts" is a technical specialist who worked exclusively in the embassy building, maintained no contacts with foreigners and speaks no foreign languages. The whole story is certainly disappointing. What is the political motive behind all this? What are the reasons — are they rooted in domestic politics or elsewhere?

As I have already said in my discussions with President Mitterand, we sincerely seek to make Franco–Soviet relations more dynamic and to co-operate with France, the French people and French political forces in areas of interest to our two countries. This does not mean however, that we will not react to unfriendly moves in relation to our country. Therefore, in this case we were compelled to take adequate counter measures.

It would be wrong to believe that the Soviet Union is more interested in good relations with France than France is interested in good relations with the Soviet Union. I believe that both countries have a mutual interest in preserving and developing good relations with each other.

R. Leroy. It is obvious that the French people have a special interest in friendship and co-operation with the Soviet Union.

M. S. Gorbachov. In pursuing our foreign policy we invariably take the interests of France and her people into consideration. This is evidenced by our latest proposals, put forth in my statement of 15 January of this year. Incidentally, when formulating our proposals we thought it natural to take account of the legitimate interests not only of France, but also, say, of such of our partners as the United States. Otherwise, our proposals would not be realistic.

I told President Mitterand in my conversations with him, and I wish to repeat it here, that we have not the slightest intention of prejudicing the security of France. In our recent proposals we proceed from the principle that France, just like Britain, will join in the process of nuclear disarmament only after the United States and the Soviet Union have implemented significant reductions in their nuclear arsenals. At present we would like to hope that in the period of practical reductions of American and Soviet arsenals, France and Britain will abstain from building up their nuclear capability.

R. Leroy. We are following with interest the progress of preparations for the 27th Congress of your Party.

M. S. Gorbachov. At our Congress we shall present in circumstantial detail our plans to bring into play ever more effectively the potentials of socialism, making maximum use of its advantages. I believe this will be our contribution to the common struggle of Communists for a better and just society. In our foreign policy we will continue vigorous steps to promote lasting peace, seeking to abolish nuclear weapons on earth. This is, of course, also highly significant in as much as it shows the strong commitment of socialism to the cause of peace.

Index

DUE DATE